The Myth of the Closed Mind

The Myth of the Closed Mind

Explaining Why and How People Are Rational

RAY SCOTT PERCIVAL

OPEN COURT
Chicago and La Salle, Illinois

To order books from Open Court, call toll-free 1-800-815-2280, or visit our website at www.opencourtbooks.com.

Open Court Publishing Company is a division of Carus Publishing Company.

Copyright © 2012 by Carus Publishing Company

First printing 2012

All rights reserved. No part of this publication may be reproduced, stored in a retrieval system, or transmitted, in any form or by any means, electronic, mechanical, photocopying, recording, or otherwise, without the prior written permission of the publisher, Open Court Publishing Company, a division of Carus Publishing Company, 70 East Lake Street, Suite 300, Chicago, Illinois 60601.

Printed and bound in the United States of America.

Library of Congress Cataloging-in-Publication Data

Percival, Ray Scott, 1956-
  The myth of the closed mind : explaining why and how people are rational / Ray Scott Percival.
     p. cm.
  Includes bibliographical references and index.
  ISBN 978-0-8126-9685-1 (trade paper : alk. paper)
 1. Reason. 2. Persuasion (Psychology). 3. Criticism. 4. Ideology. I. Title.
  BC177.P373 2011
  128'.33--dc22
                                                                2010048064

For Grace Scott Percival

Brief Table of Contents

Detailed Table of Contents   ix
Preface   xv
Prologue: People Are Rational   1

1. The Persuader's Predicament   39

2. Survival of the Truest   81

3. Does Emotion Cloud Our Reason?   169

4. Ideologies as Shapeshifters   205

Notes   275
Bibliography   287
Index   297

Detailed Table of Contents

Preface	xv
Prologue: People Are Rational	1
My Outrageous Idea	1
The Main Arguments for the Closed Mind	4
ARGUMENT #1. EMOTION	4
ARGUMENT #2. WISHFUL THINKING	4
ARGUMENT #3. LINGUISTIC OR CONCEPTUAL FRAMEWORKS	6
ARGUMENT #4. IMMUNIZING STRATAGEMS	6
ARGUMENT #5. PROTECTIVE SHELL AND ESSENTIAL CORE	7
ARGUMENT #6. BLIND FAITH	7
ARGUMENT #7. PEOPLE ARE ILLOGICAL WHEN TESTING THEIR BELIEFS	8
ARGUMENT #8. MIND-VIRUSES	10
ARGUMENT #9. DUMB DECISION RULES	11
Ghostly Logic	13
The Orthodoxy	14
The Turnover of Adherents	16
My Sense of 'Rational'	18
What Would an Irrational Human Look Like?	19
Terrorism and Emotion	20
The Problem	21
My General Position	23
The Logic in Ideology	25
Why Dawkins's Memetic Approach Is Not Enough	31

Is My Argument Open to Argument? 34
The Examples of Marxism and Freudianism 36

1. The Persuader's Predicament 39

Trading Off Closedness for Spreadability 40
    NARROW CURIOSITY OR GENERAL WONDER? 41

Truth Is an Advantage in Propaganda 43

The Struggle for Coherence in Abrahamic Religions 44
    MONOD ON PERFORMANCE UNRELATED TO TRUTH 45
    GELLNER ON BURNING FAITH UNRELATED TO TRUTH 47
    CHRISTIANITY MODIFIED BY COMPETITION FROM SCIENCE 49

The Persuasive Power of Informative Explanation 51

Popper and Bartley on Ideologies 57
    RESIDUAL DOGMATISM IN POPPER 58
    RESIDUAL DOGMATISM IN BARTLEY 60

Situational Logic 62
    THE PROPAGANDIST AND SITUATIONAL LOGIC 63

Bartley's Test Case: Liberal Protestantism 69
    KARL BARTH 73
    PAUL TILLICH 74

The Nightmare of Perfect Thought Control 76

Martyrdom as a Rational Technique 78

2. Survival of the Truest 81

Evolution and Human Rationality 82

Does the Modularity of Mind Undermine Rationality? 83

Evolutionary Epistemology 87

A Darwinian Epistemology 91

General and Specific Problem-Solving 95

An Indirect Refutation of the Existence of the
    Impervious Believer 97

Why You Are at Least as Sensible as a Snail	98
LIONEL ROBBINS AND THE MODERN CONCEPTION OF ECONOMIC SCIENCE	101
TRIAL AND ERROR IN ECONOMIC DECISIONS	102
MAX WEBER	103
The Fanatic	106
GUSTAVE LE BON AND WALTER LAQUEUR	107
SUICIDE TERRORISM PAYS	109
ABSOLUTE VALUES	113
Instrumental Rationality	115
A POSSIBLE OBJECTION	116
Rhetoric versus Theory	117
J.L. AUSTIN	118
SOCRATES	120
Unfathomable Lies	121
Exploratory Rationality	122
Wishful and Fearful Rationality	124
DAVID PEARS	125
JON ELSTER	127
GEORG LUKACS	129
WISHFUL BELIEFS AND EXPLORATORY BEHAVIOR	132
ABSOLUTE VERSUS VALUE-RELATIVE STUBBORNNESS	133
HOFFER ON THE FANATICAL COMMUNIST	136
DENISE MEYERSON ON ABSOLUTE IDEOLOGICAL STUBBORNNESS	137
Logical Thinking Promotes Survival	139
G.A. WELLS AND IMMEDIATE EXPERIENCE	142
WOLPERT: BENDING LOGIC TO PRIOR BELIEF	144
Natural Selection Doesn't Yield Perfection	146
ECOLOGICAL RATIONALITY, AGAIN	147
WASON'S EXPERIMENT	148
A General Schema for the Evolution of Ideologies under Criticism	150
RICHARD DAWKINS: THE HELLFIRE MEME	151
FLORIAN VON SCHILCHER AND NEIL TENNANT	156

Memetic Evolution of an Ideology	157
1. Occasion	157
2. Emergence	157
3. Refinement	158
4. Testing	159
5. Propagation	162
Why Some Ideologies Look Impervious to Criticism	163
The Complexity of the Learning Task	163
The Stubbornness of Important Beliefs	163
Popper's 'Dogmatism' Sociologized	164
The Early Loss of Intellectual Giants	164
Retention of the Original Terminology	164
Feeling Ashamed of Having Been Wrong	165
Bad Faith and Cowardice	166
Pressure to Conform	167

3. Does Emotion Cloud Our Reason? — 169

Ideologies as Rationalizations of Irrational Emotions	170
Hitler's Theory of Propaganda	174
Intellectual Elites and Emotional Masses	175
Evidence from Psychology	180
High Arousal Interferes with the Transmission of New Ideas	181
Intense Emotion Transmits Ideas Already Accepted	181
Suggestion as Simple Assertion	182
Suggestion as Implicit Argument	184
Influencing versus Determining Public Opinion	185
Long-term Propaganda versus Political Canvassing	188
Thinking about Abstract Ideas versus Thinking in Accord with them	190
Fitting the Theory to the Emotion	190
Moral Feelings and Factual Assumptions	194
The Relevance of Intense Emotion	199
Intense Emotion and the Theory of Advertising	208

4. Ideologies as Shapeshifters — 205

Immunizing Stratagems — 206

Popper's Examples of Immunizing Stratagems — 207

The Demarcation Problem — 211
 METAPHYSICAL THEORIES CAN BE CRITICIZED — 215
 EMPIRICAL VERSUS METAPHYSICAL CRITICISM — 217

Damaging versus Eliminating a System of Ideas — 220
 DO ALL IMMUNIZING STRATAGEMS ABANDON THE ORIGINAL THEORY? — 222
 HARD CORE VERSUS PROTECTIVE BELT — 230
 DUHEM'S PROBLEM — 235
 CHANGING DEMARCATION BETWEEN THE HARD CORE AND THE PROTECTIVE BELT — 238

Ideological Movements Split — 241
 UNFATHOMABLE IMPLICATIONS OF AN IDEOLOGY — 242
 THE GENERAL STRUCTURE OF IMMUNIZING RESPONSES TO CRITICISM — 246

Case Study: Marxism — 248

Marx's Labor Theory of Value — 249
 THE PROBLEM THE LABOR THEORY OF VALUE WAS MEANT TO SOLVE — 250
 INADVERTENTLY SELF-INFLICTED INJURIES TO MARX'S THEORY OF VALUE — 251
 THE EVOLUTION OF THE LABOR THEORY OF VALUE IN VOLUME I OF CAPITAL — 255
 ABANDONMENT OF THE THEORY OF EXPLOITATION AND PROFIT — 256

Case study: Freudianism — 259

Freud's Theory of Dreams — 262
 THE CRITICIZABILITY OF FREUD'S 'BASIC THEORY' — 269
 FURTHER EMPIRICAL REFUTATIONS — 271

Refutation versus Elimination of ideologies — 271

Conclusion — 273

Notes	275
Bibliography	287
Index	297

Preface

For as long as I can remember I've respected the power of logical argument. I've always wanted to be persuasive on account of the validity of my arguments and when tempted to substitute an immediately attractive but unsound argument for a valid but slower-to-take-effect argument, I've always resisted the temptation. This struck me as not only the noble thing to do, but also prudent in the long run. If you adhere as best you can to the truth and to valid argument, then you're guided by principles that are always there for you as you navigate life, because they are universal. You will be like a captain at sea relying on the guidance of the fixed stars to navigate. If, on the other hand, you're guided by the momentary advantages of the impressive but bogus argument, you're lost in a sea without fixed stars. You will constantly have to learn (or create) new charts to navigate.

Suppose you're convinced that some people are just impervious to valid argument, that their minds are closed to reason, but that they may be amenable to poetic or humorous cajoling, ridicule, or even barefaced coercion. It's even more tempting then to ignore the civil give and take of sincere argument. But to succumb to that temptation is a large step to a barbaric or at least philistine world. I'm arguing in this book that the temptation is much less alluring than generally supposed, because it's based on the myth of the closed mind. On the other hand, the belief in the power of sound argument can become a force for civilization and freedom.

The problem of the closed mind has been with me for a long time. For a professional thinker it's important, but also rare, to find a problem with real depth. It is in the working out of the problem that a thinker produces his ideas and they can only be as deep as the problem they are meant to solve. I'm happy to have found such a problem. For me this conundrum has been a fountain of further puzzles and enigmas that have stimulated many other fruitful ideas.

Because of the way I develop my argument, I like to think of this book as an ocean into which I invite you. In the Prologue, I walk with you down a gently inclined sandy beach to the water's edge. Even as you step into the water, the slope remains gentle and continues like this as you imperceptibly walk into deeper and deeper waters. Eventually, you will be swimming in deep water, but you'll feel in control and comfortable as you encounter slightly more difficult ramifications of my outrageous idea.

In this book, I present you with a bold thesis—I freely admit that it is outrageous—and then elaborate this by applying it to various issues, defending it against objections as I go. Though contrary to the fashion of much academic writing, this is, I believe, the best approach. Academia is almost hostage to the prevalent intellectual context, justificationism, the view that you should accept all and only those positions that are justified by experience or argument. Pick up almost any book on epistemology and its pages are likely to be exclusively dominated by chapters on justification. This intellectual context is associated with a style of presentation in which you must first marshal all your evidence, and only then announce your conclusion.

It's good to have competition, in ideas as anywhere else. Fortunately, there is a respectable alternative: the method of conjecture and refutation, otherwise known as critical rationalism. Critical rationalism is the view that truth, or closeness to the truth, and not justification is our aim. Our theories are unjustified and forever unjustifiable children of the imagination, against which we ought to marshal our best criticisms in the hope that those that survive will be at least closer to the truth.

I wish to acknowledge many friends and colleagues who have contributed to the intellectual context in which this book grew. There are times in life when one has what the psychologist Maslow calls a peak experience. One of my peak experiences was my encounter with true intellectuals—people feverishly interested in ideas, right or wrong. True intellectuals are quite rare. The first such intellectual I ever met was David McDonagh, whom I encountered while studying for my Master's in philosophy at the University of Warwick. David taught me the value of bold—almost aggressive—discussion. You couldn't really get far by searching for consensus as part of a misguided diplomacy in debate. Indeed, consensus always means the end of a productive episode of clashing ideas. Seeking consensus makes sense for business and negotiation, but debate isn't negotiation. Debate requires disagreement. So you have to stick to your guns. Of course, criticism stings, but if you're prepared to take the stings, your ideas will develop into much stronger, more interesting creatures.

During my time at Warwick I also met other outstanding intellects who have provided much encouragement but also the occasional devastating criticism that stimulated the growth of my book: Jan C. Lester, David W. Miller, and David Ramsay Steele. Criticism can sting and they pull no punches—fortunately. Another thinker who pulled no punches was William Warren Bartley III. Bartley originated the philosophical theory of Comprehensively Critical Rationalism. Bartley was true to his principles and engaged in a spirited exchange of letters with me in which he tried to defend the closed mind thesis, the result being Chapter 4 of this book. David Deutsch, Jeremy Shearmur, and Mark Amadeus Notturno also gave me encouragement and stimulating criticism.

Later, I had the great pleasure of taking afternoon tea with Sir Karl Popper. We discussed my incipient thesis of the non-existence of the closed mind and my exchange with Bartley on this topic, as Melita Mew, his secretary and close friend, served tea and scones with cream. Two other intellectual giants who gave me much encouragement and criticism were the late Donald T. Campbell (former president of the American Psychological Association) and Paul Levinson (chair of the Media and Communications Department, Fordham University).

This book was not directly supported by any awards, but it has benefited from other work I did which was sponsored by the Institute for Humane Studies at George Mason University and the Open Society Institute, New York. I thank them for their moral encouragement as well as financial help.

I also would like to thank my father Frank Percival and my brother Paul for their moral support. It was my father who gave me the precept that you should get a day's work done by noon, then you'd have the rest of the day for yourself.

Prologue: People Are Rational

My Outrageous Idea

The myth of the closed mind is the popular theory that some people, or some beliefs, are impervious to argument. Almost everyone today seems to accept the myth of the closed mind. But I want to provoke you, by getting you to consider the possibility that there's no such thing as a closed mind—or if there is, it's very rare, and cannot prevent ideas from being changed under the impact of criticism.

If I'm right, then the most menacing ideological juggernauts, such as Communism, National Socialism, or Islamic Fundamentalism, are vulnerable to criticism and can be brought down by argument—though I don't deny that they can inflict a lot of damage before they are toppled. And this applies to any future system of beliefs that may arise. It also applies to minor sects, such as Scientology, the Unification Church (Moonies), or Jehovah's Witnesses. And it applies to minority views which educated people tend to view as terribly wrong-headed, such as biblical creationism, '9/11 truth', or Holocaust revisionism.

My view—admittedly outlandish and extremely unpopular—is that people just can't help being rational. In saying that people are rational, I'm not saying that people don't make mistakes. We all make mistakes—that's an essential part of being rational (a totally non-rational entity could never make a mistake). Nor do I mean that everyone has the same opinions as you or I, or can easily be brought round to our obviously correct opinions. To the contrary, I maintain that human beings are always fallible, unfathomably ignorant, and highly prone to error. Even worse, some of them have the nerve to hold opinions contrary to yours and mine, and to cling to these opinions quite stubbornly. When I say that people can't help being rational, I mean that they can't help correcting their errors once they become aware of them. And, a lot of the time, they can't help becoming aware of them.

I'm not belittling the role of error or ignorance. I share Newton's perspective when he said:

> I do not know what I may appear to the world; but to myself I seem to have been only like a boy playing on the seashore, and diverting myself in now and then finding a smoother pebble or a prettier shell than ordinary, whilst the great ocean of truth lay all undiscovered before me. (Brewster 1855)

Newton was not suggesting that we could not sail out into the ocean of our ignorance or make corrections as we explore the world. He only meant to suggest an appropriate awestruck humility at the degree of our ignorance and the possibility for piecemeal progress. However, piecemeal progress in correcting error is all I need for my argument. As Darwin discovered, given sufficient time, repeated minute incremental change can bring about radical change in the end. I'll show you later that with ideas you sometimes get an unforeseeable catastrophic change instigated by a small change.

Our evolution has made us sensitive to the way the world is, given us a degree of general curiosity about the world, a respect for logic, and a respect for effective and efficient means. Our five senses are continually checking the world and our actions and revising our beliefs in a process that we cannot voluntarily suspend except by sleep, drugs, or suicide. We can decide to investigate some issue more or less thoroughly, but we cannot decide what we believe or decide to suspend the impact of sensory or intellectual revision to those beliefs. Philosophers have often portrayed our rational beliefs as those deriving from voluntary deliberation. It's assumed that our power to decide what we believe is essential to their being rational. However, though we are free to conceive what we will, we cannot choose what we believe. As David Hume pointed out:

> We can, in our conception, join the head of a man to the body of a horse; but it is not in our power to believe that such an animal has ever really existed. (1978, p. 39)

It's the fact that our beliefs are out of our immediate voluntary control that makes them rational—the exact opposite of what many have thought. Try an experiment on yourself, now. Take a belief that you have, say, 'The moon is made of rock' and change it to: 'The moon is made of cheese'. Your goal is to make yourself sincerely believe that the moon is made of cheese. Let me know when you've achieved this.

We can decide not to read or listen to an argument, but we can't decide to remain untouched by a telling argument that we have heard or read. We cannot decide to be unmoved by the validity of an argument that we grasp. As Plato put it, we cannot knowingly accept error (if we think it's error, then we are not accepting it).

Darwinian evolution has given us rough and ready but robust and irrepressible, specialized brain modules for solving special recurrent problems our ancestors faced during the Pleistocene: choosing a mate, detecting cheats, making inferences about the world of people, animals, and objects. However, we've also inherited the means for correcting the sometimes biased and distorted results of these problem-solving modules. We have inherited language, which enables us to frame and test ideas in sophisticated ways that make use of but go beyond the useful but limited brain modules. Indeed, most of the deductive arguments we use in language we execute outside our heads on paper or in a computer, and so they cannot be part of these modules. We have also inherited a general curiosity that goes beyond the questions our automatic modules are adapted to solve.

I'm not suggesting that evolution must give rise to rational humans. Contrary to the naive presumptions of *Star Trek*, in which most aliens are humanoid, differing only in brow-bone shape and skin colour, evolution is a contingent process, not a ladder of progress inevitably culminating in human-like people. If you ran evolution again, you would not get anything like *Homo sapiens*. Nevertheless, I'm arguing that since it did give rise to us, we ought to expect our minds to have the characteristics that a Darwinian evolutionary process would give rise to, once it happened to take the turn of producing something like us. The logic of my argument is like this. Suppose you found a car you'd never seen before and you were trying to establish how it works. Knowing who designed it and by what methods it was constructed would help you understand how it works. It wouldn't determine how it works; just help you to understand how. The same goes for evolution and how the mind might function.

Economists and evolutionary theorists are increasingly adopting the idea that all organisms are rational to some degree. Even an ant or a slug, strange as it may seem, exhibit the rational allocation of scarce resources to achieve their ends. People have other ways of rationally dealing with the world, but they also share rudimentary economic behavior with slugs. Evolutionary theorist Jack Cohen suggests that some evolved functions are contingent and others are universal. Walking on two legs, for example, is contingent, whereas the eye has evolved independently many times. Perhaps some components of rationality are universal. Therefore, even though you would probably not get humans again if you re-ran evolution, you might very well get rational organisms.

The Main Arguments for the Closed Mind

I'm now going to run quickly through the stock arguments for the Closed Mind—the idea that some people and ideas are impervious to argument. In the rest of the book I'll consider some of these arguments much more thoroughly.

Argument #1. Emotion

Some people adopt ideas because of their emotions. Emotions are independent of reason. Therefore, emotions are unaffected by our theories or assumptions about the world. However, a critical argument has to have a theoretical target in the sense of an assumption or a theory. Therefore, emotions and the ideas they maintain are impervious to argument.

Rebuttal

I hold that the Stoics were essentially right about the relation between ideas and emotions. Emotions are not in conflict with our intellect, but serve it strategically and are triggered and controlled by our theories about the world. We have the emotions we have because they have helped to solve recurrent problems our ancestors faced and are highly sensitive to information about our situation.

A husband comes home one evening and outside the door sees a man running menacingly toward his wife with an ax above his head. The husband is angry with the ax man and runs over to attack him. However, as he gets nearer, the man notices that the man with the ax is actually defending his wife from a rabid dog. His anger toward the man instantly evaporates. This switching of the direction of emotion once the facts are interpreted differently is entirely normal and typical (though often less instantaneous and dramatic than in this example).

Argument #2. Wishful Thinking

A more specific argument from the alleged irrationality of emotion is the idea that people adopt beliefs because of wishful thinking. They hold a belief, not because of evidence or inference, but because they wish it to be true. Therefore, beliefs based on wishful thinking are impervious to argument. The related (but opposite) phenomenon is fearful thinking—believing something because one fears it to be true.

Rebuttal

First, let me point out the obvious: people don't believe everything they wish were true. Everyone believes in thousands of factual states of affairs they would prefer to be different. For instance, I believe that I will die at some point in the next fifty years, that I am not going to receive a gift of twenty million dollars next week, and that no matter how hard I try, I cannot levitate. So it can't be right that people simply believe whatever they wish were true. (Similarly, it can't be right that people simply believe whatever they wish were not true.)

Presumably what's meant then is that in some doubtful or difficult cases, people have a bias towards believing that what they would prefer to be true is true. But if that's what's meant, I think we can defend wishful thinking as a useful heuristic. We live in a world of which we are mostly ignorant and in which our hypotheses are frequently refuted. This is true even of our so-called 'direct' observation. It's possible to be too sensitive to apparent counter-evidence and the best approach is to stick to our guns to see if they're loaded. It would not serve our long-term objective of getting at the truth if we were *too* ready to drop our hypotheses at the first apparent refutation. Therefore, when we seem to have counter-evidence against a hypothesis about an important issue, wishful thinking is one way of maintaining a belief so that it may be re-checked against evidence. If the stakes are high enough, it's worth re-checking the evidence.

Often, when it's claimed that people believe things because of wishful thinking, or because they 'want to believe' them, this doesn't mean that they simply believe whatever they would prefer to be true, but that they believe what fits in with their overall theory. For example, Mormons have a bias towards believing that influences from the ancient Middle East can be detected among Native American cultures, and some Mormon scholars claim to have found such influences (such as affinities with Hebrew among ancient Mexican languages). This is because these scholars recognize that, if there are no such influences, *The Book of Mormon* must be a work of fiction, not history, and the Mormon religion must be spurious.

We may say, if we like, that the Mormon 'wants to believe' that such influences will be discovered, but this is not because the fact of such influences, if it were a fact, would be inherently delightful, but because it would appear to confirm the total system of ideas, the Latter-Day Saints religion, to which the Mormon is attached. When a Mormon scholar adopts this approach, he is doing something rational: applying his currently favored theory to new areas, hoping he will find a fit. The tacit recognition that traditional Mormonism would have to be abandoned if no such cultural traces could be found is clearly a recognition that Mormon beliefs must comply with such truth-sensitive values as consistency and empirical testing. (And, of course, many former Mormons have abandoned Mormonism for precisely this kind of reason.)

Argument #3. Linguistic or Conceptual Frameworks

In the novel *Nineteen Eighty-Four*, George Orwell describes a language, Newspeak, that the state imposes on the citizens with the idea of shutting out all possible criticism (Orwell 1977). A number of subsequent writers have made Orwell's fantasy seem plausible to many. For example, Thomas Kuhn's notion of a paradigm may have contributed to the plausibility of Orwell's nightmare. Kuhn argued that each generation of scientists operates with an incommensurable set of problem solving conceptual tools and the different successive generations cannot therefore really understand one another. Benjamin Lee Whorf also made it popular to identify thought and language and to suppose that the thought of every individual is trapped inside the language of their social group (the Sapir-Whorf hypothesis). The suggestion behind Newspeak is that once learned, the sanctioned language prevents people from thinking outside the language, and it therefore is impervious to outside criticism. People then pass on the sanctioned language, unaltered and secure, down the generations.

Rebuttal

Ideologies, linguistic and conceptual frameworks that someone might suppose could monopolize our minds and shield us from outside criticism, need to be learned. However, learning involves innovation and a trial and error process that prevents any kind of Newspeak from taking over our minds. There will always be "Winstons" who fail to learn the sanctioned language and often introduce, by design or accident, innovations into this language. Someone might say that some agency could police any inadvertent deviations from the sanctioned language, nipping any incipient criticism in the bud. However, any attempt to control this only takes the learning process up to a higher level, and who then can police the thinking of the thought police?

The Sapir-Whorf hypothesis has been shown to be false: the fundamental categories applied to such matters as animal species, time, and color are basically the same in all languages and cultures. The language we use does not determine our conception of reality.

Argument # 4. Immunizing Stratagems

Some people, on encountering strong criticism, introduce what they regard as insignificant alterations in an idea to deflect criticism from it, thereby protecting it. This is the 'immunizing stratagem', analyzed by Karl Popper. For example, faced by the fact that communism did not emerge in the most industrially advanced societies first, a Marxist might resort to 'countervailing factors' to 'save' the theory from this refutation.

Rebuttal

Far from saving a theory, immunizing stratagems either empty a theory of content or encumber it with defensive baggage. In either case, the 'immunizing stratagem' changes the theory and usually impairs its ability to spread. Such ploys save the adherent from what he wrongly sees as the embarrassment of admitting error, but in doing so they transform the theory, so that it does not mean what it meant earlier.

Argument # 5. Protective Shell and Essential Core

A more sophisticated method of avoiding critical argument is to make a division between the 'core' of a system of ideas, which is maintained in the face of all criticism and a dispensable 'protective shell' that takes all the critical deformations and concessions.

Rebuttal

This defensive ploy runs into fundamental logical problems. The protectors of the system cannot fully survey the unfathomable impact of revisions to the protective shell; they therefore cannot guarantee that by modifying the nose, they will not damage the face. A look at the logical aspects of this situation indicates that these problems for the propagandist are insuperable.

Argument #6. Blind Faith

Some people adopt and maintain an idea because of faith. Faith is a blind, incorrigible belief in a system, denying the relevance of reason. We've all heard someone say, 'You will not convince me, for my belief is based on faith'. Faith and the ideas it supports are therefore impervious to argument.

To quote Sam Harris, a prominent critic of religious belief:

> The idea, therefore, that religious faith is somehow a sacred human convention—distinguished, as it is, both by the extravagance of its claims and by the paucity of its evidence—is really too great a monstrosity to be appreciated in all its glory. Religious faith represents so uncompromising a misuse of the power of our minds that it forms a kind of perverse, cultural singularity—a vanishing point beyond which rational discourse proves impossible. (Harris 2006, p. 25)

Rebuttal

Perhaps faith is mere bluff. Perhaps there is no such thing as faith, but as a defensive ploy, it works on opponents of such creeds that use it. It works not by securing the belief in a system from critical argument, but by discouraging critical argument from opponents. The widespread use of the faith ploy suggests to me that those who claim to have faith and to be beyond reason are actually tacitly aware of the tremendous force of argument.

Belief and faith are quite different. Faith is both a voluntary defensive ploy and a voluntary expression of loyalty to a creed or group. Belief, however, lies beyond our direct voluntary control and is independent of loyalty. I presume you believe the moon is made of rock, not cheese. You cannot decide to believe otherwise, even if you wanted to do so out of loyalty to someone or even if I threatened you by putting a gun to your head and could monitor your beliefs with brain implants. In *Nineteen Eighty-Four*, Winston Smith is persuaded under torture to declare that he saw five fingers even though he saw only four. I'm saying that if someone believes they only saw four fingers, then a declaration—which is voluntary—that they saw five is all that torture can force out of that person, not a change of belief.

Argument # 7. People Are Illogical when Testing Their Beliefs

If people are open to critical argument, then they must be like scientists, putting their theories to a test. People must first work out what their theory logically implies and then search for counterexamples that falsify one of these implications. However, so the argument goes, the work of the psychologist Peter Wason has shown that people do not act like scientists (Wason 1966).

Wason told his experimental subjects that a set of cards had numbers on one side and letters on the other. He then showed his subjects four cards taken from the set and asked them to test the following rule: 'If a card has a D on one side, it has a 3 on the other.' Wason then asked them to say which of the cards they would have to flip over to test the rule. The cards were D, F, 3, and 7. The correct answer is D and 7. Only between five and ten percent of subjects gave the right answer. Hence, people are hopeless at falsifying their beliefs and even have a bias towards verifying what they already believe. Therefore, people already wrapped up in an ideology are impervious to critical argument—they just cannot do the logic. The ideology is hence perpetuated, secure and even increasingly verified, down the generations.

Rebuttal

Most commentators emphasize the ninety to ninety-five percent wrong choices and neglect the five to ten percent right choices. However, those percentages mean that in a population of one hundred thousand (not a big city but a modest-sized town) between five thousand and ten thousand people will get the right answer. That's a large number of people who are like scientists, checking their opinions by logical reasoning. However, one only needs a small number of dissidents to make a big difference.

In addition, any population has a small number of opinion leaders, intellectuals who have a disproportionate influence on the opinions of others. Is this the same set as those who get the logic puzzle right? Is there at least a large overlap? It's implausible that all the logical thinkers are deceptive or bribed leaders of the many allegedly 'irrational' cults and ideologies.

Leda Cosmides later discovered that if we change the puzzle from a purely abstract one to a puzzle involving the testing of some social rule about cheating, then many people become better logical thinkers (see Barkow, Cosmides, and Tooby 1995). Cosmides conjectured that we have inherited a reasoning module specifically attuned for detecting cheating. Commentators have emphasized the typical biases in these modules. However, Cosmides's conjecture would imply that if adherents of an ideology aren't getting anything in return for adherence, then any adherent is potentially capable of discovering the deception, and they'll drop the ideology. However, it's also clear that people, having inherited language, can become aware of their errors and biases, and learn the more abstract rule of inference. My experience is that when you explain the logic of the puzzle to people, they always get the point fairly quickly.

There's another way of looking at this that puts a kinder light on our rationality. For some time, economists, whose theories were mostly developed to analyze market situations, have been successfully extending these theories to apply to contexts where no explicit market trading is involved. One fruitful idea is that the search for information involves opportunity cost: when you're making a judgment, you collect relevant information. But when do you stop? As you collect information, the value of the other things that you could be doing that are necessarily forsaken by this information-gathering increases.

One day I was scanning some pages from a book using text recognition. I had done eleven pages and was disappointed to find that the scanner produced alternating pages of text and nonsense. So I looked at the procedure I was using. I was scanning some pages in one direction, alternating pages in the other direction. I toyed with the hypothesis that the scanner can only recognize text in one direction. I devised a test: scan a page first one way then the other. The first direction I tried worked. I was tempted to take my hypothesis as confirmed and not bother with any further tests. But I remembered Wason, and so dutifully tested the other direction: gobbledygook. Would it have been irrational of me to just get on with my work? I don't think so. An alternative view is that perhaps it makes sense to make higher level conjectures about our hypotheses—guesses about guesses, such as guessing that I had done the right testing and enough testing of my scanner hypothesis and carry on with other urgent and important projects of the day. After all, continuing to test a hypothesis raises the opportunity cost, minute by minute. If the scanner had started making gobbledygook, I'd have made further guesses and done further tests.

My point is that the fact that people can improve their logic and take account of the cost of judgment hardly makes them closed to argument.

Argument 8. Mind-Viruses

Richard Dawkins argues that certain kinds of ideas are like computer viruses, taking control of people's brains to make more copies of them. Dawkins called these self-reproducing ideas memes or mind viruses (Dawkins 1990). Like computer viruses the memes that survive will be, not those that are truth-like, logically coherent and consistent with well-established knowledge, but rather those that are simply good at making copies of themselves. For example, Dawkins asserts that people adopt the religion of their parents, not after a careful rational comparison of alternative religions, but simply because the memes for that religion are what they are exposed too. Therefore, it seems, people infected by these mind viruses are impervious to argument.

Rebuttal

I completely accept that Dawkins's basic notion of memes is illuminating and captures something true. However, ideas and theories are not passed on by a process of copying in the same way someone might copy the wearing of a baseball cap backwards or the wearing of the latest stylish suit. When parents tell their children a theory about the world, the child does not simply copy this statement, word for word. If the child has understood the theory at all, then the child can extract the sense of the theory and restate it in different words than the those the parents used.

Put differently, there are some ideas we cannot adopt without understanding them—not necessarily a complete or deep understanding, but an understanding of what the idea means. The idea has to be graspable or intelligible.

The child assimilates the new ideas into his network of assumptions about the world. Children already appreciate rudimentary logic and spontaneously work out new implications from the augmented set of assumptions. However, this means that the child will say things that his parents did not, and would not, say. I remember my aunt telling me one day that God is everywhere. Later that day I was walking with her and we passed by a gap in a row of trees. Through the gap, I saw a wide-open field, apparently completely empty. I asked my aunt whether God was there in that field. (Presumably, my question was prompted by the tacit logic: God is everywhere; the field is somewhere; therefore, God must be in the field, even though it looks empty.)

Dawkins assumes that if an idea is adopted for no reason, then reason can't evaluate or reject it. This is a serious and common misunderstanding. I might adopt a choice as to which road to take by tossing a coin, but then later reject my choice because of new evidence that refutes my assumption that the road is leading me to my preferred destination.

ARGUMENT # 9. DUMB DECISION RULES

There's a seemingly endless torrent of popular books explaining how thoroughly dumb and decidedly crazy we all are. To mention just a few examples (and I give the subtitles here as well as the main titles, as they help to convey the flavor of these books): *Kluge: The Haphazard Construction of the Human Mind* (Marcus 2008); *Predictably Irrational: The Hidden Forces that Shape Our Decisions* (Ariely 2009); *Risk: The Science and Politics of Fear* (Gardner 2009); *On Being Certain: Believing You Are Right Even when You're Not* (Burton 2008); *The Hidden Brain: How Our Unconscious Minds Elect Presidents, Control Markets, Wage Wars, and Save Our Lives* (Vedantam 2010); *Sway: The Irresistible Pull of Irrational Behavior* (Brafman and Brafman 2008). All of these books have sold at least fairly well, and some of them are huge best sellers that have been through several editions.

These works are all entertaining and contain many fascinating anecdotes and insights; here I'm only concerned with the message they preach that people are generally irrational.

Here's how the typical argument goes. People's beliefs are not produced by a careful evaluation of the evidence. People are instead led to their beliefs by unjustified systematic biases. Much research has shown how bad we are at forming well-considered beliefs. We use a number of stupid heuristic rules for making decisions. One rule is called anchoring (focusing on an easily accessible value and then making our judgment by adjusting to that). Another is called the ease of recall rule (when estimating the likelihood of some type of event, we will use the rule: 'If you can remember similar events easily, then it's likely'). An example would be our over-estimation of the likelihood of dying in a plane crash because it is much easier to remember plane crashes than car crashes—the latter aren't newsworthy unless they involve the death of a famous person. Another example of the 'easier to remember' rule is that people will estimate the likelihood of a commercial nuclear disaster much higher than a disaster in similar energy-intensive industry such as gas, than is warranted by the statistics, simply because they can easily remember events like Chernobyl and Three Mile Island.

We are incorrigibly locked into these biased modes of thought, and so any ideology that could exploit these biases would be safe from criticism.

Rebuttal

There are a number of points to be made about these supposedly dumb decision rules.

1. In situations requiring rapid decision, they are a way of economizing on valuable time. We need something to work with; some idea is better than none.

2. In the search for the best decision, it does not matter how we arrive at our judgment, provided that we actively seek to check the judgment. I can decide what stock to invest in by consulting tea-leaves, and then use reason to correct the suggestions later by carefully observing the evidence. This is a fundamental methodological point. It's assumed by all this human-bias literature without so much as an argument, that we cannot operate rationally with guesses, that is, judgments formed independently of the evidence. But according to the scientific methodology of falsificationism, championed by Karl Popper, we can and must use guesswork as a source of hypotheses to test, in the quest to get nearer to the truth.

3. The tirade of books that gleefully announce Joe Public's irrational biases overlook the full import of the fact that we *have* discovered them and so we can be made aware of them. This knowledge can

even show us how to redesign institutions to minimize the incidence of costly biases. There are, after all, millions of people who have read at least one of these books, who presumably congratulate themselves that *they*, at least, don't commit these stupid blunders in reasoning.

Fine though this literature is at displaying the sometimes-surprising biases and typical errors that afflict us, it fails to affect my point that people are open to argument. It could only do so by showing that we fall irretrievably into these biases and characteristic errors: it does no such thing. Since we can learn about these typical errors and even give them names, we can escape and even prevent them and so all such errors are open to argument.

Ghostly Logic

We need both abstract logic and our material brain modules to explain the emergence, persistence and death of ideas. How can an abstract thing like logic and a material thing like our brains have a bearing on the same problem? Let me illustrate this with the belief in ghosts. We create beliefs in supernatural agents like ghosts because we are supersensitive to signs of agency; we then cannot easily get rid of these beliefs, even if they are errors, because they are logically irrefutable.

I grant that some ideas do have a degree of stubbornness against criticism. Anthropologists have found that all societies have some belief in ghosts and other supernatural agents. There are two factors working together to cause this relative stubbornness and universality. One is the way our brains are biased by evolution to produce guesses of certain kinds about our world; the other factor is to do with the logic of those guesses. We readily guess the presence of agency, but some of these guesses are irrefutable by direct observation. We form these beliefs because we are supersensitive to any signs of agency in the world. A freak gust of wind on an otherwise still day slams a door behind us and we think there is someone there; we hear voices in the wind or running water and think there is someone there. But though they are relatively stubborn, we can learn to criticize these ideas with the more circumspect methods of internal consistency and consistency with the rest of our knowledge. Our genetically inbuilt module for language helps us to do this, thus compensating for the more reflex and rough-and-ready operation of our modules for detecting agents.

In a world of uncertainty, organisms need to make guesses, to explore and check that world. But we cannot test out every guess. Our ancestors became biased to guess the presence of agency because things with agency—people and animals—were the most important and urgent things in their world (tigers out to eat us, people who may be friend or foe). Rocks, trees, and gusts of wind are not good as friends and rarely pose a threat or short-term opportunity, but people and animals do. Failing to detect a friend or foe can be costly; on the other hand, falsely detecting friend or foe, when not dealing with a consciously motivated person, has little cost—hence the bias.

We may look about for the agent and find none. Is it not rational to abandon the fancy there and then? Not necessarily, because the possible presence of friend or foe has great urgency and importance, so it is a possibility worth extra effort to re-check. However, the thought, 'There is some agent acting to cause the door to slam or the wind to make sounds like voices' is not amenable to refutation. Try as we might to find evidence against it, we can always say 'but we haven't looked in the right place'. And if we chance upon the idea that it is an invisible or remote agent, then that explains our inability to find it. But once we have the idea, we are then saddled with it, because it is logically irrefutable.

We lie awake at night without hope of removing the possibly wrong idea because there is no observation that would put our mind at rest: we look in the kitchen, in the cupboard, and so forth, but we cannot definitively show that it is not there. On the contrary, there are still the odd phenomena that seem to indicate agency and these constantly remind us of our fearful fancy. So, these ideas are irrefutable by direct observation, but nevertheless verifiable in a weak sense. How can we ever divest ourselves of these ideas? In the cold light of dawn the specters are easily removed because we are reminded of reality and can draw on our knowledge of scientific theories that imply that ghosts are non-existent. At least until the next freak gust of wind on an otherwise calm day!

The Orthodoxy

The attempt to evade criticism is familiar to us all. 'It's like talking to a brick wall', 'You can't reason with him; nothing will change his mind', and 'We'll have to agree to disagree' are all commonplace remarks that allude to this common experience and to the assumption that some people are closed to criticism. These phrases suggest, not merely a degree of stubbornness, but a relentless imperviousness to argument. Some people, we are told, have a disposition to believe things whatever the evidence to the contrary.

Many eminent thinkers hold this position. For example, Dawkins, the brilliant Oxford evolutionary zoologist, asserts that some theories can exploit what he calls "blind Faith," so that absurdity not only enhances an idea's ability to spread through the population like a virus, but also makes it secure against counter-evidence: "Another member of the religious meme complex is called faith. It means blind trust in the absence of evidence, even in the teeth of evidence" (1990, p. 198). Despite this gloomy view, Dawkins is one of the most eloquent and ingenious practitioners of rational argument.

Dawkins is not alone in the attribution of absolute stubbornness to certain doctrines. Consider this frightening declaration from Sam Harris:

> Some propositions are so dangerous that it may even be ethical to kill people for believing them. This may seem like an extraordinary claim, but it merely enunciates an ordinary fact about the world in which we live. Certain beliefs place their adherents beyond the reach of every peaceful means of persuasion, while inspiring them to commit acts of extraordinary violence against others. (Harris 2006, p. 53)

Notice that although Harris defends his recommended policy of killing people for having the wrong beliefs by reference to the likely practical consequences of these beliefs, he thinks it is okay to kill them even if the practical consequences he surmises have not yet ensued. Individual religious fundamentalists may be killed even if those individuals have not yet done anything wrong or harmed anyone. We see here (in a particularly grisly instance) how the notion that people who hold different opinions to ourselves have closed minds tends to encourage the abandonment of argument and the resort to violence. If it can be widely understood that, after all, people's minds are not as closed as Harris imagines and their belief systems are vulnerable to rational criticism, then one policy conclusion would be: More explanation, less extermination.

The revered Polish thinker Leszek Kolakowski wrote:

> Not only in the 'socialist bloc', where the authorities used every means to prevent information from seeping in from the outside world, but also in the democratic countries, the Communist parties had created a mentality that was completely immune to all facts and arguments 'from outside,' i.e., from 'bourgeois' sources. (Kolakowski and Falla 1978, p. 452)

In a similar vein, consider the words of the scholar of ideologies, D.J. Manning: "An ideology cannot be challenged by either facts or rival theories" (Manning 1976, p. 142).

I reject these pessimistic pronouncements on the power of argument. I aim to show you that there is far more openness to argument in even the most stubborn people and systems of ideas. Contrary to Dawkins and many other thinkers, I argue that the more absurd a doctrine, and the more it hides from criticism, the less its ability to spread. Investigating this issue will take us on a journey through varied terrain: psychology, sociology, logic, and the philosophy of science.

The Turnover of Adherents

I'm not asking you to deny your own experience. We do meet people who seem impervious to our well-thought-out and carefully marshalled arguments. But there's also the common experience reflected in the expression 'It takes time for the penny to drop'. Often, people change their ideas, or openly admit to changing their ideas, only some time after they have encountered a challenge to these ideas. We may have had the opportunity years later to meet some of these seemingly impervious people and discovered that they have in fact modified or completely changed their minds or that what once seemed vitally important to them now seems less so or even irrelevant. When people are overwhelmed with emotional shock, they seem oblivious to the facts because of the intense emotion, but this may again be an example of the fact that it takes time to absorb the import of the event. As Shakespeare put it: "Thou know'st we work by wit and not by witchcraft, and wit depends on dilatory time" (*Othello* II:iii, lines 376–79).

We also observe that formal organizations devoted to promoting an ideology have a turnover of membership and are subject to splits and other dramatic internal disagreements. When we look at the western Communist Parties in the 1930s, we're at first impressed by what looks like formidable discipline, strength, and staying power. But all the time, some CP members are leaving and new people are joining. Typically, in all such ideological bodies of adherents, there are a few stalwarts who remain at the helm through thick and thin, while the great body of members are continually being replaced. A similar phenomenon affects religious movements. Eileen Barker found that at least sixty-one percent of those who joined the Unification Church during a four-month period in 1978 had left within two and a half years (Barker 1988, p. 167). Others have found very similar defection rates in various minor religious sects.[1]

Of course, this ignores the interesting question of whether the defectors have given up all the beliefs in the doctrines of the movement they have quit. However, most have probably rejected at least some of the ideas, and examples of comprehensive rejection are certainly not hard to find.

If humans are rational then ideologies which fail rational standards will tend to lose support. But even if all humans were very intelligent, sharply critical beings, as well as merely rational, there are limits on how quickly they could eliminate error. It's theoretically possible, therefore, for everyone to be rational in my sense and yet for irrational ideologies to persist for centuries or longer, because large movements may have a high turnover rate. If a movement gains new members at least as fast as it loses them to critical argument, the movement's doctrine may persist for thousands of years even though no one was ever convinced for more than a year (or, more realistically, if only a comparative handful are enduringly convinced). Perhaps the many long-lived false, or futile, or uneconomic, or inconsistent ideologies cited in support of the theory that humans are closed to argument are like the Church of Scientology, where one study found that 100 percent of new converts quit the Church within five years. Tarot, astrology, '9/11 Truth', or ufology, may be systems of ideas that people adopt for a while, partly out of playfulness and curiosity, partly out of conviction, only to abandon them several years later. Even if people were to choose infallibly between correct and erroneous doctrines given several years to decide, we would still expect to see a great number of erroneous doctrines being perpetuated. You don't have to think that some people are closed to argument to explain the prevalence of error or stupidity.

The reader may suspect that by saying this I have conceded much of my case, for if wrong-headed ideologies can gain ground over a long period, then the population as a whole might be described as effectively irrational. I would respond in two ways. First, by asking whether it is totally fortuitous that most people today believe, in contrast to a few hundred years ago, that malaria is caused by mosquito bites, or whether this fact about people's beliefs is in any way connected with the fact that it's *true* that malaria is caused by mosquito bites. Second, I would clarify my position. I do not maintain that the rationally most defensible beliefs will always inevitably or quickly triumph. I maintain that they have a competitive edge, a built-in advantage, in the contest of ideas. The possession of rationally preferable qualities, such as being closer to the truth, is a net advantage, not a net disadvantage, in the survival and spread of ideas, though this inbuilt advantage may, on a particular occasion, be swamped by some other influence.

Aside from the dramatic splits and disagreements in ideological movements, I explore the less obvious, long-term drift and differences of interpretation that systems of ideas are subject to, and the logical and philosophical reasons why this cannot be avoided. The logic of evasion is rather like the logic of lying: just as one lie requires many more to sustain it, an evasion also requires other evasions and these further evasions and modifications then have an unpredictable impact even on the most cherished parts of the system of ideas one is trying to protect. Imagine the ideology as like a whole human body. Sometimes when the propagandist meets criticism by evasion it is as if in repairing the damage to some minor limb a surgeon had taken a graft from an artery to the brain, impairing the whole. This has hardly been explored because we normally think that being closed to argument is simply a matter of a person's stubborn personality or attitude. The way Richard Dawkins frames the issue in terms of blind faith obscures this, as we shall see.

My Sense of 'Rational'

Don't we just know that some people and ideas are irrational and that this imperviousness to argument is merely one reflection of their irrationality? The notion of 'rational' I use here is not equivalent to 'wise' or 'sensible' or 'immune to making mistakes' or 'well-informed' or 'being able to perform perfect calculations' or 'agreeing with me'.

I think many people are poorly informed when they overestimate the frequency of major disasters, like airplane crashes, think that crime is worse now than it was ten or twenty years ago and is getting worse, think that all scientists are agreed that there is an overpopulation problem, or think that there is only one explanation for global warming, but I don't think they are irrational. I think people are unwise for not checking the long-term statistics on crime, but instead using the impression they get from newspapers—they'd not only have the truth, but they would also be happier. Nevertheless, I don't think they are irrational. I think many people are silly when they allow themselves to say negative things without ending on an up-note to maintain a more sensible upbeat attitude, or allow themselves to become hypnotized by long-passed tragedies instead of creating a new happier life, but I don't think they are irrational.

The rationality I have in mind is more of an economic and logical conception. If we accept economic theory and evolutionary theory, both of which are powerful and testable explanatory theories, then we ought to accept their implications for how people behave. What do these theories imply? At the very least, economic theory implies that people conform to what is known as 'folk psychology'. People are agents who have beliefs, wants, and capacities. You can understand people by figuring out what they want to do and achieve and what they believe about the feasibility and cost of doing so. We are so used to this way of thinking we may overlook it. But it's also a way of thinking we cannot help. We see a man walking across the road and we automatically impute wishes and beliefs to him. For example, he's walking across the road because he wants to get to the other side and he believes he can get there without too much cost.

Many of these explanations of peoples' actions are banal and usually not worth mentioning. However, as economics has shown us, a systematic application of this type of explanation can yield surprisingly satisfying insights. I'm saying that the same holds about the issue of imperviousness to argument. Our ancestors would not have been our ancestors had they not evolved to take account of reality: if they had spent their time wasting resources and pursuing futile actions. If our Pleistocene ancestors, on observing two saber-tooths go into a cave and only one emerge, had a tendency to go into the cave, they and their genes would have been eliminated. Of the myriad competing ideas, people prefer to adopt ideas that are logical, effective, and least costly and help to render their emotions appropriate to the world. Therefore, people are sensitive to criticism that hinges on these criteria or standards. I am not arguing that logic and economics are always decisive in the life of ideas, but only that they exert a powerful influence. Other factors are at work in our adoption and rejection of ideas. However, all I need to show is that this influence is enough to prevent absolute imperviousness to argument.

What Would an Irrational Human Look Like?

Is an irrational human in my sense conceptually possible? If not, then I would merely be defining 'rational' so broadly that we couldn't even imagine an irrational human, and my thesis would lose some of its interest. I think an irrational human would actually look quite strange to us, but we can imagine such a thing. A popular view of an irrational being is a zombie, but a zombie, at least of the *Living Dead* variety, would be rational in my sense, though not very bright. Zombies act to achieve a definite goal, and in pursuit of that goal, they try to avoid obstacles and will seek the shortest and easiest route. The fact that this goal is the consumption of human brains is amusing, but does not gainsay their rationality. They have a strange goal and limited intelligence, but they don't defy logic or economics.

It's hard to imagine a truly irrational human. Let's make a more extreme thought experiment to see if we can imagine such a human being. Suppose someone was captured by aliens and they controlled his brain and his actions. Some mischievous alien children might play around with their toy human. I imagine that for fun they wish to confound Earth economists. They might make their toy human always choose less of any good for the same price, always take the larger risk with the same or lower expected returns, continually espouse contradictory opinions in the same breath, try to walk through walls, always try to pick up things he knows he cannot lift, always take what he knows is the longest and hardest route to any goal with the highest opportunity cost. Now, imagine a person doing this without first being abducted by aliens. Some Austrian Economists, such as Ludwig von Mises, have claimed that this is not conceptually possible, but I think my thought experiment shows otherwise. It is perfectly conceivable, but—except perhaps for very few people with severe brain damage—we just don't see such behavior.

Terrorism and Emotion

Surely emotion is a great barrier to reason? Am I ignoring the rise of suicide terrorism? This surely undermines the idea that we evolved as rational creatures. Does terrorism not illustrate that people can be closed to argument?

Some people suppose that the 9/11 atrocity was the result of demented minds. Weren't these people driven by irrational emotions that do not simply cloud judgement, but even eliminate judgement? For emotions, especially strong violent ones, are not connected with ideas or theories and are therefore not amenable to control by argument.

However, it's both facile and factually incorrect to represent suicide terrorists as simply demented or believing they will be rewarded by 'seventy-two virgins in paradise'. Recent analyses show that their motivations are more like the motivations of other patriots, soldiers, or political activists. They have definite political aims and definite (and often well-crafted) means to achieve those aims. When we look at the 9/11 horror, we are looking, not at an irrational cocktail of emotion, but at the successful execution of a well-planned strategy. 9/11 issued from a propagandistic network of ideas. And 9/11 was successful: the hi-jackers, nearly all Saudis, wanted US troops withdrawn from Saudi Arabia, and eighteen months after 9/11, without fanfare, all US troops were withdrawn from Saudi Arabia.

Walter Laqueur in *The Age of Terrorism* contends that the chances of success in terrorism are slight:

> The main difficulty is not that the rational model is useless with regard to people engaging in suicide missions (of which there are only few), but that it tends to ignore factors such as frustration, anger, fanaticism, aggression, etc., which are very frequent in terrorism. Above all, economic man is a rational being wishing to maximize beneficial returns; few people would go into a business in which the chances of success are as dim as they are in terrorism. (p. 153)

However, the fanatic, who wittingly sacrifices everything he values to a single cause, who is unmoved by the perceived effectiveness and cost of his actions, is a myth. It's a commonplace that the terrorist of today is often the statesman of tomorrow: Menachem Begin, Archbishop Makarios, and Gerry Adams are well-known examples. As we will see a bit later, suicide terrorism is an exceptionally effective type of operation: it gets results, and has spread since 1980 precisely because it gets results far more reliably than any alternative open to the groups which employ it.

The Problem

Western culture holds in high esteem the give and take of open debate. This seems to have originated with Thales, the founder of the Ionian school of philosophy, the first to encourage criticism of the master. Before Thales cosmology or philosophy was taught by dogmatic schools. These schools had the function of preserving the doctrine of the founder or first master. New ideas were not admitted, and their inventors were dismissed as heretics. This type of school is the general rule in all civilizations. However, Thales allowed one of his pupils, Anaximander, to criticize his own theory. Moreover, since this went against tradition, it seems likely that Thales must have actively encouraged his pupils to criticize his theories. This would explain why a mere two generations later this critical attitude is explicitly formulated in the fragments of Xenophanes.[2] I conjecture that this liberal attitude to criticism was made more popular by the rise of science, which the Ionian tradition, revived in the Renaissance by Galileo Galilei and others, made possible.

But western culture also seems to have produced systems of ideas that scorn open debate, ideas that seem impervious to criticism or counter-evidence and seem to have gained evangelistic strength through this very imperviousness. The classic examples, at least in the opinion of Karl Popper, are Marxism and Freudianism. Others, such as Bartley, have focused their analysis on systems such as Christianity. Is this imperviousness to criticism real or merely apparent? Is it absolutely rigid or a matter of degree? My answer is that the imperviousness we see is real but merely a matter of degree.

In this book I quote a number of writers who maintain that followers of various belief-systems have closed minds, that they cannot be reached by reasoned argument. Someone might say that these writers don't mean this literally; they are exaggerating for rhetorical effect and don't really intend to attribute absolute imperviousness. I think it will be clear as we go on that at least some of these writers do indeed quite literally mean what they say. Those attributing absolute imperviousness to certain systems include Richard Dawkins, W.W. Bartley III, Karl Popper, D.J. Manning, Leszeck Kolakowski, Ronald Knox, Eric Hoffer, and Gustave Le Bon.

However, the claim that some people's minds are completely closed to argument might be worth investigating even if no one who made it meant it quite literally. A theoretical problem and an associated position on that problem have an autonomous existence and may be interesting even if they cannot be attributed to any one person. Some popular theories are trivial; some 'straw men' are profoundly interesting. For example, Popper's criticism of historicism was often criticized because it was thought that the theory that Popper examined could not be attributed to anyone.[3] Nevertheless, the insights that emerged through Popper's criticism of a somewhat contrived theory made the enterprise worthwhile. So I will not allocate any more space to the possibility that some proponents of the Closed Mind theory may not mean it literally. I am simply interested in the problem of the survival of belief systems in the face of criticism, and one way to come at that problem is to scrutinize the typical allegation that such systems can be insulated from criticism by easy tricks.

I propose to look at this problem from the point of view of the propagandist, the persuader, the proselytizer, the person who takes upon himself the task of 'spreading the word'. How can a propagandist preserve his message intact against criticism, and ensure its propagation and the recruitment of new adherents? Can a propagandist protect his message from criticism by relying on clever formulation or sociological manipulations, and thereby guarantee it against losses in credibility and propagation? Can he do what Leszek Kolakowski evidently supposes possible when he asserts that:

the Communist parties had created a mentality which was completely immune to all facts and arguments 'from outside', i.e. 'bourgeois' sources. (Kolakowski 1978, p. 452)

Or in general, as Hoffer supposes:

to interpose a fact-proof screen between the faithful and the realities of the world. (Hoffer 1962, p. 75)

I am looking at the problem as the strategic problem of the propagandist. I use the word 'propagandist' in a neutral sense, neither pejorative nor dismissive. I simply mean someone who is intent on promoting some view or doctrine by persuasion. I also use the word 'ideology'. By this I simply mean a system of ideas or beliefs. The points I am making are general and apply to all promoters of ideas and all systems of beliefs. Formally worked-out ideologies or doctrines associated with formal organizations are especially interesting because they embody some of the more intricate and abstract devices for evading criticism, because they allow us to explore how evasive parts of a doctrine may affect other parts, and because we can study how they influence the long-term future of the doctrine. Evasive moves in everyday conversation are too fleeting to permit this kind of study of the effectiveness of evasion of criticism in the long term.

Looking at the problem as a problem of propaganda, persuasion, and recruitment is a useful heuristic, and should not be taken as implying that many of the processes by which an ideology is modified under criticism are necessarily a matter of planning or conscious control by the propagandist. Ever since David Hume raised the important issue of the unintended results of intentional action, unplanned and unforeseen effects of action have loomed large in the social sciences. Such patterned effects are of considerable importance to my argument, and indeed they are among the reasons why a propagandist cannot guarantee his message against criticism. I am simply choosing the most difficult case for my argument: a network of ideas to whose propagation and protection someone is devoted, someone who makes the propagation of these ideas a strategic task.

My General Position.

The purpose of this book is to offer you a bold counterblast to the popular theory that some people and ideas are impervious to argument. But

I want to focus on the types of ideas that seem to dominate the world: ideas such as Marxism, Freudianism, fascism, and various religions. I can concede the existence of some individuals who are impervious to argument, individuals who play almost no role in the life of influential ideas. But it is in the life (and death) of supposedly world-dominating ideas where we can see all the evasive tricks and manipulative ploys to evade criticism and the greatest resources spent to immortalize ideas. It is therefore these systems of ideas, often supposed to be held in an irrational way and for irrational motives, that will be a good test of my argument.

Imagine yourself as someone who simply wants to hold on stubbornly to his ideas in the face of criticism and who wants to propagate these ideas throughout a population and down the generations. Imagine yourself as a Marx, an Ayn Rand, or the leader of a religious sect. Your ideal would be a guarantee that you could: 1. propagate your network of ideas without revision and 2. completely insulate it against losses in credibility and adherents through criticism. I argue that you cannot have both. You must face a trade-off: to the extent that a network of ideas tries to save its credibility by meeting criticism, it changes itself; to the extent that it does not try to meet criticism, it loses believers.

At this point someone might ask 'What about Jonestown?' Jonestown was a communal settlement in northwestern Guyana, made by the People's Temple, a cult from California, led by a Protestant minister, Jim Jones. Jim Jones (according to some accounts) convinced nine hundred members of his sect to commit suicide on November 18th, 1978, for the sake of their religious beliefs. Was not Jim Jones a highly effective propagandist in spreading an irrational system of ideas? No. Where is the People's Temple today?

Such charismatic cults that have seemingly monopolized people's minds and induced them to self-destructive behavior are perfect examples of my point. They only succeed in safeguarding the system of ideas by sacrificing their ability to spread outside what is typically a maximum of about a thousand people. They are rather like extremely virulent viruses: they are usually poor at spreading just because they kill off their hosts too quickly. Jim Jones was apparently aware of the trade-off I am arguing for. Implicitly he must have appreciated that there was far too much critical thinking in the larger society to risk much contact with it—hence the rules of inner cohesion and the prohibition of communications with the outside world that Marc Galanter and others have described. Few have drawn the corollary which I draw: that 'rational' ideas have a better chance of spreading than 'irrational' ideas.

The Logic in Ideology

Here is my outrageous idea. If a network of ideas is false, or inconsistent, or fails to solve its intended problem, or is unfeasible, or is too costly in terms of necessarily forsaken goals, its chances of spreading may be undermined given only true assumptions and valid arguments. People prefer to adopt and spread ideologies that:

1. **are logically consistent;**

2. **are more truth-like and of higher information content than their rivals;**

3. **systematically organize their content;**

4. **solve their problems better than their rivals;**

5. **do not contain unfeasible demands; and**

6. **do not contain uneconomic (excessively costly) demands.**

In the Darwinian perspective, that which does not match the relevant criteria of survival is eliminated or filtered out. Truth and validity act as Darwinian filters on the spread of ideas. You may be tempted to object and point to all the uneliminated erroneous doctrines. Tens of thousands believe in UFOs, spoon-bending, astrology, and so forth. But such an objection is superficial, since a Darwinian filter does not have to be one-hundred-percent effective to be effective. People are fallible, hence some ideologies that violate one or more of the rational filters, #1 through #6, may escape rational elimination. However, this does not mean that having escaped some rounds of rational elimination, they will continue to do so indefinitely.[4]

My general argument flows from three main propositions:

a. **That all propaganda messages are in a logical sense criticizable**

b. **That the propagandist trying to propagate a doctrine is constrained by the logic of his situation to expose his message to criticism**

c. **That our evolutionary past has given us, if not perfect, then at least robust rationality**

a. *All propaganda messages are in a logical sense criticizable.* All doctrines and ideological platforms, not just false assumptions and invalid arguments, are criticizable in a methodological and logical sense. This is the sense in which something is criticizable if you can check or test it by some method or other. There are systematic methods of checking claims (proposals, theories, and arguments) in any field. (This is a rough statement of the core of Bartley's philosophy of Comprehensively Critical Rationalism.)

I need to assert this obvious point here, as many philosophers have contended that there are positions that you must simply accept or reject, and that cannot reasonably be said to be open to argument. For example, some have argued that if we are rational then we cannot criticize logic, for criticism requires logic and therefore would presuppose logic! My brief counter to this is that just as one can coherently use a computer to run a program on it to test the program or the computer, one can use logic to check logic. To test a hammer I don't have to assume it works correctly!

Another suggestion is that the logic of argument itself forces us to stop at some point because all argument starts from premises but we cannot justify the premises ad infinitum: therefore, we have to adopt some unshakeable privileged assumption or assumptions as a starting point for our arguments. My brief answer here is that if our goal is truth (or the closest available approximation to truth) as opposed to justification, then we can check the premises by confrontation with reality: our positions are still controlled by critical argument. Consider the following argument. 'All mammals live on land; a whale lives in the sea; therefore, a whale is not a mammal.' Even though we could never justify the assumption that all animals live on land, we might be able to show it is wrong by discovering an exception: a mammal that lives in water. Even if we cannot justify a position we can still remove one of its rivals if it is found to be false.

There are complex issues here, but I must address them briefly, because the suggestion that logic itself may justify being closed to argument might seem to undermine my case at a deep level. There are related issues to do with relativism, nihilism, incommensurable frameworks and other philosophical assumptions that would seem to place ultimate barriers to openness to argument. Some light will be shed on these issues in the course of this book.

b. *The propagandist trying to propagate a doctrine is constrained by the logic of his situation to expose his message to criticism.* Here I employ the theory of *the logic of the situation*, situational logic, sometimes called strategic analysis. In a strategic analysis we take the aims, knowledge, and skills of an agent or agents, plus the constraints they are acting under and discover the intended and unintended consequences that flow from this situation.

Strategic analysis can sometimes explain odd or costly behavior. At the main opening to my university there is a barrier for incoming traffic and another for outgoing traffic. The barrier has to be raised to comfortably walk through, otherwise, you have to bend down uncomfortably with your books. The guards are in a building with very reflective glass so that you cannot see whether they have seen you or not. If they have not and you walk under a raised barrier, they may accidentally lower it on your head. Therefore, even though it is far more comfortable to walk through the open barrier, you might choose to clamber under the lowered barrier. This must look odd to the security guards; unless they think that I think they may not have seen me.

When a general analyzes a battle, for example, especially how one side lost, this is the kind of analysis that he performs. Now imagine yourself in the shoes of the propagandist. You face a sea of already thriving ideas all competing for the minds of people. A number of things may then become apparent to you. The successful propagandist cannot ignore criticism, but rather has an interest in meeting criticism. Ignoring criticism means that the propagandist has fewer opportunity to improve his ability to convince others of the ideology, that he has fewer chances to consolidate his retention of the ideology, and that he fails to take account of competing ideas. However, if he meets criticism, he then exposes his message to criticisms he cannot predict.

A belief system or ideology is a theory. Theories have an infinite number of implications and ramifications, and I will show that these logical properties preclude propagandistic efforts to guarantee a systematic exclusion of dissent or to prevent the evolution of factions. Someone might argue that with many false doctrines, most people won't have the time or percipience to work out many of the implications. But that also applies to the leaders policing dissent. In other words, some dissent is not obvious: but non-obvious dissent is sometimes all that is needed for schism to develop, step by imperceptible step. Darwin reminded us that a significant number of imperceptible steps could yield a big step.

This issue is connected with what some have called the frame problem, originally posed by robot designers. A robot needs a goal and 'beliefs' about the world relevant to its task. Taking an action often changes the facts. But which changes are relevant? After taking an action, what beliefs need to be updated to ensure continued successful action toward a given goal? This is a fundamental challenge. Well, the same can be said about human beliefs if they are an extensive web of connected suppositions: changing one requires that others may have to be changed, but which ones are relevant? I will show that, for ideologies, you cannot give a comprehensive answer to this question in advance.

c. *Our evolutionary past has given us, if not perfect, then at least robust rationality.* People are products of Darwinian evolution with a rich set of inborn problem-solving strategies and knowledge adapted to the world. The blank-slate view of human nature is hardly defendable today. Perhaps one of the most dramatic battles in the nature-nurture debate was Noam Chomsky's devastating review of B.F. Skinner's 'Verbal Behavior'. Skinner wanted to explain language acquisition through the child's exposure to many stimulus and reward situations. But Chomsky pointed out that this was inadequate: there simply are not enough stimuli to account for how the child develops the ability to understand and produce an unlimited number of different sentences that have never been uttered before.

Chomsky's theory of language, which posits inborn rules for acquiring a language, helped to set the stage for the rise of cognitive psychology which, not to exaggerate, kicked the stuffing out of behaviorism and the over-socialized conception of people. It became clear that the debate, in any case, could not be over the question of whether there are inborn rules, but over just what those rules are. Even Skinner acknowledged the existence of evolved general rules that explain how organisms systematically respond to reinforcement schedules. People cannot be shaped in any desired way according to carefully arranged circumstances. In the light of the findings of evolutionary psychology and anthropology, which have cracked the slate in so many directions, it is no longer plausible that people can be shaped in the image of any ideology. A Stalin, a Hitler, or religious leader is constrained by people's native dispositions to think in certain ways.

Evolutionary psychology shows us that people are born already equipped with surprisingly sophisticated rules for dealing with the world. For example, consider a child's intuitive natural history. It is quite abstract. Children without any tuition will automatically assume that if one hen lays eggs, all hens will, or if one cow gives birth through live young, then all cows will give birth in the same way. If one hen lays an egg and others do not, the child will be surprised. The world has changed over our evolutionary history, but it has long-term general structural properties that people have adapted to: stable objects governed by physics, people governed by their beliefs and desires and their use of language, animals governed by other rules, tools governed by engineering rules. As a result people have evolved with an intuitive grasp of various aspects of the world: an intuitive physics, an intuitive biology, an intuitive psychology, an intuitive number sense, an intuitive economics, and a mental database with which we represent ideas and from which we infer other ideas and check others. Most importantly, people have a language with which they can use these various 'faculties' to go far beyond the partly isolated, distorted and partially ignorant account of the world that the faculties or modules provide.

Humans are rational in the following senses: they prefer to take account of the opportunity costs and benefits of their actions; they prefer to abandon what is futile; they are curious (they want to explore the unknown); they tend to develop beliefs on important issues in accord with fearful and wishful thinking, enabling these beliefs to be better tested; they try to resolve inconsistencies in their beliefs, thereby thinking in accord with the rules of logic; and they adapt their emotional reactions to what they perceive as facts.

There are qualifications to be made. People don't always make the optimal choice in logical or economic problems. We have been adapted to our ancestors' environment, not to our current advanced industrial urban society. Also, our various inborn strategies and knowledge is often adapted to specific domains and may show typical biases toward error outside these domains. But I don't think that these qualifications render our respect for logic and economics impotent. For example, our perceptual system is better than any artificial system we have built, but it also gives us illusions that we cannot change: when you look at a mirage or the apparent bending of a spoon in water you cannot help but see the illusion even when you know it's an illusion. But, unlike other animals, we can know it is an illusion and take account of it. This is where our language enables us to think beyond the sometimes distorted information provided by our ancestral problem-solving modules, to frame conjectures and make inferences about things beyond immediate inspection. A similar point can be made about other types of typical errors that people are liable to manifest. People are also fallible and take time to think. People make mistakes and could in principle think faster, but we hardly need an explanation for why we are not gods.

Someone might accept that we're creatures of evolution, but think that that only shows that we're under the control of irrational emotions. Freud's unconscious 'id' comes to mind. Aggressive territoriality, unreasoning sexual drive, inter-group hostility, are all candidates. I argue that intense emotion is no absolute barrier to argument, though it may temporarily impair the understanding of critical argument. The theory that people adopt ideologies because of thoughtless emotion seems to imply that they are closed to argument, for what would the target of that argument be? I will argue that all emotion is under the control of our theory about the world and our place within it, and so even intensely passionate ideologies have a theoretical target for criticism. Even things like respect for the flag, attachment to the nation, patriotism, devotion to the emperor or other leader, snobbery, racial hatred, religious fundamentalism, or global jihad are all under the control of some web of assumptions, some of them perhaps unexamined and not even explicitly formulated.

It makes evolutionary sense that the emotions we have are under the control of our theory of the world for how else could they be appropriate to fairly complex, subtle, remote, or hypothetical circumstances? We are born with a disposition to build up a web or database of ideas about the world. It is based on theories about what's what, what's where, who did what to whom, when, where and why. We can combine and recombine these theories with the logical operators of 'and', 'or', 'not', 'all, 'some', 'necessary', 'possible', and 'cause'. Anthropologists have found that all peoples are fascinated by stories and use these stories to explain their place in the world. Evolutionary psychology explains why. We evolved in highly social groups and so it made evolutionary sense to track and reason about social events to know whom to avoid or socialize or co-operate and trade with. The emotions we have are the emotions that are appropriate to our stories and helped to make our actions appropriate to complex social circumstances.

What do we mean by the perpetuation or change of a movement or a system of beliefs? When we talk of a movement we refer to a mass of people and an associated doctrine. There is a trade-off between the strength of belief in the movement—roughly indicated by number and turnover of adherents—and doctrinal integrity. The two principles, Darwinian evolution and situational logic, together explain the trade-off between the perpetuation of the movement and the integrity of the message. When a doctrine suffers from criticism, adherents often defect if the doctrine is not changed. The general consequence is that the intellectual leaders of the movement make marginal revisions in the doctrine in order to keep up the numbers of propagandists while retaining as much of the original doctrine intact. This may occur as a planned process, but may also occur as a result of a filtering Darwinian-like process whereby variants (themselves designed or accidental) of the original doctrine are subject to criticism, the strongest surviving and being reproduced.

Contrary to C.R. Hallpike (1988), both conscious and 'blind' selection processes may occur.[5] Because of the insuperable problem of achieving conformity in the interpretation and defense of an ideology, different propagandists will be disposed to employ different presentations of the ideology. Some of these will be better at passing the rational rejection than others, and this will be the case independently of whether the variants are deliberately constructed to evade criticism by hoodwinking the critic or constitute misinterpretations of the original position. An accumulation of marginal revisions can make a large difference, just as in biological evolution an accumulation of numerous successive slight variations can make the difference between a virus-like entity and a human being. But though these changes are taking place, they may be masked by the more conspicuous trappings of the movement: the name, the emblems, the flags, the slogans may remain the same, and the absolute number of adherents may even increase. So we tend to see an illusion of immutable ideologies careering like juggernauts down the corridors of time.

Why Dawkins's Memetic Approach Is Not Enough

Dawkins made a great advance in understanding the life of ideas by introducing the theory of memes to explain the relative success of different systems of ideas. His theory, which sees the spread of ideas on a par with the fashion of wearing a baseball cap backwards or a computer virus, forced us to see that the life of ideas is not reducible to what happens in peoples' heads. Ideas have a life of their own. The key question, Dawkins correctly argues, is how 'copyable' an idea may be. How good is an idea at making more copies of itself?

The fashion of wearing a baseball cap backwards and computer viruses spread because they are good at inducing their hosts to make more copies of them. However, when it comes to ideas that have a theoretical aspect, Dawkins fails to mention that there is a logical task. Propagating Marxism, for example, is fundamentally different from propagating wearing a baseball cap backwards. Mouthing at random the terms 'capitalism', 'class struggle', 'dictatorship of the proletariat', or 'social relations of production' will not make you a Marxist: you need to have an inkling of what these terms mean and how they are related to one another.

Dawkins does introduce the idea of a memeplex—a network of mutually supporting memes that help one another to reproduce, and this partly explains the difference between the baseball cap and Marxism. Marxism is a memeplex, and the various evasive tricks and ideas that have accreted to it supposedly help to reproduce their host and each other. Wearing a baseball cap backwards is just a fashionable habit with little or no theory behind it. Dawkins shows us that it is important to analyze the interactions within or between ideas. But the memeplex idea still overlooks the role of logic. This is not surprising in Dawkins's purely materialistic account: what could logic, as abstract relations between ideas, have to do with what happens in a materialistic account of the world?

Normally, we think of closeness to argument as a matter of a person's stubbornness. But I am asking you to consider a less obvious aspect. The propagandist's task in propagating an idea is not simply a sociological or psychological one of motivating and organizing people to pass it on. Nor is it, as Dawkins says, just a matter of copyability. It is a logical task: otherwise how can one tell that the successive generations of adherents are replicating the same doctrine? To adopt an idea is to grasp its meaning, and this involves logical relations. How can one tell whether the idea is being applied properly? Texts and speeches are not simply marks on paper or noises, but have to be interpreted the same way for replication of the doctrine to be faithful. Trying to ensure that this will occur is profoundly difficult. There is, therefore, an ever-present tendency for unintentional schism and drift to occur in the interpretation of any propagandist's message.

The concept of openness to criticism is not simply a psychological and sociological one, but is also a logical one. There may be distinctly psychological, sociological, and logical barriers to criticism. For example, wishful thinking, universally thought to be a barrier to criticism, is clearly a psychological matter; group hostility to criticism and rules and traditions against dissent are obviously sociological. Someone may try to reject the legitimacy or relevance of logic, which would—if successful—be a barrier to criticism. Using immunizing stratagems is a methodological barrier. Dawkins's way of describing memes obscures these distinctions.

I fully accept that one can specify rules which if scrupulously followed would make an ideology unresponsive to argument. One could simply stipulate that criticism be ignored: if one encounters criticism, maintain one's position. There are ways or methods of dealing with criticism which exclude taking account of criticism not as a conscious aim but as an unintended logical consequence. The evasion of criticism in such a case would not count as a stratagem, but as a systematic consequence of the method of responding to criticism. If a Christian invariably responds to criticism simply by maintaining that one cannot understand

God until one believes in his existence, then the Christian's position would appear to be secure against criticism. After all, if the critic becomes a believer he is no longer a critic. Similarly, if an extreme follower of the socialist Georg Lukács always insists that his critics cannot understand the proletarian point of view until they join the struggle, then (providing this is all he does) his position is secure against criticism.

The question, however, is whether a propagandist with the goal of propagating his doctrine and subject to certain evolutionary and current situational constraints could maintain such methods in the face of all potential criticism, and still have a good chance of satisfying his goals. I'm arguing that this is not possible. Evasion of criticism is not so easy. Even if the atheist is converted, new puzzles and questions may arise about the nature of the Christian God; for example, how is it possible for God to consist of three persons as seems to be implied in the notion of the Trinity? Believers who have embraced one another as belonging to the same flock may be shocked to find their common ground disappear before them. You often find, in the history of belief systems, that adherents of an ideology suppose that they all believe the same thing, then a new issue arises which splits the movement, with each side believing that its interpretation is the one that follows naturally from the ideas they all thought they held before the schism. Hence the fact that, throughout the history of Christianity, church councils have been convened to settle points of doctrine, to determine what constitutes correct or 'orthodox' belief.

Similarly, Lukacs's epigone may be embarrassed to find newly converted members of the proletarian movement quarrelling among themselves, or that he is alone in his own interpretation of the class struggle. I was told by an ex-member of the Socialist Party of Great Britain (SPGB) that a very prominent member would occasionally express his concern that "the members do not understand the Party case." (The SPGB, a small Marxist group founded in 1904, refers to its distinctive doctrine and world-view as its 'case', and all applicants for membership are examined to determine whether they know and agree with this 'case'.)

An extreme version of this sort of criticism-deflecting stance would be the theory that all argument is illusory, that the notions of validity and logical truth are unreal. However, one might ask: if this position is very effective in protecting an ideology, why is it not simply incorporated by every aspiring ideology? This would provide cast-iron proof against dissent, would it not? My answer is that the potential converts of an ideology are rational in the ways I have mentioned. Such an antilogical adjunct to an ideology would deprive it of its power to explain new circumstances and also of its power to defend itself against competing ideologies that happen to address themselves to people's rationality. Even such seemingly mystical ideologies as astrology and tarot pay some respect to logic in their systematic nature. Moreover, an ideology that rejects or belittles logic runs the risk of not being able to police heresy and prevent the strains of internal dissension, for it will not be able to say systematically what is and what is not part of the doctrine. Without some respect for logic it is impossible to learn a language, let alone a particular doctrine. For these reasons the rejection of logic is not feasible, while occasional rhetorical rejection of logic is usually mere bluff or confusion.

Obviously, a doctrine whose descriptive elements are true and solves all the problems for which it was produced better than its rivals is guaranteed against sound criticism in a logical sense. A true and practically optimal doctrine cannot be refuted or shown to be futile. However, epistemologically, no one could guarantee either that a doctrine is flawless or that the methodological rules that explicitly or implicitly exclude taking account of sound criticism will be followed.[6]

Is My Argument Open to Argument?

Suppose we are having an argument and I insist that all Indian elephants have five stomachs. If I'm wrong, you can in principle easily show that I'm wrong by finding just one Indian elephant that does not have five stomachs. However, if, after you embarrass me with this refutation, I insist that there might still be one elephant that has five stomachs, and that this is the only truly Indian elephant, but it just hasn't been found yet, then I'm safe from the refutation of direct observation. For no matter how far and wide you look for a five-stomached elephant without finding it, I can always insist that it is elsewhere at some other time. (I might even be so awkward as to say that, at least all elephants in the distant past had five stomachs.) My argument would have assumed the character of what Popper called a metaphysical theory: the mere assertion that something of some character exists at some unspecified time and place. Simple versions of ufology, beliefs in ghosts, or vague astrological predictions, are like this. Neither 'There are aliens' nor 'There are ghosts' nor 'Our personal life trajectories are governed by the positions of the planets' can be shown to be wrong by direct observation.

My general position is metaphysical in Popper's sense, in that it is not open to direct empirical refutation. But in this respect it is no worse than my opponents' position: that there are systems of ideas that are completely insulated from criticism. No matter how many systems of ideas are shown to be open to criticism, it is always possible for my opponents to re-assert the existence of some, perhaps as yet undiscovered, system of ideas that is completely insulated from criticism. I am forced by my opponents to examine each of their supposed examples of absolutely reinforced dogmatisms and criticize their reasons for taking them as such.

But I can also develop a more general argument by showing that the idea that some people and ideas are completely impervious to criticism is inconsistent with other powerful theories that are more open to direct refutation. This is an important point in the philosophy of science. Popper, as well as Watkins and Agassi among others, have argued that even metaphysical theories are rationally arguable and criticizable despite their not being open to direct refutation by the falsification of their empirical implications (since by definition they do not have any empirical implications that can contradict a basic statement—a statement describing an event at a spatio-temporally restricted location). One can argue, for instance, that they fail to solve the problem they were supposed to solve, or that they are inconsistent with another theory of higher informative content that is open to direct refutation, or one that is regarded as unproblematic at the time.

For example, the statement that there is an acid that can dissolve gold is logically closed to direct refutation by observation, since no matter how far one looked without finding the acid, one could always suppose it would be found sometime. However, the idea that gold has a solvent is incompatible with chemical theory, a theory rich in explanatory power and itself open to observational refutation. The idea that Indian elephants have five stomachs may be inconsistent with biological theory. I believe this is the case with my opponents' position: it is inconsistent with Darwinian theory, with economic theory, and with an analysis of the strategic logic of the propagandist. My argument is open to any criticism that shows that Darwinian evolution can be expected to develop organisms that thrive on error—not simply being fallible, with systematic biases, but predominantly prone to get things wrong. My argument is also open to arguments that undermine my strategic analysis of propaganda and to arguments that refute the basic assumptions of economic theory.

To press this point home, I'll use another hypothetical conversation. First, lets look at temperature adaptation in animals. In 1847, the German biologist Carl Bergmann observed that large animals tended to live in the colder regions of the earth, while small animals tended to live in the hotter regions. Bergmann propounded two fundamental reasons for this. The first is that large bodies have more cells and consequently produce more heat, making it more difficult to keep core body temperature down to its optimum. The second reason is that larger bodies of the same shape have a much smaller surface area relative to body volume, but the rate of heat loss is proportional to surface area. Galileo showed with cube shaped boxes that volume increases twice as fast as surface area, and a similar disparity applies to more oddly shaped masses. Having accepted Bergmann's theory, imagine someone telling you that he thinks that there is a species of mice that share all the same ecological regions as Polar Bears. I think you'd be well placed to refute this tale without having to don your big fur coat. (There are voles—*Microtus epiroticus*—that live on the island Svalbard, which is within the Arctic. However, this island is 550 miles south of the North Pole, and the voles live in abandoned buildings, not exactly Polar Bear ecology.)

By analogy, we can refute the existence of the closed mind by general arguments from economics, evolution, psychology, and logic. Of course, it's logically possible that there is a species of vole that has a special hitherto unknown mechanism for keeping its optimum core temperature in extremely cold environments. We could be surprised. But, without independent observations of voles living in these environments, the onus is on the arctic vole theorist to supply details of such a mechanism. The same point applies to the closed mind pundit: he needs to supply mechanisms that would make a closed mind. Attempts have been made to do just this, but they only succeed in finding biases and common errors, not incorrigibly closed mind mechanisms. Talk of 'cognitive traps' by theorists such as Daniel Kahnemann obscures this.

The Examples of Marxism and Freudianism

Near the end of this book I look at two propagandistic systems of ideas: Marxism and Freudianism. Karl Popper maintained that Marxism and Freudianism are closed to argument. In Popper's view, Freudianism was from the beginning closed off from criticism, whereas Marxism began life as refutable, but then in response to telling criticism used clever devices—immunizing stratagems—to save itself.

I don't think anyone would take issue with the assumption that Marxism is propagandistic, that its adherents wish its ideas to propagate through the population. At first sight, it may seem that unlike Marxism, Freudianism is not propagandistic, but simply a scholarly and therapeutic occupation. But Freud was explicit in his desire that psychoanalysis become a successful 'movement', and wrote a book called *On the History of the Psychoanalytic Movement*, in which he describes how the spread of his ideas was carefully planned. At the second Congress of Psychoanalysts in Nuremberg, in March 1910, the International Psychoanalytic Association was founded. Its declared aim was:

> To foster and further the science of psychoanalysis founded by Freud, both as pure psychology and in its application to medicine and the mental sciences; and to promote mutual support among members in all endeavours to acquire and spread psychoanalytic knowledge. (Freud 1990, pp. 50–51)

Freud was aware early on of the difficulties of keeping the adherents of a doctrine from straying from the true path. The IAP was intended to give new members a 'guarantee' of proper understanding and to monitor publications for heresy:

> There should be some headquarters whose business would be to declare: "All this nonsense is nothing to do with psychoanalysis; this is not psychoanalysis." (Freud 1990, p. 50)

Adler, representing the Vienna group, feared that "censorship and restriction of scientific freedom" were intended (Quoted in Freud 1990, p. 51).

Gellner (1985, p. 8) has pointed out that Freud justified Jung's rapid elevation within the movement against the anger of Freud's older followers by arguing that favoring non-Jewish entrants was politically essential for the successful expansion of the movement. Freud did the same thing in the United States, with the ill-fated Horace Frink, for the same reason. Freud, therefore, was interested in the propagation of his ideas and, at least initially, under the impression that this could be guaranteed by proper planning and instruction. Freudianism is thus an ideology and also a 'movement' disseminating that ideology, within the scope of my argument.

I suspect that not just the adherents of any scholarly or therapeutic system of ideas, but most people desire greater public knowledge and acceptance of their ideas. This quite harmless fact is obscured by our habit of putting the academic and the propagandistic into mutually exclusive categories. There are more or less scientific, more or less civilized, more or less violent, and more or less devious ways of propagating one's ideas; but this should not blind us to the fact that everyone is disposed to spread his word.

We will see that immunizing stratagems can't really insulate a system of ideas from criticism. Contrary to Popper, I maintain that immunizing stratagems have failed to successfully perpetuate Freudianism and Marxism either in a logical or a sociological sense.

[1]
The Persuader's Predicament

When someone asserts that people are vulnerable to irrational ideas and may become impervious to outside argument, what they often imagine is a charismatic leader dominating the attention of potential followers and simply infecting them with his ideas. Hitler's rallies come to mind in which the popular view is that Hitler played the minds of the crowd like a puppeteer. However, the situation is more complex.

When a cult leader, religious thinker, or political ideologue hatches a new idea with which to charm his followers, the idea is like a new kind of fish in an ocean of other well-established fish all competing for resources and opportunities for reproduction. The ideologue wants his idea to be copied from mind to mind and from generation to generation, but other ideas have a head start and are also trying (so to speak) to get themselves adopted and spread by people. People have only so much attention and memory capacity to devote to these ideas. Because of these constraints, people have to choose between rival ideas and the propagandist is forced to take account of the preferences of his audience and the character of his competition.

We should distinguish between politicians or others, who manipulate existing ideas without changing them very much, and long-term propagandists, who are successful in changing the commonly accepted ideas within a large population. Adolf Hitler did not so much play the crowd like puppets, but had to tailor his message to suit the dominant ideas of the time. Hitler was an adroit politician and an accomplished public speaker, but he was more a puppet of ideology than its puppet-master. Hitler was not a creator of a completely new system, but a skilled user of ideas hatched by intellectuals writing decades before him. For example, ideas favoring racial hygiene and compulsory sterilization of the unfit reached their peak of popularity and political influence in western countries, including Britain and America as well as Germany, in the 1920s.[7]

Certainly there are other factors at work, factors not directly related to argument, in the success or failure of systems of belief. Some beliefs, like those espoused by Hitler's movement, have harnessed compulsion, torture, and mass murder to suppress their rivals. There is also simple lip-service paid to a dominant ideology, independent of genuine conviction. But I would like to see how far we might go focusing on the audience's preference for truth and information. Whereas particular regimes and particular thugs may come and go, logic and truth have an eternal quality which, like a barely noticeable evolutionary advantage in biology, can have a major long-term influence.

Trading Off Closedness for Spreadability

Let's look more closely at the logic of the propagandist's situation. Suppose his two goals are 1. to guarantee the propagation of his doctrine and 2. to guarantee it against being damaged by criticism. Guaranteeing the idea against criticism is often thought to be a way of promoting its spread. However, neither goal can be perfectly fulfilled, and they must be traded off for one another. Maximizing the ease with which an idea can be copied requires making it more open to criticism; maximizing the idea's closedness to argument makes it harder to copy from mind to mind.

Any system of ideas is likely to contain a mixture of some truth and some falsity; some good arguments and some bad arguments. The truth content of an ideology and the validity of its arguments enhance its ability to propagate and its falsity content and the invalidity of its arguments diminish its chances of being propagated. Why should this be? Part of my answer is that people have an innate curiosity about the world and so prefer true and informative ideas. As a consequence, in competing with other propagandists, the successful ideas tend to be shaped to satisfy our curiosity. But an idea that says more about the world is proportionately more open to counterexamples. For example, consider the sentences:

A. All cyclists live longer than non-cyclists.

B. All non-smoking cyclists live longer than non-cyclists.

Other things being equal, we would prefer to adopt sentence A because, being more general, it tells us more about the world. We would know something about all cyclists, rather than some qualified subsection of them. However, A is open to more kinds of counterexamples than B just because A is more general. A is refuted by any cyclist (whether smoker or not) who has a shorter life than a non-cyclist. On the other hand, B is only refuted by a non-smoking cyclist who has a shorter life than a non-cyclist. We see here that making ideas more attractive for adoption (in this case, by making them more general) may have the unintended consequence of making them more open to potential criticism.

Consider the interest in UFOs. Suppose the following sentence were true: 'At 10:00 A.M. every morning at coordinates XY you can see an oblate spherical spacecraft of 100 meters diameter made of metal, impenetrable by diamond cutting equipment.' Unless immediately dismissed as obviously false, this assertion would quickly spread throughout the world's media. Compare this with the following sentence: 'Someone saw one morning at 10:00 A.M. at XY coordinates an oblate spherical spacecraft of 100 meters diameter made of metal, impenetrable by diamond cutting equipment.' Other things being equal, this would have a short lived existence in the media of the local town nearest to XY coordinates. Why? Well, because, being more general, the first sentence would be more checkable—reporters would turn up at the right time and place and find that there was indeed such a craft with the claimed properties. The excitement at discovering such a craft would spread like wildfire. Of course, someone might say, that's why real 'reports' tend to be worded in such a way as to avoid repeatable checks by independent witnesses, and it is because these 'reports' are cunningly crafted to be impervious to argument that they survive. Nevertheless, I think it's clear that the true and informative UFO story, if it were taken at all seriously, would get more press and prevail over its vaguer cousin.

NARROW CURIOSITY OR GENERAL WONDER?

But do people have a general curiosity about the world, or do they only care to think about very specific types of question related to their narrow practical interests? If people have a free-floating, general curiosity, then the propagandist can't tell in advance where his system might be scrutinized for coherence and truth. But if people only had narrow curiosities, then a propagandist might be able to fashion his ideology so as to avoid the checks of truth and coherence that these might impose. I maintain that people have a general curiosity about the world and their place in it and that religions and other systems of ideas have to accommodate themselves to this fact about people.

When teaching introductory philosophy I begin my course by asking my students to remember their childhood questions about the world. I do get some rather mundane, narrow minded questions, but I also get many questions that express a general, sometimes quite deep, curiosity in the world: Why are clouds white? Why do stars shine? Do the stars move or are they stationary? Why do we live? Why do people die? Why is water transparent? Why can't we fly? Why don't planes fall down? Why can't we converse with animals? How can we walk in a straight line? Are there people on other planets? One of my students remembers asking her mother "Why do we have to eat?" She even remembers deciding to see what would happen if she did not eat! These seem to be questions that have spurred the greatest thinkers of science, philosophy, and religion.

For a long time, cognitive psychology assumed that the mind was very much like a general-purpose computer. It has general problem-solving strategies to solve all kinds of problems, whether these are to do with people, objects, animals, or tools. However, evolutionary psychology now argues that the mind is not a general-purpose computer, but more like a bundle of domain-specific problem solving machines. This is the modular hypothesis, first put forward by Jerry Fodor. Fodor actually left room for a general-purpose creative thinking and inferring machine, but other writers have tried to argue that all thought issues from a bundle of special purpose machines. I think there's a large amount of truth in the modular hypothesis but, like Fodor, I leave room for some general-purpose creativity and deduction.

In line with this modular approach, some have argued that we do have curiosity, but that it is channeled by our desire to explain very specific things and that these explanations satisfy particular modules of the mind. Pascal Boyer (2002) offers an account of religion in which he stresses the particularity of our curiosity. He thinks that it undermines the idea that we have a general curiosity about the world and the theory that religions are, at least in part, an answer to this. He criticizes what he calls intellectualism, which he expresses as: "If a phenomenon is common in human experience and people do not have the conceptual means to understand it, then they will try to find some speculative explanation." He then points out that there are many such phenomena, but that people do not in general try to explain them: when you lift a pint of beer to your lips by willing your arm to move, you are not moved to explain this, yet how can a non-physical thing like the mind affect a physical thing like a pint of beer? Boyer says this is only a problem for those that have been brought up in a long intellectual tradition.

One of my students did wonder as a child why we are able to walk in a straight line, a significant problem in neuropsychology. More generally, I think Boyer is overly impressed by the fact that people are not trying to explain everything all the time and that people have stopped at some point in their speculative explanations or curiosity. But the world is a rich place for uncountable questions and it is multi-layered, like an infinite onion. Even science at any given point has only gotten so far in the process of explanation, as it peels off the onion layers to reveal the world's underlying structure. If you look at the childhood questions my students remember or at the ones your children ask, it is clear that many of these questions were the inspiration for great advances in science and philosophy. Should we dismiss them simply because the child does not advance much beyond them? It takes a Galileo or a Newton to do this. The fact that few people think about the mind-body problem is more a reflection of the depth to which one must go in explanation before this becomes a problem, not evidence of a lack of general curiosity. Boyer refutes the rather crude intellectualism that he mentions, but that still leaves room for a general, free-floating curiosity in the world.

And after all, if there's no wide wonder about very general matters, how can you account for the fact that you're reading this book?

Truth Is an Advantage in Propaganda

Truth and validity enhance an argument's persuasive strength. Truth acts as a Darwinian filter on ideas through criticism and it satisfies our innate curiosity, which prefers more rather than less truth in our ideas.

The propagandist who propagates a true message can also take advantage of the fact that the world reminds him and his audience of the message. Reality is a mnemonic. This effect will be greater the more truth the message contains, because it will then have a bearing on more of reality. Theories with the greatest truth content speak about the observable world, that part most likely to act as a mnemonic.

Intellectual history, particularly a comparison between science and religion, bear out my suggestions. Religion is often held to be the most stubborn of all ideologies. Freudianism and Marxism have often been described as religions, insinuating that they are closed to argument and rationality. If I can show that even religion can offer no immunity from criticism, then I will also have shown as a corollary that even if Marxism and Freudianism assume the form of a religion, they will not thereby be closed to criticism.

Religion, like science, has tried to provide an information-rich account of the world and religions which have been most indifferent to truth have tended to be eliminated. Religions attempt to satisfy our preference for coherence and truth and their history is shot through with the use of abstract argumentation and a deep concern for logic. They may not have been as successful as science in doing this, but it is hard to understand the development of religions if this is ignored.

The Struggle for Coherence in Abrahamic Religions

One of the best examples of the sustained attempt to maintain logical coherence in a religious system is the attempt by early Islamic scholars to incorporate the works of Aristotle into Islamic thought. If powerful religious leaders can ignore logic and truth, why would a succession of outstanding Arabic speaking philosophers over hundreds of years devote such mammoth efforts to square the Quran and Aristotle? Why didn't Muslim leaders just ignore Aristotle? Instead Al Kindi, Al Farabi, Avicenna, Al Ghazali, and Averroes saw the strength of Aristotle's system, which they wanted to adopt, but also saw logical problems with doing so: Aristotle's work appeared to contradict the Quran in some respects. Most of these writers went to enormous lengths to try to make them cohere. Some took the alternative path of holding on to the bulk of Aristotle, while attempting to use philosophical arguments to refute and excise just a part of Aristotle's doctrine (for example, Al Kindi and Al Ghazali). Either way, these Islamic thinkers felt forced to appeal to logic. On Pascal Boyer's view, this makes no sense.

The Arabic writer Al Ghazali is often held up as the exception to this. In his book, *The Incoherence of the Philosophers*, he attacks certain philosophical positions (Avicenna's presentation of Aristotle), arguing that theology is superior to philosophy because faith provides a better road to religious knowledge. Some have taken this as showing that some strands of Islamic thought took a very different path afterward, belittling the standing of philosophy and ushering in a subsequent contempt for logic and argument. But it's quite clear that Al Ghazali was doing philosophy. The other great Islamic philosophers had been trying to argue that in general philosophy is compatible with theology, it's just another way to the same truths. But we shouldn't take this subtle marketing ploy at face value. Theology just is philosophy in the sense of using abstract logical argument in the quest to understand the world in a deep way. Theology's attitude to open debate and specific methods of argument may differ from the attitude of the typical philosopher, but that doesn't detract from theology's immersion in a turbulent ocean of argument that it must take account of. Even denying the reality of argument would constitute a target for argument—however, none of the Islamic critics of Islamic philosophy went that far, perhaps because such a move would also deny themselves the essential tool of argument for their own purposes of intellectual defense and propagation of what they accepted. It would be like a 'Doomsday Bomb' defense that only works if it destroys all defenses on both sides. Theology or even a half-baked, poorly worded expression of faith, is also trapped into some philosophical position or other on account of the fact that all positions presuppose general assumptions about the world and thus open the door to metaphysics.

There are numerous examples of logical issues that have taxed and troubled the intellectual leaders of Abrahamic religions (Christian, Islamic, and Judaic):

1. Abrahamic religions assert that the universe was created by God and therefore had a beginning. Aristotle held that the universe has always existed and will exist forever. But this implied that it had not been created by anything and therefore not by God.

2. Abrahamic religions assert that the soul lives on after bodily death. But Aristotle maintained that the soul dies with the body, which implies that it cannot live on after the body.

3. Abrahamic religions assert that God can make prophecies. Aristotle said that God knows only abstract universals, not particulars. But a prophecy is knowledge of a particular event, so Aristotle's view implies that God cannot make a prophecy.

The reason, I suggest, that these issues troubled religious thinkers and even some religious leaders is that people in general, and religious people no less, realize that ideas have logical implications, that two or more ideas may have contradictory implications, and that they abhor incoherence. That people often fail to discover or eliminate contradictions successfully does not mean that they have contempt for logic; it just means they are fallible and that even when a contradiction is found, it takes time to deal with it. Not everyone is a Bertrand Russell, let alone an omniscient being. In everyday life we notice this fact about people, that they can't help putting two and two together. It's most painfully realized in gossip: one person is trusted with a seemingly insignificant part of a secret. But if that is released to a third person, there's no telling what that person can do with it (intentionally or unintentionally) by adding his own beliefs (true or false) to it.

Monod on Performance Unrelated to Truth

Jacques Monod attributes the power of an idea to spread to its 'performance' and certain innate structures in the mind. The sort of performance Monod has in mind is the power of an idea to give greater coherence and confidence to a society. He seems to conclude from this that the promotion value (of an idea) bears no relation to the amount of objective truth the idea may contain. The might of the powerful armament provided by a religious ideology for a society does not lie in its structure, but in the fact that this structure is accepted (Monod 1970, p. 155).

But here Monod just assumes that being "accepted" or not accepted bears no relation to truth. It may be true that a coherence- and confidence-giving idea will be spread by its beneficiaries, but Monod does not stop to examine the possibility that performance may also be facilitated by truth. A false theory may be useful, and spread because of its usefulness. However, the theory may be useful because of the bit of overlap with the truth that it does have. Therefore, while we might be able to imagine cases in which the usefulness (or 'performance') of an idea may be independent of its truth content, we cannot accept that in general there is never any relation between performance and truth or between acceptance and truth.

Usefulness and truth content are logically distinct notions. However, I find it difficult to think of examples of useful theories completely devoid of truth-content. A false theory may be useful on account of its falsehood for someone who has a theoretical interest in false theories. For example, in a criticism by reductio ad absurdum the critic takes a false premise of his opponent's position and uses it to infer an absurd conclusion. In such a case the premise remains useful no matter how low its truth content. But this is an artificial example. An example that might fit Monod's purpose is the idea that Jews are specially chosen by God. Without disputing the truth of this idea, I concede that the idea that they are the chosen people would give the Jews greater confidence and coherence, even if it were false. On the other hand, this itself is an artificial example, since this idea does not have an independent existence; it is embedded in a much larger doctrine consisting of such matters as moral injunctions and historical theories. Is the acceptance of this vast body of doctrine completely unrelated to such truth as parts of it may contain? That seems unlikely.

It can be argued that the idea that Jews are the chosen people has given them coherence and confidence at the expense of the 'promotion value' of their religion. As Gibbon argues in his *Decline and Fall of the Roman Empire*,

> The descendants of Abraham were flattered by the opinion that they alone were the heirs of the covenant, and they were apprehensive of diminishing the value of their inheritance by sharing it too easily with the strangers of the Earth. (Gibbon 1963, p. 146)

Curiously, having eliminated truth (and even verisimilitude) and structure, Monod is left with a tautology: that the power of an idea to become accepted lies in its being accepted. Monod also overlooks the possibility that a system of ideas may unintentionally give greater coherence and confidence to a society. Newton, Faraday, Maxwell, and Einstein, may not have intended their theories and arguments to promote a confident and coherent society, but it would appear that through technology (telecommunications, transport, manufacturing, medicine) they have done just that. If we attribute this technological success to the truth-likeness of their theories, then we must conclude, contrary to Monod, that the truth-likeness of our ideas may promote confidence and coherence and thus their power to gain acceptance. (I will occasionally refer to truth-likeness or verisimilitude. One theory may have greater truth-likeness than another theory, because, though both theories are false, the first theory is closer to the truth, or is a better approximation to the truth.)

Gellner on Burning Faith Unrelated to Truth

Equally dismissive of the influence of truth is Ernest Gellner:

> It is worth noting and stressing here that truth is not an advantage in producing a burning faith—contrary to Gibbon's highly ironic observations. (Gellner 1985, p. 204)

Gellner's assertion leaves a number of possibilities open. Even if truth is no advantage it may not be a disadvantage either. Alternatively, truth may not be necessary to engender a burning faith; but falsehood may be the reason for its elimination or abatement. Even burning faiths would then be subject to a Darwinian selection through falsification. To maintain this, I do not have to argue that all false ideas are eliminated. My position is tenable even if only some glaringly false doctrines have a tendency to be eliminated.

There's an interesting sophistication to Gellner's position which brings it much closer to my position than the above quotation would suggest. Gellner actually says that if psychoanalysis were true and cured eighty percent of its patients, then it would spread throughout the world. But he thinks that its very truth and success would mean that a burning faith in it would be impossible. Gellner asks us to consider two techniques A and B. A cures eighty percent of patients by a publicly testable procedure, and B cures twenty percent by an esoteric and invisible unspecifiable method which is accompanied by intense emotion. A would spread like wildfire, but would not have any magic attached to it and would generate no offense. B on the other hand would spread just as much as A. Opposition to B would come from the sixty percent of patients who remained uncured. However, those lucky to be cured by it will be bound by faith to their therapists, and they will be bound by faith just because B is untestable, invisible and unspecifiable. If they spread the word and another twenty percent are cured who in turn spread the word, then we will have an exponential growth of the movement.

Gellner does not explicitly speculate as to what the outcome of a competition between the two techniques would be. But any system of ideas must come into competition with other ideas if it is to have any chance of spreading throughout the world. In that case Gellner's hypothetical argument loses its strength, for even on Gellner's assumptions A, being closer to the truth, would have the advantage over B. Under these realistic circumstances, B would not spread as much as A, contrary to Gellner's thesis. An unintended implication of Gellner's position is that the conditions favorable for the generation of burning faiths are a positive disadvantage to their propagation.

Gellner's definition of B seems to denude it of all content. If a system is invisible and unspecifiable, it is hard to see how it could be of any use or guidance, let alone work in twenty percent of cases. Let us see if we can provide a possible interpretation that would serve Gellner's point. Such a definition would be satisfied by a book so sacred that only a certain select group of priests could inspect it for counsel on various matters. The rank and file faithful would accept the advice ostensibly taken directly or by inference from the book by the priests. But all along the book has nothing but blank pages. Such an invisible and unspecifiable system of ideas would be no system at all, merely the pretense of a system, and could not therefore be perpetuated. What Gellner could have said, but fails to bring out clearly is that what is being perpetuated in a case like this is the idea that a certain group of individuals has privileged access to knowledge or wisdom. But this is checkable since the advice of the priests can be searched for inconsistencies over time. An example of this is M. James Penton's *Apocalypse Delayed*. Penton, originally a Jehovah's Witness, shows how the so-called authoritative interpretations of the Bible by this church's Elders were inconsistent over time, producing much disaffection among followers. The same kind of criticism can be applied to psychoanalysis.

Monod's and Gellner's positions each imply that truth does not add persuasive strength to criticism or aid the propagation of an idea. (As we saw, in Gellner's case, it is burning faiths that are extinguished by truth).

But if this is so, why is it that science has had such an impact on religion? So great is this impact that new religions sometimes feel obliged to adopt the name of science—Christian Science or Scientology—and virtually all religious apologists now proclaim that their religion doesn't conflict with science. (One is reminded of the Freudian notion of identification with the aggressor, though criticism works quite differently in other respects from aggression.)

Christianity Modified by Competition from Science

The rise of science as the pursuit of truth for its own sake in the sixteenth and seventeenth centuries, with associated developments in philosophy, has made it very difficult to maintain the old religions with their old interpretations. Scientists such as Isaac Newton produced better explanations of the world than those contained in the Bible or other canonical texts. Newton's explanations had greater information content and were closer to the truth. Newton may have maintained his theistic views on the creation of the world, but his scientific theories are autonomous objects with unintended ramifications and implications. Despite Newton's intentions, his scientific theories undermined the dominant Christian cosmology.

Moreover, philosophers such as David Hume and Voltaire exposed the fallacious reasoning and inconsistencies in the Bible and the arguments of its supporters. The argument from design and the ontological argument, not contained in the Bible as such but propounded by Thomas Aquinas in his *Summa Theologica* and Anselm (1033–1109) in *Proslogion*, were two of the most prominent intellectual supports of Christianity. Hume refuted the argument from design in his *Dialogues Concerning Natural Religion*, and undermined the principle of the ontological argument in his *Enquiries*. Kant elaborated the latter in his *Critique of Pure Reason*. The ontological argument was immediately attacked on its publication from within the Christian community by a monk, Gaunilo, and by Aquinas, both using sophisticated arguments. Far from reason being irrelevant to Christian commitment, the maintenance of commitment has sometimes involved quite competent and subtle reasoning.

The design argument is that just as one can infer the existence of a designer from the order in human artifacts, one can by analogy infer the existence of a designer of the universe from its order. Hume pointed out that the two cases are quite distinct. In the case of humans and their artifacts, we have two genera whose members we have experienced to be in a certain relation. We have seen watch-makers making watches. Moreover, we have not seen watches simply emerge without a watch-maker. But in the other case, we have two unique things: the theistic God and the Universe. We have not seen gods making universes; indeed, this is logically impossible. Darwin further undermined the argument from design (in the version advocated by Paley) by proposing that both the obvious fact of adaptation and the obvious fact of adaptation's imperfections are better explained by variation and natural selection than by divine design. Voltaire pointed to inconsistencies and empirical absurdities in Genesis; for example, the assertion that God first created daylight, and only later the Sun and the stars.

Anselm's ontological argument attempts to show that denying God's existence involves a contradiction. He begins by assuming that God is a being than which nothing greater can be conceived. If we grant this, which seems harmless, then we grant that we can conceive a being than which nothing greater can be conceived. But, Anselm says, if this concept exists only in our mind, then there is a being greater than this mere mental entity: one that actually exists. Thus we would contradict ourselves if we were to deny existence to what corresponded to this conception. Kant's reply is his famous dictum that "Whatever, therefore, and however much, our concept of an object may contain, we must go outside it, if we are to ascribe existence to the object." Adapting Kant's argument, suppose one had a concept of an X that included existence. One could deny the existence of X's without contradiction. Suppose, for example, that one had the concept of a centauroid: a centaur that exists. If one then asserted that there are no centauroids one would not contradict oneself. Therefore, to assert or imply the existence of an X it is not sufficient to grant the possibility of conceiving an X: one must actually assert or imply the existence of an X.

The resulting damage to the doctrinal integrity of Christianity is not easy to see. What we find is that the original texts and ceremony are retained but radically different interpretations are placed on them. The result is that the power of argument is underestimated by onlookers. For example, the Jehovah's Witnesses, reputedly a fundamentalist Christian sect, have virtually abandoned the original interpretation of Genesis. The creation of the world is taken to mean the creation merely of the Earth and the Solar system, and each of the seven days of the creation is taken to be thousands of years long. These are attempts to make a now unconvincing account of creation more plausible in the light of the triumph of science. This is typical of Christianity as a whole. As the Claremont theologian John Hicks puts it:

> The pressure upon Christianity is as strong as ever to go on adapting to something which can be believed. (As quoted in Wells 1988, p. 66)[8]

Such examples will help us to see how it is that Marxism and Freudianism can seem to be insulated from criticism, yet to have actually changed quite considerably in response to criticism.

You can see the move away from the older literal interpretation of the Bible in the works of prominent theologians. Earlier this century theologians such as Karl Barth asserted complete freedom in the interpretation of the word of God (with the proviso that, whatever the proper interpretation is, it be thought of as true). Today the most popular theologians are those like Paul Tillich, who argue that only metaphorical interpretations can be placed on the Bible. These are Protestant theologians, theologians living in a culture with considerable exposure to science. Perhaps other religions such as Islam are more intact because they have in recent centuries had less exposure to science. We may conjecture that with a similar degree of contact, these religions would also resort to apologetics similar to those to be seen in Protestantism.

No serious attempt to determine the extent to which a system of ideas can insulate itself from the truth can ignore this general development in intellectual history. It must lead us to suspect views such as Monod's and Gellner's. But also we must answer the question: in what fundamental respect were scientific explanations of the world better at spreading than those supplied by Christianity?

The Persuasive Power of Informative Explanation

There is a similarity between being converted to a religion and being struck by the power of a scientific explanation. Science has succeeded in spreading its ideas because it promotes the values of truth and criticism. Science has a greater chance of surviving in competition with rival systems of ideas because it supplies theories of the world that are: 1. general and precise (have high information content); 2. relatively simple or unified; 3. open to public scrutiny and testing, and 4. often closer to the truth. Why should these characteristics give ideas a better chance of spreading? Because, as I have been arguing, contrary to Gellner, Monod, and others, man is a rational animal and is substantially interested in the truth. Let's see how one might apply this view to the rise of Christianity and its subsequent loss of authority.

Christianity has been successful partly because it satisfied a universal interest in an explanation of the world. But not any sort of explanation would have done. It had to be general, precise, relatively simple, and close to the truth—just the qualities commonly attributed to a scientific explanation. There are better criteria of a good scientific explanation, but these are important aspects that our best criteria have to assimilate and explain. Popper's criterion of falsifiability does just that, but for now let's see were these cruder ideas takes us. We can develop a more sophisticated conception of a good scientific explanation in the course of exploring the overlap in the standards of explanation embodied in religion and those embodied in science. We'll then be able to see more clearly why, in the sea of competing ideas, at first religion is successful, but then is later supplanted by science.

The extraordinary growth of Christianity and Islam can be attributed in part to their monotheism: they reduced the apparent diversity of causes to one divine source. One God satisfies the demand for simplicity and generality. Many pluralistic religions posit a supreme god who at least sets limits to the behavior of the other gods. But has not Christianity avoided giving definite information? A cynic might think that the last thing an adherent wants in a religion are definite claims that can clash with reality. However, the history of Christianity, at least, is replete with predictions of various kinds. The Old Testament scholar H.P. Smith listed twenty-seven different dates which were fixed as the end of the world and of the second coming between the years 557 and 1734 (Smith 1921, p. 180). This accords with a comment made by George Santayana:

> What would make the preaching of the gospel utterly impossible would be the admission that it had no authority to proclaim what has happened or what is going to happen, either in this world or in another. (As quoted by Bartley 1984, p. 38)

It is almost ubiquitous among new religious movements to make predictions, for example about the end of the world. But these prophecies can be falsified. People become dissatisfied with the vacuous 'explanations' of moribund religions because—among other criticism—once the traditional teachings have been emptied of much of their content in an attempt to deal with these falsified predictions, they become very uninformative. If the appeal of religions were unconnected to their informative content, such predictions that can clash with reality would not be so common. (And neither would the content-decreasing modifications to systems whose predictions have suffered falsification.) Falsification by actual events can act as a selective filter on the form of religions, tending to eliminate those with little or dwindling content. Objective truth, therefore, is relevant to an idea's promotion value. It may not be the only selective filter on the propagation of ideas, but I do not have to maintain that in order to refute Monod's denial of any relationship between truth and promotion value. In Chapter 4, I will explain how doctrines can become emptied of content in response to criticism, not through an explicit refutation, but through a surreptitious or unwitting abandonment of the theory in response to criticism.

It's fairly commonplace to describe science as guided by the principles of simplicity, precision, and generality. It would be interesting if we could reduce these principles to a single principle. Owing to work in philosophy this does seem to be possible. The human mind desires information from its systems of belief. However, it is not just any kind of information that will do. Émile Meyerson argues that what the mind desires are explanations that reduce diversity. Meyerson is responsible for the application of this idea, called the principle of identity, to scientific methodology. Zahar developed Meyerson's idea in his book *Einstein's Revolution*.

Meyerson argues that the same desire for such explanations is a basic property of the mind and determines what we regard as good explanation in both science and common sense. The identity principle shows itself in different forms. This is how Zahar presents Meyerson's idea:

> According to Meyerson, the whole of science is informed by the identity principle, which consists in denying the diversity of the phenomena, or rather, in deriving this diversity from one fixed set of laws. This is the so-called legal form of the identity principle. According to the causal version, nature consists of substances governed by strict conservation laws. The human mind has an irresistible tendency to hypostasize natural processes, thus turning them into things whose total quantity remains constant. This is an innate propensity, which already leads the child to a belief in the persistence of material objects. (Zahar 1989, pp. 23–24)

This principle seems to be in operation in science's preference for universal as opposed to particular facts, and theories with few premises—Zahar presents as an example the search for the unified theory in physics.

Zahar agrees with Meyerson's conjecture that this innate propensity evolved by a Darwinian process. The 'legal form' of this propensity enables animals to anticipate facts. Meyerson denies any survival value to the causal version of the identity principle, but Zahar points out that the postulation of objects that persist in time also helps an animal anticipate facts. However, Zahar is quick to maintain that even though the emergence of these principles can be explained in Darwinian terms, once they exist their application in science is strictly Lamarckian. Zahar therefore neglects to ask whether these principles act as Darwinian filters of ideas spontaneously produced partly independent of heuristics or receptions. Zahar takes it for granted that Darwinian-like and Lamarckian-like processes are incompatible, but many processes embody both: for example, the breeding of dogs, which is directed in certain respects in accord with a plan, does not eliminate Darwinian processes.

Meyerson's idea can be generalized to religions. Meyerson's theory accounts for the propagation of monotheistic religions and it also accounts for the spread of such ideologies as Marxism and Freudianism. Marxism claims to offer a comprehensive explanation of at least the social world, using relatively few premises, and Freudianism, which—at least in the beginning—reduced virtually all psychological phenomena to sexual impulses. Surprisingly, Monod takes a similar line, attributing the immense influence of Marxism to

> its ontogenic structure, the explanation which it provides, both sweeping and detailed, of past, present, and future history. (Monod 1970, p. 157)

Monod, therefore, attributes Marxism's success to the values of exactitude and generality. This contradicts his earlier assertion that the structure of an idea is irrelevant to explaining its spread. Although these criteria of a good explanation are not necessarily connected with a search for truth, it's hard for Monod to maintain the relevance of an idea's exactitude and generality in the light of his assertion that the propagation of an idea bears no relationship at all to its objective truth-content. Marxism may contain false generalizations or spurious details. But the search for generality and exactitude is hardly likely to lead away from truth in a systematic way. Moreover, Monod does not show that Marxism is completely false. The appeal of Marxism's generality and exactitude may well depend on Marxism's being successful within fairly large areas, on its having at least some objective truth-content.

Some would argue that Marxism claims to provide a metaphysical theory of the whole world that all true theories must presuppose (or at least not contradict). As Minogue points out in *Alien Powers*, Marxism overreaches itself in this respect for it even tries to explain all theory creation and debate, including itself.

Religions are not concerned with exactly the same set of problems as science, but there is an overlap. Religions are, like science, concerned with the structure of reality, but they also deal with ethical questions which lie outside the scope of empirical science. But even here they may come into contradiction since at least some ethical questions, whether for instance one should pray to God, are dependent on the actual state of the world, in this case on whether there is in fact a God, and if so, how many? At this point Meyerson's principle would come into play.

There is a problem with Meyerson's principle that helps to explain why scientific method has out-competed Christianity. An even stronger innate principle than Meyerson's principle is the demand for greater information, for a growth in knowledge. As Popper argues, science has progressed most when it has striven for an increase in the information content of its theories. Now, some ways of reducing diversity may also reduce information content (or possibly truth-likeness). Obviously, an unrestrained application of Meyerson's principle would lead to Parmenides's theory of a block universe, in which everything is one. But truth lies somewhere between the theories of Heraclitus and Parmenides. Meyerson was actually aware of this and consequently asserted only that the human mind struggles to impose its denial of diversity on the world, which resists the straitjacket. Historically, when there has been a choice science has preferred increased information content to reduced diversity. (The Greeks thought there were but four elements; today there are thought to be 109. Carnot's principle may be another example.) Also we know from Gödel's work that there are limits on the axiomatizability of theories, a result that may preclude a unified field theory: physics may be ineradicably incomplete. Therefore, while Meyerson's principle helps us to see that monotheistic religion and science appeal to some of the same standards, its occasional conflict with the search for increasing verisimilitude and information content helps us to explain why science has out-competed monotheistic religion.

In the above comparison between science and Christianity, I did not mention an important difference between them that might seem to undermine my argument. To say that science has out-competed Christianity in the competition for credibility on matters of empirical fact is a little misleading. 'Science' is a term that refers both to a collection of particular theories and to a collection of methods and attitudes. More scientific theories have been falsified and discarded than religious theories. This is hardly surprising since science (as a general approach) does generally encourage the severe testing and retesting of theories and the generation of competing theories. Thus a more accurate description would be that the methods and attitudes of science have survived and out-competed religious methods and attitudes, but at the price of refuting a great many scientific theories. (To be even more precise, we should also say that the various refuted scientific theories have lost out not to Christianity, but to other scientific theories. Even refuted and scientifically discarded theories are still far superior in terms of survival value to religious theories, and this is due to their greater truth-likeness and information content.)

Once we acknowledge that science and Christianity have competed to satisfy similar (or overlapping) standards, it becomes less plausible to suppose that there is a great gulf between science and ideology, making ideology more closed to argument. Edward Shils has expressed the opinion that:

> science is not and never has been part of an ideological culture. (Shils 1968, p. 74)

Manning goes further, asserting that

> Ideological talk, unlike legal talk, does not give us information about the world in which we live. It cannot carry the appropriate descriptive content.[9] (Manning 1980, p. 75)

But even if one regards science as non-ideological, one must admit that the paradigm examples of ideologies may incorporate and use the propositions of science. For example, classical liberalism used theorems of economics, such as the law of comparative advantage, in its arguments for the general value of freedom within a market. Marxism used a modified version of Ricardo's Labor Theory of Value to argue against this ideology (Boudon makes a similar criticism of Shils in Boudon 1986, pp. 26–27). Human beings desire an informative, general explanation of the world and their place within it. The more any system of ideas satisfies this desire, therefore, the greater will be its chances of propagation. This accounts for the relative propagandistic success of both Marxism and classical liberalism.

I am not arguing that truth always wins out in the long run. That may be false. What I am arguing is that there are no foolproof methods of saving a network of beliefs from the impact of truth. But I also want to argue that truth adds strength to a position's ability to spread, and that if pressed truth, or a closer approximation to truth, yields an advantage in argument. A true or valid position is rather like the number which is favored in a loaded die: it does not always win, but it has a certain propensity to do so.[10] My thesis is not refuted by examples of false doctrines that have survived over the centuries. My contention is that their position can never be made secure.

Popper and Bartley on Ideologies

Popper and Bartley have been central figures in the attempt to make the distinction between open and closed systems of thought; between critical and dogmatic beliefs, attitudes, and methods. In many ways they have weakened the philosophical case for absolutely closed systems of thought, showing how diverse sorts of ideas can be subject to criticism of different sorts. They have thus contributed to a more critical ethos. But they have also claimed that some ideologies and their proponents are impervious to criticism. I disagree.

My criticism of Popper and Bartley is heavily dependent on their achievements in extending the notion of criticizability. Their major achievements have been in extending the logical and methodological notion of criticizability, though even this extension remains to be completed. Their view that all (or nearly all) positions are logically open to criticism has not been generalized sufficiently to the psychological and sociological domain. I will explore the move from Popper's early conception of critical rationalism to Bartley's important generalization. We will also cover the latest extension to the logical notion of openness to criticism, propounded by David Miller. We will then see how Popper's and Bartley's principles of situational logic and Darwinism can be used to show that there are no absolute barriers to criticism even in the psychological or sociological domain.

It's important to distinguish logical, psychological, and sociological openness to criticism, so that one can then see how they are related and how they interact. It might be thought that questions of psychology and sociology should be dealt with by psychologists and sociologists rather than by philosophers. However, problems cannot always be neatly slotted in to particular departments. One could argue, as Popper has, that there are no subject matters as such but only problems (cf. Popper 1983, p. 5). In trying to solve a problem, we should not be shy of using various theoretical and conceptual tools independent of their origin. I intend to examine relationships that exist between the psychological, sociological, and logical domains, relationships that have received only scant attention, perhaps because of a too departmental attitude to this problem.

Residual Dogmatism in Popper

Bartley's major contribution is his theory of comprehensively critical rationalism, which was meant to resolve some internal problems of Popper's position on openness to criticism. Popper had championed the critical attitude, but there were unintentional dogmatic elements in Popper's presentation that Bartley showed to be unnecessary. Henceforth all positions were open to criticism. Bartley had made the notion of criticism comprehensive. It is my task to eliminate the remaining dogmatic elements in Bartley's and Popper's system. Let us first see how Popper allows a dogmatic element into his theory.

Popper has asserted that

> no rational argument will have a rational effect on a man who does not want to adopt a rational attitude. (Popper 1966, p. 231)

Popper arrives at this pessimistic position through a discussion of the relative merits of uncritical (or comprehensive) rationalism, critical rationalism, and irrationalism. Uncritical rationalism is the doctrine that all and only those positions that can be supported by argument or evidence should be accepted, the rest rejected. Popper points out that uncritical rationalism is in fact self-undermining, since it cannot itself be defended by argument or evidence.[11] Moreover, uncritical rationalism can be defeated by its own weapon, argument.

Popper generalizes the argument. Since every argument makes an inference from assumptions, it is impossible that all assumptions be based on argument. The impossibility arises because we would be involved in an infinite regress: each argument for an assumption would have to have an argument for each of its own assumptions.

> The demand raised by many philosophers that we should start with no assumption whatever and never assume anything without 'sufficient reason', and even the weaker demand that we should start with a very small set of assumptions ('categories'), are both in this form inconsistent. For they themselves rest upon the truly colossal assumption that it is possible to start without, or with only a few assumptions, and still to obtain results that are worthwhile. (p. 230)

How does this argument lead to Popper's pessimistic position on argument against someone who does not want to be influenced by argument?

Popper applies this general point to the problem of adopting a rational attitude.

> The rationalist attitude is characterised by the importance it attaches to argument and experience. But neither logical argument nor experience can establish the rationalist attitude; for only those who are ready to consider argument or experience, and who have therefore adopted this attitude already, will be impressed by them. That is to say a rationalist attitude must first be adopted if any argument or experience is to be effective, and it cannot therefore be based on argument or experience. (And this is quite independent of the question whether or not there exist any convincing arguments which favour the adoption of the rationalist attitude.) We have to conclude from this that no rational argument will have a rational effect on a man who does not want to adopt a rational attitude. (p. 230)

The adoption of the critical attitude then must be an "irrational faith in reason."

From the above quotations it can be seen that there are two aspects to the dogmatic residue in Popper's account: a logical-methodological aspect, and a psychological-sociological aspect. However, Popper does not consistently separate the two. Clearly, one can specify a methodological rule to the effect that one maintain one's position in the face of all argument. Such a rule is logically consistent, and if scrupulously applied would mean that all criticism would be ineffective. But Popper seems to think that if irrationalism is logically tenable then it must be psychologically tenable. Popper first says that the rationalist attitude must be adopted to make criticism effective, but then immediately retracts this implicitly by saying that this is independent of whether there are any convincing arguments for adopting rationalism. Is Popper saying that a convincing argument can fail to convince? If there are arguments that can persuade one to adopt the rationalist attitude in general, then one can be affected by rational argument without having first adopted the rationalist attitude. Popper could mean that there might be arguments in favour of the rationalist attitude that can strengthen this attitude only after one has made the faithful leap in adopting rationalism. But this is unclear.

Bartley wanted to develop a methodology that kept Popper's emphasis on the critical attitude, but which did not have to rely on Popper's "irrational faith" in reason. More generally, Bartley wanted a critical rationalism that avoided Fries's trilemma: 1. infinite regress; 2. vicious circularity; 3. dogmatism. Bartley successfully solved this logical-methodological problem by his arguments for comprehensively critical rationalism. Bartley's solution was to clearly distinguish between justificationism and criticism. Traditionally, criticism had been defined implicitly as an attempt to show that some position was unjustified. But, Bartley says, if justification is impossible and our primary interest is, and always has been, truth, then it would make sense to define criticism with respect to truth, not justification. We can then go on to define the rational attitude in a coherent manner that avoids the circularity. We may not be able to prove or justify our positions or our methodology itself, but we can nonetheless diligently search for the truth by keeping our positions as much open to criticism as possible. Popper accepted Bartley's argument and rejected his own earlier call for an "irrational faith" in reason. This was no longer necessary. (Popper's acceptance of Bartley's argument is recorded in his 1982a.) Thus, methodologically there was then no dogmatism in Popper's position. However, both Bartley and Popper have retained the psychological-sociological aspect of their residual dogmatism.

Residual Dogmatism in Bartley

The problem as presented by Bartley is an unresolved crisis of identity in contemporary rationalism which can be clearly analyzed in terms of contemporary Protestant theological thought. Bartley argues that the Christian intellectual reaction to the failure of Liberal Protestantism is able to defend its retreat to commitment, its use of unargued faith, only because rationalism, with which it identifies itself, has admitted that it must itself appeal to unargued, unjustified assumptions. Bartley pictures the Christian saying to his conventional rationalist critic: Why should I be moved by your demonstration that my faith cannot be justified? After all, you yourself must dogmatically accept some starting point. The fault, as Bartley sees it, lies in the ubiquitous adherence to what he calls a justificationist metacontext. Argument and even criticism itself is generally understood as dependent on justifying some position. A criticism in this context is an attempt to show that a position cannot be justified.

Bartley's proposed solution is to separate criticism from justification. In this way Fries's trilemma is avoided. All we need for rational argument is a willingness to keep our positions, all our positions, open to criticism. This method, of course, applies to itself. But this self-applicability does not suffer the same problems that Popper attributes to uncritical rationalism. Neither does it suffer, like critical rationalism, from the need to rely on an ultimate terminus in argument. I would not want to leave the impression that Bartley's comprehensively critical rationalism is without its critics; it is in fact the subject of considerable debate, in which the principle figures have been Watkins and Post.[12]

Bartley's analysis of the reaction to the failure of Protestant Liberalism serves to illustrate his answer to the main problem of his book:

> ... what can be done to (systems of ideas), how can one tinker with them, to enhance or reduce their criticizability. In particular, the book is concerned with how men use ideas to protect ideas from competition, to remove them from the selective process that is the heart of criticism. (Bartley 1984, p. xix)

Bartley's general position on psychological-sociological openness to criticism is that

> ideologies are retained regardless of the facts; they are not abandoned when they clash with the facts; rather they die out or are eliminated, if at all, together with their carriers. (p. xvii)

The claim is that there are networks of theories making certain claims about the world whose proponents continue to maintain and propagate them whatever facts are presented against them. This view is reminiscent of Planck's view of science. Planck held that new theories in science become accepted only because the proponents of the old theories die off, leaving it to the young generation of scientists to adopt and develop the new theories.

Bartley takes this as a rough and ready distinction that can easily be expanded to treat the main case study of his book, Protestantism and its successors. But this qualification does not repudiate the implication that humans are irrational. Indeed, Bartley begins with the assumption that humans are irrational:

> I do not for a moment believe that man is a rational animal, let alone that men are born with a 'faculty' of reason. Rather, rationality, like consciousness itself, is a comparatively late, and still rather rare, and, where it exists, fragile development. Most individuals exist in a troubled, slumbering fantasy world, and, when most awake, are bound by rigid habits and unconscious patterns of behavior. Comparatively few persons enjoy the give and take of criticism or think to any purpose other than to dominate. (p. xxi)

On this view, the rise of science becomes a puzzle. Bartley recognizes this and attributes the rise of science to the influence of competition and imitation through the rise of open markets. It paid individuals to copy the exploratory, entrepreneurial behavior of their more successful competitors in the provision of commodities. Reflecting critically on one's own behavior to eliminate unsuccessful trials also allowed one to shift one's energies more quickly to meet consumer demand. These attitudes of exploration and self criticism became generalized, making science possible. This is what Popper and Bartley would call a situational analysis of the market and the rise of science. Bartley does not consider the possibility that the situational logic of the market may have been part of the genetic selection pressure acting on our ancestors; if he had he may not have dismissed so quickly the existence of a rational faculty. In any case, the same sort of analysis that Bartley applies to the emergence of rationality can be applied to ideologies to show that they are more open to criticism than Bartley or Popper suppose.

Situational Logic

Now let's look at two questions:

1. Can the propagandist simply avoid criticism, refusing to listen to or read counter-arguments?
2. Can the propagandist control the more subtle defenses of the doctrine and build up membership? (For example, through the often supposed monopoly of interpretation that the Catholic Church has on the Bible, in traditional Catholic communities.)

My answer will be that due to the logic of the propagandist's situation, neither of these strategies are available to those propagandists who are keen to propagate their ideas. First we must explore Popper's notion of the logic of the situation.

In situational logic, according to Popper, what we do is to construct a model of the situation in which an agent acts. The situation will be made up of his knowledge and his aims plus the constraints on his action, constraint understood in a very general sense. We then assume that the agent acts appropriately to the situation as we have modeled it. What we learn is how and why the agent saw his action as appropriate to the situation as he saw it. But the model is not confined to how he sees it: for it must include information that describes his limited experience, his limited or overblown aims, his limited or over-excited imagination, and so forth. We thus learn how the agent's action was adequate, within the limits of his inadequate view of the situational structure.

Popper points out that we can use the rationality principle even to explain the actions of a madman:

> We try to explain a madman's actions, as far as possible, by his aims (which may be monomaniac) and by the 'information' on which he acts, that is to say, by his convictions (which may be obsessions, that is, false theories so tenaciously held that they become incorrigible). In so explaining the actions of a madman we explain them in terms of our wider knowledge of a problem situation which comprises his own, narrower, view of his problem situation; and understanding his actions means seeing their adequacy according to his view—his madly mistaken view—of the problem situation. (Popper 1994, p. 179)

Popper's view overlaps with my own, since he thinks the rationality principle can be applied in the great majority of cases as a useful approximation. But I hold that all people are rational and no one is incorrigible. In this chapter I will be arguing that the logic of the propagandist's situation impels him, on pain of failure to spread his ideas, to be—among other things—corrigible. In the next chapter, I will argue that Darwinian theory suggests that no person is incorrigible in their beliefs.

THE PROPAGANDIST AND SITUATIONAL LOGIC

Both Popper and Bartley regard Marxism and Freudianism as examples of irrational ideologies: their proponents have made them closed to argument. However, if we view these systems from the point of view of the propagandist's situation, there are important pressures and constraints that render them more open to criticism than we might at first suspect.

Marxism and Freudianism are propagandistic sets of assumptions that are subject to a situational logic peculiar to the endeavour to recruit and retain new followers. Think of the logic of the situation facing the ideologue who wants his ideas to catch on, to propagate, but also wants to protect them from criticism.

When he first contrives the ideas he could decide there and then never to utter them or write them down. They will be safe from outside criticism, but certainly will not spread far and may well be forgotten. Suppose he decides to speak them but not to write them down, thinking that if he comes across a strong counter-argument, he can more easily deny having asserted the theory in this vulnerable form. The costs here are quite high: even if his ideas do spread by word of mouth, they are likely to be distorted and changed significantly without reference to a canonical text, perhaps even spawning new ideas that come into competition with the original idea. It's a matter of common observation that rumor distorts initially innocent tales, often contravening the purpose of their originator. It also becomes clear that, contrary to popular opinion, pride may actually work against the survival of an ideology, since in avoiding the shame of error the ideologue abandons it by denying he even asserted it.

The propagandist could write the text for a new creed and then promptly lock it away in a safe. It would then be free from possibly damaging criticism, but it would also be safe from propagation. Gibbon attributes the propagational success of Christianity partly to the fact that it threw off the fetters of the Jewish religion, which kept the teachings and promise of salvation confined to the descendants of Abraham (Gibbon 1963, p. 147). The Gnostic heretics of early Christianity claimed to possess secret knowledge that was only given to those few they deemed spiritually mature. One could argue that this practice was partly responsible for the ease with which Gnosticism was suppressed by the orthodox church. (On the Gnostics' claim to secret knowledge see Pagels 1979, pp. 44–47.)

The propagandist who restricts his propagandistic efforts in the hope of evading criticism and rival positions has to incur a number of costs:

a. A loss in his skills of argument and persuasion. Preaching only to the converted breeds laziness: attempts to persuade novices require attention to details and more difficult counter-arguments. If a shy doctrine is exposed one day to an avalanche of criticism, the skills to defend it against criticism would be unavailable.

b. A loss in clear recollection and understanding of the ideology. There's nothing as effective as meeting criticism to maintain and improve the memory and understanding of an idea or theory.

c. A failure to take account of competing ideas. In the modern world in which many ideas are easily available through TV, radio, and the Internet, as well as print media, any new idea aiming at maximum spread is likely to have more critics than defenders.

To combat competing ideas, one needs to understand them and the attitude that their adherents have toward them. One has to understand the rival theory as an objective entity and also come to know to what extent and accuracy the rival propagandist understands his own theory. Sometimes a refutation bears on a part of the rival's theory that lies outside his current grasp. To make it a persuasive refutation one has to connect the refuted part to the part already grasped. Paradoxically, one needs to be in a position to teach the rival his own theory! Moreover, if one is in this position, one's arguments cannot be so easily dismissed as lacking understanding of the doctrine. Without such knowledge of the rival ideology intrinsically very subtle and excellent arguments may be wasted because they do not address the adherent's premises, problem and styles (or methods) of thinking. An example from science would be Newton's work on Cartesian Vortex theory in order the more thoroughly to refute it. Newton elaborated more precisely the implications of Cartesian Vortex theory to show that it was incompatible with Kepler's laws, which the Cartesians had accepted.

Thus we see that the logic of the propagandist's situation involves an implicit trade-off between the reproducibility and fidelity of his message and protection from criticism. His situation forces him, as it were, to make his message into some sort of publicly inspectable record: to encapsulate it in catchy verses, or better still, to write it down in a book or to make a sound recording. The message is then accessible to more potential converts, but it is then also available for critical inspection and is more openly in competition with other networks of ideas. To propagate the ideology, its adherents need to present it to others who may express doubts about it. Those who will agree with the message and pass it on and those who will hesitate to accept the message and offer criticisms cannot be determined in advance, so the avoidance of criticism cannot be guaranteed. Furthermore, maximizing persuasive refutation of rival ideologies requires mastery of these ideologies, thus exposing oneself to possibly demoralizing criticism. The logic of the situation is that the propagandist must meet counter-argument.

The propagandist may not be able simply to avoid encounters with criticism without cost to the copyability of his message, but perhaps there are subtler defenses of the ideology that do not incur such a risk? There are indeed subtler defenses, but the defenses cannot be controlled to prevent unintentional schism or drift of interpretation.

The propagandist's message, then, is no longer a changing and vague subjective idea but an object open to public criticism. This much is fairly obvious, but there are unforeseeable consequences of giving the message an objective form, and these flow from the logical character of any theory. It might be thought that the propagandist could prepare his message in advance to protect it from criticism. Perhaps by engendering a monopoly on the interpretation of the doctrine, as the Catholic Church is commonly supposed to have done at some stages in its history (discouraging anyone but priests from reading the Bible, for instance). However, there are certain properties of the message that cannot be fully surveyed or known to the propagator and therefore cannot be controlled by him in such a way as to anticipate and avoid all or even most criticism. These properties are called the information content and the logical content of the message. They correspond roughly to what we might call the implications of a theory.

When one questions a theory one questions its implications. But there are an infinity of non-trivial implications of any theory, and therefore an infinity of possible criticisms. This is true even if we're considering only the falsity content, and thus sound criticisms, of an otherwise true theory. And because no one knows all the implications of a theory, doctrine, or ideological platform, no one can anticipate all criticisms which will be made as the movement grows. The propagandist cannot fully prepare his theory or his recruits to answer criticisms which will be made in the future, but which no one has yet thought of. Furthermore, given a modest amount of technological and social change, even the loyal adherents of a belief system will find themselves obliged to apply the doctrine to situations which the founders of the system never encountered and possibly never imagined.

If movements are so good at protecting themselves from criticism, why is it that they so often have a tendency to split? An important factor is that different individuals faced by the same criticism must improvize a defense there and then. Since criticism cannot be completely predicted and prepared for in advance, and since no two people understand a doctrine or theory in exactly the same way, these improvized defenses are almost bound to be somewhat different. It follows therefore that differences of opinion must arise about the interpretation of the doctrine and how to best defend it. Interpretation is partly a matter of seeing the implications of a doctrine relative to criticism. In understanding some criticism one is seeing some of the implications of the doctrine being criticized. It follows that the supposed monopoly of interpretation of the Catholic Church may well have impeded the search for truth, but it could not fully protect its doctrine from criticism because it could not truly establish an effective monopoly of interpretation.

What about the general strategy to dub all criticism of Marxism as bourgeois or class treachery, or criticism of the Church as evil heresy? It is not always obvious what counts as criticism. It is often a difficult task to determine whether a statement follows from or contradicts or is compatible with a complex web of assumptions. A new doctrine seemingly supportive of an orthodox position may be taken on board and only later discovered after protracted chains of argument to be incompatible with it. This vulnerability exists even if all members understand the orthodox doctrine in the same way. But no two people understand the same system of beliefs in exactly the same way: an individual cannot grasp a system of ideas without making it his own. But even if two persons' understanding of a doctrine did overlap exactly to begin with, when they start to examine different unforeseen criticisms this overlap must begin to diminish. For in understanding a criticism one is seeing how it relates logically to some of the, perhaps unsuspected, implications of the theory.

There is a strong counter-argument that is worth considering. My above argument depends on the assumption that different propagandists improvize defenses of the doctrine independently. But suppose each new criticism is presented to a leader (an individual or a committee) who decides on what defense to use, or perhaps it is discussed at a conference and a vote is taken. This, one might argue, would eliminate unintentional differences in defensive responses.

This institutional approach can achieve something, but it does so at a cost. It works most effectively where there is a hierarchical organization with little or no pretense of empowerment of the rank-and-file, the assumption being that the leadership is somehow guaranteed against error. The Catholic Church, headed by the Pope, and the Communist movement in the 1930s, headed by Stalin, are examples. In a more democratic movement, there would be resistance to the pronouncements of the governing body. For if there were disagreement about the best way to counter an argument from the movement's opponents, many members would be in the awkward position of being required to employ an argument that they themselves did not find persuasive. And here we should notice that the governing body may make a mistake (from the standpoint of propaganda effectiveness): in such a case, dissenting members may perceive that their own favored mode of arguing would be more effective than the officially sanctioned one.

We observe that when an authoritative body is convened to resolve possible differences in interpretations of the doctrine, this body's pronouncements narrow the differences but do not abolish them. Controversy shifts to the interpretation of the body's pronouncements. Furthermore, the institutional structure now becomes part of the ideological package that the propagandist has to defend. It is easier to defend the proposition that Jesus died for our sins than to defend the twin propositions that Jesus did for our sins and that a little group of men sitting in the Vatican are alone able to determine exactly what is meant by Jesus dying for our sins. The opponent can point out that the Pope or Stalin or Mao might make mistakes, and can criticize the notion that these individuals are always right.

There is another more subtle and extreme form of defense that might be thought to obviate the problem of spontaneous differences in interpretation of the doctrine and its defense. The idea is embodied in Orwellian Newspeak, a language that so embraces the thought of people that it is impossible to think outside its framework. Gellner, for example, thinks that economic liberalism is a perfect example of Newspeak:

> Within this system, the notions which carry and imply this vision allow no alternatives, and those who have internalised these notions generally simply cannot conceive any alternatives to them. (Gellner 1979, pp. 282–83)

Gellner's position on this issue is not without ambiguity.[13] However, both sorts of defense succumb to a general characteristic of copying processes, independently of the problem presented by the unfathomable content of any doctrine. Reflecting on the learning of language, Hattiangadi argues that strict conformity is extremely difficult to achieve. When people learn a language they make conjectures about word meanings. If the guesses overlap sufficiently then communication is feasible. But there is at the same time a degree of unintentional and unforeseeable innovation in the language, simply because the overlap is not perfect (Hattiangadi 1987). We may infer that the same imperfection would hamper any attempt to achieve conformity in the interpretation and use of defensive responses. The prescribed defenses might be copied with devotion by the 'faithful', but copying errors would be almost inevitable. For the same reason, any attempt to impose a form of Newspeak would founder because of the unintentional innovations introduced into the language when different people learn it. Darwin argued that new species emerged from earlier species by numerous, successive, slight modifications. One can easily see how copying errors in the interpretation of the doctrine and its defenses can lead in a similar way either to a drift in the whole movement from the original doctrine, or to the emergence of factions, each claiming to be the carrier of the true message. In either case, the defenses would have failed to guarantee the doctrine against criticism.

Given such an analysis of the propagandist's situation it becomes less plausible, for example, for all Marxists to stick rigidly to the evasive tactic of dubbing all criticism of Marx as bourgeois. And so it is not surprising to find that there are Marxists who do not use this rhetorical tactic, and would argue against its validity and use. And there is nothing like criticism from within the ranks to undermine morale. Of course, each splinter group may adopt the habit of calling all other splinter groups bourgeois or class traitors, but as the number of splinter groups grows, this rhetorical device wears thin.

A similar phenomenon occurred in regard to the belief in miracles. G.A. Wells points out that when rivalry between different religions arises, the miracles of the rival have somehow to be discredited:

> The Protestants in Europe denied the reality of the Catholic miracles, and the Catholic enemies of the Jansenist Port-Royal refused to credit the miracle of the Holy Thorn. Mutual criticism on the part of rival faiths tended to undermine and discredit the whole system of miracles. Attention was more and more directed to the possibility of error and fraud. (Wells 1988, p. 133)

So we may conclude that due to the unforeseeable depths and ramifications of any theory and copying errors in the interpretation of the doctrine, it follows that sociologically an ideology cannot be guaranteed against criticism; and moreover, it will have a tendency to split both logically and sociologically. Schism and drift have a tendency to occur even in the absence of criticism, but the attempt to deal with criticism adds another source of schism and drift.

The propagandist cannot simply conceal his message and avoid criticism, since he sacrifices potential new adherents. He must give it a permanent public form, open to competition from other ideas. Having done that he can no longer control the evolution of the ideology through centralized control or through the imposition of a special language that excludes innovation, because different propagandists will interpret the doctrine differently and improvise different defences to unforeseeable criticism.

Bartley's Test Case: Liberal Protestantism

We are now in a position to apply these considerations to Bartley's own test case: liberal Protestantism. Are liberal Protestantism or its successors ideologies in Bartley's sense? Are they being retained regardless of the facts? On Bartley's own account it appears that liberal Protestantism has been largely abandoned in response to criticism. But more importantly, it has been replaced by systems of thought that, although less openly critical, are systematically but unintentionally more vulnerable to propagandistic failure. They have jeopardized the propagation of their message by allowing too much room for variation in its interpretation, for both schism and drift.

In the introduction to *The Retreat to Commitment*, Bartley had provided a general definition of ideology and contrasted this with science. At best this introductory classification of types of networks of ideas is highly misleading. To recapitulate somewhat, Bartley implies that there are only two ways in which ideas can be eliminated:

1. Elimination of inadequate ideas through deliberate criticism. This is the attitude of the scientist, whose success in at least approximating the truth, depends on his deliberately seeking error in his theories by deliberately subjecting them to the severest criticism.

2. Elimination of inadequate ideas through the death of the carrier. Bartley illustrates this with Popper's example of the Indian community that died with its belief in the sanctity of tigers. Other examples might be the eleven-century Albigensians, who were exterminated by the Church, and the Shakers, a religious community which believed in abstaining from sex, and therefore died out.

This contrast is reminiscent of Edward Shils's inadequate contrast between ideologies and science, criticized above. Despite Bartley's extensive and insightful application of Popper's notion of the unfathomable content and ramifications of our ideas, he neglects to incorporate this approach into his general account of ideologies. He overlooks an extremely important third possibility: the unintended and unforeseeable encounter with effective critical argument. This criticism can come either from outside or from inside the movement. It is especially interesting when the criticism comes from its own propagandists. As I made clear above, however circumspect are the rules of study (in general, thought) the leaders of a movement enforce on its propagandists, they cannot determine which paths of study or argument will be free of troublesome conclusions. Even the most innocent route to the aggrandizement of an ideology may lead to its destruction and shame. Liberal Protestantism is one such ideology.

Bartley's suggestion also overlooks the possibility that an idea may lead simply to a lowered reproduction of the carriers, not necessarily their death. As I pointed out in the introduction one has to look at the rates of loss and gain in adherents. Even if members of a community are dying because of there belief in the sanctity of tigers, this belief may survive them if they pass it on quickly enough. However as Trigg has pointed out, it is surprising how quickly even isolated and technologically primitive people will abandon myths in the presence of counter-evidence, as witness the success of missionaries in the nineteenth century. South Sea islanders discovered after the arrival of missionaries that taboos and rituals connected with sailing and fishing could be given up without anything terrible happening (Trigg 1985, pp. 97–98). Perhaps the hypothetical sanctity of tigers would be part of a larger belief system that assumes that even more horrible things may happen if tigers are killed.

In the early twentieth century Albert Schweitzer, the principal critic of the liberal picture of Jesus, wrote:

> Therefore there is hopeful significance in the fact that modern theology with its study of the life of Jesus, however long it might resist by the invention of fresh shifts and expedients, must in the end find itself deluded in its manufactured history, overcome by real history and by the facts. (Schweitzer 1914, p. 32)

Schweitzer was acutely aware of the possibility of what Popper would call immunizing stratagems: the "shifts" and "expedients". It was not long before Schweitzer's hope was fulfilled. As Bartley says himself:

> Thousands of Protestant liberals soberly abandoned their Christian affiliations because they could not accept what appeared really to have been the 'Christian Ethic' as objectively determined by biblical scholarship. (Bartley 1962, p. 65)

Bartley goes on to show how various Protestant theologians reacted to the collapse of the liberal picture of Jesus. Bartley points to the degeneration of the critical spirit in the theologians Paul Tillich, Karl Barth, R.B. Braithwaite, and Reinhold Niebuhr. However, none of them exemplifies Bartley's general definition of an ideology, for every one of them in fact espouses a doctrine that is tantamount to an abandonment of orthodox Protestant Christianity in response to criticism. To be accurate, none of them represents an explicit, forthright acknowledgment of error, but rather an unintended and confused abandonment.

Bartley sees a pattern in these differing attempts to reconcile Christianity and reason: any statement of the essence of the Christian message is revisable, but whatever the message turns out to be assent or commitment to Jesus is required. Recall that Bartley's general characterization of an ideology is a system of ideas that is retained regardless of the facts. It is this commitment to Jesus that constitutes for Bartley the non-critical constraint on the fluidity of this new Protestant liberalism. Now Bartley's original characterization of the collapse of Protestant liberalism is consistent with this. Protestant liberalism, says Bartley, began as a self-critical system of ideas, but then in response to its own critical findings it became an ideology, closed to critical argument, and therefore able to be retained come what may. However, far from the system of ideas being saved and perpetuated regardless of the facts the strategy of the new Protestant thought can only amount to a face-saving exercise at the price of propagandistic success. For the commitment to Jesus itself, being vague and arbitrary, cannot operate as an effective constraint on interpretation. The symbol system is retained but the range of interpretation has become even more flexible to accept diverse viewpoints and thus maintain membership of the movement. The movement is then defined as all those who adopt the same symbol system, whatever the meaning they attribute to it.

The unintended consequence of this strategy is that there is more room for undetectable dissent and fluctuation in interpretation of the symbol system. The various interpretations may be safer from explicit analysis and criticism and the explicit acknowledgement of error, but this may be bought at the price of propagational failure. Trigg makes a similar point, but on the assumption that the system becomes totally empty of meaning, which is not necessary for my argument (Trigg 1973, pp. 58–59). An accumulation of numerous successive slight deviations may leave very little of the earlier interpretations left for propagation. The liberal Protestant propagandist would then have failed.

Before the complete abandonment of liberal Protestant through accumulated slight deviations, there is a reduction in the information and moral content of the system. If information is related to the number of possibilities closed by a message, then increasing the range of possible interpretations of Christianity decreases information. Neo-Protestant liberalism is then less able to offer adequate cosmological explanation and moral guidance. To say that one is committed to whatever Jesus happens to have said is not only to abjure any specific and explicit moral position, but is also to run a profound risk of immorality.

The thought of two of the most prominent neo-Protestant liberal theologians, Barth and Tillich, illustrate the general characteristics of this movement.

KARL BARTH

Barth rejects the methods of traditional apologetic theology as useless and irreverent. To argue for the Word of God is useless if one has already made the commitment to it and doubly so if the gift of faith is entirely in God's hands, not dependent on argument. It is irreverent because one ought to be awed, trusting, and obedient, rather than subject the Word of God to critical test against mere human standards.

The theologian should rather limit himself to the description of the Word of God and the critical discussion of the supposed content of the word of God. But argument about whether the Word of God is true is forbidden.

This is quite different to fundamentalism since the Bible, and indeed all theological statements, are explicitly treated as fallible conjectures. The only theological statement that is treated dogmatically is the statement that the Word of God is true, whatever that happens to be.

Barth's proposal that assent to God be unconditional became the price of admission to many ecumenical organizations. Bartley conjectures that its popularity lay in the fact that it offered an island of stability and definiteness in a sea of tempestuous confusion about the essence of being a Christian. It allowed theologians of diverse opinion to be at least definite about their common ground.

However, even Bartley sees that the ostensible definiteness is merely ostensible:

> Barth's formula was not of course without its own dangers, ones with which he never satisfactorily dealt; if the character of the Jesus or the Word of God to whom assent was required was indefinite, and if such commitment was required no matter what Jesus was and did, at best the subjective commitment itself would be definite. Its object would be an (I know not what and I care not what)—perhaps a less satisfactory object of worship. (Bartley 1962, p. 48)

Barth was scornful of the liberal Protestants for their use of argument and critical discussion in the search for the historical Jesus cast in the mold of social reformer. Barth's method amounts to an exclusion of certain sorts of questions and critical discussions while allowing others. But it is not altogether obvious that such a method will not become just a weak gesture of defiance toward the encroachment of argument. The license for certain sorts of argument may well function as a Trojan horse for other unintentional, unforeseeable and more damaging arguments, just like the methods of historical study of the liberal Protestants.

Paul Tillich

Tillich creates a theology more open to an accumulation of interpretative deviations by re-defining many Christian concepts in such a way as to deprive them of specific content, defining God in an extremely abstract, almost contentless way, repudiating the Bible as historical report, and his habit of creating an impression of profundity by using prepositions and abstract nouns uninterpreted by context.

Tillich rejects the traditional Christian definition of God as a unique, all knowing, all powerful, benevolent being, who makes personal contact with the believer. This conception, Tillich says, is far too abstract. One wonders what Tillich means by 'abstract' for he himself defines God in an even more abstract way as the ground of all being. Actually, Wells has shown that Tillich has a number of definitions of God, nearly every one of which looks to me to be more abstract than the traditional conception:

1. **The infinite and inexhaustible depth and ground of all being**
2. **Depth**
3. **The depths of your life**
4. **The source of your being**
5. **Your ultimate concern**
6. **What you take seriously without reservation**
7. **The infinite and inexhaustible ground of history**
8. **The depth of history**
9. **The ground and aim of your social life**
10. **What you take seriously without reservation in your moral and political activities**
11. **Hope** (Quoted in Wells 1988, p. 80)

Although Tillich rejects the traditional conception of God, none of these definitions rules it out as such, so Tillich's conception can easily accommodate a traditional Christian. But whereas the traditional conception was very definite, applying to a single unique being, Tillich's various conceptions are so indefinite and abstract that nearly everyone can find an application of at least one of them to something they think important or real. Even benevolence and justice, or any other virtue, is not required by these definitions. One could be a murderer, a liar, and a thief and still be committed to 'God': for these could be things you take seriously without reservation. So broad are these definitions that one critic disparagingly characterized Tillich's method as conversion by definition.

From Tillich's writings it is unclear what it is that a Christian is committing himself to by committing himself to Jesus. Tillich seems to be aware of this need for one's commitments to have content and creates an impression that the commitment is profoundly meaningful by a liberal use of prepositions and abstract nouns. For example, he says that the yoke of Jesus

> is not a new demand, a new doctrine, or new morals, but rather a new reality, a new being, and a new power of transforming life. . . . it is a being, power, reality, conquering the anxiety and despair, the fear and restlessness of our existence. (Quoted in Wells 1988, p. 90 from Tillich 1949, p. 99)

What being? What power? What reality? The definite reference is left open for the reader to supply.

Having repudiated the Bible as a historical report, any particular interpretation is less subject to criticism. One might think that this would be ideal for retaining and propagating a particular interpretation. However, the gain from a diminution of criticism may be offset by the greater difficulty of policing interpretations: the Bible plus historical research can no longer be used as a constraint on interpretation.

It might be argued that the intellectual reaction to the failure of liberal Protestantism was not a system that is retained despite the facts, but rather a symbol system open to more diverse interpretations. To some degree these interpretations are less open to criticism, for they are poorly expressed, if at all. Thus the resultant system is less open to explicit criticism and debate, but more prone to schism.

I do not want to suggest in this account of liberal Protestantism that the move from the literal and specific to the vague and metaphorical is the only evolutionary path in response to criticism. The Catholic Church, for example seems to have become more and more specific. The early Catholic Church regarded the infallibility of the Pope and the immaculate conception (the miraculous conception of Mary) as questions that should be left to the believer's own conscience. Though many Catholics had long accepted these claims, it was only in 1870 that the first Vatican Council laid these down as requirements of Catholic belief.

An earlier issue was the interpretation of the Eucharist. Early Christians interpreted this custom quite freely, many of them apparently regarding it as a memorial ritual. Later, church councils ruled that the bread and wine were literally the flesh and blood of Christ. Since Catholics are rational people and not blind, the literal interpretation could only be maintained by the distinction between the manifest (or accidental) features of the sacramental bread and wine and its essence (or substance). The sacramental offering was the flesh and blood of Jesus only 'in substance', not by the standards of physics, chemistry, or common observation. All Catholic theologians accept that you can get just as drunk on consecrated wine as on unconsecrated wine, and that you will not find any hemoglobin in consecrated wine. In the short term, this distinction was apparently a doctrine-saving move, but over the longer haul it has landed the Church in the odd position of maintaining that physical materials possess a 'substance' which is totally undetectable, has no observable effects in the world, and yet is of the utmost importance. Despite its apparently adroit way of closing off an issue to criticism, this literal interpretation of the Eucharist (transubstantiation) was not adopted by the Eastern Orthodox Church (Ware 1963).

More recently, Catholic Modernism seems to have made great inroads despite official condemnation, and to have heightened the urgency of the problem of what makes one a Catholic. As just one example of this seepage, Higher Criticism (analysis of the biblical texts, revealing their inconsistencies and other shortcomings) used to be confined to Protestants or skeptics in traditionally Protestant communities. Up to the mid-twentieth century, Catholic propagandists would smugly point out that Higher Criticism was a disease of Protestantism. But Higher Criticism is now accepted among Catholic scholars, so that we have the standard Higher-Critical work on the Nativity clearly indicating that the historical evidence is against the Virgin Birth, written by a Catholic Priest in good standing (the late Father Raymond Brown), with an Imprimatur and Nihil Obstat on the copyright page, certifying that the work is free of doctrinal or moral error.

The Nightmare of Perfect Thought Control

The central thread of this book is the question whether it's feasible for a propagandist to guarantee the propagation of his doctrine, perhaps by protecting it against encountering any criticism or simply ensuring it will be maintained in the presence of any criticism. I have considered Bartley's examples and found them wanting. But in order to test a theory in the severest way it is sometimes necessary to provide stronger examples than one's opponents have come up with. I now intend to construct such an example and to examine the logic of the situation that the propagandist would then find himself in.

Suppose a world government has discovered a method by which to make everyone incapable of innovative thought. Perhaps a drug or brain surgery would bring about this effect. I do not rule out the possibility of such a nightmarish world in which everyone is, if not in complete conformity, at least something disturbingly like a docile mental clone. The people in this world would be more like Bartley's view of people in our world: slumbering fantasizers, only under this mental despotism they would all have the same fantasy, day after day, night after night.

Criticism depends on the ability to produce a new thought or apply an old one in a new way. Therefore the citizens of this world would be rendered incapable of criticizing the approved ideology. They might be given perfect memories so that they would simply repeat the ideology unchanged even by copying errors. In this hypothetical world, assume that the world government has complete control over societal processes to rule out deliberate or accidental deviations from the approved ideology. Is the propagandist's doctrine guaranteed against criticism and guaranteed in its perpetuation?

Providing no physical catastrophes occur, it has to be admitted that the propagandist's doctrine is safeguarded against criticism. But there is no guarantee against physical disasters that put the society in peril, and therefore imperil the perpetuation of the ideology. Coping with a physical disaster may, and often does, require innovation. By definition, innovations are unforeseeable. They cannot be specified in advance, except sometimes in outline or in terms of the need they are to satisfy and the means available for their creation (and even here innovative thought is sometimes required to properly assess needs and means). The situational logic facing the world government, therefore, would require that it at least temporarily suspend the suppression of innovation. But the freedom for innovative thought allows the unforeseeable creation of criticisms of the approved ideology. What might the government do to prevent this? It might be thought that the world government could insure against that by restricting the areas or subject-matters in which innovations would be allowed, by a discriminatory use of drugs or brain surgery. However, even if one has a definite description of the problem that the innovative theories are to solve and even an outline description of the innovation, one cannot derive from this all and only the problems on which it might have a bearing. To do this one would have to survey the information and logical content of each new theory, and this we have seen is impossible. One cannot therefore exclude its critical bearing on the approved ideology. To have any chance of perpetuating the ideology the government would have to take the risk that the innovation required to maintain the society may produce a competing ideology or the means of combating the government's repressive use of drugs or brain surgery.

We can develop a more general argument from the observation that innovation is important in the maintenance of any highly populated and advanced industrial society. Hayek has argued that innovation is necessary and has made possible the perpetuation and growth of our own society, to the maintenance and growth of living standards and population (Hayek 1960, especially Chapter 2). It would follow from this that even in the normal running of a society free from cataclysmic perils a world government that sought to perpetuate an ideology by the suppression of free thought would run a grave risk of reducing the number of its converts and the technological means used in the reproduction of its ideology.

Throughout history one can find horrible despotisms that attempt to perpetuate a doctrine by school-indoctrination, TV and radio advertising, violence, censorship, spying, encouraging family betrayal, border guards, death squads, and so on. My point is that the perpetuation of a doctrine against criticism is an extremely difficult, delicate, costly, and uncertain project. The extremes that some governments have gone to in their attempts to achieve this goal and their failure to impose perfect conformity only testifies to the difficulty of completely taming the voice of doubt, which, eel-like, slips out of the policeman's grasp when he least expects it to do so.

Martyrdom as a Rational Technique

Martyrdom and other religious sacrifices are rational decisions of people trying to achieve their personally conceived ends by what they regard as effective and efficient means. Economics, seen as a general and abstract theory of human action in all fields, not only in pecuniary contexts, can explain martyrdom.

The history of religions is littered with examples of people enduring grotesque torture and sacrifice, culminating in a sacrifice of their lives on behalf of their religion. When social scientists have asked 'How could rational people sacrifice even their lives for unseen supernatural entities?' their answer—as Rodney Stark has observed—has been that they must be irrational. Typically, they have either adduced the irrationalist thesis about humans in general or claimed that these particular individuals must have suffered from some psychopathology. A popular theory asks us to accept that martyrs are masochists attracted by the exquisite pleasures of bodily mangling, galling, ripping, or burning.

Social scientists who have thought this way have apparently assumed that it is irrational to have aims that can only be attained in the afterlife. This may, of course, be mistaken and misguided, if there is no afterlife, or if the afterlife is not constructed the way certain religious believers suppose. But mistakes are part and parcel of rational behavior. In some versions, theorists come perilously close to assuming that only self-interest can be rational. But rationality relates to the use of reason and the adjustment of means to ends; it cannot exclude some ends (except by assuming that they are subordinate to other ends). It is just as possible to be rational for altruistic or self-sacrificing motives as for motives of direct personal benefit.

It is therefore entirely rational, for example, for an individual to sacrifice his own life or well-being in order to bring about some state of affairs after his death. People do this routinely when they make provision for the future welfare of their children or other loved ones. Even some people who do not believe in their own personal survival after death do sometimes sacrifice their lives or their happiness for the future success of a cause, such as liberalism, socialism, nationalism, fascism, democracy, or some particular religious system. There is nothing irrational about this: these individuals are taking sensible steps to further that which they value. If they also happen to believe in an afterlife, and to believe that things will go better for them in the afterlife, this provides a possible further inducement for them to sacrifice their lives if the occasion arises. If they are mistaken about their reward in the afterlife, and they sacrifice their lives on account of this mistaken judgment about future outcomes, this is in principle the same kind of mistake as investing heavily in stocks (to the extent of buying on margin) just before a stock market crash. All judgments are fallible.

[2]
Survival of the Truest

Darwinian evolution has made us rational. We prefer effective and economic means, we prefer truth to falsity and have a general curiosity about the world, we prefer logical arguments and consistent theories, and we are disposed to check our hypotheses against the facts. Even our wishful and fearful thinking is a means of thoroughly testing hypotheses that are important and urgent to us. These dispositions are not always decisive and there are other factors at work in our preference and rejection of ideas. We are lazy, distracted, fallible, incredibly stupid, and vastly ignorant.

However, we are born with the tools to curb the excesses of ideological deception. Cognitive psychology has shown that children already have an intuitive grasp of the world. They have an intuitive physics, an intuitive natural history, an intuitive psychology and an understanding of tools. Children have the robust rudiments of an understanding of logic. They also have the capability of forming hypotheses (jumping to conclusions) and then being surprised if their hypotheses turn out to be wrong. For example, if a child sees a frog squashed in the road revealing its insides, the child will be surprised if the next frog is not the same inside. If a child sees a cow give birth to a live calf, the child will be surprised if told the next one will lay eggs. Children are born with a categorizing disposition that places animals into natural exclusive classes, all the members of which are assumed to have the same characteristics. This is their intuitive natural history.

If a child sees someone walk across the road or pull something out of a pocket or press a button or do anything, the child will automatically assume that the person is trying to achieve something—that they have a desire to get to a goal and have beliefs about how they can do that. This is children's intuitive psychology. This disposition is so strong that they will impute desires and beliefs to dots moving and 'bumping' into one another on a computer screen, providing only that the dots move in the right way. No one has to teach the child to perceive the dots as 'chasing one another', 'attacking one another', or 'helping one another', depending on the pattern of movement.

Any propagandist wishing to disseminate his message faces a multitude of innate critics—perhaps not sophisticated, but effective to a degree. We cannot easily be shaped in the image of any false, ineffective, uneconomic, or illogical ideology. A Hitler or a Mao has to take account somehow of the character of the material to be molded or chiseled: only certain things can be made out of quartz. The view that we are playthings of ideologies was plausible only before the blank slate view of human beings was shattered by the combined assault of cognitive psychology, economics, and evolutionary theory.

Evolution and Human Rationality

Darwin's fundamental intellectual puzzle was that the world is teeming with life forms that have the mark of being designed. A fish's fins are made to swim better, a hawk's eyes are made to see prey at great distance, and so forth. William Paley (1743–1805) in his *Natural Theology* had put the question memorably. If you were walking in the countryside and came across a smooth stone, you would think that its shape had been made by a river. However, if you came across a watch, even never having seen a watch before, after inspecting its intricate complexity, and noting how its parts are delicately dependent on one another, you would conclude that it had been made for a purpose. You would conclude there must be a watchmaker. What natural force could have brought together the parts in such an improbable arrangement? If there appears to be design, there must be a designer. If such reasoning is valid with a watch, then why not with every living thing? Indeed, why not go further? The world looks designed, therefore it is.

As a Cambridge undergraduate Darwin was deeply impressed and completely persuaded by this argument. But later he was to explode it by suggesting a powerful alternative explanation. Darwin conjectured that the myriad forms of life we see today derive ultimately from one or a few life forms by gradual change over millions of years. Each generation of life forms was slightly different from their parents and from one another. In the competition for resources, some of each generation would, by chance, be more successful in surviving and leaving offspring. Their offspring would inherit this advantage and the variation might be a little further in the direction of advantage. The same selective pressure from competition would be felt again. When this process of variation and selection is repeated millions of times, hardly noticeable increments of change could lead from a fish to a reptile and from a reptilian form to a mammalian form.

In Darwin's explanation there is no design or planning required for organisms to become increasingly more adapted to survival. The process of variation and the later process of selection between the variants are blind. This was a tremendous intellectual leap, because prior to Darwin, Lamarck's theory had held sway, in which life forms evolve by the action of use and acquired characteristics. Giraffes developed long necks because their ancestors benefited from stretching their necks to reach fruit higher on the trees and their longer necks were inherited by their descendants. More fundamentally, Darwin's theory also contradicted our intuitive natural history, which assumes that there are species with essences. A fish is a fish and cannot change into a reptile.

Sophisticated people can see how, say, the domestic dog evolved from quite different wild varieties of wolf, but need extra coaching to see that the wolf in turn could have evolved from something very different, the creodont, which lived at least sixty million years ago, ancestor also of cats, bears, weasels, raccoons, civets, and hyenas. This is a nice paradox, that Darwinian evolution, which gave us our intuition of species, refutes the simple intuitive idea of species. This may be the greatest, but not insurmountable, barrier to the acceptance of Darwin's theory. In any case, Darwinian evolution is change involving blind variation, selection, and reproduction.

Even Darwinism's major critics such as Stephen Jay Gould maintain Darwinism's key insight: that natural selection is the only way of explaining the emergence of complex and subtle adaptations. Gould simply disagrees with certain types of gradualism. Gould still relies on the idea of natural variation and natural selection.

Does the Modularity of Mind Undermine Rationality?

Does the fact that we evolved according to Darwinian evolution guarantee that we are rational? The old theory of evolution due to Lamarck did seem to guarantee this. Lamarck postulated a ladder of evolution, beginning with bacteria or other simple life form and step by step rising up the ladder, through fish, reptiles, mammals to finally arrive at human beings. Lamarckism implies that if you ran evolution over again, then you'd get human beings again, and that if you run it long enough with other creatures, then you'll also get humans as a the final step. If you also believe that humans are rational, then for you Lamarck's vision guarantees rationality. In science, Darwin's theory supplanted Lamarckism. However, Lamarckism is still a popular assumption: many of the *Star Trek* episodes portray aliens as advanced humanoid with larger brains. The search for extraterrestrial intelligence is based on looking for radio signals, that is, on the idea that intelligent beings would likely be humanoid.

The popular imagination thinks of aliens as little green men. Jack Cohen, the reproductive biologist who specializes in plausible alien biology, once said: "I don't believe in little green men. Not so much because they are green, but because they are men." But Darwinian evolution is blind—it has no direction. It has no long-term goal. If you run it again, you may not get humans. We therefore have to be more careful in setting out an argument from evolution to human rationality. However, if there were non-humanoid green aliens, I would place a bet that they would be disposed to avoid failure or excessive cost. The ability to be effective in the world and not squander resources seems to be a minimum requirement for survival and reproduction. Whether the aliens had self-consciousness, general curiosity, language, an appreciation of complex logical relations, and the ability for long term planning would be less sure bets.

Evolution has adapted organisms to their past environment and mode of life, which may not be the same as their current or future environment and mode of life. We are adapted to the Pleistocene epoch. As Cosmides puts it:

> Our species spent ninety-nine percent of its evolutionary history as hunter-gatherers: the genus *Homo* emerged about two million years ago, and agriculture first appeared less than ten thousand years ago. Ten thousand years is not enough time for much evolutionary change to have occurred, given the long human generation time; thus our cognitive mechanisms should be adapted to the hunter-gatherer mode of life, and not to the twentieth-century industrialized world.

Cosmides calls the resulting rationality "ecological rationality." This is in contrast to Aristotle's conception of humans as 'rational animals'. The idea that humans have a general problem-solving mind dominated thinking in psychology and philosophy for thousands of years.

Cosmides's revolutionary approach has led many thinkers to conjecture that the human mind is not a general-purpose problem solver, but has many special-purpose problem solving machines built into it by the very specific demands of our ancestors' hunter-gatherer life. Our ancestors encountered certain problems for hundreds of thousands of years, and encountered other types of problems never. Our ancestors had to recognize objects, make tools, find mates, understand animals; they never had to solve or even understand the general and abstract problems of set theory or Goldbach's Conjecture, or wonder whether there might be life on other planets or why we can't fly like birds. Instead of being like a general-purpose computer our mind is more like a Swiss army knife.

This approach fits well with what psychologists have found. Our reasoning abilities are domain-specific and have their own biases and limitations. Jerry Fodor (1983) was the first to conjecture that the mind has a collection of special-purpose machines. Fodor said they are mandatory (you cannot stop them), fast-acting, domain-specific, encapsulated (they don't affect one another's operation), and break down independently of one another. For example, if you open your eyes, then you can't help but see a stable three-dimensional environment before you, this is instantaneous, what you see is not affected by what you hear and vice versa, and if you damage your brain in a car crash, then you can lose your sight without losing your hearing.

Fodor's original idea was that this was true of our senses and perceptual abilities. Fodor thought that there was a general-purpose thinking ability responsible for creative thought and deductive reasoning. But other writers have suggested that the general-purpose thinking itself can be divided up into a host of modules. Your mind is a herd of little Terminators that "simply will not stop."

Now, you may ask, does this undermine my whole approach? In talking about instrumental rationality (the preference for effective means), economic rationality, and logical rationality, am I saying that rationality is general, not specific? And if I admit that human rationality is fragmented into modules, each with its own biases and typical errors, then must I also concede that cleverly-constructed ideologies may survive the scrutiny of this weak "ecological rationality"?

Any such conclusion would be unwarranted. I maintain:

1. **The reasoning within each of these modules is not only effective but tough.**

and

2. **We can correct or compensate for 'errors' produced by the separate modules.**

1. *The reasoning within each of these modules is not only effective but tough.* The highly effective operations they perform are reflex-like and cannot be conditioned out of us. They are innate and come into operation at or just after birth. Our Swiss army knife is made of titanium and it was our first birthday present.

2. *We can correct or compensate for 'errors' produced by the separate modules.* We can and do discover our own natural biases and typical errors and make allowances for them. When you look at something, light falls on your retina to form a two-dimensional image. One of our modules converts a two-dimensional retinal projection to give us our stable three-dimensional perception of the world. This is an amazing feat of computation. However, it has its typical errors. Sometimes you see illusions—mirages, sticks bending in water, and so forth. But you know (or can easily find out) that they're illusions, and with a little more knowledge you can even use the illusions as a source of information (for example, humans fishing with spears learn to adjust the angle at which they throw the spear to compensate for the bending of the light by the water). There are better and worse ways of using our Swiss army knife. We come to know its idiosyncrasies and even invent new uses for some of the tools.

We do not seem to be trapped inside these modules. Somehow, it seems that there must be room for a general-purpose idea creator and reasoning ability, in addition to the specific modules. We do seem to be equipped with a set of hard-wired domain-specific modules that work on their problems automatically. It makes sense to have some of these. When chased by a tiger or when chasing lunch, undistractable, decisive speed of calculation and action count. Also, the knowledge required to solve some problems is irrelevant to solving other problems. The effect of the slant of an object on its luminance is irrelevant to choosing a mate; the effect of lying on tone of voice will not enable you to judge the shape of an object.

However, even as children, we do wonder why we can't fly like birds, whether there are people on other planets, how we can walk in a straight line and why the moon does not fall, if it's a rock. We have a general curiosity about the world, the ability to create new ideas and goals, and we can make abstract generalizations. Combined with our language these general abilities allow us to use our automatic 'Terminators', audit the output of these drones and make appropriate corrections and inferences.

I can still maintain my argument. I can say that economic, instrumental and logical rationality exist in a general form as a first approximation and then make qualifications when required by special circumstances. This is what we do in everyday life. We assume, following our innate folk psychology, that people have beliefs and desires and will pursue means they think are effective in obtaining things that satisfy their desires. If we learn that a particular person has a certain bias or typical error, we take account of this special circumstance. But it's also true that many ideologies are concerned with just those areas of thinking to which the modules are beautifully adapted.

Marxism, national socialism, liberal democracy, and various religions are concerned with the distribution of costs and benefits in a social context. They make use of the 'logic of exchange' that Cosmides explored. So, either we have general rationality or we have specific rationality. If our rationality is completely general, then it can stand up to the manipulations of ideologies; if our rationality is domain-specific, then also it can stand up to the manipulations of ideologies. Therefore, our rationality can stand up to the manipulations of ideologies.

To handle the question of whether our minds may be more closed to argument on account of our having an 'ecological' or modular rationality, I need to look at how knowledge and its growth is possible. We can then see more clearly whether a modular and problem-specific structure of the mind would make us open or closed to argument.

Evolutionary Epistemology

Let's take a step back from psychology, economics, and biological evolution to see them in a larger perspective. Human beings produce and use a larger range of knowledge than any other organism. Whether it's our assessment of effective and economic means, the truth or falsity of ideas, or their logical consistency, we're attempting to produce and use knowledge. What implications should this have for the survivability of systems of ideas that are trying to hide themselves from critical argument? What broader perspective should we take in dealing with this problem? The answer lies in the theory of knowledge: epistemology. To be more precise, we want evolutionary epistemology. This is the idea that evolution explains the mechanisms for the production and use of knowledge, and that these very mechanisms or adaptations are knowledge.

Popper and Campbell were early developers of this line of thought. A more recent contributor is Henry Plotkin who, in his Darwin Machines, elaborates their point that an animal's organs and behavior embody knowledge, understood as information, about the world. Even the way we try to find out about the world, the way we learn and explore it, uses biologically embodied knowledge about the world that has evolved over millions of years.

Evolution explains these mechanisms in two senses: their emergence and how they work. Some of these mechanisms may actually embody evolutionary principles. For example, our ability to produce new ideas may be a combination of blind variation followed by selection according to imposed criteria related to our goals. Edison's production of the idea of the light bulb involved thousands of freely created trials, most of which were duds. But some of the mechanisms may be more routine, hard-wired, and domain-specific, such as our ability to derive a three-dimensional environment from a two-dimensional retinal image.

One or both of two instincts drive philosophical enquiry: wonder and control. We have a deep wonder about the world, its structure and origin, and in ourselves and our place in the world. We also possess a general desire for control, and, as Schopenhauer pointed out, understanding is partly a sort of vicarious mastery over the world. We share these instincts with other animals. Psychologists have found that monkeys confined to rooms without a view will perform tasks in order to obtain a view through an opened window, and will perform tasks in order to be able simply to manipulate objects. This is not to equate knowledge and power, as the philosopher Francis Bacon does in his aphorism "Knowledge is power," for wonder and its satisfaction is its own delight and some delightful knowledge is of no other practical use.

Unlike the mystic, who is content to savor a mystery, the philosopher wishes to solve it, reveling in the expectation of even deeper problems within the cracked shell of the first problem. The mystic monkey would stay in the room simply savoring the question 'What is outside?', whereas the monkey-philosopher would jump through hoops to open the window. My suspicion is that there are in fact no mystic monkeys—or that they are so few that they play no appreciable role in the life and death of ideas. I also suspect that the great majority of people are closer to the philosopher than the mystic.

The fundamental questions of epistemology are: What are the source, the nature, scope, and limits of knowledge? Often neglected in current commentaries is perhaps the more fundamental problem: How do we advance the growth of knowledge?

My problem is related to this problem but different. The problem I'm trying to solve here is a problem in evolutionary epistemology applied to ideology. The traditional epistemological question is: How can we know? But my approach starts with the question: How can we avoid knowing? How can the propagandist evade or overcome the effects of human rationality? Can we argue that because of humankind's origin as a creature of Darwinian evolution humans can always correct their errors? The question is not so much why people get things wrong, for any system capable of knowing is fallible. But rather, having fallen into a pit of error by accident or foul play, can people in principle, alone or with help, always climb out? My answer is that they can. There are no evolved mechanisms in our psychology that perpetuate error come what may, but there are fallible mechanisms or dispositions for correcting error.

I am not arguing, as some have, that because of our evolutionary history we must necessarily make progress in the growth of knowledge. Science may degenerate into a stale perpetuation of sacred texts, or it may, for example, unintentionally help to produce a society in which any one can easily construct weapons of mass destruction and destroy the whole population. But, short of destruction, humankind can always reverse regressions in the search for truth, or at the very least continue correcting error.

I argue that, provided we are careful, Darwinian evolutionary theory must play a central role in our understanding of human thought in general and therefore also in our understanding of openness to argument. As Karl Popper says:

> I do conjecture that Darwinism is right, even on the level of scientific discovery; and that it is right even beyond this level: that it is right even on the level of artistic creation. (Popper 1981, pp. 89–90)

By "Darwinism" here Popper means something encompassing Darwin's biological theory but more abstract. Any explanation of the evolution of a population of entities by a combination of their blind variation and selection or, more accurately, their differential elimination.

In a later article, Popper argues for a much more general application of Darwinism, following Darwin's own assertions (in his *Essay* of 1844, his Origin *of Species*, and his *Natural Selection*) that the mental powers of animals and man are products of natural selection. Popper asserts that if conscious states exist then we should, according to Darwinism, look for their adaptive function (Popper 1987, pp. 148–49). At the conclusion of his article Popper remarks that

> the process of variation followed by selection which Darwin discovered does not merely offer an explanation of biological evolution . . . but also of . . . "the entire range of phenomena connected with the evolution of life and mind, and also of the products of the human mind. (pp. 152–53)

The psychologist and philosopher Donald T. Campbell clearly stated the relevance of evolution to a philosophical treatment of man:

> An evolutionary epistemology would be at minimum an epistemology taking cognizance of and compatible with man's status as a product of biological . . . evolution. (Campbell 1974, p. 413)

It is specifically Darwinian evolution that Campbell has in mind, which has the following form:

1. **Blind variations in heritable characteristics;**[14]
2. **Elimination of unadapted variations;**
3. **Reproduction of selected variations.**

Now recall what Popper said about the closed mind:

> no rational argument will have a rational effect on a man who does not want to adopt a rational attitude. (Popper 1945, p. 231)

And Bartley:

> ideologies are retained regardless of the facts; they are not abandoned when they clash with the facts; rather they die out or are eliminated, if at all, together with their carriers. (Bartley 1984, p. xvii)

But if Popper and Bartley mean what they say, then their theory of ideology ought to be consistent with both a Darwinian account of our biological evolution and with a Darwinian account of our world of ideas. Even though Popper does not explicitly mention ideology in this connection, he does see how a Darwinian account is applicable both the biological world and the world of ideas. However, Popper has overlooked certain relationships that we will now look at.

If we adhere to a Darwinian approach to our biological evolution, we should expect humans to be rational in ways that undermine the plausibility of pessimistic positions on the power of argument to undermine ideologies. For convenience of exposition, the relevant ways in which humans are rational can be classified as:

1. **Economic,**
2. **Instrumental,**

3. **Exploratory,**
4. **Wishful and fearful, and**
5. **Logical.**

They are examples of man's responsiveness to truth, and once in place, as it were, act as Darwinian-like filters in the evolution of ideologies. The three processes mentioned above (blind variation, selective elimination, and retention) work through human biological evolution to produce certain rational dispositions that tend to eliminate irrational variations in ideas in general and therefore also in ideologies.

A Darwinian Epistemology

What epistemology is consistent with a Darwinian perspective? It is the method of conjecture and refutation. First, we are surprised by an event or a puzzle is raised by our curiosity in the world. Using our imagination we then make guesses to explain our problem. Knowledge grows by advancing varied unjustified guesses, which we then subject to destructive criticism.

Our theories are like the blind variations in Darwinian evolution, criticism is like the sometimes brutal encounter with reality that organisms face. When natural variation among organisms produced the first rudiments of vision, say a mere sensitivity to light, this was not justified or instructed by the environment. It just happened to be useful for the organism solving its problem of survival and reproduction. Similarly, Einstein's conjecture that the speed of light was a constant was not justified or instructed by the data. It just happened to help solve the problem he was working on. Both science and biological evolution are knowledge-producing processes and, because of logical constraints, they both use the same method. The mind, as an evolved organ, is then likely to operate by conjecture and refutation.

This is a rather eccentric proposal, I know. So let me put it in context. The old theory of how science should be conducted was due to Francis Bacon, who proposed that one should collect much and varied observations. The correct theory would, somehow, emerge from or be derived from this careful enumeration of data. Nature was manifest and one had only to purge one's mind of prejudices and look carefully at the world to discover its lawful nature. This is the method of induction. Don't we reason from our numerous experiences of things to generalizations? We see some hens lay eggs and conclude that all hens lay eggs.

As I said earlier, even very young children do this. Yet even though we do *seem* to use this method in our thinking, that's an illusion. The method of conjecture and refutation can simulate induction.

But what's wrong with induction? It became clear that there were insuperable logical problems with this approach. The nineteenth-century polymath William Whewell pointed out that at least some prejudices were necessary just to be able to classify data of the same kind relevant to the same problem. Data does not come ready labeled for us. It also became clear that statements of natural law are not equivalent to enumerations of observations: they go far beyond all possible observations. David Hume pointed out that one could not deduce a law from any number of observations. Nor could one even make a law probable by collecting observations. A law, for example 'All planets move in elliptical orbits', talks about all planets, in the past, present, and future. And not only about planets that happen to have existed, but also all these that could have existed but didn't and all those that could exist in the future but won't.

The law therefore talks about an infinity of things of a type. Scientific laws are extremely bold, informative statements about, the world. But the boldness doesn't stop there. Each law is a selection from an infinity of other possible laws, and so excludes an infinity of other possible cases or types. So laws speak about activity at two levels: at the level of particulars (this or that planet) and at the level of types (this and that type of ellipse). But our rules of probability go a little crazy when you try to feed infinities into them. Normally, when we work out the likelihood of something we know the size of the main population of things of the type we are talking about. Suppose we have a bag of twenty balls, each one of which has a different number on. If we want to know the likelihood of drawing a ball from a bag with a particular number, we divide the number of favorable outcomes by the total number of possibilities. In this case, it is 1 over 20, so the likelihood is 1 in 20. Now, what is the population of actual and possible planets? It is infinite. What is the number of our observations of elliptical orbits. It has to be a finite number, say 10,000. Therefore, we might want to say that the likelihood that the next planet we observe moves in an ellipse is 10,000 divided by infinity. But this leads to strange results.

There is another fundamental problem about our knowledge of the world that surfaced, further frustrating the idea that we learn and acquire knowledge through repeated observation. The philosophers Popper, Quine, and Duhem all pointed to the fact that for any given set of sense-data, there is literally an infinity of explanations logically consistent with it. Many of these would seem bizarre to us given our background assumptions, but we are looking at how you are supposed to justify these assumptions in the first place. In practical terms this was brought home to the first computer engineers who tried to simulate how the human eye forms a three-dimensional theory of the world from the two-dimensional visual data it receives. They discovered that the problem involved a breathtaking amount of computation. But, more to the point, they discovered that the visual system had to be already equipped with the right answer in some respects. In other words, important truths about how the world is structured must already be wired into our senses by evolution. That general point further frustrates the idea that organisms learn and adapt by using their sense-data and some general purpose problem-solving mechanism such as association.

Are these conclusions frustrating? Our frustration is due to a deep presupposition in western culture that we should only accept positions that we can justify, either from sense-data or reasoning. The assumption goes back to Plato's discussion of the difference between knowledge and mere opinion, the idea being that unlike mere opinion, knowledge has been or can be justified. In the *Meno* Plato describes a thought experiment. Suppose you are on a journey to a city and you come to a fork in the road. You have to choose between them, for one leads to the city and the other somewhere else. Suppose you merely guessed it was the right fork and this was correct. Would you have acted any differently if you had chosen the right fork with knowledge? Suppose that you were justified in choosing the left fork, but by hypothesis you fail to get to the city. Plato concludes, rather surprisingly since it has nothing to do with the discussion, that knowledge differs from mere opinion in being more consolidated in memory. Since Plato, however, most philosophers have assumed that knowledge is both true and justified. Knowledge is defined as justified true belief. A whole vast 'philosophy of justification' has been developed with this as the sacrosanct assumption. Whereas Plato thought the crucial thing about knowledge was its consolidation in memory, later philosophers looked more at the source and procedures whereby the belief was acquired.

But what I think Plato's thought experiment shows is that for practical purposes, truth is enough and that justification is not necessary, and the search for justification may even be misleading. All action and all technology only require truth or at least truth-likeness, verisimilitude, approximation to truth. Would you want to choose the horse that wins or do you want to choose the horse that is likely to win? Of course, you will say 'But don't people use form to bet on horses?' I'm suggesting that using form is a way of eliminating the horses that will lose. But these methods are themselves guesses, even though they have been honed over thousands of years. A bridge constructed in the light of the truth is preferable to one the justification for whose methods of construction is impeccable, but collapsed. We have methods for telling whether a bridge will stand or collapse—I'm suggesting that these again are guesses which can in principle be wrong. But the same applies to our curiosity about the world. What we want is truth about what's happening in a black hole, the truth about the big bang, whether there is a theory that can unite the quantum and relativity theories. The goal in either case seems to be truth, not justification.

But what about the control of error? We can't sensibly go around just guessing the truth. Popper proposed that, inspired by a deep question about the world, scientists propose theories that can in principle clash logically with observational reports about the world—'All planets move in ellipses', for example—and then try to show by observation that the theory is incorrect or at least not as close to the truth as an alternative explanation. Our guesses are free and always totally unjustified, but we use the strongest methods at our disposal for destroying them. Our guesses are trial balloons that we try to shoot down. The ones that remain aloft may be true, or if not actually true, closer to the truth than the ones shot down.

The analogy with Darwinian evolution is strong. Just as the variations in biological evolution are blind, our conjectural explorations of the world in science or, indeed, any field, are blind. Just as the world extinguishes organisms that don't fit it, the world, through our careful observations, can extinguish our guesses. Of course, we have to make the right logical inferences from observation and this may become quite complex.

Talking about these abstract philosophical issues is important, for we are then better able to see just how irrational or rational people are in their production and use of knowledge. We can also evaluate and understand more accurately the new science of evolutionary psychology and its postulation of innate mental modules. The view I have developed allows me to portray these modules in a way that makes sense in terms of the conjectural nature of our knowledge, not just as in science, but all the knowledge embodied in our organs.

Let's look again at our apparently inductive habits of reasoning based on the module for thinking about animals. That they are inductive is merely apparent. When looked at more closely, you will see that it is better seen as deductive thinking. Actually, what has happened is that our evolution has given us the general hypothesis that all animals belong to species and that species belong to higher level groupings. Each grouping has its own set of distinctive characteristics. So, when a child sees a hen lay eggs, the child doesn't reason inductively to all animals of the same species. That would simply be invalid, a logical error. That we seem to do this troubled Hume. However, we don't really do it. Rather, the child combines two assumptions, one from our instinctive set of inborn knowledge, and one from the child's particular observation, and then reasons deductively that all hens lay eggs. Even children are deductive thinkers. Humans think more logically than Hume supposed.

The philosophical approach I have just outlined is called 'critical rationalism'. One important result of critical rationalism is that a theory is not at fault if it is not based on evidence, and a belief is not irrational if it is not based on evidence. In fact, in a deep foundational sense, no theory or belief is ever based on evidence, or ever could be. It does not matter in the least where a theory or belief 'comes from'. What does matter is how that theory or belief can be tested, and what would lead us to abandon it. Dawkins and other atheists sometimes dismiss theistic religion because it has not based itself on evidence. From the standpoint of critical rationalism, it's more to the point to find out whether any particular theistic doctrine can be tested or criticized, whether its proponents encourage or discourage criticism, and whether they might conceivably abandon that doctrine under the impact of criticism.

General and Specific Problem-Solving

My argument assumes that there are both general and specific strategies for solving problems. Leda Cosmides, the advocate of ecological rationality, has argued that general problem-solving strategies are woefully inadequate to solve the problems that our ancestors faced. Cosmides infers that we do not have a general problem-solving ability or strategy. I want to suggest that in the light of evolutionary epistemology, we should expect at least one general problem solving strategy: that modeled on an abstract conception of evolution. We should expect something along the lines of blind variation and selection.

For example, Edison produces thousands of ideas without knowing in advance which would work; this 'inspiration' stage is then followed by the 'perspiration' stage, in which the ruthless demands of engineering and economics play their part. This is an idealized view, but it is characteristic of our general approach to solving problems, after our reflex-like automatic modules have had a go at cracking the problem or at least limiting the range of information worth looking at. The analogy between biological and scientific evolution is not merely analogy. What is true in logic must also be true in psychology. If conjecture and refutation is the only valid method by which knowledge is acquired and grows, then our psychology will itself embody this method. We seem to have a fundamental argument for a general problem-solving strategy. Cosmides may not have looked at a high enough level of abstraction in the search for workable general strategies.

I also think that the method may be incorporated into the specific constraints of each individual module. So, even though they are 'content'-rich (embody lots of specific knowledge), they are implemented in accord with a scheme of variation and selection. For example, our visual system gives us a stable perception of the world, but only because it continually tests alternative models about the three-dimensional structure of what we are looking at. Necker's cube is a depiction of a transparent cube by drawing the lines of the cube's edges. Look at the cube, and you will see it appear alternately in two apparent 3-D orientations that are consistent with the 2-D line drawing. This suggests that the visual system is testing out alternative hypotheses and has insufficient data to settle on one. Cosmides does acknowledge that general-purpose problem-solving strategies can work well if they are set in a context of specific problem solvers that already have specific knowledge of their domain built into them (Tooby and Cosmides 1992, p. 113).

I suggest that the mind consists of a bundle of specific problem solvers, with their own typical errors and biases, and a more general, supervisory, language-based system that uses the specific problem-solvers as 'first attack' troops, cannon fodder.

The person most responsible for discovering various typical human errors of reasoning and judgment, Daniel Kahneman, seems also to have found evidence that can be explained by assuming there are two systems at work when people are given problems to solve. There is a quick, lazy judgment that shows typical errors and biases, and a secondary system, which given more time to solve the problems, shows fewer typical errors and biases. This is evidence that we are not trapped in these modules and that we can become more aware of our typical errors and correct for them.

An Indirect Refutation of the Existence of the Impervious Believer

We cannot directly refute the idea that there are ideologists who are completely immune to criticism. No matter how many supposed examples of such ideologists are shown to be spurious, the advocate of the irrationalist thesis can always maintain that we have not looked hard enough for an example. It is as if someone had claimed that there is a pink elephant. No matter how far and how long you look without finding it, the pink-elephant-believer can always say that you have not looked far enough. The animal is extremely shy. However, we can apply what can be called a theoretical refutation. When trying to refute an opinion we can sometimes refer directly to a counterexample. For example, if someone claims that no hammerhead shark ever attacks humans, one could in principle point to just one actual attack to dispose of that claim. But often one has to approach the matter in a more circumspect manner by pointing to a theory we already hold because it is both strong and itself directly testable.

If Darwinian evolution is taken as background knowledge, then we are obliged to reject the closed mind thesis on pain of inconsistency. Bartley has used Darwinian theory in this way to undermine anti-realist positions in the philosophy of science (Bartley 1987, pp. 7–45). For example, if a philosopher of science thinks that an evolutionary theory like Darwin's is part of our science, and that, as explained, there has to be something doing the selecting or eliminating the 'unfit', then it becomes a puzzle as to what, on an anti-realist view, is doing the eliminating, if not the objectively stern reality that reduces the reproductive prospects of individual organisms. The anti-realist view does not seem to have a plausible answer.

If someone returned from a pioneering trip to a previously unexplored land in deepest Africa with tales of animals similar to ants in all respects but the size of elephants, the biologist would easily refute such a tale. As I pointed out earlier, animals are the size they are in accord with certain constraints imposed by physical, chemical, and geometric considerations. In the science-fiction movie *Them*, ants the size of houses terrorize the inhabitants of Los Angeles. In reality, ants that large would overheat and die. As an object increases in size its volume increases at a faster rate than its surface area. But the rate at which a body loses heat is proportional to its surface aea. Thus there must come a point in the hypothetical expansion of an animal's body when the rate at which it loses heat is lower than its heat production. At that point and beyond, the animal will heat up so that its biochemistry malfunctions and the organism dies. Biology is very far from solving all its problems, but the tale of the giant ants would remain roundly refuted. I contend that the absolutely stubborn ideologist is just as non-existent as the elephant-sized ant. Armed with a Darwinian theory of our origins and evolutionary epistemology, we may launch an indirect theoretical refutation of the myth of absolute imperviousness to argument.

Why You Are at Least as Sensible as a Snail

Alan Sugar, Osama Bin Laden, you, and a microscopic snail all have something in common: they (or you) are all subject to the reign of economic laws. This can be seen if we apply two elementary concepts of economics: choice at the margin and opportunity cost.

Suppose someone builds a hospital on a piece of land. As a consequence, nothing else can be built on that land. A school or a factory could have been built, but these are mutually exclusive alternatives with the hospital. Suppose the most valued of these forsaken opportunities is the school. In economics this is called the opportunity cost of the hospital. In general, the opportunity cost of a given action is the next-best alternative action that is necessarily forsaken by the given action. Why focus on the greatest forsaken value? Because it is this alternative which, if it had had a slightly greater value, would have prevented the construction of the hospital. People do seem to take account of their forsaken opportunities when they make decisions and when they are considering arguments. People are able to see the alternative consequences of various possible actions open to them.

If there were types of action that paid no heed to opportunity cost, then one might be able to argue that ideologies based on such action and its motivation were closed to argument as far as economic rationality were concerned. However, both Darwinian theory and economic theory, plus experiments on animals and humans, go against this idea.

If economic postulates are true of all organisms then we have a strong indication that there is at least a general tendency for Darwinian evolution to produce economizing organisms. Some experiments have explored the assumption that all organisms are economically rational by testing very simple organisms.

David Rapport, for example, has investigated a microscopic animal, *Stentor coeruleus*, and found its behavior 'simple-minded but rational'. When its food was hard to get, the Stentor made do with second-rate food. However, when the cost of the 'better' food was lowered, the

Stentor would spit out the less-preferred food and concentrate on the more preferred. Rapport concludes with the following observation:

> The use of optimizing principles has been implicit in much theoretical biology. As Rosen points out, "the idea that nature pursues economy in all her workings is one of the oldest principles of theoretical science" (Rosen 1967). The assumption of optimizing food selection behavior appears valid provided natural selection is efficient in weeding out species or individuals which failed to make optimum food choices. (Rapport 1971, pp. 757–787)

Neither Rapport nor I are implying that this microscopic animal consciously compares the future marginal utility of future alternative mouthfuls of the two foods. (In that strict sense, we agree it is not at all rational; that is, it doesn't make decisions by conscious deliberation.) Its mechanism of assessment may simply use a proxy, such as amount of effort, as a rough and ready way to decide which action is the most costly and most beneficial.

You might ask, why should humans be any the less economically rational than a microscopic animal? It is often taken for granted that the irrational pursuit of a goal dictated by a fixed idea is a product of primitive animal impulses that lie beyond the economist's ken. But experiments like Rapport's undermine the idea that the more primitive an organism's motivation, the more economically irrational its behavior will be. In reality, the behavior is explained by economics, and the applicability of economics is in turn explained by the Darwinian theory of evolution. The argument is not that snails are rational, therefore humans are rational; but that Darwinian theory and economics, both powerful theories with many unfalsified explanations to their credit, can be used to explain an aspect of the behavior of all organisms. The point of bringing in *S. coeruleus* is to show that the theory has been severely tested and passed, and that the theory also explains the results.

If our capacity for argument has been tailored by evolution to serve economizing, we might expect humans to be open to arguments about the economic implications of their ideologies. An example is the fall of the ideology of the Soviet empire and with it the empire itself because of its extreme economic inefficiencies. Even the supposed closed mental state that Kolakowski spoke of is subject to economic rationality.

One possible counter-argument is that while economic rationality may hold for the consumption of foods, warmth, shelter and other 'basic needs', and thus explain the demise of the Soviet empire, it fails to hold for other traits that have evolved in man, traits that make him far more unpredictable than *Stentor* and other simple organisms. It is these traits that make ideologies based on them closed to argument.

To answer this counter-argument we can look at psychotic patients. Psychotic patients may be conjectured to represent the full range of extremes of human mental characteristics and thus include whatever economically irrational traits are alleged to be responsible for ideologies closed to argument. Hence by testing the economic rationality of psychotic patients we thereby test the assumption that humans have evolved economically irrational traits that might make them closed to argument. Many experiments have now been performed in psychiatric institutions using what is called a token economy. In a token economy psychotic patients are rewarded for certain types of behavior by tokens they can exchange for any of a range of things they desire. Such experiments have found that psychotic patients will change their behavior in order to obtain the tokens (Winkler 1973). In addition, if the prices of goods are changed they will do exactly as economic theory predicts; the psychotics purchase more of those goods whose prices have dropped and less of those whose prices have risen (Battalio 1973).

The evolutionary pressure to economize may be partly responsible for the economy of thought represented by the preference for systematically organized networks of assumptions of high information content that are axiomatizable with organic fertility. The axiomatization of a theory undoubtedly often presents formidable difficulty, but once achieved gives the theory great 'promotion value', to use Monod's phrase. It would be hard to argue that the highly systematic character of Euclid's *Elements* had little to do with its reproductive success. However, let us concentrate on the economic implications.

When we consider economic rationality in humans, we find that there is an influential opinion that economics looks at just one narrow slice of human behaviour, and that there are major other areas of human activity about which economics has nothing to say. Perhaps, then, there is economic behavior, which is rational, and non-economic behaviour, which could be irrational. The view that economics can only account for a particular slice of human activity goes back to John Stuart Mill:

> [Economics] does not treat the whole of man's nature as modified by the social state, nor of the whole conduct of man in society. . . . It is concerned with him solely as a being who desires to possess wealth, and who is capable of judging the comparative efficacy of means for obtaining that end. (Mill 1874, Essay 5, paragraphs 38 and 48)

Later writers referred to this view of the human individual as 'economic man' or *Homo economicus*. They contrasted this view with what they called *Homo sociologicus*, a supposedly richer conception of humans, shaped by values other than wealth, that both undermined and went beyond economics. However, the development of economic thought after Mill has shown that there are no uniquely economic motives, and that economics can analyze behavior that is not wealth-maximizing as well as behavior that is. Some sociologists unaware of economic theory have tended to perpetuate John Stuart Mill's misleading conception of economics.

LIONEL ROBBINS AND THE MODERN CONCEPTION OF ECONOMIC SCIENCE

In his path-breaking *Essay on the Nature and Significance of Economic Science*, Lionel Robbins undertook to provide a more adequate conception of the scope of economics. Robbins points out that the definitions of the various sciences has followed, rather than preceded, their development as theoretical explanations. In the case of economics, various disparate problems—price determination, balance of payments, capital investment—were explored and then brought together, around the beginning of the twentieth century, by theoretical advances. This view harmonizes with my evolutionary view of scientific development, in which problems, both practical and theoretical, are prior to the theories and definitions they stimulate.

Robbins suggests that the bad definitions of economics have misdirected investigations into the exploration of superficial and trivial aspects of human activities. He covers many narrow definitions such as that economics is the study of phenomena that relate to the price of goods or of the market. The definition he thought most misleading and most common was that voiced by theorists such as Cannan, Marshall, Pareto, and J.B. Clark, which saw economics as the study of material wealth.

Along with other arguments, Robbins explodes this conception by considering the theory of wages. Clearly, Robbins says, wages can be used to buy 'material' satisfactions such as butter or meat. But equally, those wages can be spent on aesthetic or cultural satisfactions such as the theater or books. More fundamentally, Robbins points out that even with regard to the so-called material satisfactions, it is not their materiality that is important in our valuations, but rather the services that we can obtain from the objects. It's the subjective taste and feeling of enjoying a good meal that we want from the butter and meat and this could conceivably be satisfied by other material means. To use a modern example, once we relied on copper—millions of tons of it—to convey our communications around the world. Now, those same services are increasingly provided by a couple of tons of aluminium in a satellite. Robbins echoes Fisher here. Services must be conceived as "immaterial," says Fisher (1906). To paraphrase the words of Fisher: from the dancer, the opera singer, and my valet, I obtain an income that "perishes in the moment of its production."

Robbins reflects that:

> From the point of view of the economist, the conditions of human existence exhibit four fundamental characteristics. The ends are various. The time and the means for achieving these ends are limited and capable of alternative application. At the same time the ends have different importance. (Robbins 1945, p. 12)

Robbins argues that the most abstract characterization of the problems that economics had dealt with was that economics is the science that studies human behaviour as a relationship between ends and scarce means that have alternative uses. It covers all the special avenues of explanation, but is far more general:

> It follows from this, therefore, that in so far as it presents this aspect, any kind of human behavior falls within the scope of economic generalizations. We do not say that the production of potatoes is economic activity and the production of philosophy is not. We say rather that, in so far as either kind of activity involves the relinquishment of other desired alternatives, it has its economic aspect. There are no limitations on the subject matter of Economic Science save this.[15] (Robbins 1945, p. 17)

TRIAL AND ERROR IN ECONOMIC DECISIONS

When I said earlier that humans weigh up the costs and benefits of their actions, this could easily be misunderstood. People often make mistakes. We decide on what we think is desirable, and what constitutes its cost— the desirable objective we have to give up. But often we find that we were wrong about what was most desirable or about the actual cost. The closed mind theorist sometimes sees this fact as devastating to a view of humans as rational, but to me it is an inescapable aspect of rational behavior. In economic decision-making, as in science, we make guesses and then disprove some of our guesses, replacing them with new guesses. It's a process of trial and error. We're always fallible and we're always capable of correcting our mistakes.

Max Weber

The most influential and comprehensive opposition to the view I'm offering may be Max Weber's theory of human action. Weber classifies action into the following categories: instrumentally rational; value rational; affectual; and traditional. I'm going to quote Weber to head off any charge that I'm misrepresenting his views by misinterpreting hyperbole as a serious position. I contend that Weber's terms 'value-rational action', 'affectual action', and 'traditional action' connote action which lies outside the influence of criticism based on cost or effectiveness, and that Weber's classification breaks down, as Ludwig von Mises has shown, since plausible examples of each class involve Weber's 'instrumental rationality' (or more accurately, actions subject to choice at the margin). Mises shows that every example of a supposedly economically irrational action that Weber gives can be interpreted in terms of economic theory, and hence that Weber is simply begging the question.

Weber defines "value-rational" action as that which is

> determined by a conscious belief in the value for its own sake of some ethical, aesthetic, religious, or other form of behavior, independently of its prospects of success. (Weber 1968, pp. 24–25)

Humans, then, try to effect actions independently of their success. This could mean either that humans strive to engage in actions that they believe to be impossible, or that humans strive to engage in impossible actions to approximate an ideal. Remember that according to Weber value-rational action is not action as a means to an end, so Weber could not say that the striving is an attempt to approximate an ideal. Hence, Weber must be asserting that value-rational action chooses unattainable ends. This implies that value-rational action cannot be criticized on the basis of its practicability. I do not deny, of course, that humans value some behavior for its own sake: in these cases, performing the behavior is itself the end and this is therefore not an instance of behavior performed independently of its prospects of success.

I am not attacking a straw man. Weber goes on to claim much more.

> Examples of pure value-rational orientation would be the actions of persons who, regardless of possible cost to themselves, act to put into practice their convictions of what seems to them to be required by duty, honour, the pursuit of beauty, a religious call, personal loyalty, or the importance of some 'cause' no matter in what it consists. In our terminology, value-rational action always involves 'commands' or 'demands' which, in the

actor's opinion, are binding on him. . . . On the other hand, the actor may, instead of deciding between alternative and conflicting ends in terms of a rational orientation to a system of values, simply take them as given subjective wants and arrange them in a scale of consciously assessed relative urgency. He may then orient his action to this scale in such a way that they are satisfied as far as possible in order of urgency, as formulated in the principle of 'marginal utility'. . . . from the latter point of view, however, value rationality is always irrational. Indeed, the more the value to which action is oriented is elevated to the status of an absolute, the more 'irrational' in this sense the corresponding action is. For the more the actor devotes himself to this value for its own sake, to pure sentiment or beauty, to absolute goodness or devotion to duty, the less is he influenced by considerations of the consequences of his action. (p. 25)

Weber is making the following claims:

1. That people engage in some types of behavior whatever the cost. However, an important basis for criticism of a network of ideas is often its costliness, what other values have to be forsaken to implement its injunctions or plan. Value-rational action precludes this, thus restricting criticism.

2. That value-rational, affectual, and traditional behavior are incompatible with instrumentally rational behavior (and thus not subject to marginal analysis). These types of behavior then become impervious to economic criticism.

3. That devotion to a form of action for its own sake implies a lack of consideration of its costs and benefits.

Economics analyzes all action that involves a choice among scarce means to satisfy given ends. Weber erroneously restricts the range of economics.

Deliberation about consequences (marginal costs and benefits) itself involves increasing marginal costs because it consumes the scarce resource of thought power, which generally can serve different but incompatible projects. Thus shortening deliberation in the pursuit of important ends is subject to marginal analysis and is rational from this perspective. Also, devotion to an end for its own sake may well be the result of a protracted consideration of the consequences of doing so.

The most fundamental criticism of Weber's position was propounded by Mises (Mises 1960). He showed that Weber's classes of action are not incompatible and that nothing that Weber says undermines the idea that marginal theory is applicable to them all. Mises considers the following example of value-rational action:

> If someone not only wants to earn his livelihood in general, but also in a way which is "respectable" and "in accordance with his station in life"—let us say as a Prussian Junker of the older camp, who preferred a government career to the bar—or if someone forgoes the advantages that a Civil Service career offers because he does not want to renounce his political convictions, this is in no way an action that could be termed non-rational. Adherence to received views of life or to political convictions is an end like any other, and like any other, it enters into the rank order of values. (p. 84)

Mises suggests that a more accurate way of describing behavior devoted to ideals

> is to say that there are men who place the value of duty, honour, beauty, and the like so high that they set aside other goals and ends for their sake. (p. 84)

That is, the consequences (more accurately, the opportunity costs) have been considered, but are not high enough to make the man renounce his pursuit of these goals.

Mises maintains that the same point applies to traditional behavior:

> When an aristocratic landowner rejects the proposal of his steward to use his name, title, and coat of arms as a trade mark on the packages of butter going to the retail market from his estate, basing his refusal on the argument that such a practice does not conform to aristocratic tradition, he means: I will forgo an increase in my income that I could attain only by the sacrifice of a part of my dignity. In the one case, the custom of the family is retained because—whether it is warranted or not is of no importance for us—it is considered more "rational"; in the other case, because a value is attached to it that is placed above the value that could be realized through its sacrifice. (p. 85)

Again, Mises points out that the opportunity costs are considered and not ignored, as Weber would suggest.

The same is true of affectual action:

> He who endangers his own life in rushing to the aid of a drowning man is able to do so because he yields to the momentary impulse to help, or because he feels it his duty to prove himself a hero under the circumstances, or because he wants to earn a reward for saving the man's life. In each case,

his action is contingent upon the fact that he momentarily places the value of coming to the man's aid so high that other considerations—his own life, the fate of his family—fall into the background. (p. 85)

Mises makes the general point that all these forms of action are similar in that they all

choose between given possibilities in order to attain the most ardently desired goal. (p. 85)

Mises speculates that Weber's fundamental error which has led him astray in his classifications is his failure to understand the universality of the propositions of sociology (here Mises takes economics as a subset of sociology). Weber continually falls into the mistake of restricting the applicability of the laws of economics, seeing them only from the point of view of the businessman. Thus:

The theory of marginal utility treats . . . human action as if it took place from A to Z under the control of a business-like calculation: calculation based on all the relevant conditions. (Weber as quoted by Mises, p. 93)

Where money is involved Weber is constantly thinking in terms of the businessman's maxim 'Buy cheap, sell dear' (this for Weber is the quintessence of rational action). Modern economics has seen a great expansion and elaboration of the theory of the consumer's behavior. The theory is easily able to encompass non-pecuniary motivations, as in the case where a buyer of soap may deliberately pay more for it from an invalid veteran than he would have to pay to buy it from a regular store, or where an employee takes a job at a lower wage with a not-for-profit foundation because he believes in the aims of that foundation. Weber's mistaken arguments cannot be used to limit the rationality of human behavior without also rejecting fundamental postulates of modern economics, a theory of great information content, and without also rejecting the fruitful application of economics to the evolutionary explanation of animal behavior.

The Fanatic

Is the fanatic open to criticism? Fanatical terrorists, revolutionaries, *kamikaze* pilots, hunger strikers, and others, are put forward as examples of violent ideological emotion completely devoid of reason. Weber might have put this sort of behavior in the class of 'value-rational action' or 'affectual behavior'. If this were admitted, then the associated ideologies might be beyond effective criticism. We will see that, despite seeming imperviousness, the fanatic is open to both self-criticism and external criticism.

GUSTAVE LE BON AND WALTER LAQUEUR

Gustave Le Bon, an influential writer on ideology and argument, held just such a view. Speaking of terrorists he says:

> The mentality of martyrs of every kind is identical, whether political, religious or social. Hypnotized by the fixity of their dream, they joyfully sacrifice themselves to the triumph of an idea without any hope of recompense in this world or another. . . . Persecution of them is powerless and only renders their example contagious. . . . These facts and all those of the same order are very instructive. They prove the power of the mystical mind which is capable of triumphing over pain and dominating feelings considered to be the very basis of our existence. What could reason do against it? (Le Bon 1979, pp. 214–15)

Le Bon's position confirms the soundness of the present approach, for he generalizes his point to political, religious, and social martyrs. Le Bon is indeed an important influence, which can be traced through prominent figures such as Adolf Hitler, whose views on propaganda are similar to and ultimately derived from Le Bon's.

An echo of this sort of theory can be heard in more recent writing. Laqueur in *The Age of Terrorism* maintains that

> The main difficulty is not that the rational model is useless with regard to people engaging in suicide missions (of which there are only few), but that it tends to ignore factors such as frustration, anger, fanaticism, aggression, etc., which are very frequent in terrorism. Above all, economic man is a rational being wishing to maximize beneficial returns; few people would go into a business in which the chances of success are as dim as they are in terrorism. (p. 153)

The fanatic, who wittingly sacrifices everything he values to a single cause, who is unmoved by the perceived effectiveness and cost of his actions, is a myth. It has always been acceptable to romanticize and mystify the fanatic, either to portray him as subject to otherworldly laws or as unintelligibly crazy. The fanatic himself often has an interest in projecting this image of his own personality, since it makes his threats more convincing (consider Paul's behaviour, near the end of *Dune*, in convincing the Emperor and the Guild that he really will wipe out spice production if he does not get his way).

The fanatic is as subject to the laws of economics as Adam Smith's greengrocer. The hunger striker in the Maze prison or the *kamikaze* pilot, both fighting for what they believed to be justice, were acting under a rational assessment of their goal and the price they thought they would have to pay in terms of forsaken opportunities. That price could have been too high. In fact for some potential recruits to the IRA the price was too high, as is evident in declining recruitment at the time of the hunger strikes. Le Bon's contagion evidently has its limitations.

Laqueur himself seems dimly aware that skilful negotiation with terrorists has had some successes, but he does not draw the conclusion that this must be so because they are not zombies but rational beings who act in the light of what they perceive to be effective and economical means. The fact that their beliefs and values may be wildly at odds with our own does not place them outside the field of economic analysis, and likewise does not make them immune to argument and criticism. This position of Laqueur's is odd considering that in his introduction he points out that increased repression decreases terrorism: terrorist incidents were more frequent in Spain only after Franco died, while terrorism in West Germany and Turkey grew under a movement to more social democratic or left-of-center governments (p. 6).

Laqueur states that "few would go into a business with as little success as there is in terrorism." Really? The great majority of new businesses, well over ninety percent, fail permanently in their first few years. The percentage success of terrorism in attaining its political objectives is higher than that. But even if Laqueur's factual claim were true instead of demonstrably false, it hardly supports his conclusion. Suppose that 99.9 percent of new businesses failed almost immediately; still, there would be the other 0.01 percent; would their proprietors be acting outside any 'rational model'? Laqueur's argument here is like saying that since only a small percentage of the population become directors of international banks, economic theory cannot apply to those who strive to become directors of international banks. The chances of becoming a world champion boxer are exceedingly slim for most men. Does that mean that world champion boxers pay no heed to such things as the sacrifices involved and the financial incentives held before their eyes? Just as there is natural variation in height, weight, hair color, there is natural variation in personality traits and values. Economic theory is not tailored to one personality type or even the average man, nor confined to certain sorts of values and the means for their attainment; economic theory applies to all values and all scarce means. Mises argues that marginalist economic theory, properly interpreted, implies that wherever there is action there are subjective costs and benefits and marginal theory applies just as strictly in non-financial as in financial contexts.

Are the chances of success in terrorism very thin? If the objective is to terrorize, it would seem that anyone can be a terrorist. If Laqueur responds by denying that terrorism is that simple, but rather involves delicate planning and has complex ulterior motives, then it becomes difficult not to view terrorism as rational action. Complex and delicate planning and execution does not logically entail sensitivity to cost, but it does rule out a zombie-like state or a mind excessively disturbed by anger or frustration. Without a rational model of human action how could one explain why the terrorist plans at all? Laqueur supplies no answer. Is the terrorist indifferent to how long he spends planning, even when the opportunity cost of increased planning may be fewer or less well prepared missions? Laqueur could say that the terrorist just picks a mission at random and blindly tries to see it through even if it means sacrificing many other certain and easy missions to this one highly costly and ineffective mission. But this would not explain Laqueur's own point about repression curbing terrorism. I am not arguing that an alternative model is logically impossible, only that Laqueur has not supplied one.

Laqueur's mention of terrorists involved in suicide missions is misleading (though Laqueur was writing before the great expansion of suicide terrorism). The terrorist who plans his own death reasons that the attainment of his end will involve his death and is prepared to sacrifice his life for this end. There is nothing irrational in choosing to sacrifice one's own life because one values the end one hopes to attain sufficiently highly. Costs that would deflect others from their path may fail to deflect the terrorist. Nothing that Laqueur says contradicts the conjecture that if the terrorist could achieve his objective without sacrificing his life, he would do so. But even if the terrorist valued suicide for its own sake, committing suicide would still be rational. However, the facts about actual terrorists do not bear out the conjecture that this is a significant part of terrorists' motivations. Laqueur does not present us with an example that cannot be interpreted in terms of economically rational action.

SUICIDE TERRORISM PAYS

Are suicide terrorists crazy? Are they attacking us because of who we are? Does their religion make them do it? These questions trouble many people. Robert Pape, author of *Dying to Win*, actually took the trouble to find out the facts and get the answers. As a matter of fact, the answers are No, No, and No.

Pape set up the only comprehensive database on terrorists. At the time Pape wrote his book, the database contained every suicide bombing and other attack around the globe—315 attacks in all—from 1980 through 2003. Drawing on this careful work, Pape argues that terrorists are not in the least crazy. All terrorists are rational agents with definite goals and use definite means to achieve them.

Neither Pape nor I are defending the *morality* of the terrorist's actions. Being rational is not the same as being good. The murderer who meticulously plots the killing of his aunt so that he can get his hands on her life's savings is highly immoral, but no one would dispute that his murderous plotting is completely rational. Let's have a look at Pape's account.

Pape found that suicide terrorists are guided by the definite goal of repelling foreign military occupation. It's not aimless, unplanned violence.

> Most suicide terrorism is undertaken as a strategic effort directed toward particular political goals; it is not simply the product of irrational individuals or an expression of fanatical hatred. The main purpose of suicide terrorism is to use the threat of punishment to compel a target government to change policy, and most especially to cause democratic countries to withdraw forces from land the terrorists perceive as their national homeland. (Pape 2005, p. 27)

Suicide terrorism is a strategy for weak actors in a conflict. The terrorist, being militarily weak, cannot conquer the target country, but he can impose an unacceptable cost on its government.

> So the only coercive strategy available to suicide terrorists is punishment. Although the element of "suicide" is novel and the pain inflicted on civilians is often spectacular and gruesome, the heart of their . . . strategy is the same as the logic of states when they employ air power or economic sanctions to punish an adversary: to cause mounting civilian costs to overwhelm the target state's interest in the issue in dispute and cause it to concede to the terrorists' political demands.

The suicide terrorists magnify the coercive effects of punishment because they have the following advantages:

   a. suicide attacks are generally more destructive than other terrorist attacks, because an attacker who is willing to die is more likely to complete the mission and cause maximum damage, the attackers can conceal weapons on their body and make last minute adjustments more easily than ordinary terrorists, they can more easily infiltrate heavily guarded targets, because they don't need escape routes or rescue teams, and they can use especially destructive methods such as suicide vests and ramming vehicles. Between 1980 and 2003, suicide attacks amount to 3 percent of all terrorist attacks, but accounted for 48 percent of total deaths due to terrorism.

b. The willingness to die is itself a signal of more pain to come, as it suggests that they cannot be deterred. This can be orchestrated by the terrorist organisation and portrayed as martyrdom and sacrifice for the religious and political community. The threat of further attacks then looks more plausible.

c. Suicide terrorist organisations can better heighten the fear of future attacks by breaching taboos on potential targets.

Terrorists have learned that suicide terrorism works. Between 1945 and 1983 there was almost no suicide terrorism. The recent rise in suicide terrorism goes back to the perceived success of the Hezbollah in ousting the United States from Lebanon in 1983 when terrorists drove a truck loaded with explosives into the marine barracks, murdering hundreds of marines and killing themselves. Ronald Reagan pulled the troops out shortly afterwards, exactly as Hezbollah had hoped and intended. Observing this, other terrorist groups learned that suicide terrorism pays.

Nationalist politics is the main cause, not religion. They are not attacking us because of who we are or because of our religion. The terrorists see their actions as national defense. The religious difference between the occupying power and the occupied country's people only reinforces the feeling among the occupied that their society will be radically transformed and is an easy way of demonizing their enemy. It also makes it possible to justify martyrdom as a tactic. But the pivotal cause is foreign occupation. Hamas and Al-Qaeda have concentrated their attacks on the respective occupying powers: Hamas on Israel, Al-Qaeda on the United States, UK, and allies who have troops stationed in what they see as their homeland countries. These terrorist organizations have never done joint operations or shared information. The overwhelming majority of suicide terrorists in Al-Qaeda have been recruited from occupied countries or their adjacent neighbors, very few from the largest populations of Islamic fundamentalists: Pakistan (149 million), Bangladesh (114 million), Iran (63 million), Egypt (62 million), Nigeria (37 million). The most active terrorist group in the world, the Tamil Tigers, are not religious (in the theistic sense) at all—they are Marxist-Leninists and therefore atheists, and are actively hostile to religion.

Seeing this latter point about the Tamil Tigers as fatal to his position—that suicide terrorism must be due to religion—Sam Harris tries to defend it by an exercise in what can only be called associative thinking:

> the Tamil tigers are often offered as counterexamples to the claim that suicidal terrorism is a product of religion. But to describe the Tamil Tigers as "secular"—as R.A. Pape . . . and others have—is misleading. While the motivations of the Tamils are not explicitly religious, they are Hindus who undoubtedly believe many improbable things about the nature of life and death. The cult of martyr worship that they have nurtured for decades has many of the features of religiosity that one would expect in people who give their lives so easily for a cause. (Harris 2006, p. 229 n2)

Millions of people throughout history have believed improbable things about life and death without becoming suicide terrorists. The fact that there is a sociological phenomenon that Harris chooses to call "martyr worship" within a Marxist-Leninist group that has a similarity to religious martyrdom, carries as much weight for his case as the fact that organized criminal gangs will often have their own rituals and heroes. Are all groups with rituals and heroes religious? This style of argument—in which "martyr worship" is cross-blurred with "hero admiration"—is as flawed as a court finding someone guilty by association. Pape's argument is more subtle, because religion can—sometimes cynically—be used as a way of cultivating community support for what is a secular goal and the means of achieving it.

Harris cannot see that nationalism may be a much more potent force for deathly conflict than religion. Most wars for the last several centuries have been national, not religious wars. Harris overlooks the extent to which ordinary and non-religious people engaged in what they regard as a national conflict will sacrifice themselves for the goal of repulsing an invading nation. But one only has to remember World War II. Think of the Royal Air Force in the Battle of Britain, for example. The life expectancy for a spitfire pilot was four weeks, but this grim statistic did not still the flow of British, Polish, Canadian, Czech and other volunteer pilots. Hundreds of pilots flew bombing missions over Germany from which they knew they would not return.

As Caldararo argues, many writers have overlooked the spate of examples from Europe of suicide bombers:

> Forgotten in the western analysis of present suicide attacks is the wave of terror against Royalist governments that followed the atrocities of the revolutions of 1848, whose sacrifices by republicans are today glorified in cute theater pieces under the title of *Les Misérables*. (Caldararo 2006, p. 128)

We may also cite other examples of non-religious, but nationalist motivated suicide bombings that fit Pape's theory that it is the strategy of the militarily weak; Following World War II, Viet Minh 'death volunteers' fought against the French Colonial Forces by using a long stick-like explosive to destroy French tanks; the Turkish PKK, founded on revolutionary socialism and Kurdish nationalism, conducted suicide attacks against police headquarters and some tourist areas.

Pape's investigation helps us to see terrorism, even suicide terrorism, as the admittedly abominable actions and strategy of rational individuals. Pape could have made it clearer how nationalism works. Nationalism can, after all, be represented as an irrational force of feelings or instinct and conducive to the closed mind. There is a better view of nationalism, one that sees it as involving a partly unconscious theory. A nation, Benedict Anderson said, is "an imagined political community." This is an improvement, as it brings in the imagination as the binding agent: it's not just feelings, it's a cognitive model about the social world. I would argue that it's the modern tribalism, with the—almost unexamined—moral sentiment: if one of you hurt one of us, you have hurt all of us; thus all of us will hurt all of you. I surmise that terrorist organizations exploit this tribalistic, perhaps unconscious, presupposition that is rapidly growing in strength all over the world. But it is a kind of theory that can be made conscious and examined, and so open to critical debate. Before 1918 you could travel anywhere in the world without a passport. Now, as an unintended by-product of many separate nationalisms, except for the super rich, we are all potentially prisoners of our own nation.

Absolute Values

Some values are urged by ideologists as absolute or unconditional. The fanatic, impelled by irrational emotion to sacrifice everything to some ideal end, personifies this. Can we accept this? Not really, if we accept economic theory. It follows from economic theory that ideological values (however one delimits them) cannot in practice be categorically binding on anyone, not even the ideologist who peddles them.

The theory of choice at the margin implies that any values are exchangeable with one another, bit by bit. That is, people act as if their values are relative to one another. An individual will sacrifice some of any value for a sufficient increment in any other value. And as values Y are sacrificed for increments in X, the value of an additional increment in X decreases and the value of an additional increment in Y increases. Eventually, an increment in X is worth less than an increment in Y, and therefore no more of X is sought. Most choices are of this incremental kind, not categorical. To take an example from political philosophy, Rawls (1972, pp. 3–4) depicts justice as categorically binding: it is not incrementally inferior to any other value. It is allowed that some aspects of justice may be sacrificed for some other aspects of justice, but not in the slightest degree for any amount of any other value.

Adam Smith held that some justice is necessary for any of the other desirable features of a society, but that not all increments of justice invariably outweigh increments of other things, and that the attempt to carry through into practice the categorical conception is doctrinaire and counter-productive. I would add that it never is carried into action. An individual can choose to violate the true laws of economics but he cannot succeed in doing so, no more than one can violate the law of gravity. If they are true laws then by definition they cannot be violated, since their violation would refute them. If someone rejects their status as laws then it is incumbent on them to supply alternatives that have at least the same truth content. Not even Rawls, I suspect, would hold fast to his principles if he thought that the attempt to fulfil them would result in mass starvation. If we are to countenance absolute values then we must reject marginalist economics, a theory that has had much explanatory success.

You may agree that economic theory denies the absolute character of values, but then ask: How do we explain the fact that some values do at least appear to be held in an absolute way? I think a possible explanation is that some value systems can simulate absolute values. For example, some people may find murder so loathsome that the incentives required for them to violate that value simply cannot be physically realized, either because of natural laws or because of technical obstacles. It may be that our world rarely tests our adherence to some of our values to an extreme extent: rarely are people called upon, for example, to choose between murdering two people to save ten. (This hypothetical choice is formulated to exclude the option of not murdering anyone.)

Instrumental Rationality

The manufacture and use of tools is the use of knowledge of causes and effects to obtain a goal in the presence of obstacles. Cognitive psychologists have found that we seem to be born with a rudimentary understanding of tools in this sense. This understanding is quite abstract and extends also to the understanding of the functional parts of animals. Three-year-olds understand that the thorns of a rose are useful to the rose, but not that the barbs on barbed wire are useful to the wire. They think that the jaws of a lobster are useful to the lobster, but not that the jaws of pliers are useful to the pair of pliers. Later we understand more abstract applications of the same concept. We see economic systems, communication systems, financial institutions, various social arrangements, even knowledge as "instruments" designed or at least used for certain ends. Marxism or National Socialism were accepted by some because they were thought to be effective instruments or means to certain ends. And they were abandoned because they were thought to be ineffective. Any propagandist spreading a message has to answer the questions: Why should I accept your idea? What will it do? Why will it do that?

Humans only pursue those ends they think attainable and use only those means they think effective. Humans are always capable of abandoning what is futile, whether this is a means or an end. A person's use of tools and other means in the pursuit of goals is based on his theory of the world and his ability to test that theory. Theory is involved because even the conception of a tool (or means) and its end involves a theoretical interpretation; and tests of the tool or means themselves have to be interpreted.

This theory may be unconscious in the sense that a person has never articulated it in language or in self-conscious thought. But even such inarticulate theories can be revealed when one is surprised that a tool, machine, or scheme of action has broken down. It might be objected that people use herbal medicines without any theory about how they work. But they do have a theory that they do work, a claim that may happen to be false. Arguing that everyone operates with a theory about the use of an instrument or means may not be necessary for my point. It may be sufficient that the use of any means can be brought under theoretical control so that the person can abandon its use under criticism.

One might apparently pursue what one thinks is unattainable as a means of approximating it or as a means of achieving some other end as a by-product. However it is clear that here one's goal is not the ideal but the approximation or some other end. If one thought that neither end were attainable one would desist. (For example, one might playfully strive for a goal one knew to be impossible to achieve; but then the goal would be playfulness, which, if one came to think it were also impossible, would be abandoned.)

Humans abandon what they see as futile. Seeing something as futile is often (at least partly) caused by its very futility. We don't hear people say that something must work because it has been found not to work. Here there is a clear advantage to truth, or a good approximation to truth.

Why should we conjecture that humans control their pursuit of goals by a theory of the world? From a Darwinian point of view organisms that persist, come what may, with futile actions tend to be eliminated, while organisms that can abandon the futile tend to reproduce the genes responsible for that ability. As explained below, an ideal strategy would not be overly sensitive to signs of futility: the organism must not be discouraged too easily. Nevertheless, the organism must be capable of correcting its mistakes.

A Possible Objection

A skeptic anent human rationality might question whether humans are interested in the truth or in reality when they act. He might grant that humans abandon what seems to be futile, but, he insists, it is the experience of futility as such and not futility that matters to humans. As long as they seem to be doing what they want to do, they are unconcerned. Without this concern there is no disposition to adapt to reality as such. Indeed on this theory, it might pay people who adhere to an ideology to avoid contact with counter-arguments and evidence, since, they might reason, as long as we believe our ideology, that is all that matters. To rebut this possible objection, consider the famous thought-experiment devised by Robert Nozick. Nozick actually uses this thought-experiment to undermine eudemonistic utilitarianism, the idea that people simply want the pleasurable experiences in life; but the argument can also be applied in a different way.

Nozick poses the question: 'What matters to people other than how their experiences feel from inside?' To help answer this question he supposes

> that there is an experience machine that would give you any experience you desired. Super duper neuropsychologists could stimulate your brain so that you would think and feel you were writing a great novel, or making a friend,

or reading an interesting book. All the time you would be floating in a tank with electrodes attached to your brain. (Nozick 1974, p. 42)

A somewhat similar idea forms the basis of the film *Total Recall* (1990), adapted from the short story by Philip K. Dick, 'We Can Remember It for You Wholesale', though here it is not a question of being in a tank, but of having one's memories reconstructed.

Would anyone plug in to such a machine? Various informal surveys of college students suggest that almost no one would, though this has yet to be tested rigorously. Nozick adduces a number of reasons why most people wouldn't plug in. People want to do things, not simply have the experience of doing them; people also want to be a certain way; and, being plugged into the machine would limit us to a man-made reality, to a world no deeper or more important than that which people can construct. Nozick concludes that "Perhaps what we desire is to live (an active verb) ourselves, in contact with reality. And this the machines cannot do for us" (p. 45).

This argument harmonizes quite well with the argument of this book. People want to use real means to achieve their ends, and want to abandon really futile means or ends: the means and ends of fantasy are not enough. The implication here is that to the extent that an ideology has practical implications it is subject to instrumental rationality and therefore open to criticism.

Rhetoric versus Theory

D.J. Manning maintains a position similar to that of Bartley's on ideologies:

> An ideology cannot be challenged by either facts or rival theories. (Manning 1976, p. 142)

Manning's position differs from Bartley's in that Manning portrays ideas like Marxism as non-theoretical, but rather rhetorical devices to inspire people to do certain things or express commitment to a group. In so far as an ideology describes the world, Manning says, the world has no existence independent of the "practical understanding prescribed" (p.142). The implication is that ideologies cannot be undermined by sound criticism because they do not actually make any factual claims, and this follows from their being rhetorical or expressive. Furthermore, even if ideologies did make factual claims, the ideologists would be closed to sound criticism because the ideology acts as irremovable blinkers: the ideologist cannot conceive anything outside his ideology, let alone deal with criticism.

Manning actually equivocates on this point. He sometimes asserts that ideologies have no descriptive content at all: "Ideological talk, unlike legal talk, does not give us information about the world in which we live. It cannot carry the appropriate descriptive content" (Manning 1980, p. 75). But sometimes he admits that ideologies contain descriptive content: "Ideologists do make use of the findings of academic disciplines, but they confer on them a political significance which the methodology of those disciplines cannot confer" (Manning 1976, p. 142).

Professor Minogue made it clear to me that there is a middle-ground: the point of theories like Freudianism and Marxism is not merely locutionary (to explain, to describe) but also practical, their point being revolution or therapy at least as much as finding out the truth. This important observation must be faced by any theory that gives an important role to truth in the elimination of ideologies. Does this practical or rhetorical element exclude truth? What precisely is the relationship between rhetoric, theory, and truth? In answering this question we will look at the role of deception in rhetoric. I will argue for Socrates's position that rhetoric can be improved by knowledge and the use of valid argument. Even the mendacious propagandist must take an interest in the truth. I will also argue that the effectiveness of deception in protecting a doctrine from criticism is constrained by certain logical properties of theories, specifically the way in which the lies combine logically with other assertions.

We must begin by noting that even rhetoricians are guided by a theory as to the most effective way to motivate and direct peoples' action, and thus we have an instance of instrumental rationality, and hence an avenue for a challenge from facts or rival theories. Manning's claim that the expressive or in general rhetorical function of ideologies rules out the logical relevance of truth and hence by implication the psychological relevance of truth can be examined more thoroughly by reference to the work of Austin.

J.L. Austin

The theory of rhetoric has in recent years belittled the role of truth in persuasion, forgetting important contributions from Socrates. This development can be traced to the work of Austin, though perhaps more precisely to a misunderstanding of Austin's later thought. Austin's earlier work made a very strong distinction between utterances that do things (which have no connection with truth) and others that can be evaluated with respect to truth. Austin's later work rejected this analysis, but it is his earlier work that is remembered.

Austin's most acclaimed work is his contribution to a symposium on 'Other Minds' (1946). In this article he uses an analogy between 'knowing' and 'promising'. Knowing was usually thought of as a special mental state, and to assert that 'I know that S is P' is to report that I am in that state in relation to 'S is P'. This false dogma rested, Austin thought, on the descriptive fallacy, the supposition that words are used only to describe, and not for any other purposes. Austin maintained that when I assert that I *know* that S is P, I am not describing my state, but giving others my word, my authority, for saying that S is P, just as to promise is to give others my word that I will do X. This reasoning led Austin to distinguish between performatives and descriptives, the former being utterances that do certain things, the latter being utterances that describe. In this early work the two categories were taken to be mutually exclusive.

In 1962 Austin raised profound doubts about his former hard and fast distinction. First he restates the distinction more precisely. The word 'descriptive' is abandoned as having too narrow a scope. Performative utterances, he suggests, are 'happy' or 'unhappy' but they cannot be true; it is 'constatives' that can be true or false. For example, 'I name this ship Queen Elizabeth' cannot be false. It is 'unhappy' if I am not entitled to name ships or if it is not the right time to do it. 'He named the ship Queen Elizabeth' is on the other hand, true or false, not happy or unhappy.

Austin then shows that the idea of putting particular sentences exclusively into one or the other of these categories has to be given up. Happiness and the question of truth apply to both performatives and constatives. The happiness of a sentence always depends on something's being true: that the formula is the correct one and that the circumstances are the right ones. Happiness and truth also interact in the case of constatives. For example, the sentence 'John's children are bald' is unhappy if it refers to John when John has no children.

Those who would put ideological language outside the scope of an evaluation in terms of truth have a more difficult task in the light of Austin's findings. Austin shows that an attempt to separate the 'practical' from the 'theoretical' in the use of language is logically impossible. It seems that in all uses of language, humans are concerned about what is true. (It's not being denied that language users have other concerns.)

Having evolved under the pressure of tailoring our plans of action (whether in deed or word) to reality to avoid frustrating our needs, we make conjectures, theoretical guesses, about the possible effectiveness of our actions in advance. In this way our ancestors could eliminate some incipient futile actions before they caused any damage or harm to the organism (and thus reduced its genetic reproducibility). Language, considered as a form of action, has evolved to fit this need, making for a ubiquitous connection between the concern over the truth and 'happiness' of our utterances.

Socrates

This last point connects well with a neglected insight of Socrates. In the *Phaedrus* Socrates poses the question:

> Well, if a speech is to be classed as excellent, does not that presuppose knowledge of the truth about the subject of the speech in the mind of the speaker? (Plato 1988, p. 71)

Phaedrus answers with what is now the common view:

> But I have been told, my dear Socrates, that what a budding orator needs to know is not what is really right, but what is likely to seem right in the eyes of the mass of people who are going to pass judgment: not what is really good or fine but what will seem so; and that it is this rather than truth that produces conviction. (p. 71)

Socrates's response to Phaedrus is that even a speaker who wishes to mislead will be successful in so far as he is not misled himself. Socrates's argument for this is that misleading someone about reality requires small steps away from reality for it is slight differences between things which mislead. It then follows that the deceiver must know the true state of affairs in order to know that he is proceeding by small steps from reality to the false position. Thus the logic of the propagandist's situation seems to demand that he cultivate an interest in the truth.

However, Socrates's argument may have limited scope. This argument covers the case of substituting a false position for an originally true position, but it does not cover the case in which the deceiver is trying to substitute one false position for another false position. It might be said that deceivers are not so much concerned simply to mislead but rather to mislead to a definite view; so it does not matter what the original position was. Hence it might be maintained that what the deceiver is normally concerned to know is what will seem true to his audience.

Nevertheless, notice that the logic of a mendacious propagandist demands that he cultivate a healthy interest, if not in the truth, then at least in his opponents' theories, in order to judge their distance apart. We then have another pressure on the propagandist to learn the criticisms of his position, for an opponent's criticism provides excellent clues about how he sees his own theory, what he would regard as a large distance between theories and what a small distance between theories.

Socrates neglected an important ally of truth and validity in rhetoric: mnemonics. We are comparing two propagandists: one who intends to spread an erroneous doctrine by deception and one who intends to spread a non-erroneous doctrine by sound argument. Why should truth and validity help to spread the latter doctrine? Because:

1. Reality itself acts as a mnemonic, constantly reminding us of the truth. Hence a true doctrine will not only be consistent with all our other veridical observations of the world, but we shall also be reminded of the doctrine by those observations that are implied by the doctrine alone or in combination with other assumptions.

2. The validity of an argument helps us to understand, learn, and recall it. It is easier to remember a telling argument, and a telling argument will probably display a definite logical shape. Experiments have shown that learning and recall are most efficient when the items to be learned or recalled are organized according to a schema imposed by the subject, and the more familiar this schema the better it is in facilitating memory. Logic itself is such a schema. Indeed our learning and understanding of language itself is dependent on a grasp of logic and the ability to impose this schema on the tools of language.

Unfathomable Lies

As we saw in Chapter 1, all theories have an infinite number of implications in conjunction with other theories. To be precise, a theory's logical content and its informative content are each infinite. This has an interesting bearing on the old rhetorical trick, discussed by Socrates, of telling a small lie, L, in conjunction with a larger amount of truth, T. Our hypothetical propagandist reasons that glaring falsehoods are liable to detection and elimination; but if he surrounds his small lie with truth, it will escape detection and be propagated throughout the community. This is another and more formal way of putting Socrates's assertion that it is slight differences between things that mislead.

Now the propagandist is faced by the following problem. Since all theories have infinite logical and informative content, the propagandist cannot survey the whole content of his doctrine. It follows that he cannot survey the changes to the content he has committed himself to by conjoining T and L. As Gellner points out, all propagandists operate with a vast amount of opinion that they take for granted (Gellner 1979, p. 124). This may include a great deal of knowledge that they accept without at the time understanding it, as when we accept the contents of a chemistry text book when we have only dipped into it. Call this 'unknown knowledge' G. Assuming that propagandists do learn new things over time, there will be statements that they will accept in the future that they cannot now be aware of. Call this set S. Even though T and L may be consistent, certain unfathomable elements of T, L, and G may be inconsistent.

From an inconsistency any conclusion whatsoever follows. This can be demonstrated by the application of just two logical rules of inference. We have already assumed that some statements are glaring falsehoods that cannot be sustained and propagated. Therefore, if 'T & L & G & S' is inconsistent then the propagandist is committed to glaring, unsustainable falsehoods. The propagandist cannot forestall this possibility by performing a consistency proof on the conjunction 'T & L & G & S' since G is far too large, and S does not even exist yet.

We may conclude, therefore, that there are deep constraints on the use of deception by a propagandist to help along the propagation of his doctrine. Deception may very well backfire because of the unfathomable depths of the theoretical changes he is committed to in combining a small lie with a large amount to truth. Even deception, perhaps the oldest rhetorical trick, offers no guaranteed net advantage to a false doctrine in the competition of ideas.

Exploratory Rationality

All primates and most animals will learn complicated behaviors if being allowed to explore a new environment or object is used as the reward. Humans, more than perhaps any other animal, have a strong instinct of curiosity. They are substantially interested in and responsive to the truth, to what the world really is like. Individual humans vary in their desire to explore. The value of exploration is not absolute; curiosity can be encouraged or discouraged. But there is in every human an instinct to discover, to know. The evolution of curiosity explains why humans prefer to adopt ideologies that are of higher information content and closer to the truth.

Popper argued that we should expect humans as creatures of evolution to have a drive for exploration:

> So far as the knowledge is not, somehow, genetically built in to them, animals and men can only gain knowledge if they have a drive or instinct for exploration—for finding out more about their world. Their very existence, to be sure, presupposes a world which is to some extent 'knowable' or 'explorable', but it also presupposes an innate disposition to know and to explore: we are active explorers (explorers by trial and error) rather than passive recipients of information impressed upon us from outside (Lamarckism, inductivism). (Popper 1974, p. 1060)

Such a view is hardly compatible with Bartley's picture of the average human existing in a "slumbering fantasy world."

Exploration can be undertaken by movement or sensory scanning (which itself consists of small movements).[16] But it may also be done mentally. It can be done efficiently if our beliefs have some tendency to change spontaneously. Thus Popper also argues that natural selection will favour those organisms that are able to explore the world vicariously, with the help of internal models of the world. This vicarious process of trial and error allows fatal projects to be eliminated before they are executed (Popper 1977, pp. 151–52).

It follows that our beliefs are never completely stable and from time to time admit of doubt. This makes sense if we see humans as actively discovering things about their environment by continually making hypotheses and testing them. Organisms that try out (at least mentally) different possibilities, if only momentarily, are surely better able to take advantage of new opportunities and thus enhance their genetic reproducibility. As in the case of wishful thinking, we have to admit that different sorts of belief will be differently weighted with respect to doubt: some beliefs may admit of only momentary doubt, others would be prone to more persistent doubts. Every Marxist and every Christian has experienced doubts about their creed; that is exactly why doubt is given the stigma of petty-bourgeois pseudo-objectivity or heresy. Faithfulness requires a great deal of effort in the way of constant revision of the doctrine. But even if our memory were perfect we would never quite achieve faith because of these fundamental characteristics of our psychology.

Belief, then, is like a searchlight, continually scanning possibility space. To continue the metaphor, our beliefs (or better, our attitudes to issues) differ in their range of scanning, some with a narrow scan, others with a wide scan.[17]

Wishful and Fearful Rationality

Many agree with Popper that if an ideologist does not want to be affected by rational argument, then even if he has to face it as a consequence of the logic of his situation, he can resolve to keep his cherished beliefs, come what may. A variation on this thought is that wishes are a barrier to argument. An ideology is often said to be based on wishful thinking and hence closed to rational argument. Bertrand Russell put it this way:

> The cause of belief, here, is not, as in science, the evidence of fact, but the pleasant feelings derived from belief. (Russell 1938, p. 144)

Many other influential thinkers have held the same view. Ludwig Feuerbach, for example, held that religion was the result of a projection of the essence of man onto a supernatural being, the projection being caused by a wish:

> it is not human misery in itself that creates the Gods, but the satisfaction this misery finds in the imagination, as the instrument of wish fulfilment, which creates and appropriates the objects of these wishes and desires; which in effect, objectifies them, so that they can be appropriated. (Quoted in Wartofsky 1977, p. 216)

However, it's not clear whether Feuerbach regarded wishful thinking as a barrier to argument.

Focusing on wishful thinking overlooks the fact that people often believe what they fear. They believe that the opposite of what they would wish for is true.[18] But it is true that both wishful and fearful thinking are almost ubiquitous in the systems of ideas that have enchanted large fractions of mankind. Christianity is a good example with its heaven and hell, eliciting wishful and fearful thinking respectively. Marxism with its promise of superabundance also enlists wishful thinking. Freudianism is a less obvious case, but nevertheless conforms to the pattern. Freudianism promises a liberation from unnecessary repression of urgent desires plus a deep understanding of other people's minds, an understanding that surpasses their own.

Many writers hold that wishful thinking is irrational because it makes us impervious to counter-evidence and impedes us in the pursuit of our goals. Against this popular view, I intend to argue that wishful thinking is:

1. an efficient way by which any organism may seek goals, because it generates and maintains beliefs that are relevant to goal attainment so that they can be tested to a degree proportionate to the urgency of the desired goal;
2. open to argument, in the sense that beliefs sustained by it may be undermined.[19]

Wishful thinking is often thought to be irrational because of the widespread assumption that only justified beliefs are rational. Justifying a belief requires a certain procedure. Since it is thought that coming to a belief via wishful thinking is not a process of justification, it is concluded that such beliefs must be irrational. Pears, Elster, Lukacs, and Denise Meyerson, among many others, all make this leap. The role of wishful thinking as a guide in goal attainment becomes clearer when the fallacious doctrine of justificationism is discarded.

Both wishful and fearful thinking are rational and open to criticism. All beliefs are unjustified guesses, and believing what you wish or fear is one type of unjustified guessing. There are other types of unjustified guessing, for instance believing whatever you're told, or the opposite of whatever you're told. Rationality does not lie in how you come up with your guesses, but in how you test them once you have arrived at them. Nonetheless, some guesses may be more fruitful than others, for example because they are more relevant to your current problems or goals. Wishful and fearful thinking have evolved through Darwinian biological processes because they facilitate the organism's exploration of reality in the pursuit of its goals. Failing to generate wishes and fears relevant to one's desires and failing to persist (up to a point) in a wishful or fearful belief in the presence of some counter-evidence is likely to place organisms at a disadvantage in survival and reproduction.

DAVID PEARS

The wish that something be true sustains the belief that it is in the face of evidence to the contrary. This is what is thought by many to be one reason for describing wishful thinking as irrational. David Pears in *Motivated Irrationality* is a typical example.

> reason itself has certain bad habits. . . . For example . . . a person's first formulation of a theory is obstinately retained even when further evidence is telling heavily against it. (Pears 1984, p. 9)

Pears asks us to consider the slightly different case of a driver who goes against evidence already in his possession:

> he judges it best that he should stop at two drinks in spite of the pleasure to be had from more. Nevertheless, when he is offered a third drink, which we may suppose is a double, he takes it. . . . If the guest persuaded himself that doctors are just wrong about the amount of alcohol that can be taken without loss of judgment or slowing of reactions, he was going against the evidence in his possession and merely making a wishful guess at the facts. That would be a clear case of incorrect processing of information and so, by the suggested criterion, a clear case of irrationality. (Pears 1984, p. 13)

This argument implies that retesting a hypothesis whose importance has increased is irrational. But this is not so. It is true, of course, that alcohol degrades performance and increases the risk in driving. But under the influence of alcohol the driver's values have changed, and the marginal cost of incurring increased risk is worth less than the marginal value of an extra drink. But as a consequence the value of testing the belief that three drinks is too risky has increased. The fact that the test involves increased risk to the life of the driver does not alter this fact. The fact that a wish prompted the man to entertain a false proposition which he earlier had rejected does not make the man irrational, since being liable to error is something that only gods can avoid. The relevant question is: is the driver now beyond persuasion by even stronger arguments?

A clearer case than the one Pears presents is that of the jealous lover who suspects there is a rival round every corner. This makes sense as a strategy for the rigorous testing of a very important hypothesis: that the lover is faithful. Rivals are more liable to detection and thwarting if the lover is always on the lookout. This is a case of fearful thinking. A parallel case of wishful thinking is when a jilted lover thinks he sees his lover all over the place and finds himself running up to strangers only to be embarrassed. This example illustrates how wishful thinking might serve the interests of an individual. (Admittedly, this is not ideological thinking, but it can easily be generalized.)

In Pears's argument we may discern a strong element of justificationism. For Pears, any rational belief or action must be based on evidence; mere guesses prompted by wish are irrational. But a guess can be true, and one can act no better then in the light of what is true.

Jon Elster

Jon Elster argues that there is no tendency for wishful thinking to promote goal-seeking. Elster acknowledges that a wishful belief may happen to be true or efficient. However, this is a chance affair and therefore irrational:

> A belief about instrumental means-ends relationship, if true, is no less efficient because it is arrived at by wishful thinking. But of course, instrumental beliefs shaped by interest will serve interest only by fluke. (Elster 1985, p. 142)

Wishful thinking would be "even more irrational than weakness of will" because "a desire could never rationalize a belief." For Elster, the generation of a belief through a wish could never make a belief rational, because this is not a justificatory procedure. Elster is fairly subtle though, since he does point out that a wishful belief may happen to be justified on other grounds. So a wishful belief may happen to be a justified true belief: a piece of knowledge as traditionally defined. But this is pure coincidence.

In general, Elster argues for the following proposition:

> There is no reason to suppose that beliefs shaped by interests tend to serve these interests. (p. 143)

> On general grounds, distorted beliefs cannot be expected, any more than illusionary beliefs, to be very helpful for goal achievement. (p. 141)

The "general grounds" that Elster speaks of are not forthcoming. His arguments consist of envisioning hypothetical situations in which wishful thinking leads to erroneous beliefs or (detrimental consequences) in which the individual's interests are thwarted by the way others react to his wishful thoughts.

Consider this argument of Elster's:

> If out of wishful thinking I form a belief that I am about to be promoted, my subsequent display of unwarranted self-confidence may destroy once and for all my chances of promotion. (p. 141)

It's also possible that my belief I am about to be promoted may motivate me to display self-assurance, causing me to be promoted.

Elster points to the Lysenko affair, the disastrous nature of which, Elster asserts, was brought about by scientific beliefs being formed by wishes. Quoting Paul Veyne, he points to the possibility that the "exploited and oppressed classes" may out of wishful thinking suppose that their fate is just and proper.

These examples show at most that wishful thinking can produce error and thwart interest and desire. But someone arguing that wishful thinking acts as a guide in the pursuit of goals is not committed to the view that wishful thinking is infallible. Nowhere does Elster show, or even attempt to show, that wishful thinking leads either systematically or by tendency to erroneous beliefs or the thwarting of interest or desire. We can just as easily cite hypothetical cases where wishful thinking leads to favorable outcomes.

Elster is led astray in his analysis of wishful thinking by his acceptance of justificationism. This is most clearly seen in his book, *Making Sense of Marx*.

> Summing up, the presumptions that a socially caused belief will not be rationally grounded, and that a belief which is not rationally grounded will be false, creates a case for the falsity of socially caused beliefs. To repeat, such beliefs may well be true, like the broken watch that tells the correct time once every twelve hours. The point is only that we cannot expect them to be true. (Elster 1985a, pp. 474–75)

Why, according to Elster, are socially caused beliefs irrational? Because

> a belief is rationally caused if (i) the causes of the belief are reasons for holding it and (ii) the reasons cause the belief qua reasons, not in some accidental manner. Conversely, they are shaped in the wrong way if irrelevant causes enter into their formation or they are irrelevantly shaped by relevant causes. Among such irrelevant causes we may cite the interest or position of the believer; hence socially caused beliefs are not rationally caused. (p. 474)

Elster accepts the traditional definition of knowledge as justified true belief. Elster points out that a justified belief may be false, because a justified belief is one that has the right relationship to the evidence, not the world. But, Elster continues, justificatory procedures are chosen because they are conducive to the goal of truth. Since wishful thinking is not a justificatory procedure we cannot expect it to help discover the truth.

Georg Lukacs

Elster's position is fairly sophisticated and does not fall into the same error that many sociologists of knowledge since Karl Mannheim have: the self-undermining idea that since all theories are socially caused they are all false, or at least presumptively false. Elster is right to reject the solution offered by Georg Lukács and others that Marxism has a privileged character, but his own solution is really superfluous.

Georg Lukacs tried to defend the special character of Marxism, by arguing that Marxism is the theory of the proletariat, a class acting in the interest of humanity and not in its own narrow class interest. Georg Lukács assumed that a class whose beliefs are shaped by its own peculiar interests must have a false consciousness: its understanding or theory of society must be false. Lukács's explanation for the systematic error of a narrow class is that it would be against its interest to have a true understanding of society. But a class whose interest coincided with that of humanity as a whole (the proletariat) must have a true consciousness: its theories of society must be true. Why did Lukács think that the proletariat were infallible in this regard? Because, he assumed that for the proletariat, its self-understanding and its process of achieving humanity's interest (communism) were identical.

Elster contests that social causation is social causation and rational causation is rational causation; and a belief caused by social position or interest is not made any more rational by the social position or interest being that of humanity as a whole rather than some sub-group. Marxism, Elster insists, needs another answer to this problem.

Elster's answer begins by distinguishing between an ideology that arises spontaneously and independently in the minds of many individuals and a belief that arises in the mind of some individual and is then accepted by many others because it corresponds to their material interest or social position. In the latter case, Elster's argues, the belief will be socially caused for many but that will not create a presumption against its truth, because there is no reason to believe that the originators of ideas that subsequently end up as the ideas of the ruling class are similarly under the sway of irrational forces.

Elster asserts that even if all widely accepted theories are socially grounded, this does not create a presumption against their truth if the social grounding operates via their diffusion and acceptance. Thus, on Elster's argument, Marxism is justified if Marx came to his theory via a justificatory procedure, that is, if his beliefs were rationally caused.

Throughout his discussion Elster assumes that accepting a view because it corresponds to one's interest is irrational. But this may help in furthering the pursuit of one's goals, by allowing one to try out, to test a hypothesis relevant to one's goals; and this applies whether the view was generated by one's interest or accepted from another. The belief may not be understood as a hypothesis in the way a scientist views his hypotheses, but the belief will function as one nonetheless. Moreover, nowhere does Elster show that beliefs accepted on account of their conformity to one's interests are immune to change through argument. But if a belief is open to argument then its origin (whether it is justified or not) is irrelevant.

The terms of the whole debate between Lukács and Elster are wrong. The concern over the origin of beliefs is misleading, for it ignores what is done with beliefs once they have been acquired. Beliefs cannot be justified. But even a belief arrived at by, let us suppose, the finest justificatory method may be held in an uncritical, dogmatic way. The belief that a belief has been justified (or has been as well justified as any belief could be) combined with a belief in justificationism, may give rise to the arbitrary supposition that it must be true, thus reducing the urgency of confronting criticism.

Elster's definition of a rationally-caused belief is perilously close to absurdity. If, as Elster insists, a belief is rational if and only if its causes are reasons for holding it, then Elster must also assume that there are reasons that are not constituted by beliefs. Such non-belief reasons would have to form the beginning of any chain of causes causing a rational belief if Elster is to avoid an infinite regress. If all reasons are rational beliefs, then according to Elster's definition any rational belief would have to have a rational belief for its cause and this belief in turn would have to have a belief for its cause and so on, ad infinitum. But Elster fails to hint at what kind of non-belief reasons these would be. Immediate experience cannot serve this role, for all our experience is belief-impregnated. The best-tested theories in psychology imply that even apparently simple visual experiences involve complex beliefs.

Epistemologically, it does not matter how a belief was produced. All that matters is whether it is open to criticism, and what is done with it in response to criticism. Mannheim and Lukács fell into their insuperable problem by taking justificationism for granted. Justificationism searches for authorities, whether in reason, experience, gods, or intuition. Lukács thought he had found an ultimate authority in the consciousness of the proletariat. But there just is no authority. Nothing can ever justify any belief.

A defender of Lukács's position might retort to Elster's argument by saying that it is the bourgeoisie's dogmatic stand on their ideology that is important: and it is their type of narrow class interest that maintains the ideology against argument and appeal from other classes. In fact this is what Lukács seems to be saying when he says that the capitalist class cannot understand the proletarian viewpoint because it is against their interest. But then Elster could respond by pointing out that Lukacs does not show that the proletarian interest is any different: the proletarians may be just as dogmatic as the bourgeoisie. Lukács failed to see this possibility for he had already concluded that the proletarians had a privileged epistemological position: they just could not be wrong, even in principle.

Lukács's position is possibly the most extreme statement of the irrationality engendered by interest (which we may equate with wishes). Not only is the capitalist class prevented by their wishes from agreeing with the proletarian position, but their wishes prevent them from even understanding it. (Lukács complicates this slightly by saying that one can only understand the proletarian position by being involved in the struggle for communism. So there are two barriers to criticism.)[20]

We may deny the premise of Lukács's argument. Commentators on positions such as Lukács's take for granted his contention that the interests of the two classes, the working class and the capitalist class, are incompatible with respect to communism. However if, as Marx sometimes seems to suggest, everyone will eventually have a higher standard of living in communism it would clearly be in the interests of the capitalists to promote communism. But even if the richest of the capitalists are to be reduced from fabulous luxury to merely comfortable adequacy by communism, they might still embrace it, for the same reasons that so many of the most successful capitalists have become major philanthropists. Stepping closer to reality, we might take note of the sad truths that no significant fraction of the real-life proletariat has ever had the slightest interest in communism (this being a matter for the self-appointed leadership of the proletariat, to wit bourgeois intellectuals like Lukács) and that any attempt to abolish market competition will reduce the living standards of the workers as well as those of the capitalists.

In assessing the presumption that wishful ideologies lead systematically away from truth, impede goal attainment, and are closed to argument, let us return to an eagle's eye view of man as a creature of evolution. Let us construct the logic of the situation facing our ancestors (plus their close relatives who failed to cope with it).

WISHFUL BELIEFS AND EXPLORATORY BEHAVIOR

Imagine yourself in the desert. You've gotten lost and are trying desperately to find water. You see a lake some distance of, and run toward it, only to find that it was a mirage. This happens to you over and over again. Do you disregard the next impression of a lake? No, because you want to find water so much, your belief is sustained by the wish. This is perfectly rational behavior (in a desperate situation). But, in terms of our evolution, why are we like this?

In the efficient pursuit of any goal an organism must discover the possibilities open to it. Since it is fallible and mostly ignorant of the world, it must explore some hypotheses. Now its ignorance is literally infinite, so there are an infinity of possible hypotheses to test. It would be inefficient to pick hypotheses without any constraints. Could evolution have eliminated some ranges of these hypotheses? Could evolution have given the organism a higher-level conjecture about what kinds of hypotheses are worth testing? I suggest that it could have eliminated from consideration all those that are irrelevant to the pursuit of its goals. Already, it appears that we have a tendency for the organism's beliefs to be related to its interests. Can this relationship be brought still closer?

Very desirable or fearful possibilities are worth testing for. Organisms that do not test for very desirable or fearful possibilities would tend to be eliminated in favor of our more circumspect ancestors, or they would at least suffer a diminished reproductive potential. (I assume that evolution has already made desires and fears fairly well correlated with reproductive needs, though the correlation need not be exact.) But for a possibility to be tested, a relevant belief has first to be generated. Moreover, the more desirable or fearful the possibility, the more testing it is worth; hence the belief ought sometimes to be retained in the presence of some counter-evidence.

I assume here with Popper that all organisms—indeed, all knowledge acquiring systems—are fallible. That means that organisms can be wrong not only in their initial hypotheses but also in their interpretations of tests. Even the results of observational tests are provisional, and are sometimes worth retesting. Beliefs that concern very valuable things are often for this reason difficult to dislodge (for example, obsessive jealousy, beliefs in ghosts of lost relatives, belief in a world of superabundance, belief in a simple way to get rich quick, belief that choosing one leader rather than another will make us vastly better off).

Thus we see that the action of natural selection working on organisms subject to certain properties of theories and methodological considerations can be expected to produce organisms that have a tendency to wishful and fearful thinking.

This analysis of wishful and fearful thinking by applying Popper's principles is necessary if we are to take account of the stubbornness of some systems of ideas. This is an important element of truth in Popper's and Bartley's idea that ideologies are unresponsive to criticism. However, by placing them in the context of an evolutionary view of humans, we are also in a better position to see that wishful and fearful thinking are no impenetrable shields against criticism, but in fact are ways of making the most of criticism. For the stubbornness with respect to criticism is not absolute, but proportional to the importance of the values at stake.

Absolute versus Value-relative Stubbornness

But what prevents the propagandist from making himself absolutely stubborn? Eric Hoffer maintained that:

> The readiness for self sacrifice is contingent on an imperviousness to the realities of life. . . . Strength of faith, as Bergson pointed out, manifests itself not in moving mountains but in not seeing mountains to move. And it is the certitude of his infallible doctrine that renders the true believer impervious to the uncertainties, surprises and the unpleasant realities of the world around him. (Hoffer 1962, pp. 75–76)

Is it possible through argument, experience, or commitment to get into such a state? Are there evolutionary reasons why this is unlikely? In answering this question we need to understand the nature of belief in the context of evolution.

Popper describes the ideologist as if he had a choice whether a. to resolve to adopt a belief in a position or b. to resolve to continue believing in the position come what may:

> Thus when those who praise commitment and irrational faith describe themselves as irrationalists (or post-rationalists) I agree with them. They are irrationalists, even if they are capable of reasoning. For they take pride in rendering themselves incapable of breaking out of their shell; they make themselves prisoners of their manias. (Popper 1994, p. 180)

However, neither a. nor b. is possible, because belief is involuntary. This statement is easily misunderstood, so I shall expand on it. It does indeed derive from Locke's doctrine, but Locke put severe restrictions on its generality which are unnecessary.[21]

We can choose to listen to, read or participate in an argument. We can choose to follow a lifestyle that encourages or discourages seeking out views contrary to our own. We can also set out to argue ourselves into or out of certain beliefs. (Indeed, maintaining a belief requires maintaining the memory of the relevant information revision—which itself is clearly a matter of choice). This is another important element of truth in Popper's and Bartley's account. Indeed, it is this truth that makes the cultivation of the critical attitude and associated institutions of fundamental importance.

But at the end of an argument or after having heard or read a counter-argument, we find that we have involuntarily retained or lost the belief. Believing is rather like seeing: we can choose to open our eyes but once they're open we will see something independent of our wishes or resolutions to the contrary. This is not meant to imply that sight is infallible, or that it is a completely passive process. Indeed, it involves many low and high level hypothesis testing active scanning mechanisms (Gregory 1966). What is implied is that we can be surprised by what we see. If we hear someone come into the room and look toward the door expecting to see Bill, and Mary has in fact come in, we see Mary and not Bill. Even if we make a supreme effort before looking, determined to see Bill, we will be out of luck (or, perhaps, in luck); if Mary's there, we see Mary, not Bill.

Seeing is not believing, but there is a close analogy in this respect. We cannot choose what we will see when we open our eyes, and we cannot choose what we will believe when we turn our minds to some topic. Our beliefs regarding states of affairs not immediately inspectable by our sense organs are dependent on various tacit or explicit arguments. And we can be surprised by what we encounter in an argument, abruptly upsetting our beliefs.

Popper has pointed out (in personal correspondence with me) that this might look like a deterministic account of belief, which would then raise the obvious problem: Do we believe what we believe because of the truth or just because we were determined to do so? If this were the case, then my argument that truth is important would be vitiated. However, involuntariness does not imply determination, though the two notions have often been confused.

I broadly agree with Popper's opposition to determinism, as expounded in his *The Open Universe*. I conjecture that the formation of beliefs is an indeterministic process. Indeterministic patterns exhibit constrained randomness.[22] Beliefs are formed by a process that involves some randomness, but there is a propensity for them to be about important issues, that is, wishful and fearful. There are other constraints on their formation, but these are irrelevant to this particular problem.

Someone might say that we certainly don't always believe what we believe because of its truth, since a lot of the time we believe what is false. What we believe is what we suppose is true, whether we're right or wrong. This is certainly correct. Popper's concern was that if we believe what we believe to be true because we have been determined to believe it, our acceptance of what is true and false may have nothing to do with the truth. However, even on Popper's view, where a belief comes from is irrelevant, so long as it's still open to argument. I think there is a connection between being open to sound argument and Popper's propensity interpretation of causation.

If you favor a probabilistic account of belief, as I do, then this is perfectly compatible with saying that the truth has a propensity to stimulate belief. When I open my eyes in the morning, there is a high propensity that I will believe I am in my bedroom: in other words the fact that I'm in my bedroom has a propensity to cause my true belief that I am. Popper had a propensity account of causation (see Popper 1990), so I imagine if this point had been put to him it may have changed his view. The point about the involuntariness of belief is not that it is determined (there are only propensities), but that it is not open to an individual to decide to ignore all facts, to decide one day 'Oh, I will believe what I want from now on'. Every one of us has been in the situation of becoming unhappily and uncomfortably aware of some relevant facts. If our ancestors had been sealed off from any such possibility, they could not have survived; at least, they could not have survived as conscious beings whose actions are in some way connected with their beliefs. Evolution is ruthless and has no truck with 'inner peace' or 'personal equilibrium'. If it can improve the genetic reproducibility of the individual by making him a little unhappier, it will.

Fodor argues (Fodor 1983) that our perceptual systems are "mandatory" in the sense that you cannot stop them processing the input and generating a belief—the visual system takes a two-dimensional input and generates a perception of a stable three-dimensional world. Suppose someone could monitor your beliefs via some brain implant. Suppose also that you are sitting in your London flat watching TV. Now suppose the brain monitor puts a gun to your head and says: 'If you don't start believing that you are swimming under water in the Caribbean, I'll blow your head clean off.' And you believe he's serious. Your mandatory visual system will not allow you to change your belief in that way. You just can't do it. No one can. Our evolution has rigged up our visual system so that there is a 'high propensity' between a given type of input and our beliefs about visual matters and others to which they are logically connected. This account allows for the possibility of illusions (trees seen as men; and vice versa) and the visual system has its own biases and typical errors.

On this view there is no hard-wired deterministic connection between the truth and belief. I also think that even in the absence of propensities, there could still be valid arguments and we could still entertain true hypotheses. But it then would be hard to arrange situations that would not only test our theories, but also prompt us (probabilistically) to accept the results. So I think causation is important in being rational, specifically, open to argument in a non-random way.

On evolutionary grounds why should we expect beliefs to be involuntary? The answer might be that organisms that persist in beliefs comewhat-may tend to be eliminated. We must expect there to be a limit, therefore, to the extent to which wishful and fearful thinking can sustain beliefs against contrary evidence, since any genes responsible for absolutely impervious wishful and fearful thinking would tend to be eliminated. Organisms that persist indefinitely in seeking food simply on the basis of where they wish it to be, or try to escape predators by wishing them away, will leave few descendants. So from an evolutionary point of view we can expect even wishful and fearful thinking to be open to argument.

Hoffer on the Fanatical Communist

Eric Hoffer, like Kolakowski, picked the fanatical Communist as an example of his claim:

> The fanatical communist refuses to believe any unfavorable report or evidence about Russia, nor will he be disillusioned by seeing with his own eyes the cruel misery inside the Soviet promised land. (Hoffer 2002, p. 79)

This assertion may be reinforced by the elastic term 'fanatical'. Many former Communists have become disillusioned, but maybe they weren't fanatical enough. When Hoffer wrote this, there were far more former fanatical Communists, at least in the English-speaking world, than there were currently fanatical Communists. Sequel volumes to *The God that Failed* could have been published by the thousand, if they had been written about non-celebrities.

Hoffer is really making two assertions: that the fanatical Communist won't believe the reports of bad things in Soviet Russia, and that even if he witnesses those bad things (and does therefore believe that they exist) he will still not be disillusioned, presumably meaning that he will remain a Communist. So the Communist thinks the bourgeois media are lying about Russia, and if they're not lying after all, the bad things are due, say, to capitalist encirclement and the activities of imperialist saboteurs. Yet there were huge desertions from Western Communist parties following Moscow 1939, Budapest 1956, and Prague 1968. Not only did Western Communist parties dwindle, but the parties themselves eventually became infected with 'Euro-Communism', which involved a measure of independence from Moscow, and sometimes quite forthright criticism of Soviet conditions and Soviet policies.

Hoffer and Kolakowski could have presented a more subtle argument. Following Popper, they could have pointed out that our experiences are interpreted by our theories about the world. As David Hume argued in more particular terms:

> as force is always on the side of the governed, the governors have nothing to support them but opinion. It is, therefore, on opinion only that government is founded; and this maxim extends to the most despotic and military governments. (Hume 1904, p. 29)

Thus if Soviet citizens were convinced that there was no alternative to their miserable existence, or that the other alternatives would be worse, or that their misery was only a temporary and regrettably necessary step to profound happiness, it might not be surprising if they still thought Soviet Russia to be the best society in the world. This would be what Hume called an opinion of interest. It might also be an opinion difficult to criticize and thus undermine psychologically. However, as we have seen, argument against the economic mismanagement and moral outrages of the Soviet Union eventually penetrated the supposedly impenetrable barriers to criticism.

Wishful and fearful thinking engender stubbornness in our beliefs, but as in all organisms capable of belief it is a relative stubbornness proportionate to the importance of the belief to the organism. Wishful and fearful thinking is a way, perhaps a crude way, by which an organism makes the most of its hypotheses and the counter-evidence within the constraints of the organism's fallibility and in the light of the varying urgency of its values.

Denise Meyerson on Absolute Ideological Stubbornness

Denise Meyerson is one writer who acknowledges the value of a degree of conservatism towards our beliefs in the face of counter-evidence, but who still thinks that ideological stubbornness is absolute. She fails to consider the possibility that the degree of conservatism may be proportionate to the degree of importance of the issue; stubbornness for Meyerson is either reasonable or absolute. Meyerson asserts that there is a difference between a scientist's "charitable" protective attitude to a theory's predictive failures and the digging-in that acceptance of an ideology involves, which is maintained 'come-what-may' (Meyerson 1991, p. 61).

According to my approach, it is not surprising that a scientist's defense of a possibly refuted theory whose truth or falsity has little emotional significance is relatively less stubborn than the ideologist's defense of a theory whose truth or falsity has great emotional significance. It does not follow that the defense of the latter is come-what-may, and Meyerson furnishes us with no general argument that this defense would be absolutely stubborn. Of course, methodologically one ought to positively look for sound criticism, and one might out of fearful thinking avoid what one suspects to be counter-evidence. Like Pears, Meyerson thinks that she has obviated the paradox of self-deception, convincing oneself of a belief that one contradicts, by using the word "suspicion" rather than belief (Meyerson 1991, p. 65). One only suspects that there may be counter-evidence, without actually believing that there is.

But this seems to be a verbal sleight of hand. Suspicion seems to be weak belief, rather than no belief at all. The strength of a belief may be indicated by how much a person is willing to sacrifice in action based on it, and all action is based on belief, whether weak or strong. It follows that Meyerson's fearful avoiders of counter-evidence must be willing to make some sacrifice to avoid the possible counter-evidence. But then it follows that their 'suspicion' must amount to some belief, that they actually doubt their cherished belief. It's also hard not to surmise that people who are fearful of criticism of their position understand that their belief may be involuntarily undermined by the evidence despite their wishes to the contrary.

But is this weakened belief at least guaranteed against undermining counter-evidence? No, for even our most fervent desire or fear cannot act infallibly to exclude from our view all possible counter-evidence. The belief may still be discarded in response to the right argument, whether looked for or not.

The major weakness in Meyerson's case is that she overlooks the evolutionary origin of our psychological make-up. As a consequence she feels free to postulate absolutely stubborn beliefs generated by wishful thinking, just as a science-fiction writer unconstrained by physics feels free to postulate rockets that travel at the speed of light. Like most writers who ignore our evolutionary origins, Meyerson assumes that the way we deal with counter-evidence is tailored to our desire for contentment or a life free from doubt and uncertainty. However, what maximizes the reproduction of genes may not maximize the attainment of contentment; our evolved mechanisms for registering error may wake us rather unpleasantly from Bartley's "slumbering fantasy world."

In the light of the involuntariness of belief in response to counter-evidence, and the fallibility of fearful attempts to avoid counter-evidence, we may reject Popper's conclusion that only those who have chosen the rationalist attitude can be impressed by an appeal to experience and logical argument. Every person begins life with a disposition to correct falsified beliefs, despite his wishes or dispositions to the contrary.

Logical Thinking Promotes Survival

People prefer to adopt means that are logically consistent and abide by the rules of logic. To sustain this, I need not be committed to the thesis that the rules of logic are descriptive laws of thought, as Kant and later Boole thought. All we need to suppose is that the human mind strives, fallibly, for consistency as a result of our evolutionary history.

Logic is the study of abstract relationships between statements or propositions, such as logical implication, logical contradiction, and logical independence. It attempts to explore and test proposed rules of correct reasoning, of valid inference or demonstrative proof, and also the axiomatization of proofs within systems, and their consistency and completeness. By 'logical rationality' I mean our psychological disposition to, and interaction with, abstract logic. The rules of logic were once called the laws of thought, but this is misleading, though understandable. The rule of non-contradiction states that a proposition and its negation can't both be true (in the same way at the same time). For example, 'Iron is magnetic' and 'Iron is nonmagnetic' cannot both be true. If you try to believe at the same time 'I'm reading this book' and 'I'm not reading this book', you will fail, and it is this sort of thing that suggested that logic was also the laws of thought. Now, this compulsion we feel shouldn't be ignored; indeed it should be emphasized. Nevertheless, although we can err in reasoning, an erroneous law of logic is a contradiction. The writings of those who argue for the closed mind are apt to confuse the two and even when these writers do make a distinction, they don't explore the interaction between these very different realms.

A valid argument is persuasive because it is valid, and validity is persuasive in general because it has helped us to adapt to the world. It helps us to respond to facts that are not part of our immediate environment. In logic we can distinguish the general and the particular, and once we do this, our reasoning is unleashed from immediate concerns, and can explore the lawful structure of the world and remote and perceptually inaccessible domains. It's a fascinating question why the world has logic, as it is why it has mathematics, and why both of these are applicable to reality. I conjecture that a future 'unified theory' will not simply use mathematics and logic with which to state itself, but will attempt to incorporate these abstract domains within its explanatory grasp. But that's another question. I can assume here without much trouble that just as mathematics has an uncanny applicability to reality, so does logic. We don't need to countenance what I regard to be one of the major stumbling blocks to the acceptance of a multi-layered world containing something other than atoms and force-fields: the idea that only factors of the same domain or type can affect one another. This idea was already exploded by the time Faraday had shown the interaction of electricity and magnetism. (Materialists have a charming tendency to appropriate any new phenomenon and simply call it 'material', thereby denuding their theory of any content.)

I'm arguing that logic is an abstract structure. While not determining our beliefs, it makes one hell of an impact. More importantly, it enables us to escape from our errors in specific domains. But how did this appreciation for logic arise? If I can argue that we must have the appreciation of logic we do have because it must have evolved, then I can argue that our appreciation of logic must be both universal and fairly robust, even if imperfect. And if its appreciation is universal and robust, then closed minds are less plausible entities.

We cannot easily suppose that our ancestors had a habit of regarding a snarling sabertooth as at the same time both dangerous and not dangerous. Those pre-*Homo sapiens* that had a propensity to neglect the law of contradiction became extinct. Similarly, to ignore the law of the excluded middle—holding that it's not necessarily true that the tiger must be either dangerous or not dangerous—would have produced fatal outcomes. I might add that an inability to reject the contradiction of a given belief would have produced fatal degrees of hesitation in general. An evolutionary explanation of a function or organ allows that it could have evolved from something quite different by numerous successive intermediate stages. Even an incipient propensity to think in accord with the laws of logic would be of reproductive advantage. This is a serious consideration for any Darwinian-like explanation. My argument does not commit me to the hypothesis that somehow logical rules as such are present in the brain, but only that thought tends to occur in accord with, or simulates, the following of these rules. As John Searle (1984, p. 51) points out in his criticism of Noam Chomsky's theory of generative grammar, the fact—if it be a fact—that all human languages conform to essentially the same set of grammatical rules ("deep structures") does not mean that human brains contain these rules, just as the fact that falling stones obey the laws of gravitation does not mean that stones contain instructions or rules in order to obey these laws. Indeed, the admission of the sudden phylogenetic emergence of logical rules would work against the Darwinian mode of numerous small steps.

A very early step toward logical thinking was perhaps the ability to act as a single individual, where a number of actions can be co-ordinated and incompatible actions decided. The emergence of a central nervous system obviously enhanced this ability. The fact that human brains evolved a tendency to think in a way that simulated following rules of logic first made possible the development of a descriptive language (*Homo habilis*) and later a formal understanding of logic, an argumentative function. This formal understanding of logic may well have made its incipient appearance as simple rules of thumb or maxims similar to modern expressions such as 'You can't have your cake and eat it'. These early developments may have had a feedback effect on brain structures responsible for thinking in accord with logical rules. Those pre-*Homo sapiens* who were more logical in their thinking would presumably remember these maxims with greater efficiency and thus gain more from them, perhaps setting up a positive evolutionary feedback loop. Once the appreciation of elementary rules of logic (such as the law of contradiction) had emerged, coded in the nervous system or in language, these propensities would have themselves acted as evolutionary pressures in the evolution of our appreciation of other rules of logic (such as the modus ponens).

Ruse (1986) has made an excellent case for the evolutionary origin of our appreciation of logic, though Ruse appears to confuse the questions of the origin of our appreciation of logic, our tendency to think in accordance with it, and the origin of logic as such. Once evolved, logic, like mathematics, has its own autonomous properties that cannot be explained as conducive to reproductive advantage. These properties may take deep insight to discover and can astonish us. An example is Gödel's theorem. But perhaps this should not surprise us too much. That a tool developed for one use has properties (even useful ones) that are irrelevant to this original use is hardly surprising. Our opposable thumb evolved perhaps because of its usefulness in grasping tree branches, but this humble origin does not prevent a pilot using it to turn dials flying the space shuttle. We might well say that our traditional conception of, say, the excluded middle (P vs. not-P) covers undecidable Ps, but that such knowledge did not make a difference to behavior, and so its origin could not have resulted from differential selection over behavioral variants. We could then say that we originally developed an intuitionistic appreciation of P vs. not-P for reasons not connected with its now classic contribution to knowledge, and then built the classic P vs. not-P on this original with the aid of language, at least partly independently of genetics.

G.A. Wells and Immediate Experience

I am arguing here that humans are open to argument and counter-evidence. Now someone might object to my line of argument by saying that, while it's admittedly very difficult and often impossible to reject what we encounter in our immediate sensible environment, this applies only to beliefs and memes concerning our immediate sensible environment, and therefore not to the abstractions of religion, science, and modern ideologies. The strongest version of this line of argument is propounded by G.A. Wells in his attempt to explain why religious ideas survive criticism:

> When our ideas about our immediate environment are very incomplete or erroneous, our behavior is likely to be ill-adapted to our needs, so that we expose ourselves to some immediate unpleasantness. But in this way attention is called to our mistake, and we may be led to rectify it. If, for instance, we act on the belief that ether is a good fire extinguisher, we shall be in for a rude shock, and if we survive the experience, the belief will not survive with us. On the other hand, any ideas we may have formed about the nature of the universe, or about the distant future or past, are unlikely to lead to any noticeably inappropriate reactions on our part. Thus we may well persist in erroneous beliefs of these kinds all our lives without experiencing the smallest surprise or disappointment. (Wells 1988, p. 219)

There is something in this: false beliefs remote from everyday experience have better survival chances than false beliefs relied upon in everyday activities. My idea is that an appreciation of logic evolved because of its utility in handling problems presented by our ancestors' immediate environment, first perhaps in the avoidance of predators and then in the construction of tools, and later in organized hunting and still later in the capacity to learn and transmit a language. This grants the element of strength in Wells's argument: a deficiency in coping with immediate practical problems is a great selection pressure.

However, the appreciation of logic was not tied exclusively to thought about the immediate environment. There was no evolutionary reason for this new general ability to be tied to immediate problems, so general logical reasoning was not eliminated. Analogously, one may learn to count colored beads, but then automatically also be able to count, as an incidental by-product, apples, oranges, cars, and stars. General reasoning ability may have been a lucky advantageous by-product of the selection pressure on our ancestors to deal efficiently with their immediate environment. Our ancestors were then able to compare alternative plans of action, whether short- or long-term. Their decisiveness would be enhanced by the very fact that they could see more readily which plans really were alternatives. And the more abstract their grasp of logic, the longer the time span over which they could plan.

More productive processes often require more time to put into effect: for example sacrificing today's fish caught by hand to make a net that will bring in more fish tomorrow. In addition, they were able to discard those plans, or parts of plans, which were internally inconsistent or conflicted with a general theory about, say, the whereabouts of game animals. They were able to do this before they committed themselves to a hunt, for instance, instead of having to test directly every promising plan. Borrowing Popper's phrase, our pre-*Homo sapiens* ancestors could begin to let their ideas die in their stead. They would also be better at fashioning a tool whose manufacture required a sequence of actions of limited permutability (Holloway, 1983). They could make better use of general theories by inferring their consequences for many particular circumstances, and finally, they could override the sometimes over-generalized effect of Pavlovian conditioning. This evolutionary analysis of the origin of our appreciation of logic explains the fact, noted by cognitive dissonance theory, that people prefer to adopt consonant beliefs, attitudes, and behavior. We could also argue that the notion of dissonance in this theory covers not only logical inconsistency, but also what might be more aptly described as infelicity (Austin 1962). However, even felicity, as Austin later argued after dropping his earlier exclusive categories of performative and constative utterances, is dependent on truth.

The evolutionary pressures also explain why all the world's logics are extremely similar. As Staal (1967, p. 520) says, "Although it remains uninfluenced by Western logic and stems from an entirely different tradition, Indian logic offers striking parallels to Western logic." The same is true of Chinese logics.

There is something a bit misleading in Wells's conclusion (p. 219) that "beliefs which admitted of no practical demonstration and could be checked by no intelligible test could be entrusted only to words or to other equivocal ciphers and symbols which each generation had to interpret afresh according to its lights." This is not the entire picture, because it suggests that all intelligible tests depend on the immediate environment and neglects the check of consistency and more remote and roundabout checks of logical reasoning generally. Moreover, it overlooks the possibility that an appreciation of logic evolved in connection with immediate problems of the environment while its scope transcended this parochial domain.

Wolpert: Bending Logic to Prior Belief

Lewis Wolpert (2006, p. 6) argues that people use logic, but they are apt to bend it to their preferred beliefs. Wolpert says that if people are presented with a logically correct argument whose conclusion agrees with their beliefs, they accept the validity of the argument, but otherwise they are more likely to question the validity of the argument. For example, subjects will accept the following argument nearly one hundred percent of the time:

No cigarettes are inexpensive.

Some addictive things are inexpensive.

Therefore, some addictive things are not cigarettes.

By contrast, only fifty percent of people thought the following argument to be valid, even though it is logically correct:

No addictive things are inexpensive.

Some cigarettes are inexpensive.

Therefore, some cigarettes are not addictive.

But Wolpert jumps too readily to take this as evidence of a closed mind or even of a logically flawed mind. Wolpert speaks about logically valid arguments. In logic we have to distinguish logically valid arguments and sound arguments. Valid arguments are correct by virtue of their form alone, but sound arguments also require that all the statements in the argument are true. A valid argument is one in which, if the premises were true, then the conclusion must also be true. The key words here are 'if', 'were', and 'then'. They help to construct what is known as a subjunctive or hypothetical sentence. For example: "If I were to jump off the Burj Khalifa building, Dubai, then I would be dead." This hypothetical can be true, even if I never jump off the building. There is a similar situation with a valid argument: it can be valid, even if the premises are false:

All professors are birds.

All birds read.

Therefore: All professors read.

An argument can be valid even if all the statements, premises and conclusion, are false:

All camels are fish.

All fish are nocturnal.

Therefore: All camels are nocturnal.

Of course, we want our arguments also to use true statements for premises.

If you call an argument valid, you're not saying the premises and conclusion are true; you're saying that the form will never lead you from true premises to a false conclusion. You're saying, strictly, the premises may be false, but if they were true, then the conclusion would also have to be true. The only possibility prohibited by a valid argument is all the premises being true and the conclusion being false. Now, if a valid argument has a false conclusion, then it makes perfect sense to be alert to a defect somewhere in the argument. At least one or more of the premises must be false. So the reaction these subjects had to the arguments whose conclusion they disagreed with made sense. But let's pursue this a little. Even if you know that the argument is valid and the conclusion is (from your point of view) false, you can't tell which of the premises is causing the trouble. All you can say is that at least one must be false. The possible true-false distributions are shown below.

No addictive things are inexpensive.	F	T	F
Some cigarettes are inexpensive.	F	F	T
Therefore, some cigarettes are not addictive.	F	F	F

Is it any wonder that subjects were reluctant to accept the argument? There are two ways an argument can go wrong: either it has an invalid form or one or more of its statements is false. It's plausible that subjects may start to re-evaluate the premises, but that's an extra cognitive task. In other words, there is much room for 'reasonable' hesitation over accepting the argument.

Natural Selection Doesn't Yield Perfection

Karl Popper (private correspondence) has objected that Darwinian theory does not imply that organisms are perfectly adapted to their environments. Darwin himself was well aware of this:

> Natural selection tends only to make each organic being as perfect as, or slightly more perfect than, the other inhabitants of the same country with which it has to struggle for existence. . . . Natural selection will not produce absolute perfection. . . . The correction for the aberration of light is said, on high authority, not to be perfect even in that most perfect organ, the eye. (Darwin 1859, p. 229)

Indeed, there are organs and behaviors that reduce the reproducibility of the relevant genotype. Maladaptive characteristics survive and are reproduced on the back of adaptive characteristics. I may add that if organisms were perfectly adapted it would be hard to understand extinction. The very fact that species become extinct implies that they were not perfectly adapted to whatever made them extinct. Therefore our inferences from the principle of Darwinian evolution have to be carefully qualified. We can only argue that there is a rough and ready tendency toward the evolution of economic, instrumental, exploratory, logical, and wishful rationality.

However, it's interesting to compare Darwinian and Lamarckian evolution in this regard. Darwinian evolution has at least a tendency to produce rational organisms; Lamarckian evolution (on its own) could easily produce irrational organisms. Lamarckian evolution relies on the inheritance of acquired characteristics, but many acquired characteristics are injuries. Brain damage impairing reasoning abilities would be passed on to the next generation, and (without Darwinian selection) accumulated down the generations. Without extinction—that is, Darwinian selection—organisms would tend eventually to reproduce mindless heaps of poisoned, lacerated flesh and fractured bone.

Thus Popper points out that there is no general tendency in Darwinian evolution to produce flexibility; it may well issue in highly inflexible behavior. Popper drew the implication that there is no general tendency in Darwinian evolution to produce flexibility of belief, which I argued was useful for exploring the world.

Popper's criticism can only be met by pointing to the importance of the kind of selection pressures to which humans have been subject. When we look at the evolutionary conditions from before the emergence of *Homo sapiens sapiens* to the present, it becomes clearer that being economic, abandoning the futile, thinking logically, exploring the unknown, wishful and fearful thinking, and being flexible in belief have all been reproductive advantages. Wasting resources, pursuing the futile, ignoring the unknown, flouting logical rules, failure to persist in beliefs of importance, and being utterly rigid in one's beliefs has been a reproductive disadvantage.

More particularly, I pointed to *Homo sapiens sapiens*'s origin as a maker of tools, a hunter and a user of symbols. We can imagine that both of these practices were part of the selection pressure acting, perhaps indirectly, on our ancestors' genes. This point of view is consistent with Popper's theory of orthogenic trends in evolution.[23]

To maintain the general thesis I only need to argue for a propensity to correct errors in the ways I have specified, so perfect adaptation is unnecessary. Thus O'Hear's criticism (1988, p. 85) of Munz's argument for evolutionary epistemology is misplaced, for evolutionary epistemology is not committed to the idea that organisms together with their perceptions, skills and knowledge are perfectly, or even near-perfectly, adapted to the world. The central point of evolutionary epistemology is that organisms can adapt and have adapted to the world, that they can correct and have corrected errors. Perhaps all that is needed for a good adaptation, as for a good scientific theory, is verisimilitude; and if organisms can correct errors, then they can increase the verisimilitude of their beliefs plus the efficiency with which they eliminate error.

Ecological Rationality, Again

When I say to you 'Prime Minister Cameron is a man; All men are mortal; therefore, Prime Minister Cameron is mortal', you understand the force of the logical inference. Tacitly, you apply the general rule 'an x is a B; All B are C; therefore, x is a C'.

Suppose you are meant to meet your friend Harry at Luigi's restaurant in downtown Chicago. You know Harry will use anyway to get to the restaurant to meet you. But Harry has just two ways of getting there: by bicycle or by car. You are trying to work out whether your friend will get there. A mutual friend of yours tells you he spoke to Harry and that Harry had said his tyres had gone flat, but your friend did not manage to hear what vehicle he was talking about before the signal on his mobile phone broke up. Logic to the rescue. You know that either the car or the bicycle is unusable. So you reason thus: 'If Harry uses the car, then he'll get there; if Harry uses the bicycle, then he'll get there; either way, he'll get there'. Such an inference rule has the fancy title 'disjunctive syllogism'. But despite the fancy label, this sort of reasoning is as easy as falling of a log and you do it all the time.

But logic problems can be tougher. There are some archeologists, biologists, and chess players in a room. None of the archeologists are biologists. All the biologists are chess players. Using all the premises, what follows? A majority of people infer that none of the archaeologists are chess players, which is invalid. No one concludes that some of the chess players are not archeologists (which is valid). Does this show we are illogical? No, just that problems can be tough. But there's a fashion for writing books on how stupid and illogical we are. Researchers have found typical biases and errors in the way we reason and this is seen as ammunition for the view that 'we're all irrational', and therefore that logic is a feeble force in human affairs. However, all it shows is that we're not gods, we sometimes make mistakes, we're fallible. And it does not show that we are locked into these errors.

But do we have brains that are equipped with general rules of logic with which we solve any kind of problem that is put before us? My argument appears to presuppose this. But some research seems to show that we don't look at problems in a general way and apply general rules of logic, but tackle them in terms of rules specially tuned to the situation. Logic appears to have arisen to deal with social situations in which cheating may occur. When the problem does not involve cheating, our performance deteriorates. Logic, as Cosmides might say, is just another tool on the Swiss army knife of our mind.

Wason's Experiment

The best known example of our supposedly irrational reasoning was discovered by Peter Wason. Wason wanted to explore the extent to which people follow Karl Popper's advice to scientists: advance a hypothesis and test it by looking for counter-instances. If our hypothesis is 'All swans are white', this means that if something's a swan, then it's white. The rule or law has the form: If P then Q. This is only false when P is true and Q is false. If you fail to find any swan, you can't infer anything. If you find a swan and it's white, you cannot infer that the general rule is false, nor can you infer that it's true. So to test the hypothesis, we have to look for a non-white swan.

The inference rule has the form:

1. **If P, then Q;**
2. **P but not Q;**
3. **Therefore, not (if P, then Q).**

This is the only circumstance in which the rule can be counted as false; all other circumstances (P not being true and Q being true; P not true and Q not true) are consistent with the hypothesis.

Peter Wason devised an experiment in which people were given a set of cards. They were also told that each card has a number on one side and a letter on the other. They had to test the rule: if a card has a D on one side it has a 3 on the other. They were shown four cards and asked to say which ones they would have to flip over to test the rule.

| D | F | 3 | 7 |

Reportedly most people choose either the D card or the D card and the 3 card. But the correct answer is D and 7. The 3 card is irrelevant because the rule does not say that if a card has a 3 on one side, then it has a D on the other. Commentators make much of the fact that only five percent of those tested get the right answer.

Now, what does this experiment show about us? Does it show we have no disposition to test our hypotheses? The import for human rationality is partly a matter of attitude: is the glass 95 percent empty or 5 percent full. Most people at least get one of two crucial cards, the D. So perhaps the optimists might be allowed to say the glass is nearly half full. However, let's allow that people are only 5 percent logical. Darwin showed that an accumulation of small changes can make a big difference, and this applies here too. Even if people eliminate their errors only 5 percent of the time, when this error elimination is repeated over time, very large errors can be discarded. The point is, we are not victims of our poor performance as logicians; we are not trapped in our erroneous doctrines.

Someone might insist that people really are irrational in some ways. The word 'irrational' has many meanings attached to it. It's not my intention to tell people how to use this word. My intention is to argue that any of the other ways in which humans can be called irrational erect no absolute barrier to criticism, and do not give a net evolutionary advantage to false ideas. Humans may sometimes be called irrational because they are ignorant, make mistakes, or often entertain inconsistent beliefs.

They have been called irrational because their values change with time. But none of these insulate an ideology from criticism, or give a net advantage to false ideas. Ignorance and mistakes are simply due to our less than omniscient and infallible nature.

A General Schema for the Evolution of Ideologies under Criticism

The evolution of ideologies under criticism may be analyzed with the help of a schema. We will make use of this schema later in the analysis of the immunizing stratagems in Chapter 4. But it will help us to see how the biologically evolved forms of rationality (instrumental, economic, exploratory, wishful or fearful thinking, and logic) fit into the general pattern of the cultural, or memetic, evolution of an ideology. They in fact provide important mechanisms for the elimination of error or maladaptiveness in ideologies.

Bartley provides the following schema for the evolution of ideas which mirrors the evolution of genes:

1. **Blind or unjustified variation.**
2. **Systematic selection and elimination.**
3. **Retention and duplication.**

Bartley's and Popper's suggestion here may be taken as a contribution to the theory of what Dawkins has called memetic evolution, 'memes' being the ideational equivalent of biological genes.

Writers who have noticed an analogy between genetic and memetic evolution have been keen to point to the disanalogies. Two often noted disanalogies are that genetic evolution is slower than memetic evolution and memetic evolution is Lamarckian (Ruse 1986, Chapter 2). Schilcher and Tennant (1984, pp. 118–19) and Hallpike (1988, p. 36) supply many more. Most writers assume that cultural evolution must be completely Lamarckian or completely Darwinian, but they are not mutually exclusive. For example, in brainstorming one deliberately applies a heuristic for the generation of ideas and for their elimination, but this heuristic, the Lamarckian aspect, is but a guide and does not determine the range of ideas or their elimination. Also one can imagine that brainstorming will be used in slightly different ways and some of the variations will be unintended but will survive because they work.

How are memetic evolution and genetic evolution related? My answer is that an important mechanism of Bartley's Stage 2 is supplied by the kinds of rationality I have argued for. The systematic selection and elimination of ideas is carried out by economic, instrumental, exploratory, wishful and fearful, and logical rationality. That is, ideas are eliminated by people generating beliefs about important possibilities, exploring the unknown, trying to avoid waste, trying to think logically and trying to abandon the futile.

I am not arguing that these genetically evolved traits are the only eliminators of error. Nor am I denying that truth may also be eliminated and false positions maintained by processes working against the elimination of error. All I need for my argument is humankind's capacity to correct its errors in the sorts of ways I have outlined above.

I will now deal with my potential critics. We will see that none of them attribute a rational element to Stage 2, to the elimination of error. This stage is regarded by them as either irrational or as ineffective: memes are either eliminated by things other than truth and validity or not eliminated at all.

Richard Dawkins: The Hellfire Meme

In *The Selfish Gene* Richard Dawkins developed the theory that with the emergence of the human brain a new type of replicator had come into existence. He called this the *meme*, a general term which includes ideas, theories, designs, tunes, and fashions. Dawkins thinks it is worthwhile trying to explain culture in Darwinian terms, but that not all cultural phenomena can be reduced to genes and their evolution. The Darwinian process of selection is a much more general notion than that, and it can be applied to the evolution of memes. Dawkins holds that memetic evolution can be quite independent of our genetic evolution. The meme for celibacy, for instance, Dawkins argues, is clearly independent of genetic evolution: it hardly increases the genetic reproducibility of those humans who replicate the meme.

The right conditions for a Darwinian evolutionary process seem to be present: variation in ideas; differential elimination of ideas; and ideas are reproducible. Dawkins points out that the same three characteristics that make for high survivability in genes must be the same for memes: longevity, fecundity, and copying-fidelity. In other words, the longer a meme exists the greater is the chance of its being copied; the higher the rate at which copies are made the greater is the chance that copies of the meme will exist in the future; and the higher the precision with which copies can be made the greater the chance that true copies will exist in the future.

We can now make clearer the idea that a propagandistic advantage can be conferred on an ideology by insulating it from criticism. Any such insulation would have to operate by enhancing the ideology's longevity, or its fecundity, or its copying fidelity, or a combination of these.

We can also see here a partial explanation for the success of Marxism and monotheistic religions that neatly harmonizes with Meyerson's identity principle. A very general theory using only few premises clearly has more copying fidelity, since there are less distinct items to learn; and being general it has greater fecundity, since it lends itself to application on many problems. Less plausibly, it could be argued that it has greater longevity, as there is less danger of the parts being separated.

Dawkins deals with two possible objections to his generalization: the question of discreteness of the units of selection; and whether competition exists between memes. It is easy to see that memes are in a state of competition. The main means of replication for a meme is a person's brain, but a brain has limited processing capacity—limited storage and recall. The other problem presents a slightly greater difficulty:

> At first sight it looks as if memes are not high-fidelity replicators at all. Every time a scientist hears an idea and passes it on to somebody else, he is likely to change it somewhat. . . . The memes are being passed on . . . in altered form. This looks quite unlike the particulate, all or nothing quality of gene transmission. It looks as though meme transmission is subject to continuous mutation, and also to blending. (Dawkins 1976, pp. 194–95)

In Chapter 3 of *The Selfish Gene* Dawkins defines the gene, not in a rigid all-or-none manner, but as a length of chromosome with just sufficient copying-fidelity to be treated as a unit by natural selection. The same sort of definition, Dawkins argues, can be used to establish the particulateness of memetic evolution. Thus, an idea-meme is defined thus:

> An entity that is capable of being transmitted from one brain to another. (p. 196)

He illustrates this with Darwin's theory of evolution. Dawkins points out that different writers have their own way of interpreting Darwin's theory. However, we can say that:

the meme of Darwin's theory is that essential basis of the idea which is held in common by all brains that understand the theory. The differences in the way people represent the theory are then by definition not part of the meme. If Darwin's theory can be subdivided into components, such that some people believe component A but not component B, while others believe B but not A, then A and B should be regarded as separate memes. If almost everybody who believes in A also believes in B—if the memes are closely "linked" to use the genetic term—then it is convenient to lump them together as one meme. (p. 196)

Does this solve the problem? Yes it does, but in a way that requires an unnecessary detour. For we know that theories are built of discrete units. These units may be called atomic propositions. It is already clear that one can have a fraction of a proposition, namely a rational fraction of a compound proposition, where the denominator is the number of atomic propositions. But one cannot have *any* sort of fraction of a proposition. For example, consider the compound proposition: 'It is raining and it is windy'. One could have one half of the conjunction: 'It is raining', but to divide further would reduce the proposition either to nonsense or simply words, which, though individually meaningful, would not express any proposition at all.

Therefore Dawkins's worry about the discreteness of memetic evolution as applied to theories was unwarranted, and his solution is superfluous. Propositional and predicate logic have already discovered the ways in which propositions can be analyzed into discrete units.

Dawkins's original intention, remember, is to argue that the evolution of memes cannot be completely explained in terms of their contribution to genetic survival:

> We do not have to look for conventional biological survival values of traits like religion, music, and ritual dancing, though these may also be present. Once the genes have provided their survival machines with brains that are capable of rapid imitation, the memes will automatically take over. We do not even have to posit a genetic advantage in imitation, though that would certainly help. All that is necessary is that the brain should be capable of imitation: memes will then evolve that exploit the capability to the full. (p. 200)

This general position is true, but in failing to look at the logic of the situation facing our ancestors (plus the variants that succumbed to it), Dawkins falls into the error of assuming that humans can be made immune (or impervious) to evidence and argument. It is therefore in his treatment of particular cases that Dawkins fails to carry through his program.

In applying his general position to religion, Dawkins attempts to show that the memes of Heaven and Hell are self-perpetuating, and also that blind faith is possible. Dawkins's account portrays religion as more rigid than it is. It is worth quoting Dawkins's argument in full. First the argument that Heaven and Hell are self-perpetuating:

> The idea of hell fire is, quite simply, self-perpetuating, because of its own deep psychological impact. It has become linked with the god meme because the two reinforce each other, and assist each other's survival in the meme pool. (p. 198)

Dawkins attributes the perpetuation of the Hellfire meme to an unanalyzed "psychological impact." This does not allow us to explore the degree to which it is open to argument. Our analysis of wishful and fearful thinking, however, allows us to explain the 'impact' of the Hellfire and God memes. Humans engage in fearful and wishful thinking about important possibilities. This tendency has evolved because it contributes to goal attainment. Admittedly, the Hellfire and God memes as such did not evolve genetically, but they arouse tenacious beliefs because of genetically evolved wishful and fearful thinking.

Being without an evolutionary analysis of fearful and wishful thinking, Dawkins finds it easy to assume that blind faith exists:

> Another member of the religious meme complex is called faith. It means blind trust, in the absence of evidence, even in the teeth of evidence. . . . The meme for blind faith secures its own perpetuation by the simple unconscious expedient of discouraging rational enquiry. (p. 198)

There are two interesting things here. Strictly, what Dawkins says is not incompatible with my thesis, but its inaccuracy makes it misleading at best. In saying that beliefs are sustained in the presence of counter-evidence Dawkins commits no error, but in failing to qualify this statement, his intention is to maintain that the beliefs would be sustained comewhat-may. But as we saw, this would not make evolutionary sense. Evolutionary theory suggests that there must be some responsiveness to argument. Beliefs cannot be blind.

Dawkins has confused two senses of being closed to argument. Clearly, one can follow a lifestyle that would reduce encounters with counter-evidence to one's beliefs. This is one sense of being closed to argument. But there still remains the question whether the human mind can be completely closed to evidence that has, as it were, got past the dogmatic lifestyle. Dawkins supplies no argument to answer this question.

There's another problem with countenancing the existence of blind faith. As Dawkins says, the survivability of a meme depends, among other things, on its competition with other memes for embodiment in people's beliefs. If blind faith really existed, then the first meme to exploit it would soon have completely dominated all minds capable of it, providing it replicated quickly enough before any rival memes exploiting blind faith emerged and attached themselves to untouched minds. There would now be only one religion. But even if there had been more than one, there would be no conversions from one to another. But since there are many religions, many conversions, and also continually developing factions in any one religion, it is hard to maintain the picture that Dawkins paints. The same points can be made about any sort of system of ideas: political, economic, or social.

Dawkins's account has many virtues, but it lacks an explanation of the interaction between logic, psychology, and genetic evolution. In his enthusiasm to show how memetic evolution can be independent of genetic evolution, Dawkins has overlooked some relationships that can easily explain the fluidity of ideological organizations.

It's perhaps an anticlimax, and not really relevant to the principle of Dawkins's argument, to point out that, as a matter of fact, belief in Hell is today one of the most fragile of religious beliefs. In the US, belief in Hell dropped from 71 percent in 2001 to 59 percent in 2008. It was observed to decline in even the most conservative of evangelical circles (Honey 2008). The evidence of the last couple of centuries suggests that people more readily give up belief in Hell than belief in Heaven, and more readily give up both than belief in God. The main reason people offer for abandoning belief in Hell is that it would be unjust of God to consign people to torture for millions of years.

These numbers mask a much bigger decline, virtually a collapse, for originally Hell was assigned for non-believers, Heaven for believers, and Hell was imagined as a place of real, unending physical torment. (According to the official doctrines of all the main branches of Christianity, people have physical bodies in the afterlife, able to experience literal pain; they are not disembodied spirits.) Most Christians who still believe in Hell believe that it is for comparatively few people who have been very wicked, like Hitler, not for those who can't swallow the doctrine of the Trinity, and that Hell is 'separation from God', rather than literal torture in a fiery pit. So much for Dawkins's casual intuition that the doctrine of Hellfire has an especially powerful "psychological impact."

FLORIAN VON SCHILCHER AND NEIL TENNANT

> The selective filter through which memes must pass has both a rational and an emotional component. And to a certain extent these interpenetrate: as Kuhn (1970) pointed out, scientists can become so emotionally committed to certain theories that they cannot abandon them when they are falsified; and almost every reader will have experienced the intense emotional and aesthetic pleasure that can be derived from artifacts that serve their functions perfectly (Schilcher and Tennant 1984, pp. 119–120).

Schilcher and Tennant clearly wish to separate the two components they see making up the selective filter: the emotional and the rational. I have already touched on the big question of the irrationality of emotion in ideologies in Chapter 3. But let's say a bit more here.

Just suppose that curiosity, the driving force behind science, is the emotional aspect of the preference for information-rich and truth-like ideas. Emotional and rational filters are then not mutually incompatible. Is the puzzle-solving that Kuhn emphasizes in science nonemotional? And is the frustration of an attempt to solve a puzzle a non-rational filter? Stubbornness born of pride or aesthetic attachment to a theory may unintentionally goad its critics into producing a much more devastating criticism of the theory than they would if its defenders abandon it at the first hint of disagreement. A few die-hard theorists may be a springboard for the launch of a very successful and popular rival theory.

Schilcher and Tennant allow some "interpenetration" between the emotional and the rational. However this may be interpreted, it suggests that there are irrational (or at least non-rational) emotions. I have already stated my view that all emotion is cognitive and all cognition is emotional, and more importantly that all our emotions are under the control of our theory of the world and our place in it.

Interpreting Schilcher and Tennant sympathetically, one might say that emotions less conducive to the search for truth may become dominant. They could have mentioned Lysenkoism, as others sometimes do in this connection. However, the case of Lysenkoism does not show that curiosity, or the preference for information-rich and truth-like theories, was completely overwhelmed. I have argued that for evolutionary reasons we are creatures of curiosity and exploration. But we also tend to promote that which is instrumental in the attainment of our goals and abandon the futile or uneconomic. It is often thought that the two are incompatible, but as I argued in Chapter 1, a theory may be useful because it is close to the truth.

For as much as we can tell, Joseph Stalin genuinely believed that Lysenko's Lamarckism would promote Soviet agriculture. However, Mendelian genetics, on account of its greater verisimilitude, was also much more useful. Because of this and because it became apparent that Lysenkoism had held up the development of Soviet agriculture for thirty years, Lysenkoism was eventually replaced by its 'bourgeois' but much more useful, because more truth-like, rival. Within Soviet Russia itself, we should recall, people were killed, on the orders of Stalin, for criticizing Lysenko. Lysenkoism was not an emotional contagion that welled up within Russian science. If Soviet society had been politically more open, there would have been serious debate, and Lysenkoism would have been discredited, just as it was in the more open West.

Memetic Evolution of an Ideology

The memetic evolution of an ideology can be broken down into the following processes: 1. the occasion, what prompts the idea; 2. its emergence; 3. its refinement; 4. its testing; and 5. its propagation. This rough model will summarise our findings so far and help us later, in Chapter 4, to analyze the use of immunizing stratagems to protect ideologies from criticism.

1. Occasion

Perception of a problem. Some problems may be simply felt, but all problems seem to be capable of being formulated. This implies that proposed solutions can always be checked against the problem in a publicly inspectable way. It is the problem or problems to which a network of ideas is addressed that gives those ideas their semblance of a coherent whole. The assumptions, themselves quite distinct logically, are intended to co-operate in the solution of the Problem or Problems.

2. Emergence

Half-baked, unjustified, spontaneously generated theory to solve the problem. The attempted solution, like a variant in Darwinian evolution, is not determined by the problem, but merely prompted by it. Neither is the theory justified: which is not surprising, since no theory can ever be justified. The ideology may use earlier concepts and theories, as Marxism drew on Ricardo and the Saint-Simonians. It may on the other hand, be radically new. But in both cases its emergence is beyond scientific prediction, for both logical and ontological reasons. Popper has argued that it is logically impossible to predict new ideas in a scientific way. Popper's argument, roughly, is that we cannot predict now what we will only know tomorrow. For such a prediction requires that we state the knowledge now, so it would be known now and not only tomorrow. Popper regards this as a good argument but not quite a logical proof, which he supplies elsewhere (Popper 1982, Section 22).

Popper's argument can be generalized to all new ideas and creations of the human mind. The argument, however, does leave room for the prediction of the general form of new ideas, or disjunctive predictions in which we can say that one of a range of possible ideas will emerge. In addition to this logical proof, there are also Popper's arguments for ontological indeterminacy (Popper 1982; 1990). The world has a random aspect, even though the randomness may have certain constraints. An ideology has a non-deterministic origin, though it may be influenced by certain factors. Each ideology lives in a sea of radically unpredictable rivals and critics, and in order to survive it improvises defenses as and when required.

3. Refinement

Attempts by intellectuals to generalize, make precise, clarify, simplify the theory. Attempts may be made to axiomatize the theory, giving it greater information content through Watkins's organic fertility requirement. Versions with loosely related assumptions will tend to be abandoned. All of which, if successful, contribute to the theory's survival value, for they make the theory easier to remember and communicate—its copyability is increased. Moreover, as explained in connection with Émile Meyerson, there is a universal need for simple and general explanations, which springs from our instinctive curiosity.

We often witness new theories, prompted by initial success in a narrow field, generalized beyond their immediate problem situation. The appeal of a simple but comprehensive explanation cannot easily be overestimated. As we saw in Chapter 1, the popularity of both religion and science is based on this important feature. A religious conversion experience may be very similar to the experience of seeing a good simple explanation in the sciences. On the other hand, as an unintended consequence, the theory becomes more vulnerable to criticism. It's easier to find counterexamples to a theory which ranges over many fields, has higher information content, than to one which has narrower scope. So in being given greater copyability the theory also becomes more vulnerable to competing ideas.

4. TESTING

Encounters with criticism. The content and timing of criticism is in many circumstances impossible to predict, and for the same reasons that new theories cannot be predicted. (Marx could not have predicted in a scientific way the occurrence in the 1870s of the marginal revolution in economics, which was to facilitate strong criticisms of his own economic theory.) The involuntary nature of the impact of counter-evidence or criticism on beliefs allows error elimination to work even on beliefs produced by wishful thinking or associated with deep commitments. The involuntariness of belief applies in all forms of rationality, so this point is quite general and applies to all types of criticism.

In *The Retreat to Commitment* Bartley starts his enquiry by assuming that there are systems of ideas that are retained regardless of the facts. This is his general position. However, when he analyzes liberal Protestantism, his case study, he finds that it is open to argument, after all. He finds that Protestant theologians agree on a number of criteria of sound criticism. Bartley makes a list of types of criticism that no network of ideas can avoid completely. In expounding these types of criticism, I will use some of my own examples to reinforce the importance of this surprising concession of Bartley's.

a. Inconsistency. Is the network internally coherent? To be more precise, does the system contain at least two statements which cannot both be true under any interpretation? Leon Festinger, thought by many to have provided an irrationalist theory of man faced by counter-evidence, makes considerable use of a similar notion in his idea of cognitive dissonance. Festinger's main point is that humans value consistency and will try to change their beliefs in order to reduce inconsistency, hardly an irrational motive; certainly not a motive that would close their beliefs to criticism.

b. Empirical refutation. Are there observable counterexamples to the system? For example, the price of unproduced goods like land, which sells for a price, are a counter-example to any simple form of the labor theory of value. Even passionately held religious systems of ideas can succumb psychologically and sociologically to empirical refutation.

Festinger, in his book *When Prophecy Fails*, supplies many examples. Festinger's theory is often adduced in arguments in the theory of ideology (by Elster and by Paul Veyne, for example). Superficially Leon Festinger's work looks contrary to my own, but it is in fact in complete agreement with what I am saying in this book.

Festinger attempted to show that groups highly committed to an idea will often increase their efforts to convince others after a disconfirmation of their beliefs. Those who have heard of Festinger remember this point. However, it is rarely remembered that he goes on to show that with further disconfirmation morale drops and the movement disintegrates. As Festinger points out, the details of the messianic movements he comments on are poorly recorded. However, two of the groups that he deals with, the Millerites and the Sabbataians, although at first increasing their proselytizing after initial disconfirmation, disintegrated after repeated disconfirmation.

The Sabbataian movement strikingly illustrates the phenomenon we are concerned with: when people are committed to a belief and a course of action, clear disconfirming evidence may simply result in deepened conviction and increased proselytizing. But there does seem to be a point at which the disconfirming evidence has mounted sufficiently to cause the belief to be rejected (Festinger, Rieken, and Schachter 1956, p. 12).

It may be retorted that these are just a few examples conforming to my thesis. But I am not looking for confirmation of my thesis, but for a refutation of the common idea that if people hold an idea with passionate commitment they are thereby closed to argument. It is interesting to find refutations of this idea in a work held by many to support the irrationalist thesis. Furthermore, my intention here is to undermine the impression, spread by poor scholarship, that Festinger's theory supports the irrationalist thesis, that under certain conditions systems of ideas are closed to argument in an important psychological sense.

The Jehovah's Witnesses are a further illustration of the impact of empirical refutation. The Witnesses have made numerous predictions for the end of the world, which have all been disappointed. So much is obvious. Few have looked closer to discover that the interpretations placed on these predictions have been radically changed. For example, when the world did not end in 1914 as they predicted the Witnesses reinterpreted the prediction to mean that "the coronation of Jesus Christ in heaven" had taken place in that year. The point is that the Witnesses knew that the predictions had failed, as they had hitherto been understood, and abandoned the original prediction. They have an extremely high turnover of membership, and new recruits are given the new predictions, not the old ones.

The Witnesses are not dominated by blind faith or by wishful thinking. Though the movement continues to grow (with a doctrine increasingly different to the original laid down by Charles Taze Russell in the nineteenth century), many thousands of individuals leave, many because of these failed predictions. During 1985, 36,638 individuals had to be disfellowshipped from the Witnesses' congregation. Here we have a clear case of the psychological, sociological, and logical impact of empirical refutation.

Ignoring the distinctions I made in my Introduction to this book, between the movement, the doctrine, the total membership, and the turnover rate of members in ideological movements, can easily give rise to misleading comments. G.A. Wells, while at other points admitting the losses that the Jehovah's' Witnesses have suffered, nevertheless says that

> the movement, like many others within and outside Christianity, has shown that it can survive destructive criticism of any kind by reinterpreting the primary data. (Wells 1988, p. 14)

If the rate of gain of new members is at least as great as the loss of members, then the movement can survive. (Despite their huge defection rate, the Jehovah's Witnesses have actually grown as a percentage of the total population.) But it hardly follows that the movement can survive destructive criticism that leads to a rate of loss greater than the rate of gain. And Wells does not present any argument to show that movements can be guaranteed against this sort of criticism. Wells fails to put sufficient emphasis on the fact that the predictions are being reinterpreted. If he did then it would be more apparent that they were being abandoned. The strange but true conclusion must be that a movement may survive empirical criticism without retaining either its members or its doctrine.

c. Unscientific character. Is the system inconsistent with scientific theories? This form of criticism is so strong that nearly all popular networks of ideas try to emulate at least the appearance of science and try to find confirmation of their doctrine in scientific theories. Their other tactic is to argue that science deals with a fundamentally different realm; but they at least feel obliged to meet this possible source of criticism. Both Marx and Freud saw their theories as scientific, and one of the most potent criticisms of their doctrines is that they fail to meet scientific standards.

d. Does the system fail to solve the original problem? This form of criticism seems to apply to all systems of ideas without exception. It can also take the form of comparing the relative success of rival ideas in solving the problem. Whether the ideas are meant as an empirical description, explanation, rhetorical device, to reinforce social cohesion, to inflame people's passions, or with some other object in view, they are open to criticism in so far as they may fail to satisfy their purpose. This is another way of looking at what I earlier called instrumental rationality.

Bartley takes the failure to solve a problem as one type of criticism. But one might even define criticism in general as the assessment of the degree to which a proposed solution is a solution to its intended problem. All problems can be formulated in a publicly inspectable way, and hence both their formulation and their intended solutions can be criticized. Some problems are extremely difficult to formulate in detail, and Russell was keen to point out that, at least in philosophy, getting the question right was more important and difficult than finding the answer. But even a vague formulation will give criticism some targets to work on.

5. Propagation

The ideas that survive testing are propagated. As I have already pointed out, those features that make an ideology an appealing explanation—clarity, generality and simplicity—also make it easier to propagate. It is at the stage of propagation that irrationality is often thought to be paramount. Sloganeering, emotionally stirring speeches, repetition—the use of advertising techniques—are all thought to be evidence of a reduced scope for rational criticism. But I argue in Chapter 3 that advertising techniques and the use of rhetorical devices are all rational and cannot protect the message from criticism.

The role of advertising and rhetoric can be understood as the production of messages which are attention-grabbing and memorable. Much of the sinister power attributed to advertising by writers such as Vance Packard lies in a failure to properly estimate the importance of these necessary features of successful advertising. I say necessary and not sufficient, because even after having contrived the most arousing and memorable form for a message it is still an open question whether the audience will agree with it.

Both Russell and Le Bon laid great stress on the role of affirmation and repetition in accounting for the acceptance and propagation of ideas. Moreover, both thought that affirmation and repetition were irrational. On our theory of advertising, however, they simply enhance the memorability of the message. The element of truth in Russell's and Le Bon's positions is that complex argument does not lend itself easily to propagation. It takes longer to transmit and is less memorable. However, there is no suggestion here that shorter arguments or assertions having been spread by affirmation and repetition are more closed to criticism. Affirmation and repetition may help spread an ideology, but they do not provide a barrier to criticism.

Each of the processes can itself be analyzed as incorporating these processes, so that, for instance, the perception of the problem and an attempt to formulate it may itself be subject to refinement and testing. Refinement may have its own problems and tests. Hence the model consists of a number of nested critical feedback loops.

Why Ideologies Look Impervious to Criticism

In Chapters 1 and 2 I have tried to show that we should expect all systems of ideas to be open to criticism in a logical, psychological, and sociological sense. In other words, there are no absolute barriers to criticism. However, this account would be seriously flawed if it did not acknowledge the fact that some systems of ideas do seem to be closed to argument and seem to persist regardless of the facts presented against them. I will summarize some points made earlier and point to some other important factors that explain this apparent imperviousness to argument.

THE COMPLEXITY OF THE LEARNING TASK

Seeing the full import of sustained criticism on a complex network like Marxism or Freudianism is a complex learning task. These systems take a long time to learn and it should not surprise us if they take a long time to unlearn. The transition from, say, Marxist to Classical liberal or the reverse obviously takes considerable time and effort.

It is rare for an ideologist to abandon one system of assumptions without a substitute. Marxists or Freudians cannot easily be drawn away from these ideas even if they see the faults in Marxism and Freudianism, for in the absence of an alternative explanation, a false system may rationally be preferred as at least an approximation to the truth.

THE STUBBORNNESS OF IMPORTANT BELIEFS

We have already seen the role of wishful thinking in sustaining a belief in a system in the face of counter-evidence. This contributes to the appearance of absolute imperviousness of some systems of ideas. Christianity, which involves the promise of Heaven and the threat of Hell has perhaps derived a great deal of its staying power from wishful and fearful thinking. From our analysis of wishful and fearful thinking we should expect this kind of stubbornness to be greater, the more important the issues at stake. And, indeed, we do observe that religions, which deal with the most important values in human life, are often the most stubborn in this sense.

Popper's 'Dogmatism' Sociologized

Popper maintained that theories should not be given up too soon, for their real strength may only become apparent at a later stage of the argument. Hence even if a Marxist or Freudian encounters overwhelming counter-argument, it may still be rational to press on with his defense of his system.

There's also a sociologized version of Popper's point about dogmatism. For every theory or ideological doctrine, there is a group of people who attack it and a group of people who defend it. Whichever side turns out to be right, both sides perform a valuable and necessary job in testing the doctrine.

The Early Loss of Intellectual Giants

There is a tendency for a moribund ideology to become more stubborn before it finally implodes, not through any deliberate strategy, but because of a sociological effect. Arguments work like judo tricks; the more intelligent the opponent the more quickly he will succumb to a sound argument. Therefore, with a seriously flawed ideology we will expect its intellectual giants to leave earlier under the impact of sound criticism. In all movements there are a relatively small number of intellectual leaders whose views are consulted, both in the event of threats to the system, to supply defenses psychological, logical, and sociological, and to interpret new events and problems in the light of the system.

When these intellectual leaders leave (or die off without being replaced by leaders of comparable caliber), the movement is liable to lose credibility to existing members and potential recruits. But more to my point here, the remaining members, being less mentally limber, will give the impression that the movement is woodenly unreceptive to criticism, and an observer who catches the movement only at this time will receive an exaggerated impression of the knee-jerk stubbornness of movements in general.

Retention of the Original Terminology

An important element in the appearance of imperviousness is the retention of old terminology. Today's Liberal Party in Britain, for example, is quite different to the Liberal Party of the early nineteenth century. Meanings and theory change while the labels linger on for far longer. It is easier to police conformity to rules about ritual, ceremony and word-use than it is to police conformity in interpretation of these symbols. The founding fathers of the orthodox Catholic church, represented by Irenaeus and Tertullian, then later reinforced by the council of Nicea, laid great emphasis on the observance of certain rituals, in contrast to the Gnostic heretics, who argued for the importance of an intuitively grasped spiritual maturity as constituting the essence of being a follower of Jesus. This may help to explain why orthodox Christianity out-competed the Gnostics' 'secret knowledge'.

When Eduard Bernstein, a friend of the late Karl Marx and Friedrich Engels, began to preach 'revisionism' in the 1890s, it was seen as an attack on the hallowed doctrines of Marxism. Revisionism was bitterly attacked by the Social Democratic leaders. It has often been observed that Revisionism was in complete conformity with the actual practice of the Social Democrats. Most of what Bernstein said was tacitly accepted by the Party and by many Marxist intellectuals. But it was presented as an explicit rejection of key postulates of Marxism. It therefore had to be officially denounced.

If you want to reform the ideas of an ideological organization, without leaving that organization by resignation or expulsion, present your revisions as the true fulfilment of the strict letter of that organization's original principles and objectives. That way, you may stand a chance of success.

Feeling Ashamed of Having Been Wrong

When argument does have a psychological impact, even to the extent of getting the propagandist to modify his message, he rarely announces the fact. People often do not like admitting error in public. Hence argument often seems impotent even when it is successful.

Shame at one's errors need not be a barrier to criticism, for it is itself open to criticism. Not being gods, we are all liable to error. There need only be shame in perpetuating error, by keeping the possibly erroneous ideas closed to public scrutiny. But that is the last thing a propagandist wants to do with his ideas in any case, for then they cannot be propagated.

Actual shame may be supported by discreet caution. The adherent of the ideology may think 'Well, that does seem to show that the ideology is wrong on those points. But who knows, if I think it over and ask one or two wiser heads for their input, I may come back round to my old way of thinking. So I won't publicly acknowledge right away that I have been convinced by these criticisms. For then I'll look a bit of an idiot when I switch back again'.

Bad Faith and Cowardice

I should not ignore the influence of outright bad faith and cowardice. People may sometimes pretend to believe in things they don't really believe in. They may be afraid of persecution by those in power, or they may gain social or business benefits from membership in an ideological movement. Perhaps in eighteenth-century England, there were many intellectuals who disbelieved in Christianity, but nevertheless acted to perpetuate Christian belief and prevent criticisms of it from being made or heard. They had goals other than the pursuit of truth, and they sometimes sacrificed the pursuit of truth to those goals. Staying alive could be one such goal. This would lead to fewer people being persuaded against Christianity, because the actions of the dishonest or cowardly would mean that anti-Christian arguments would not survive, so each generation would start afresh, with all the Christian arguments well mustered, but the critical arguments lost. Even in the Middle Ages, often perceived as an Age of Faith, we have clear evidence of widespread skepticism about God, the afterlife, and other claims of the Church.[24]

Similar influences probably occurred in Marxism and Freudianism. Gellner notes such a case in Freudianism, quoting from Anthony Storr's article 'The Concept of Cure':

> The American Psychoanalytic Association, who might be supposed to be prejudiced in favour of their own speciality, undertook a survey to test the efficacy of psychoanalysis. The results obtained were so disappointing that they were withheld from publication. (Gellner 1985, p. 161, quoted from Rycroft 1966, p. 58)

I suppose the APA knew that when revealed, this concealment of unfavorable evidence could itself serve as a strong argument against psychoanalysis, but reasoned that this would involve fewer lost believers than publication. They may not have realized that such concealed counter-evidence would acquire greater rhetorical power from its very concealment. But at least the concealment shows that the APA recognized the power of truth, for if the truth were impotent, why conceal it?

However, it's worth pointing out that the originators of the most popular ideologies—Marx, Freud, and others—have generally been sincerely convinced of the truth of the central beliefs they promulgated. Belief provides the strong motivation necessary for the arduous task of building up a system over many years.

Mendacity may serve to propagate sincere beliefs. This may seem paradoxical. A Marxist, convinced that Marxism is true on the whole, may well lie about what he regards as details in an argument in order to propagate this doctrine.[25] This hypothetical Marxist reasons that the benefits from the widespread adoption of Marxism will more than compensate for relatively small errors in Marxism. Therefore this form of mendacity is dependent on sincere belief. Freud, as has now been documented in considerable detail, habitually misrepresented the facts of his psychoanalytic cases when he wrote them up for publication. But this is quite compatible with his sincere conviction that psychoanalytic theory itself was true. It is parallel with the phenomenon, in the late nineteenth and early twentieth century, of spirit mediums who faked spirit manifestations to convince doubters, and incidentally line their own pockets, though they may well have strongly believed in the reality of the spirit world.

The influence of dishonesty or cowardliness must be qualified, for it need not prevent the emergence and spread of arguments against the relevant doctrine. In the case of Christianity, all that the cowardly needed to affirm was their belief; intellectual speculation and argument about the existence of God or some other Christian principle could then be seen as fairly innocent and harmless. David Berman points out that in eighteenth-century controversy, many writers denied that atheism was a possible state of mind for a human being, and yet went on to argue against it. Dishonesty can work in both directions.

Pressure to Conform

Certain experiments in social psychology have strengthened the popular idea that conformity is an overwhelming factor making for the preservation of ideologies. The pressure of conformity, it is said, can suppress the expression of dissent and even control belief; criticism is therefore severely limited. Once an ideology is adopted by a large number of people, it becomes virtually self-perpetuating; indeed it becomes self-reinforcing, because as the number of adherents rises the pressure to adhere rises also. This is perhaps part of what Gustave Le Bon was referring to when he spoke of the contagion of the crowd.

The most famous experiment is that conducted by Solomon Asch. Asch found that when subjects were asked to judge the relative length of vertical lines after confederates of the experimenter, posing as subjects, had given their deliberately false judgments, the subjects tended to judge wrongly in agreement with the majority. This is how the results of the experiment are often reported, but there are very important qualifications that are neglected by those (such as Hassan) who use Asch's experiment to support the irrationalist thesis.

If the subject is presented with only one ally, his tendency to conform to an erroneous judgment by the majority is reduced sharply (Asch 1951, pp. 117–190). If there is unanimity, then the size of the group need not be very large to elicit maximum conformity. Surprisingly, increasing the size of the majority beyond three people does not lead to increased conformity.

In the original Asch experiment, the subjects had to express their judgments in the presence of the majority. There was no way, therefore in which to test for sincerity. There's a huge difference between actually believing what the other group members say they believe, and pretending to believe it to go along with the group. But some accounts fudge this distinction, making it appear that most people can't see that one line is the same length as another, if other people tell them it's longer. Further experiments found that a minority's conformity is mostly mere pretense: the greater the privacy in which to express judgments after exposure to a false majority view, the less conformity there is (Deutsch and Gerard 1955; Mouton, Blake, and Olmstead 1956; Argyle 1957).

Conformity is a factor in the apparent imperviousness of an ideology to criticism, but a much over-rated influence. An ideology will be faced with criticism from within the ranks if only two of its adherents dissent from the ideology, because the leaders cannot suppress it simply by appeal to the majority or by increasing membership. And even isolated members who reject parts of the ideology and find no one to take the same view as themselves, will go on harboring their private dissent, while perhaps outwardly conforming—for the time being.

[3]
Does Emotion Cloud Our Reason?

Can intense emotions associated with ideologies make the ideologists irrational and therefore insulated against all criticism? And would the ideology then be more likely to spread? Almost all writers take the irrationality of ideological emotion for granted, but I intend to show that the ideologies at issue are rational (though they may be mistaken or even foolish) and open to argument.

The implicit assumption of much talk about ideology is that ideological emotion is thoughtless and therefore independent of theory, and therefore critical argument is irrelevant for it has no target. I grant that intense emotion engendered by an ideology may impair the appreciation of critical argument, but I insist that argument is always relevant because our emotions are under the control of our theory of the world and our place in it. When people are overwhelmed with emotional shock, they seem oblivious to the facts because of the intense emotion, but this may again be an example of the fact that it takes time to absorb the import of the event. Shakespeare put it well:

> Thou know'st we work by wit and not by witchcraft, and wit depends on dilatory time. (*Othello*, II, iii, 376–79)

It's just because our emotions are imbued with theory that it takes time for critical facts or arguments to be appreciated. We can imagine that bad news can bring shock after shock, until it is all fully taken in. For example, it may be that a man's wife is leaving him when he has always loved her dearly, and he had thought that she valued him likewise. He discovers the facts, one by one and each may give him a fresh shock. She has another man. She had been having an affair for two years. The children also hate him, and they are also moving out with her. She has also emptied their joint account and given all the money to her boyfriend. His life savings were in it, and he has no other money. His yearly paycheck is automatically paid into that account, and she waited to leave till he had just been paid a year in advance; an arrangement that his wife got him to negotiate with his boss just two weeks previously. Well, the first item may well take some time to adjust to, and that just may crowd out all the other aspects for a while. He may even stop reading at that point or he may read on but simply feel that first point so greatly that he misses the import of the later points. There is an element of distraction, but there is also the time required to work out the innumerable implications and ramifications of the shocking revelations. This is a logical and theoretical task.

Because our emotions have such a theoretical basis, they are subject to the rational filters I outlined in Chapter 2. It makes evolutionary sense that our emotions are under the control of our theory of the world and subject to the rational filters, for how else might they be made appropriate to subtle, complex, remote and even merely hypothetical circumstances? Inappropriate emotions lead organisms to shun the beneficial and embrace the harmful, and as a probable, though not necessary, consequence impair genetic reproduction. Of course, human beings are often foolish, but this does not mean that they cannot correct their errors; it only means that they are fallible and may take time to readjust their emotions to the facts.

Ideologies as Rationalizations of Irrational Emotions

There are two closely associated ideas about the role of emotion and morality in the emergence and spread of ideologies, both of which are thought to support the idea that ideologies are closed to criticism. The first is that ideologies spring from and thrive on irrational emotions, emotions that are not subject to reason, abstract theory, or argument: gut feelings of anger, resentment, envy, or greed, unadorned by ideas. In this theory emotion and thought are placed in radically different compartments. Pareto seems to have held such a theory.

Raymond Boudon states that Pareto thought that ideologies were rationalizations of feelings, and outlines what he conjectures to be the general argument behind Pareto's theory:

1. **people believe in the objective truth of all kinds of propositions, both unproved and unprovable;**

2. **by definition, their conviction cannot be founded on the objective truth of these propositions;**

3. **therefore it must have its basis in an irrational act of faith;**

4. **which can only be based on feelings.** (Boudon 1989, p. 60)

Boudon argues that both Durkheim and Weber also held this sort of theory. He makes a good case that it is implicit in Durkheim's discussion of respect for the flag (see below), but Weber's analysis of respect for charismatic leadership attributes a leader's success to his followers' assessment of his actual performance.

The second idea is that what is most important or even necessary and sufficient in the emergence and spread of ideologies is a high level of agitated, usually violent, emotion evoked by the ideologue in potential followers. Those who espouse this view have in mind the turbulent emotions of the parades and rallies that adorn political regimes and the riots and assassinations that attend their demise. Can the emotions that drive the terrorist to plant a bomb, the protester who goes on hunger-strike, and the kamikaze pilot all be rational? Surely, it is thought, such emotional people, especially the violent ones, are outside the scope of abstract theory and argument, and therefore beyond the reach of criticism.

Even if ideologies appeal to emotions and passionate moral aspirations, this is no insurmountable obstacle to abstract critical argument. Even the most violent and anti-intellectual ideologies are steeped in abstract theory and argument, and their origin and spread is traceable to conspicuously intellectual sources. All the great ideological movements have had rather undramatic beginnings with the writing of an abstract text by some obscure scribbler fascinated by some abstract problem, and they have been sustained or demoralized by abstract argument.

The intellectual content of even anti-intellectual ideologies is no surprise once it is realized that all emotion is cognitive and all cognition is emotional. There is no thoughtless emotion, and no emotionless thought. All thoughts, even of particular things, can only be constructed from abstract ideas and arguments. It seems implausible to suggest that anti-intellectual ideologies arouse people on account of being empty of meaning. It is hard to avoid meaning. Even 'nonsense' poetry or humor excites us on account of the meaning that we impute to it. Caroll's "Jabberwocky." for example, contains many words that are not in the dictionary or part of any natural language, yet the poem conjures up in our mind all sorts of strange creatures.

Some writers, such as Durkheim, might say that since at least some emotion is instigated by particular objects, abstract theory is sometimes irrelevant. If this type of emotion were responsible for maintaining ideologies, then they would be immune to theoretical attacks against the emotion. However, Popper has argued that even the identification of particular objects involves abstract theory that goes beyond the immediate observational data. Popper argues that even to describe something as simple and concrete as a glass of water involves attributing to it a set of dispositions that have not yet been fulfilled:

> The statement, "here is a glass of water" cannot be verified by any observational experience. The reason is that the universals which appear in it cannot be correlated with any specific sense-experience. . . . By the word "glass", for example, we denote physical bodies which exhibit law-like behavior, and the same holds for the word "water". (Popper 1934, p. 95)

This is a broad notion of theory, but a defensible one. The extension of the notion of theory is parallel to the extension of the notion of information, allowing us to speak of computer programs or genes as containing information. Indeed, just as the concept of information has been severed from its connection with language, Popper's broad notion of theory allows us to conjecture that even a cat and mouse have instinctive theories about each other's law-like behavior, theories which guide their responses to one another. A corollary is that even if an ideology or some of its components are non-linguistic responses to particular objects, as their emotional elements might be, a theoretical attack may still be appropriate.

Even if we admit that ideological emotion can sometimes spring from particular objects, this does not by itself make the ideology immune to theoretical criticism. A better example in this context would be the statement 'This is my father'. A father is clearly a particular object that arouses much emotion, but it is a particular object that is only understood through a complex and not easily testable theory, a theory that goes far beyond immediate experience. One can easily see how this line of argument can be extended to straightforwardly ideological notions such as 'leader', 'follower', 'heretic', 'class traitor', and so forth. Thus theories that ascribe the success of an ideology to a charismatic leader who arouses deep emotions, or to a particular object such as a flag cannot exclude the relevance of theory to that propagandistic success. For it is the theories held by the leader's audience that makes him a charismatic leader and that endow the flag with its emotional significance.

Thus I agree with the Stoic idea that "men are not moved by things but by the views they take of them" (Epictetus), though I argue (as

Epictetus would no doubt have agreed) that the views we have of things are at least partly explained by the way things are. Therefore the way we feel about things is at least partly explained by the way things are. Perhaps closer to my position is that of Dubois:

> If we wish to change the sentiments it is necessary before all to modify the idea which has produced them. (Quoted in Beck 1976)

I add that changing the ideas is not only necessary but sufficient, and moreover is always possible.

It follows that abstract critical argument is always relevant. On the other hand, emotion does have an effect on the spread of an ideology. So although truth and validity are always relevant they are not the only relevant factors. Nevertheless, I argue that the effect of emotion on the competitive strength of an ideology can be analyzed in terms of a basic theory of advertising, and that such an analysis shows how it need not be a barrier to criticism.

One may distinguish for the purpose of argument between the emergence, maintenance, and abandonment of an ideology. Even if I concede that ideologies spring from and are maintained by noncognitive emotion, I can still argue that critical argument can prompt the abandonment of any ideology. Maintaining an ideology would then be like the reflex function of the heart which continues until voluntary action brings it to an end. Some subset of emotions may be like the reflex functions of the body: they will control certain behaviors without conscious thought, but conscious thought can intervene at any moment to override the reflex, just as a coughing reflex might be consciously suppressed out of regard for etiquette, at a concert or a formal dinner.

We must concede that intense emotion may sometimes impair reasoning, but this does not mean that it eliminates it. Conceding an element of the irrationalist case, I grant that an argument may engender an emotional attitude so intense that some subsequent critical arguments requiring sharp, coherent, complex thought become ineffective. But the proposer of the irrationalist thesis must grant as common observation that intense emotional perturbations cannot last a lifetime, though a disposition to such emotions may. Therefore, there will be times when the appreciation of even difficult arguments will not be prevented by intense emotion. I will also argue that this barrier depends on the correct identification of criticism, which, as we saw in Chapter 1, is not always easy.

Hitler's Theory of Propaganda

Adolf Hitler held that successful propaganda is based on appeals to emotions devoid of abstract content, and in particular to agitated or violent emotions. Hitler is worth quoting at length since, as he was so remarkably successful in achieving power, his views on propaganda are regarded by many as at least close to the truth. Hitler expresses quite eloquently ideas about persuasion still held independently by many worldly-wise intellectuals of all political affiliations.

> The broad masses of a nation are not made up of professors and diplomats. Since these masses have only a poor acquaintance with abstract ideas, their reactions lie more in the domain of the feelings, where the roots of their positive and negative attitudes are implanted. They are susceptible only to a manifestation of strength which comes definitely either from the positive or negative side, but they are never susceptible to any half-hearted attitude that wavers between one pole and the other. The emotional grounds of their attitude furnish the reason for their extraordinary stability. It is always more difficult to fight successfully against faith than against knowledge. Love is less subject to change than respect. Hatred is more lasting than mere aversion. The driving force that has brought about the most tremendous revolutions on this earth have never been a body of scientific teaching which has gained power over the masses, but always a devotion which has inspired them, and often a kind of hysteria which has urged them to action. (Hitler 1939, p. 283)

According to Hitler, the most successful movements are those with the most intense or agitated, abstractionless emotion behind them, for these are most lasting intrinsically, and the most resistant to any counter-appeals. I suspect that many theorists have been influenced by this view of ideological change.

Edmund Wilson, famed for his eloquent exposition of Marxism, expressed his predilection for a similar theory of propaganda and ideology:

> You cannot reason an English Tory into a conviction that the lower classes are not unalterably inferior to the upper; and it would be useless to dispute with a Nazi over the innate inferiority of non-Nordics. . . . you can only appeal to them by methods which, in the last analysis, are moral and emotional. (Wilson 1967, p. 389)

It was, in Wilson's view, Marx's moral genius, inherited from his Jewish background, to have grasped this truth and exploited it to the full. The persuasive power of Marx's *Capital*, we are to believe, has no connection with its claims in economic theory, or its historical assertions; it lies rather in its ability to instil a moral fervor to abolish capitalism and institute communism. Zombie-like the proletariat or its leadership somehow acquires from *Capital* a hatred for capitalism and on they march to the revolution.

It's surprising that Wilson should have overlooked cases such as William Ewart Gladstone, the greatest of English Liberal politicians, who began his parliamentary career as a High Tory, and reasoned his way out of Tory doctrine and into classical liberalism, to which he then made an enormous practical contribution.

The idea that one cannot reason with a Nazi or a racist is one of the key ideas behind the intimidatory tactics of many left-wing student groups. These groups reject free speech. Their resort to physically obstructing those who want to attend a speech by a racist or chanting during such speeches flows from their disillusionment with argument. But if argument and reason have nothing to do with racism, it is somewhat ironic that they go to so much trouble to suppress arguments in favor of racism. Or is it being suggested that one can be persuaded by argument into racism but not out of it? I have found that, when prompted, some members of these student groups suggest that argument is a waste of time because racism is instinctive. In this vision, Apartheid and Nazi Germany are a product of instinct rather than theory.

Racism may build on an instinctive suspicion of strangers, but such a suspicion is hardly sufficient to explain those particular regimes. Such glib attempts to understand a phenomenon they are trying to eliminate is probably the sad but predictable effect of an inveterate contempt for argument and debate. To such people, racists are animals without any regard to theories and argument, who, therefore, can only be opposed by physical obstruction and censorship.

Intellectual Elites and Emotional Masses

Hitler did see a role for abstract argument and theory in propaganda, but this was confined to the intellectual elite. Serge Chakotin, a socialist leader at the time of the Nazis' rise to power and pupil of the Russian scientist Pavlov, held very similar thoughts on political propaganda.

In his study of totalitarian political propaganda, *The Rape of the Masses*, Chakotin portrays the masses as puppets of leaders, "soul engineers," who supposedly make use of suggestion to manipulate them.

Some of the ideas of Hitler and Chakotin were anticipated by Durkheim in 1915 in his book *Elementary Forms of the Religious Life*.

Although Durkheim was more concerned with the analysis of primitive cultures, he occasionally applies his thoughts on totemic religion to phenomena such as the glorification of the national flag and charismatic leadership. Durkheim's theory suffers from a vague distinction between the abstract and the concrete and an odd variant of Pavlov's theory of conditioning. Both Chakotin's and Durkheim's theories succumb to more recent research which has refuted the absolute dichotomy between emotion and cognition.

Speaking of suggestion Chakotin says:

> The question of suggestion, especially through the spoken word, or through any symbol, plays an important part here. . . . If we analyze the possibilities of resistance to suggestion—a question, as we shall see, which is of the utmost importance—we find that, apart from pathological cases of congenital inadequacy or sickness or poisoning, these possibilities are largely a function of culture . . . which makes up the psychical mechanism of the individuals concerned. Ignorance is the best medium for the formation of masses who easily lend themselves to suggestion. This is a capital fact in the domain of politics and the social order. . . . It is often said that consciousness varies inversely with susceptibility to suggestion. (Quoted in Walsby 1947, pp. 51–52)[26]

Chakotin divides communities into two classes: 1. those who are largely immune to suggestion but who are receptive to theoretical, rational, persuasive argument and to doctrine; 2. those who are passive, non-intellectual, unobjective, or subjective, and greatly susceptible to emotion and suggestion. The relative numerical proportions of the two classes are 1 to 10 respectively: ten per cent. are active and thinking, ninety per cent passive and emotional.

Since there were two sorts of persons, Chakotin reasoned, there must be two forms of propaganda:

> one addressed to the 10 percent who are sufficiently sure of themselves to be able to resist crude suggestion, and the other to the passive 90 percent., who are accessible to suggestion, especially suggestion working on the first (combative) instinct. . . . These two forms of propaganda, addressed to these two groups of persons, thus differed in principle. The first acted by persuasion, by reasoning; the second by suggestion, by means of fear, now of its positive compliment, enthusiasm or excitement, sometimes ecstatic, sometimes furious; these reactions also proceeded from the combative instinct. (pp. 53–54)

Here we see loud echoes of Hitler's theory.

Chakotin stresses that the intellectual ten percent of the population require propaganda with an idea behind it because they are "immune" to emotional propaganda:

> Far be it from us to suggest, indeed, that propaganda of any sort can usefully be carried on with no idea behind it, merely an appropriate technique. The "10 percent." must be enlightened and guided by some idea.... (p. 54)

But the ninety percent are converted by purely emotional appeals through suggestion, without any idea behind it. Such a view is clearly opposed to Epictetus's theory and more in accord with those of Pareto, Weber, and Durkheim. Chakotin constantly refers to the use of "signs" and "symbols" to carry through what he calls suggestion. Durkheim's flag may be an instance of one of these suggestive, but untheoretically interpreted, signs.

Durkheim holds that abstractions are a net hindrance to the arousal and maintenance of what we might call ideological emotion and behavior, such as respect for the flag and nationalism. Such behaviors, Durkheim contends, are aroused not by abstractions but by concrete symbols. The emotions that something arouses in us spontaneously attach themselves to the symbol that represents them. There are both abstract and concrete ways of representing something, but these emotions attach themselves more readily to the concrete symbols. This is because representing something abstractly is laborious and confusing, whereas a concrete symbol is simple, definite and easily representable. At this point Durkheim introduces an odd assumption to the effect that the emotion originally aroused by something attaches itself exclusively to its concrete symbol. Thus a country, Durkheim says, may arouse in someone feelings of loyalty, and this feeling will become associated with the country's flag and other signs of nationality; but then these feelings of loyalty may be completely transferred to the flag and other symbols.

> Whether one standard remains in the hands of the enemy or not does not determine the fate of the country, yet the soldier allows himself to be killed to regain it. He loses sight of the fact that the flag is only a sign, and that it has no value in itself, but only brings to mind the reality it represents; it is treated as if it were the reality itself. (Durkheim 1915, p. 220)

The flag in Durkheim's analysis is a totemic symbol, which is a sign of common moral life and communion. As such, individuals imbue it with a mysterious force that is felt to transcend their society even though it actually receives all its apparent power from its capacity to represent society's moral force. Durkheim's analysis of the totem is thus rather like Feuerbach's analysis of the God of the Christian religion, in which God is an unconscious projection of man's idealized virtues and power, but is nonetheless felt as a transcendent power.

I think Durkheim has captured some truth about emotional symbols. Some symbols are clearly better able to represent and arouse emotions. Good novelists are keenly aware of this.

Durkheim's analysis of the soldier's behavior is a little unfair as he fails to consider any possible tactical rationale behind a perilous or life-sacrificing attempt to regain the standard from the enemy. The fate of the country does not depend on who holds a particular standard, but then, the fate of the country rarely depends on any isolated individual action by a person of lowly rank. But winning each battle of a war is partly dependent on morale. Seeing the enemy with the flag brings the image of defeat to mind. The heroic soldier may be trying to correct this demoralizing state of affairs. More importantly for my case, would the soldier correct his behavior on re-evaluating the costs of his action? Even if we make the fantastic assumption that the soldier is only concerned with wresting flags from the enemy, it seems incredible that he would attempt to rescue a standard if he thought it impossible, or that as a remote consequence more flags would fall into the hands of the enemy, or that letting the enemy keep a flag would lead to their defeat. In fact soldiers are concerned with other possible costs to their action, such as the loss of other men, especially in their own company.

The psychological theory behind Durkheim's analysis is surprisingly poor. When he talks about a symbol being charged with the feeling originally aroused by the object of the symbol, one is reminded of Pavlov's theory of the conditioned response. But then he says the feeling may be completely transferred to the symbol, and for this strange assumption he offers no argument. The theory of classical conditioning is the most elaborate version of Durkheim's sketchy associationist theory of emotion. Let us see how it fares in comparison.

In Pavlov's theory the unconditioned stimulus remains effective after the conditioned stimulus has been made effective. Although Pavlov's theory has been refuted in some details, this implication of Pavlov's theory has remained unrefuted and forms part of the current theory of conditioning.

In conditioning, either an unconditioned or conditioned stimulus may be used to establish a conditioned stimulus. The original stimulus could become inactive only if it were not the stimulus to an instinctively unconditioned response; that it itself has been made effective only through conditioning. But this ineffectiveness is brought about by the process of extinction, in which the conditioned stimulus is repeatedly presented in the absence of the original (conditioned or unconditioned) stimulus. But the extinction of a conditioned stimulus will transfer to any stimuli that have been conditioned with it. Hence if one's emotional response to a country depends on a set of unconditioned stimuli that forms a part of that country then that country will always have this emotional significance; if, on the other hand, these stimuli are purely conditioned, then if they become extinct any other stimuli associated with them (such as a flag) will also become extinct. In either case Durkheim's hypothesis of a complete transfer of all emotion from the original emotional object to its symbolic representation is thwarted.

It is not obvious that less abstract concepts or symbols are always more effective in eliciting an emotional reaction than more abstract symbols. Extreme fear may be conditioned to the very abstract concept of redness. People develop phobias about open spaces, itself a fairly abstract concept. Neither is it clear that the most difficult concepts to fully represent are always the most abstract: it may be easier to form an image of the color green than it is to represent to oneself all the important features about one's wife, friend, or brother, and again, these are objects of much emotion. We can imagine that changes in some of the abstract features of the world would strike terror into the most insensitive: if, for example, people could walk through normally impenetrable objects. The terror would not be lessened by the fact that these changes are very abstract.

Psychological research, on non-human animals at least, shows that the range of conditioned responses that can be established depends on the species of animal. Animals display a certain selectivity in which stimuli can be paired with which responses. Rats, for instance, will learn to avoid saccharine-flavoured water whose ingestion has been followed by illness induced by X-radiation, but visual or auditory stimuli cannot be so conditioned. Contrariwise, an avoidance response to electric shocks to the feet can be conditioned to auditory and visual stimuli but not to saccharine (Garcia and Koelling 1966, pp. 123–24). Perhaps there is selectivity of emotional learning to certain ranges of stimuli in humans, a selectivity which is not so easily captured, as Durkheim suggests, in the contrast between abstract and concrete concepts. The selectivity in humans' emotional response may, as with the rats, cut across the distinction between abstract and concrete.

Both Chakotin and Durkheim rely on the notion of a purely noncognitive emotion, which presumably is equivalent to the physiological arousal we associate with emotions. But it is hard to see what use purely physiological arousal can be either to a politician like Hitler or to someone concerned with long-term propaganda. If the aim is to induce people to organize and work toward a given goal, then simply increasing their respiration rate and heart beat will be futile. If the aim is to spread ideas then, again, a purely physiological stimulus with no ideas behind it will be useless. A major weakness of Chakotin's and Durkheim's theory is that the relationship between emotion and cognition is insufficiently explored.

Evidence from Psychology

Experimental research into emotion suggests that in a normal state cognition and emotion are invariably connected. Everyone agrees that an emotion can involve both physiological states—blood pressure, heart rate, perspiration—and thoughts, for example, feeling angry toward someone for some reason. Now research seems to show that these two aspects of emotion can only be separated under the influence of drugs or surgery. In these abnormal conditions people can, for example, know that they are in great danger, but remain quiescent; or when injected with a drug that causes the above physiological perturbations, seventy percent of subjects report no emotional experience, the rest report what may be called pseudo-emotions, that is, they say such things as 'I feel as if I were angry' (Maranon 1924).

More recently, Schachter and Singer tested the theory that both cognition and physiological arousal were necessary for a genuine experience of emotion. Simplifying their report somewhat, they found that subjects injected unknowingly with epinephrine, a drug that stimulates the above physiological correlates of emotion by activating the sympathetic nervous system, experienced anger or euphoria depending on their interpretation of these physiological conditions plus environmental clues. Subjects knowingly injected with epinephrine and with an explanation of its effects on physiology did not experience anger or euphoria. Subjects not injected with epinephrine but presented with the same environmental clues also did not experience anger or euphoria. Both arousal and interpretation were necessary and sufficient for emotional experience (Schachter and Singer 1969, pp. 379–399). Schachter conjectures that arousal of the sympathetic nervous system is necessary for emotion but does not provide any distinctive cues with which to tell different emotions apart. The various emotional states are distinguished by our cognitions about the world.

High Arousal Interferes with the Transmission of New Ideas

High levels of arousal will certainly interfere with propaganda. Experiments have consistently born out what is known as the Yerkes-Dobson law relating learning efficiency to degree of cortical arousal, and this law is not dependent on the type of learning involved. As arousal is increased from a state of sleep, performance increases up to an optimum point beyond which further arousal leads to a deterioration in performance. Plotted on a graph the relationship is expressed as an inverted U-shape.

The Yerkes-Dobson law is really a precise statement of common observation. People rarely excel when half-asleep or paralyzed by fear or anger. It is ludicrous to suppose that Kautsky, Lenin, Trotsky, Stalin, Mao, or Castro absorbed Marx's writings in a frenzied state of emotional arousal. *Capital* alone takes weeks of sober, concentrated reading. If one accepts that intense emotion can distract even exceptionally astute minds, Chakotin's ten percent, from the learning of an ideology, it's hard to suppose that intense emotion can help those less skilled in the handling of abstract ideas, Chakotin's ninety percent.

Intense Emotion Transmits Ideas Already Accepted

While rejecting Chakotin's theory, I will try sympathetically to salvage some truth from it. While high arousal may be detrimental to the learning of complex and novel ideas, it may assist the transmission or reinforcement of simple, more familiar ideas. Experiments have shown that the more familiar or simpler the items to be learned the higher is the optimum level of arousal. So the propagandist's method of whipping up of emotion (and I grant that the type of emotion may not matter much) could assist in getting people to do something simple or something that they are already predisposed to do. The ironic result is that emotionally charged speeches are only useful in getting people to act on ideas that they already accept or on some watered-down version of the full-blown doctrine. Given that intellectuals, Chakotin's ten percent, are more familiar with the abstract, it follows from the Yerkes-Dobson law that they could make more use of higher levels of emotion in the transmission of new ideas than could the non-intellectuals, Chakotin's ninety percent.

Intense emotion may help sustain a position once acquired. Racism, for example, may be instilled with calm argument or assertion, but once acquired may generate intense emotion that interferes with the understanding of critical arguments. But in general intense emotion cannot be used to instil the new idea in the first place (whether it really is a radically new idea or a subtle combination of old ideas). What the irrationalist thesis gains on the roundabout it loses on the slide.

It must be noted, however, that this barrier only applies in those cases in which the racist has correctly identified the critical bearing of a message. This leaves open the possibility that he can learn something that is only later identified as having a critical bearing. This is a common phenomenon. It is common because almost everyone possesses a vast number of moral and factual assumptions about the world which cannot themselves be fully surveyed, let alone checked for all the implications that would flow from combining new ideas and theories in various logical ways with them. Simply determining whether idea c follows logically from a theory T is often an arduous task.

Suggestion as Simple Assertion

Chakotin's notion of suggestion is vague, so we can only propose alternative defendable interpretations and examine each in turn. The notion seems to be open to two interpretations: suggestion as groundless assertion, and suggestion as implicit argument. On either interpretation, however, Chakotin's theory looks doubtful.

If suggestion is simple assertion, then it cannot really be called non-intellectual, unless Chakotin is drawing attention to a matter of degree: that some people are better able and inclined to cope with more complex and abstract arguments and debate. But in that case the force of his argument is vitiated. All explicit arguments are connected series of assertions; one could call them complex assertions. In this sense reason is still required for interpretation of the assertions and there is not a vast gulf between argument and suggestion. If suggestion is meant to refer to what is implied by the propagandist's assertions, then again it doesn't seem apt to describe this as non-intellectual or as purely emotional, because the implications of an assertion are a matter of logic, and the mind's answer, right or wrong, to a problem of logic cannot be reduced to physiological arousal, but involves reasoning. And if it involves reasoning, there is then an avenue for criticism to undermine the ideology sustained by suggestion.

Western culture is permeated by justificationism, the idea that reason or rationality is equivalent to the giving of grounds for one's assertions, plus the idea that to criticize a position is to show how it violates a standard of justification (Bartley 1984). Bald assertions without reasons are taken to be less rational or reasonable. This may have been one of the ideas guiding Chakotin when he contrasts suggestion and reason and Pareto when he argued that if ideologies are unsupported by proven propositions they must be supported by irrational feelings. Others who have attributed great importance to suggestion have explicitly defined suggestion in this way. For example, J.A.C. Brown defines suggestion as

> the attempt to induce in others the acceptance of a belief without giving any self-evident or logical ground for its acceptance. (Brown 1972, p. 25)

Others have taken the use of simple assertion in propaganda as irrational. Bertrand Russell had this to say:

> Non-rational propaganda, like the rational sort, must appeal to existing desires, but it substitutes iteration for the appeal to fact. The opposition between a rational and an irrational appeal is, in practice, less clear-cut than in the above analysis. Usually there is some rational evidence, though not enough to be conclusive; the irrationality consists in attaching too much weight to it. (Russell 1938, p. 144)

And how are people led to attach too much weight to it? By their desire and the frequent repetition of the message:

> Belief, when it is not simply traditional, is a product of several factors: desire, evidence, and iteration. (p. 144)

Vilfredo Pareto went so far as to define ideologies as scientifically unprovable positions and therefore based on irrational faith, which in turn can only be based on feelings. Behind every ideology there are simply feelings: the ideology is simply an attempt to rationalize these feelings by invalid scientific reasoning. Such spurious reasonings Pareto called "derivations." Pareto thought that people did not want to admit that their feelings on an issue were without scientific proof because they thought that an unprovable position was without authority.

Brown's and Pareto's position is quickly vitiated once it is realized that there can be no self-evident grounds for a belief or assertion, and in general no certain proof of any non-tautological statement. Moreover, the merit of science does not lie in its being able to prove its conjectures, but in its being able to offer better explanations of the world and in keeping its conjectures open to criticism.

I agree with Popper and Bartley that there are no self-evident grounds for any belief. The idea of self-evidence was introduced to avoid the main problem of justificationism. If every assertion has to be justified then there is no end to justifying any assertion since each of the assertions provided to justify the first assertion itself requires another for its own justification, and so on ad infinitum. The only justificationist alternative to this infinite regress, a vicious circle in which the justifying proposition is itself justified by the proposition it justifies, is equally untenable.

The notion of self-evidence was meant to avoid this infinite regress and vicious circularity. But no candidates for self-evidence have survived a critical examination. Intuition is liable to error and perception is liable to illusions and hallucinations. Even work in mathematics and logic is hypothetical, since, as Quine put it, one never knows what one has overlooked. All positions are irretrievably hypothetical. As Xenophanes put it, everything is but a woven web of guesses.

It follows that Chakotin's division of the community into those susceptible to and those not susceptible to suggestion collapses if suggestion is defined simply as the assertion of some position, for as we saw in Chapter 1, all argument (no matter how complex) must take some assumptions for granted.

Russell's position does not rely on the notion of self-evidence, but of rationally apportioning weight to evidence. It is thought that to have one's beliefs grow stronger or weaker in proportion to one's desire is irrational. However, if one views wishful and fearful thinking as possibly useful heuristics, ways in which we can pursue our goals more efficiently, the appearance of irrationality dissolves. Humans, like other animals, seek their goals by producing and testing hypotheses about the world. Because we're fallible and liable to make mistakes not only in our initial hypotheses but also in assessing the evidence provided in the tests (for example, we may wrongly interpret the non-sighting of some prey as the non-existence of prey in the neighbourhood) we might attain our objectives if we hold onto our beliefs even in the face of some apparent counter-evidence. If our ancestors had been disposed to give up their search for food or shelter at the first disappointed expectation, they would not have been our ancestors.

SUGGESTION AS IMPLICIT ARGUMENT

We could also interpret Chakotin's argument as referring to the fact that, particularly among those with little interest in theoretical ideas *per se*, much argument remains at an implicit level. Often, one or more of the premises of an argument will be left unspoken, the speaker leaving it up to his listener to supply the silent premises. The speaker may even neglect to assert the conclusion, again leaving it up to the listener to supply the unspoken item. Either of these omissions may be for rhetorical effect or simply for convenience. In all of this, reason is evidently needed, even though not all the steps are spelled out.

But one might still ask whether the unstated premises are protected from criticism on account of being hidden from view. This is unlikely, as they are unvoiced precisely because both parties know that both parties accept them; each knows what the other is thinking. But what of outsiders, potential new converts? They may be ignorant of the unspoken items and so communications directed at them cannot make the same use of such arguments without spelling them out. Hence we have the paradoxical conclusion that mere suggestion cannot be used to obtain new recruits to the movement. Naked suggestions cannot easily be transmitted outside the initiated to a wider public, so any ideology that assumes this form will run a risk of ultimate extinction. Moreover, it is more difficult to police implicit assumptions and interpretations, which may then easily stray from the original position. So although they may be safe from outside criticism, they are also safe from maximum propagation and are subject to transmission errors within the initiated. Such is the logic of the propagandist's situation.

Influencing versus Determining Public Opinion

Chakotin's idea that the masses are the puppets of their leaders, of their 'soul engineers', seems to be a gross exaggeration. A more defensible position is that the authority that any leader has is imputed to him by his followers by virtue of a theory they hold about him, and the followers accept or reject commands from the leader in accord with this theory. Moreover, this theory is open to revision in the light of arguments and experience, both moral and factual. This position is in accord with the modern economic theory of democracy.

Boudon assumes that both Durkheim and Weber agree that charismatic leadership overrides reason. However, Weber's position on this point is closer to my own since Weber attributes a leader's authority to his actual performance: if the leader fails to lead his followers to victory or to prosperity, his authority will be taken away from him by his disappointed followers:

> He must perform miracles if he wants to be a prophet, acts of heroism if he wants to be a leader in war. Above all his divine mission must 'prove' itself in that those who entrust themselves to him must prosper. If they do not, then he is obviously not the master sent by the gods. (Weber 1968, p. 229)

As an example, Weber cites the Chinese monarch's extreme deference to his people, sometimes shown by committing suicide, on failing to extricate his people from a calamity such as a flood or defeat in war.

Durkheim's almost mystical position can be taken as representative of theories attributing charismatic leadership to factors impervious to reason:

> We say that an object, whether individual or collective, inspires respect when the representation expressing it in the mind is gifted with such a force that it automatically causes or inhibits actions, without regard for any consideration relative to their useful or injurious effects. When we obey somebody because of the moral authority which we recognize in him, we follow out his opinions, not because they seem wise, but because a certain sort of physical energy is imminent in the idea that we form of this person, which conquers our will and inclines it in the indicated direction. (Durkheim 1976, p. 207)

At least Durkheim, unlike Chakotin, recognizes that moral authority is given by the follower and not imposed on him by the leader. Durkheim fails to analyze what this "idea that we form of the person" may amount to.

Boudon agrees with Durkheim's analysis, adding the qualification that the feeling of respect for a leader may have something to do with his message. Nevertheless, Boudon says, what is said is believed because it is the leader who says it, and this is because leaders are often thought to be infallible (Boudon 1989, p. 56).

I have already dealt in Chapter 2 with the general question of whether humans can act without regard to the feasibility and costs of their actions. However, we might ask whether a command from a charismatic leader would always be obeyed if either the follower thought that obeying it would render him incapable of obeying any more commands or he thought that the command conflicted with another command, or that obeying it would endanger his chosen leader. Given conflicting commands, the follower must make the choice by himself since there can be no reliance on command, and how are we to explain his choice except in terms of his reason? And if we're going to assume that he is rational when given conflicting imperatives, it seems arbitrary to assume that he is irrational otherwise.

Even identifying a leader is a theoretical achievement. Whether someone is the leader is a question that cannot be settled conclusively on immediate inspection, and certainly not just on his say so, just as identifying one's father is a theoretical achievement whose implications go far beyond even a complete physical description. Boudon admits that if the Ayatollah Khomeini were to repudiate Islam his authority would suffer. But he could lose his authority if people simply thought he was an impostor. If the person called "Ayatollah Khomeini" were discovered to be an impostor, a finding that might require very subtle, abstract detective work, his authority over "his" people might vanish.

A difficulty for the almost mystical theory of charismatic leadership is that the authority of a leader is always circumscribed to a particular field of competence, a fact of which Weber was aware. The Pope or the Ayatollah would not be asked for their opinion on car maintenance. Their judgment on matters outside their ascribed field is not thought to be privileged or special. However, this is easily explained on the assumption that we choose leaders on the basis of a theory about them and their abilities: their ascribed field of competence is the set of problems that we conjecture their skill or knowledge can solve.

If one leader could determine the opinions of his audience, then there would be no room for contrary views, for criticism. Some small communities might approach this state of affairs. In 1978 more than nine hundred people died in Jim Jones's Jonestown, Guyana. At first it was thought that they had all committed suicide on Jones's command as part of a religious ritual. This alleged mass suicide has strengthened many in the belief that charismatic leaders can completely control the minds of their followers. However, this initial theory has not held up. Investigators generally conclude that the majority did not die voluntarily, but were coerced. Some maintain that as many as seven hundred of the deaths were involuntary. But even if one accepts that all the members committed suicide on Jones's command, it does not follow that he controlled their minds. One could argue that the followers of Jones already shared much of his worldview before they joined the People's Temple and that his influence consisted principally in channeling these beliefs into certain activities.

Moreover, even if an individual could control the minds of a thousand people, no leader could be so influential as to determine the opinion and feelings of millions of people, even if we confine ourselves to matters of important governmental policy. The turn-of-the-century

German Social Democrats illustrate this ineradicable intransigence of the 'masses'. The German Social Democrats were led by Marxists but the mass of social democratic voters reserved some opposition to their leaders despite their support of the party. The Marxists advocated proletarian internationalism and opposition to war, but the rank and file were no less nationalistic than the voters of other parties in Germany and elsewhere, and some were quite prepared to die on the battlefield for their nation. Again, the overwhelming majority of recent politicians and opinion leaders in Britain have been strongly against capital punishment; but the majority of the population have steadfastly favored it.

Still, there is some truth in the important role that Chakotin attributes to intellectuals, but it is not simply in converting other intellectuals (the ten percent) to new ideas. The ideas of intellectuals form the framework, the background assumptions, in terms of which the masses identify, interpret, accept and reject leaders and their messages. Walter Laqueur in his book on the Weimar Republic mentions that views similar to National Socialism were popular in the universities before they became generally popular. Hayek makes the same point in his *Road to Serfdom*. In general as Keynes said:

> The ideas of economists and political philosophers, both when they are right and when they are wrong, are more powerful than is commonly understood. Indeed the world is ruled by little else. (Keynes 1936, p. 383)

Long-Term Propaganda versus Political Canvassing

Hitler, Edmund Wilson, and Chakotin were led into their positions on the immutability of political beliefs because they took the politician's view of ideological change: from one election to the next there is little fundamental change in peoples' views and values. The politician's aim is power for his party at the next election (or in the upcoming *coup*). There is no time to change public opinion on fundamentals; the politician's only recourse is to try and convince the public that he already holds their views, or views acceptable to them, and that his party will most effectively implement them.

The politician struts on a stage already fitted out by a long process of abstract intellectual argument. Politicians who have flouted this constraint, who have been more concerned with promoting an unpopular opinion, have suffered a loss of actual power. Enoch Powell, Barry Goldwater, and George McGovern are politicians who forsook the possibility of power for their greater concern with trying to persuade the public of their policy ideals. By contrast, Lyndon Johnson, Edward Heath, Harold Wilson, and Richard Nixon, all of whom adapted to public opinion rather than trying to change it, were notably more successful in the power game. After he was no longer in any contest for leadership, Edward Heath became more concerned with long-term objectives, such as a federal European state.

This view of the behavior of politicians is borrowed from the new economics approach to politics, substantially developed in the University of Virginia, particularly by Gordon Tullock (McKenzie and Tullock 1975; Tullock 1976). In this model voting and buying are seen in the same light: the same man behaves in an economic way whether in the supermarket or the voting booth; he will choose the product or candidate he thinks is the best bargain for him. Seen in this light, Powell's, Goldwater's, and McGovern's approach to politics is like trying to sell the Ford Edsel or New Coke long after they flopped. Of course, political policies do not strictly coincide with popular opinion, as the example of capital punishment shows, but unlike Chakotin's theory, the Virginian theory does not have to assume that there is strict control running from the controllers (in the Virginian School, the voters) to the controlled.

Edmund Wilson's Nazi and Tory were reasoned into their positions. Decades of abstract argument by intellectuals such as Oswald Spengler, Friedrich List, Werner Sombart, and Arthur Moeller van den Bruck preceded and made possible Hitler's rise to power. The German people have been depicted as puppets of Hitler's emotionally stirring speeches. But perhaps Hitler was expressing in a clear, simple, and dramatic way what had already become the predominant ideology. It may have been this facility to distill the common sense of his time that helped to make his speeches so stirring. Hitler finally gained power through adroit wheeling and dealing, but he got into the position of being a contender for power because he was able to convince a large segment of the German electorate of his superior ability to govern in accordance with goals and theories that they had already embraced, not because he was able to excite an agitated cocktail of thoughtless emotion, or because he was able, single-handedly, to inculcate in a few years in the minds of millions the ideas behind National Socialism.

Thinking about Abstract Ideas versus Thinking in Accord with Them

Durkheim's, Chakotin's, and Hitler's intuition that there is an important difference between the ideologue and the broad masses in their attitude to abstract ideas was correct but not quite accurate. The masses are indeed poorly acquainted with abstract ideas, but it does not follow that they do not think in accord with them. Many of the concepts and presuppositions that we take for granted in daily life are susceptible to quite complex and intricate analysis. Everyone uses numbers to count their groceries without having to understand philosophical debates about the ontology of numbers or ever giving a thought to 'what numbers really are'.

The same point can be applied to more political concepts. While democracy, patriotism, and leadership are for the broad masses abstract principles they take for granted as means for solving social problems, for the ideologue, these concepts themselves are objects of thought and argument.

At the same time, a good case could be made that the broad masses are more familiar with the abstract notion of democracy than with the particular institutions that effect it. Only a minority of Britons or Americans can explain specifically how Parliament or Congress operates, but they can all state that democracy is the rule of the majority. This is a problem for a Durkheimian theory for it would imply that if given a choice between the concrete (totemic) parliamentary building and abstract democracy, the populace would automatically opt for the building (which is itself absurd) because, in Durkheim's theory, the particular object is more familiar and easier to represent than an abstract characterization of it.

Fitting the Theory to the Emotion

A more recent exponent of the theory that the emotion and morality in ideologies is prior to and independent of theory is Kenneth Minogue. Minogue's theory, similar to Pareto's, differs from that of Durkheim, Chakotin, and Hitler's in that it attributes a greater role to theory. Minogue argues that it is moral censure that engenders the Marxist's acceptance of the Labor Theory of Value, not the other way round. The Marxist hates capitalism anyway, with or without the economic theory. The Labor Theory of Value is just consonant with the prior feeling that capitalism is exploitative, and the Marxist adopts it despite the fact that

> An inquirer who discovers realities deserving of censure is more impressive than a censor who picks and chooses his theories to support his emotions. (Minogue 1984, p. 58)

The rich have throughout history been censured for greed, luxury, idleness and much else. The ideologist simply picks and chooses his theories to fit these emotions. Therefore, even if the theory succumbs to criticism, the moral censure will prevail; censure survives theory.

Minogue illustrates his point with the Labor Theory of Value. He quotes Bertell Ollman:

> The labor theory of value forces the capitalist to justify his role and the benefits he receives in a context where no justification is possible. It puts him in a corner from which there is no escape other than the practical one of keeping the workers from realizing their situation. (Minogue, p. 57)

Minogue attempts to show how confused such a position is. The Labor Theory of Value, Minogue points out, is normally advanced as a scientific account of reality, revealing the laws of motion of capitalist society. But laws of motion are no basis for an indictment; on the contrary they render both indictment and justification logically pointless.

The term 'capitalist', Minogue says, has acquired an ambiguous meaning. In one sense it refers to a social type created by the inexorable laws of social evolution; in the other sense it refers to the class of employers who have been caught out committing the crime of robbery. Ollman's certainty that no justification is possible derives from the supposedly scientific theory connected with the first sense; it is the second, quite different and incompatible theory that makes it appear to Ollman that the indictment is at all meaningful in this context.

Is it true, as Minogue asserts, that a scientific law cannot in principle be the basis for an indictment? The following syllogism might be taken as a possible counter-example:

Anything that necessarily involves unpaid labor should be swept away.

Capitalism necessarily involves unpaid labor.

Therefore, capitalism should be swept away.

Compare this with a feminist argument:

Anything that necessarily involves patriarchy should be swept away.

Capitalism necessarily involves patriarchy.

Therefore, capitalism should be swept away.

Each of these is a valid argument. One of the premises must be a value judgment, but it still seems to be a counter-example to Minogue's assertion. The law-like statement, the second premise, makes it possible to validly infer the moral conclusion, which is an indictment.

Perhaps Minogue's point is that an indictment presupposes that the indicted could act differently, and so cannot apply to strictly inevitable behavior. Minogue does speak of laws as such, not of statements of inevitable developments. However, if the Marxist abandons his talk of inevitability, and instead talks of laws in a scientific sense, then indictments are not strictly futile. Indictments may be considered as part of the initial conditions determining human behavior. By taking certain drugs one places oneself under the influence of certain laws of physiological psychology which predispose one to aggressive behavior. But it is still quite appropriate for others to censure me, if the censuring is thought likely to stop me taking the drug in future.

Vacillation between one interpretation and the other helps to deflect criticism, but the rhetorical impact of Minogue's analysis of the ideologist's maneuvers should not be underestimated. Ollman may well succumb to Minogue's dissection. Still, Minogue contends that even if Ollman's confusion were cleared up and he were also convinced that the labor theory of value is false, his censure of capitalism would survive. There is some truth in Minogue's position. George Bernard Shaw was persuaded of the falsity of the Labor Theory of Value, but his repugnance for and censure of the capitalist continued, albeit as a non-Marxist socialist. Two more recent examples are the Marxists John Roemer and Ian Steedman:

> the labor theory of value was intended to emphasize the fact that capitalists exploit workers in a capitalist system. Although the labor theory of value is false, I think the conclusion is true. (Roemer 1988, p. 2)

Roemer entirely discards the classic Marxist definition of exploitation in terms of surplus value and instead defines exploitation in terms of the inequality of outcome associated with the unequal ownership of property.

Steedman has explicitly rejected Marx's theory on the grounds that even if Marx had succeeded in transforming input prices his argument is internally inconsistent. Steedman has opted for the theory developed by Sraffa, in which the conditions of production and the real wage paid to workers, both specified in terms of physical quantities of commodities, suffice to determine the rate of profit. In this model labor values are not proportional to prices, and neither is the total surplus value equal to total profit. The connection with exploitation in Steedman's eyes, like Morishima's, is retained because in Sraffa-like models it can be shown that profit will be positive if and only if there is surplus value, that is, capitalist exploitation (Steedman 1977).

But is it true that the censure would survive the demise of any theory? Popper has emphasized that our empirical experience is theory-impregnated. But equally, theoretical interpretation also pervades all our moral experience. It is sometimes difficult to point to the exact theory that lies behind a moral position, if only because people's avowed reasons for holding a position are not always the same as the real reasons. Matters are further complicated by the fact that in many cases an emotion is supported by more than one theory. It might be that though the emotion can prevail in the absence of one or more of its theoretical supports, it cannot prevail if they all collapse. Nevertheless, in saying this it is admitted that the reasons are there. Through this admission we again have an avenue for the impact of theoretical criticism.

Although Minogue may have accurately represented recent Marxist intellectuals, he fails to capture one of the reasons behind the original Marxist repugnance towards capitalism. What offended Marx and Engels most about capitalism was that it is unplanned, a conspicuously intellectual complaint. There is a lot of planning within the market, for instance in the way labor is organized within each factory, but there is no overall planning. Each car company might plan to make a certain number of cars per year, but the total number of cars produced in any one year is not planned by anyone, (nor could it be without abolishing capitalism). To Marx this was irrational and therefore inefficient, and communism would replace this anarchy of many plans with a rational system based on a single plan. This conception explains why Marx and his early followers saw a trend towards larger business firms as a welcome move toward socialism. Engels hailed the monopolistic 'trusts' whose growth he witnessed in the late nineteenth century as the development of socialist organization of production within moribund capitalism.

The Labor Theory of Value is perhaps an attempt to give some theoretical embroidery to the already existent feeling that the wealthy exploit the poor. The wealthy, as Minogue says, had always been censured for this, but they had rarely before been censured for being disorganized. Such a complaint bears little kinship with the much more spontaneous untutored envy that Minogue speaks of. Marx's complaint requires more intellectual sophistication. (On this neglected aspect of Marx's thought see Steele 1992.)

Minogue's account makes a mystery of the ideologist's use of theory, for if the requisite emotions exist willy-nilly, why bother with the theoretical embroidery? To appear academic or scientific, perhaps, and thus steal some of the authority of academia and science. But does not the authority of science derive from its success at discovering truths? Perhaps truth, and thus reason, is important to ideologies, after all. Now if one grants that theory sets the stage for all our moral and emotional experience, then why not take the Labor Theory of Value as at least one of the factual theories behind the Marxist's rejection of capitalism?

Moral Feelings and Factual Assumptions

Marx and Engels's advocacy of communism is based on the postulate that it is possible, that it really could come into existence. Roemer clearly takes this postulate for granted when he says that

> The private property system is just one possible way of organizing economic activity; it may have been the best way for a certain period but is probably not the best way today, nor will it be in the future. (p. 11)

This is typical of moral ideals: they are rarely advocated if they are thought to be unattainable. Some ethical theorists even claim that this is a necessary truth: 'Ought implies can', from which it would follow that 'Not-can implies not ought'. It cannot be morally required to do something which cannot be done. Some ideals are advocated as goals to be approximated, but if they could not even be approximated the injunction would lapse. Even the advocacy of ideals in a cynical, manipulative manner is based on certain factual assumptions.

All moral and amoral feelings are based on factual assumptions. All cognition is emotional and all emotion is cognitive. Emotions such as anger, love, disgust, and so forth, have objects to which they are directed by thought. One does not simply feel anger, one feels angry about some object of one's thought. The fact that someone holds an emotional, perhaps even violent, position does not mean he is irrational: for these emotions are under the control of that person's conjectures about the factual state of the world. As David Hume put it:

> The moment we perceive the falsehood of any supposition, or the insufficiency of any means, our passions yield to our reason without any opposition. (Hume 1978, p. 158)

If a Marxist is convinced by argument that the market system is not the cause of poverty, or of the other things he loathes, his righteous anger against the market will subside. The moment the Marxist is convinced that communism is impossible his ardor for revolution will wane (unless, of course, the revolution has become for that person a means to other ends, but then the same argument applies to these new ends). To obtain the Marxist's approval of or resignation toward capitalism it need not even be denied that capitalism exploits workers, for there may be no better alternative. To return to our syllogistic moralizing, one might have the argument:

Anything that involves murder should be abolished.

Society involves murder.

Therefore, society should be abolished.

No one is going to suggest that we all kill ourselves or live as hermits, in order to eliminate society. A certain amount of unpreventable murder is accepted as a necessary price for all the benefits of living in societies, along with many other unwelcome attributes such as the possibility of contracting contagious diseases. So we may conclude that the Marxist's argument, even if it did establish that capitalism were exploitative, would not be conclusive. One would have to look at his alternative. Even if Ollman were right about exploitation, he would be wrong to say that the defender of capitalism must be "in a corner" without any escape but deception.

If all emotions are cognitive, it follows that if ideologues succeed by appealing to emotions, they must do so by appealing to reason. But they can only do that through theory and argument. As a corollary, the fact that ideologies are based on emotion does not protect them from factual criticism.

The only possible counterexamples that I have been able to think of to the theory that all emotion is cognitive are perhaps moods and the psychological states brought on by certain drugs (for instance caffeine apparently induces anxiety in some individuals). It's hard to imagine caffeine having anything to do with the acceptance or rejection of an ideology. A mood can be understood as a succession of similar thoughts. For example, a depressed mood is a series of depressing thoughts. Alternatively, a mood may be interpreted as a disposition to entertain emotions of that mood because of some temporarily accepted theory which colors a person's interpretations of events. It's not uncommon for people who have been burgled, for instance, to find themselves in a depressed mood, this because of a temporarily lowered opinion of people in general.

The moral element in ideological systems might seem to rule out factual criticism right from the start. The Fascist feels that the state is morally good; the anarchist feels the state is morally bad: and that is an end to the matter. Many philosophers have denied any logical connections between moral and factual claims. They have taken to heart Hume's argument that no moral position can be logically derived from a factual statement.

Many have gone as far as to endorse G.E. Moore's verdict that

> No truth about what is real can have any logical bearing upon the answer to the question of what is good in itself. (Moore 1903, p. 118)

Hume's conclusion still stands, and so does Moore's verdict. Suppose it had been established that humans are instinctively prone to aggression; it would not follow logically that humans ought to be aggressive. Equally, if they were shown to be instinctively communal; this would not license the logical derivation of the idea that humans ought to be communal. However, we can't conclude that facts have no logical bearing whatsoever on moral positions. Although no moral position can be derived from factual statements alone, facts may undermine moral injunctions.

If one advocates communism and communism, however defined, happens to be impossible, then one's moral injunction is undermined by the facts. The injunction that one ought to help bring communism about seems to imply that one can actually contribute to its emergence, and would therefore be undermined by the impossibility of complying with it. In many cases, it does appear that 'Ought implies can'. Bartley supplies an instructive example:

> Suppose that it is argued that one ought not to punish criminals but to treat them all psychologically in order to cure them of criminal tendencies. To

this proposal it is retorted that "ought" implies "can", and that there exist some criminals—for example those with certain genetic defects—whom it is impossible to cure by psychological treatment. The example is not fanciful: the XYY chromosomal abnormality has been widely associated by researchers with criminal behavior and/or low intelligence in adult males; and recent studies show that one male in every 300 may be born with just this abnormality. This factual information, which bears logically on the original proposal for a different public policy, will if taken seriously lead to a modification of the proposal. Thus Dr. Park S. Gerald of the Harvard Mecial School has urged that a large scale study of XYY incidence should be done because "a great deal of social planning could be related to this. These people [with XYY syndrome] might still get into trouble despite present welfare programs." (Bartley 1984, p. 200)

Still, Moore's position represents a problem for my approach since it would imply that different ideologies simply have fundamentally different values. There are ends of human action and there are means to those ends. One can argue about the correct or most efficient means to a given end, but when it comes to those given ends themselves, there is no fact of the matter.

My answer to this argument is as follows. The adoption of a moral end is like the adoption of a factual position in this respect: they are both conjectures. In the one case we guess what's true; in the other case we guess what's morally good. In either case we can be wrong. (The idea that morals are conjectures is neutral as to whether morals are feelings, tastes, or objective realities.) How do we check our guesses? In the case of factual guesses, we can compare what we think with the world in observation and experiment. Perhaps we cannot do this with moral guesses, but we can compare one guess with another to check for coherence. We can also check the costs of each moral value in terms of the others. Often the relationship between our morals and our factual assumptions is not obvious and needs an argument or a different perspective to bring it to light.

For example, Roemer concentrates on the alleged greater inequality of income and ownership in capitalism on the assumption that this is the decisive issue between capitalism and socialism. In taking this approach he neglects to examine an unconscious assumption: that inequality and poverty go hand in hand. This explains why he fails to consider the following moral choice between two types of society: a society of great inequality and a society of great equality, but whose poorest (or average) are as badly off or even worse off than the poorest in the former society. A type of society which produces considerable inequality may also be that type of society which lifts the poorest (or the average) to the highest level. If this relationship does hold then any choice between the societies would have to check the cost of each of two moral values in terms of the other: the marginal cost of an increment in equality in terms of a loss of income on the part of the poorest (or the average). Any such balancing of moral values depends on the assumption that their satisfaction in reality is related, and that this makes relevant factual criticism of a moral position. Someone conceivably *might* take the view that equality should be implemented even if this were bound to produce universal wretchedness, but in my experience people who would make that judgment are very few.

Another possible answer to the argument derived from Moore is to assert that there are no fundamental differences in values. What are taken as fundamental differences in values are really differences of opinion on factual matters. Why should we entertain this position, since it seems to fly in the face of the myriad varied religions, moralities, and political positions we see in the world? Such a position will appear less strange once we bear in mind that all human beings evolved from the same ancestors, and although their anatomy and physiology varies, along with their tastes, their most urgent values could be the same the world over. Writing in 1949, with the examples of Fascism and National Socialism still fresh in memory, Ludwig von Mises maintained that all peoples have the most urgent values in common:

> This fundamental fact is often ignored. People believe that differences in world view create irreconcilable conflicts. The basic antagonisms between parties committed to different world views, it is contended, cannot be settled by compromise. . . . However, if we pass in review the programs of all parties—both the cleverly elaborated and the publicized programs and those to which the parties really cling when in power—we can easily discover the fallacy of this interpretation. All present-day political parties strive after the earthly well-being and prosperity of their supporters. They promise that they will render economic conditions more satisfactory to their followers. With regard to this issue there is no difference between the Roman Catholic Church and the various Protestant denominations as far as they intervene in political and social questions, between Christianity and the non-Christian religions, between the advocates of economic freedom and the various brands of Marxian materialism, between nationalists and internationalists, between racists and the friends of interracial peace. It is true, that many of these parties believe that their own group cannot prosper except at the expense of other groups, and even go so far as to consider the complete annihilation of other groups or their enslavement as the necessary condition

of their own group's prosperity. Yet, extermination or enslavement of others is for them not an ultimate end, but a means for the attainment of what they aim at as an ultimate aim: their own group's flowering. If they were to learn that their own designs are guided by spurious theories and would not bring about the beneficial results expected, they would change their programs. (Mises 1949, pp. 180–81)

Mises did not explain why this should be so. Darwinian theory combined with the common and recent origin of the world's human races might suggest that all humans should have broadly the same set of urgent wants and dislikes. Hominids seem to have originated in Africa. Most of the detectable evolution of the hominids from pre-hominid to *Homo sapiens sapiens* occurred in the African population. Circumstantial evidence corroborating a considerable overlap of basic preferences is the fact that the market for mass-produced goods is world-wide. Western technology and consumer goods are very rapidly absorbed even by the most technologically primitive societies. The worldwide clamor for 'western' goods (most of them now made in the East, of course) is so conspicuous that it has been called 'cultural imperialism'. But two temples made of the same brick may be temples to different gods. Better evidence may be found in the so-called social universals found by anthropologists, such as sanctions against murder and theft and pervasive similarities in the institution of marriage.

The Role of Intense Emotion

Emotion does have a role to play in the evolution of an ideology, though I believe this role has been exaggerated. Emotion presupposes theory, and therefore pure emotion cannot be the source of an ideology. My assertion that "emotion presupposes theory" may appear strange, but all I mean is that emotional responses to various events and institutions are governed by an understanding of the world, an interpretation of reality.

If pure emotions could be the source of ideology, one might expect original ideological texts to be poems, novels, or movies, since these artistic forms evoke the most powerful emotions. But this is usually not what we find. Nevertheless, works of art may well help to perpetuate an ideology already developed by applying it to particular circumstances and thereby evoking strong emotions. There was a socialist movement long before *The Ragged Trousered Philanthropists* or *The Iron Heel*, an anti-slavery movement long before *Uncle Tom's Cabin*, and an anti-imperial movement long before *A Passage to India* or *Burmese Days*.

The closest thing to an ideological movement founded by works of art would be Ayn Rand's Objectivism, launched by her two best-selling novels, *The Fountainhead* and *Atlas Shrugged*. However, much of Objectivism—all the economic and strictly political aspects—is simply classical liberalism, identical with the views promoted by Herbert Spencer or Ludwig von Mises. The other aspects of Objectivism, the distinctive theories of metaphysics, morality, and art, do not have a very big following, and what following they do have comprises people who, after reading the novels, went on to read Rand's non-fiction works and those of her followers like Leonard Peikoff. It would be impossible to grasp these theories, even in outline, just from reading the novels.

Novelists and journalists know well that it is concrete and particular things which most excite interest and emotional involvement, although as I mentioned in connection with Durkheim, the difference between more and less emotive writing is not fully captured by the abstract-concrete distinction. Most popular novels and movies just take the prevailing ideology for granted, and are preoccupied by particular people, their hopes and fears, their successes and failures—in short, by the vicissitudes of their day-to-day existence.

We should distinguish between movements and the ideologies that those movements help to perpetuate. There are new movements with new ideas, and old movements with old ideas; there are also old movements with new ideas, and there are new movements with old ideas. According to my view of the role of emotions, I would expect that intense emotion, provided by poets, orators, and novelists, would be most useful to old and new movements with old ideas.

Hitler was wrong to think that the most intense emotions are necessarily the most long-lasting. Emotions of the agitated sort—the emotions of parades or riots—cannot alone be responsible for the creation and the initial fostering of an ideology, for they are too short-lived to sustain the intellectual creator of the ideology through the thousands of hours of writing and arguing his case. Neither can the perpetuation of the ideology once accepted be imputed to intense emotion alone. It is psychologically impossible to be intensely emotional for more than half an hour or so. Of course, a disposition to intense emotion may persist for years. But is Hitler right in his claims that love is less subject to change than respect or that hatred is more lasting than mere aversion? Respect may outlast love and aversion may outlast hatred because love and hatred require more effort, and also because the more intense emotions may burn out more quickly.

The propagandist who pursues long-term effectiveness must have a profound taste for theory and argument themselves, independent of the excitements of righteous anger and missionary zeal. Emotion arises when a person applies his ideology to a particular right or wrong. Contemplation of the abstract structure of the ideology itself arouses little agitated emotion, save that connected with the beauty of the theory.

Eric Hoffer, author of *The True Believer*, said that

> the readying of the ground for a mass movement is done best by men whose chief claim to excellence is their skill in the use of the spoken word. (Hoffer 2002, p. 131)

Hoffer probably got this idea from Hitler. In the introduction to *Mein Kampf*, Hitler expressed his belief that more converts to mass movements had been won through the spoken word than through the written word. The suggestion is that the spoken word is more moving than the passive text. Hitler lived at the end of the period when large public meetings were the core of political campaigning. The classic example of this use of the spoken word is Daniel O'Connell's 'monster meetings' held throughout the Catholic parts of Ireland in the 1840s. Later, as Hitler was growing up, the spoken word was given a final fillip by the radio. Today, ninety years after Hitler wrote *Mein Kampf*, it may be too soon to say that the reign of the spoken word is over, but a look at Facebook and Twitter suggests that it could well be in eclipse.

In any event, the building of a political mass movement is a late stage in the development of an ideology. It is not the man of words as such but the man of abstract theory and argument who lies behind the origin of mass movements, and this man or woman is usually a writer who could not hold a crowd if there was free beer next door. If we bear in mind the distinction between a movement and its ideas, we may agree with a more precise statement of Hoffer's and Hitler's view: that the spoken word is important for the creation and maintenance of a new movement with old ideas. Hitler's error lies in his contention that all of "the most tremendous revolutions on this Earth" were created by intense "hysterical" emotion.

Hitler asserts that none of the tremendous revolutions have been inspired by scientific teaching. Yet the abolition of the mercantile restrictions on trade and the rise of liberalism is in no small measure attributable to Adam Smith's economic analysis in *The Wealth of Nations*, a scientific work not lacking in abstract argument. The American Revolution and its ensuing constitution were created by scholars steeped in the scientific political theories of David Hume and John Locke. As we read the *Federalist Papers*, it's hard to spot the decisive role of hysterical emotion.

Hitler's account tends to support the view that the creator of a mass movement must be concerned with particulars. I do not want to deny that those preoccupied by particulars may play an important role in the evolution of ideologies. Historians and journalists, for instance, often provide information about particular events which may serve to refute the factual assumptions of an ideology and thereby undermine its authority. But even here in the field of refutation as opposed to theory creation, it is often the connoisseur of abstract theory and argument who makes the most of the material provided by the journalist and historian. As a rule, the journalist and historian take for granted the abstract theories they use, of which they may only be dimly aware, while they focus on the uniqueness of the historical phenomena they have chosen to describe or explain.

INTENSE EMOTION AND THE THEORY OF ADVERTISING

Even though emotion is not the source of an ideology, perhaps it still has some role in the acceptance and rejection of ideas? An objective account must tease out what truth there may be in those theories in which emotion plays such a central and often exclusive role. There is good and bad poetry—effective and ineffective, quite apart from the logical rigor of the poem. Perhaps there is something analogous to poetry that could be used to manipulate people.

Contrary to Hitler, Chakotin, Wilson, Sargent, and many other writers, the effect of intense emotion—parades and dramatic speeches—is not the direct inducement of belief, but simply the conveyance of a message. Effective advertising packages the message in an attention-grabbing and memorable form, and effective propaganda must do the same. Most writers underestimate the problem of simply conveying a message, and have attempted to discern all kinds of strange and insidious powers behind modern advertising techniques. The power of advertising is easily overestimated because we do not often see the advertisements for goods that fail to sell, simply because such goods are taken off the market. Successful goods make for successful advertisements.

The extravagance and eccentricity of much advertising is seen as a sign that it appeals to the irrational in man. But the attraction and maintenance of attention, and the making of a memorable message seem to be the main function of successful advertising, something that is eminently rational. There is no implication here that the recipients of such communications are led to endorse an idea independently of their reason's grasp of some theory, and thus no suggestion that what they endorse or their endorsement itself is immune to criticism.

I would summarize the role of emotion in ideologies as:

1. **Facilitating advertising: making an attention-capturing and memorable message;**
2. **Eliciting already available or easily learnable behaviors;**
3. **Inducing relatively simple messages (recall the discussion about the Yerkes-Dobson law).**

[4]
Ideologies as Shapeshifters

If we want to guarantee our belief system—our theory or our ideology—against being destroyed by criticism, we may try to formulate it in such a way that it can survive any criticism, because it can be reinterpreted so that no criticism could really touch it.

A crude example would go like this. I predict that the world will end on a certain date. Lots of people believe me, and I attract a big following. That date comes and goes without the world ending. My critics say that I was wrong: what I said would happen did not happen, therefore my belief-system is false. I then scornfully reply that my belief-system is still entirely correct. My critics are making a silly and superficial blunder, because the world really did end on that date (and I intend to go on reporting the fact that the world did end on that date). It's just that the end of the world is not detectable by the normal methods of observation, as my very foolish critics have carelessly supposed.

It doesn't matter here exactly how I develop this idea: I may say that God destroyed the world, and then instantly re-created it exactly as it had been before, or I may say that the new world is different to the old world (which really did come to an end, don't doubt it for a moment) because in the new world certain trends have begun which did not exist before. There are hundreds of other ways I might develop the idea. I might even be very obscure about just how it is to be developed, which would go to show that I am inordinately wise. All that matters here is that I have given an interpretation to my old belief which saves it from being rejected. I deny that I was ever wrong, by giving an interpretation to my old belief which squares it with the criticism it has encountered. Criticism of my belief has been rendered impotent, and my belief has been guaranteed against ever being demolished by criticism. I've won—haven't I?

Immunizing Stratagems

If we frame our theory so that, logically, no possible criticism (or perhaps merely no actual or likely criticism) could touch it, we have immunized it against criticism. The device we use to immunize our theory is called an *immunizing stratagem*. We give our belief-system protection against criticism by setting up a logical barrier to criticism. It may seem that if we can do this, then we will have given our ideology an advantage in the competition of ideas.

My aim in this chapter is not to demonstrate that a system of ideas cannot deflect criticism by logical means, but rather to show the limitations and the costs of doing this. What I will show is that immunizing stratagems either abandon the belief system they're supposed to protect or else lower the survivability of the system.

Karl Popper originally used the term 'conventionalist stratagem', but then adopted the term 'immunizing stratagem' from Hans Albert to describe an aspect of the unscientific methodology of certain ideologies claiming to be scientific: Marxism and Freudianism. Arthur Pap had already anticipated this usage.[27]

Popper argued that Marxism, which was originally an empirically testable theory, had been recast in the form of empirically irrefutable metaphysics. This maneuver, Popper claimed, saved Marxism from refutation and immunized it against further attacks (Popper 1976, p. 43).

Freudianism was, Popper claimed, irrefutable from the beginning. The basic theory of Freudianism does not need any immunization to make it irrefutable. Nevertheless, it does incorporate immunizing stratagems. Popper contrasted Marxism and Freudianism with the theories of Newton and of Einstein which, he said, were full of testable content. Thus Popper's employment of the term 'immunizing stratagem' arose in connection with his attempt to solve the problem of distinguishing scientific from non-scientific (including pseudo-scientific) theories—the demarcation problem. Popper's solution was the methodological rule to allow into science only empirically falsifiable hypotheses. If a theory can be shown to be false by an observation—an empirical test—then it is scientific; if no observation could show it to be false, it is not scientific.

Furthermore, Popper maintained, theory development ought to proceed from less to more testable, meaning more informative, theories. If a theory is refuted and an alternative sought, it had to be more testable, not less, and the more testable the better. For to reduce testability is to reduce knowledge, whereas in science we desire the growth of knowledge. An immunizing stratagem is always a development in theory that reduces testability.

Popper's Examples of Immunizing Stratagems

Popper says that immunizing stratagems save theories from refutation. However, Popper's own examples of immunizing stratagems undermine the claim that an ideology can maintain itself against criticism by logical means. Popper's examples are not examples of saved theories but of repudiated theories: to immunize a theory in these cases is to abandon it.

The two main effects of these immunizing stratagems are saving the theorist from embarrassment at the price of abandoning the original theory, and clouding the issue while reducing information content. The latter obviously interferes with the growth of knowledge. To go back to my earlier crude example, my belief that the world ended on a certain date is really a new belief, because when I predicted the world would end on that date, I actually meant it would end in a way that everyone would be able to observe. The old belief has been replaced by a new belief, which is formulated in the same words as the old belief. The verbal formula has been saved, but the actual belief is different. I think that Popper was dimly aware that immunizing stratagems do not strictly save theories (in some cases he puts the word 'saved' in scare quotation marks), but he did not see the full implications of this, especially for the survival of an ideology.

Consider the simplest of Popper's examples. Popper asks us to consider the case of a man who makes the bold claim that all swans are white, and on being presented with a black swan promptly denies that it is a swan. After all, this man says, whiteness is part of the definition of the word 'swan'. Popper states that the theory that all swans are white has been 'saved' from refutation. But has the theory really been saved? What had been an empirical theory about the world has now been turned into the application of a definition. The original theory, supposedly protected by the immunizing stratagem, has actually been replaced by an implication of a vacuous definition.

The original theory was empirical in Popper's sense: it was capable of clashing with observable reality. The statements 'All swans are white' and There is a black swan' cannot both be true. A definition or implications derived exclusively from a definition, however, cannot clash with reality for they say nothing about the world, only about the way we choose to describe the world. The statement, 'All swans are white', which used to convey information about how the world is, has been transformed into a statement which tell us nothing about the world, but only about how we shall use the word 'swan'. The original theory implied: 'You will never come across a black swan'. The new theory implies: 'You cannot possibly come across a black swan because we have redefined the word 'swan' so that being white is part of being a swan'. Thus the original theory has been repudiated, although the words of the original theory ('All swans are white') have been preserved. The repudiation is implicit and unacknowledged, thus saving face despite abandoning the original claim. Once this point is seen, we can derive some implications about the evolution of an ideology under criticism.

In real life people do not simply make such bold assertions out of the blue. Rather, they are made with a certain intention, background assumptions, and more or less clearly formulated problems. It is this context of assumptions and problems that both guides us in identifying an immunizing stratagem and in refuting the original assertion. For example, the sentence 'All swans are white' might be derived from a biological theory of coloring in birds. Knowing this allows us to exclude a whole range of immunizing stratagems that contradict this biological theory or seem to make irrelevant the intention of maintaining the biological theory as a solution to the problem of coloring in birds.

Provisionally, we may define an immunizing stratagem as an evasion of falsification by the reinterpretation of a theory or the modification of its assumptions so that the modified theory is then consistent with the critical evidence. The reinterpretation or modification must consist in a reduction of information content, which is defined as the class of all and only those statements that are logically excluded by the theory.

Scientific development can be described in terms of concepts, theories, problems, method, and evidence. We can classify immunizing stratagems with respect to these categories.

Conceptual immunization. For example, conventionalist interpretations of Newton's laws of motion portray them as definitions and thus taken alone these laws could not contradict the results of any imaginable experiments.

Theoretical immunization. A theory that is contradicted by a true observation report, e, may be weakened just so that it no longer implies not-e, or it may be weakened in this way but also strengthened by the addition of a new auxiliary hypothesis so that e becomes a consequence of the altered theory. (The theory cannot be made consistent with e simply by adding extra assumptions, something I examine below.)

Immunization through change in problem. A theory may escape a specific criticism by a change in the problem supposedly being solved by the theory. We will see that Freud does this with his theory of dreams in order to deal with the contrary evidence of anxiety dreams.

Methodological immunization. One's theories might be associated with a method which, either deliberately or unwittingly, excludes certain domains of potential falsifiers. For example, if a Freudian only considers evidence from the couch, then, providing he sticks doggedly to this method, lots of non-analytic evidence will be made impotent. He may be alarmed to discover that he has been wrong for many years, or he may be simply ignorant of the relevance of such evidence.

Immunization by reinterpreting or denying the evidence. The evidence itself may simply be denied or reinterpreted. (A report of a black swan may be put down to hallucination.)

Metaphysical immunization. One's theories may be attached to a metatheory that interprets them in a certain way. For example, one might combine catastrophe theory with the metatheory that all argument is illusory. (This hybrid is purely hypothetical.) If taken seriously and heeded, this would amount to an exclusion of all possible criticism of catastrophe theory since it would exclude all possible criticism of any theory.

Popper's demarcation criterion is useful methodological advice if our objective is to promote the growth of knowledge. The term 'immunizing stratagem' helps us to designate those moves in theory development that flout the criterion. In other words, if we're interested in gaining new theoretical knowledge, we'd better look our for immunizing stratagems and try to avoid them.

But as protection against criticism, 'immunizing stratagems' possess serious limitations, and certainly do not provide an easy and thorough logical means of ensuring the survival of a theory or an ideology. Many immunizing stratagems involve abandoning the ideology for whose protection they have been introduced, an unplanned, often unforeseeable, process that consists of numerous successive slight modifications extending sometimes over hundreds of years. Other immunizing stratagems seriously lower the survival value of the ideology through the acquisition, sometimes over a long period, of a burdensome and confusing 'protective belt' of hypotheses, each of which acted at least in the short-run, to deflect criticism away from a privileged sector of assumptions.

Moreover, I see the use of immunizing stratagems not as a sign of an ideology in Bartley's sense, as a complete disregard of truth, but rather of a confused and incompetent attempt to take account of criticism. Those resorting to immunizing stratagems are rather like the American officer in Vietnam who said that a village had to be destroyed in order to save it. Thus I also disagree with Antony Flew. Flew characterizes evasions of falsification as involving "surreptitious" and "arbitrary" maneuvers (Flew 1975, p. 48). They also show "that your concern is with what you would like, rather than with how in truth things are" (p. 54).

My rather different take is that the changes may not be designed, but may be the unintended consequence of an attempt to deal with criticism and retain the theory. To the extent that the maneuvers abandon the original doctrine in response to the specific falsification involved they cannot be wholly arbitrary. This reinforces my point that falsification can act as a Darwinian-like filtering device on ideologies even if evasive (intentional or unintentional) moves occur. It may be that although each successive immunizing stratagem is intentional and introduced in the knowledge that the ideology is being altered only slightly, the whole sequence of immunizing stratagems and their accumulated effect is unplanned and unforeseeable. An analogy with the evolution of language might clarify my point. Even if every change in the language were a conscious innovation, the total effect of all the unintentional ramifications of these intentional changes cannot be foreseen. No one living in medieval England, for example, could have predicted the shape of today's English language.

Can it be correct to say that the introduction of an immunizing stratagem displays complete indifference to the truth? If ideologists are indifferent to truth then why do they employ immunizing stratagems at all? There may well be cynical ideologists who have more dominant concerns than truth, who are more interested in the perpetuation of their doctrine. But their audience is interested in truth. Perhaps the use of immunizing stratagems is an attempt to satisfy these conflicting interests. In any event, whatever the intentions of the propagandist, his audience selects those elements that pass the filters of rationality that I discussed in Chapter 1. The rationality of the propagandist's audience is part of the logic of his situation. Thus I see this chapter as reinforcing my general thesis that truth acts as a Darwinian filter on ideologies.

Marxism and Freudianism are vast rambling structures, so I intend to focus on a small segment of each: Marx's Labor Theory of Value and

Freud's theory of dreams. On the other hand, with the aid of the notion of the immunizing stratagem I aim to show that Marxism and Freudianism are less rambling than they appear. The immunizing stratagem helps us to link up the various stages of evolution of these structures by relating the changing theories to the changing problem-situations facing Freud and Marx, a sequence of problems itself partly created by the use of immunizing stratagems.

The term 'stratagem' may suggest a dishonest move, but some immunizing stratagems might be implemented in all sincerity. Popper is concerned to promote intellectual honesty, partly because this would go a long way to prevent content-decreasing evasions, but even from the point of view of the growth of knowledge, a dishonest and an unwitting reduction of information content have the same effect. And since I'm concerned with how the propagandist's audience selects elements from his message, a process independent of his intentions, there would be no loss in generality if I spoke of a move rather than a stratagem. In most cases 'immunizing stratagem' can be interpreted as any immunizing move.

The Demarcation Problem

How do we distinguish science from non-science? This is the Demarcation Problem. Popper concluded that science makes statements which can be checked against observations—that is, tested empirically.

Popper wished to characterize a romantic and heroic conception of science, a conception that captured the spirit and method of great scientists such as Galileo, Kepler, Newton, Einstein, and Bohr (Popper 1974, Sections 5–8 of 'Replies to My Critics'). Popper's main concern in his philosophy of science is to account for and to promote the growth of knowledge. Popper believed that these outstanding scientists made possible a tremendous growth of knowledge by championing bold ideas and subjecting them to severe attempts at refutation. Popper's criterion of demarcation is the outcome of a logical-methodological analysis of what has counted as bold ideas and severe criticism, and thus of what promoted the growth of knowledge.

Popper begins with a rough characterization of bold ideas: a theory is bold if it is a new, daring, hypothesis. It is daring if it takes a big risk of being false. Popper argues that this risk can be analyzed ultimately in terms of the amount that the idea excludes, the degree to which it forbids states of affairs. Severe attempts at refutation are severe critical discussions and severe empirical tests.

Popper illustrates these ideas by examining the development of cosmology, from the heliocentric theories of Aristarchus and Copernicus to Einstein's general theory of relativity. He argues that this development illustrates not only the growth of knowledge but an improvement in method, in which theories become ever more daring and subject to severer tests. It becomes apparent that riskiness and testability are linked: the greater the former, the greater the latter.

Aristarchus and Copernicus conjectured that the sun sat at the center of the universe, in opposition to the prevalent Earth-centered view of their own times. The heliocentric[28] theory was exceptionally bold because it clashed with both common sense and the prima facie evidence of the senses. It went beyond the appearances to posit an unobserved reality; the appearances were explained in terms of this unfamiliar reality. This was bold in itself, for it broke with the Aristotelian idea that to explain something is to reduce it to the familiar.

However, Popper says, neither Aristarchus nor Copernicus were fully scientific because neither of them was bold enough to predict new observable appearances and thereby expose their theories to new empirical tests.[29] They explained the known appearances, but did not explicitly suggest the existence of unknown appearances, appearances that might decide between the heliocentric and Earth-centered views. If they had made such predictions their theories would have been much more informative, and would therefore have taken a larger risk of being false, but they would also have better promoted the growth of knowledge.

Kepler comes closer to Popper's idea of good science. Kepler had a bold theory of the world, but he also made detailed predictions of new appearances. Not only that, he abandoned many of his ideas in the light of the observations furnished him by Tycho Brahe. In accordance with a promise he had made Tycho, Kepler tried to fit Tycho's model of the solar system to these observations. Tycho accepted neither Copernicus's nor Ptolemy's model, but like all other astronomers Tycho took for granted their Aristotelian-Platonic assumption that orbits must be circular. Nevertheless, he subjected this idea to empirical testing. Kepler made seventy different trials to fit the model to the data and failed. He then took the bold step of proposing that the orbits of the planets were not circular but elliptical. The data fell snugly into place.

Kepler's three laws, though good approximations to the truth, have been refuted. But, Popper says, though false, Kepler's theory is regarded as scientific. Newton's theory is also regarded as false but scientific.

Hence it is not truth which decides whether a theory is scientific. Why should this be? Each theory, though false, represented an attempt to increase knowledge, and did so because even though each was false, it had greater truth-content than its predecessor and exposed itself to more tests. Popper's answer, then, is that it is a theory's openness to empirical refutation that makes it scientific. But more generally, it is whether the theory is an attempt to expand our knowledge, whether it represents an increase of information on the theory it replaces.

Marxism or Freudianism would not be counted as unscientific because they have been refuted, but because of the evasive way Marxists and Freudians have dealt with possible refutations. What is most important for the demarcation criterion is a critical attitude and the proposal of increasingly falsifiable theories in response to refutations. Kepler's elliptical orbit hypothesis represented just this sort of increase of information content in response to empirical refutation.[30]

What impressed Popper most about Eintstein's theory of relativity were the following characteristics:

1. Like Kepler's and Newton's theories, Einstein's theory was very bold, differing fundamentally from Newton's.

2. Einstein derived from the theory three predictions of vastly different observable effects, two of which were radically new, all of which contradicted Newton's theory.[31]

3. Einstein explicitly declared in advance of the experimental tests of his theory, that they were crucial: if the results did not match his predictions, he would abandon them as false.

4. Einstein regarded his theory as simply a better approximation to the truth. For a number of reasons, he was convinced that it had to be false. He specified a number of characteristics that a true theory would have to satisfy. (Popper argued that Einstein's attitude to his theory clearly showed that belief in the truth of a theory is unnecessary to working on it as a promising candidate. It is worth noting, though, that Einstein believed that the theory was closer to the truth than its rivals; so Einstein's disbelief in his theory could not warrant the inference that belief is irrelevant to explaining why Einstein worked on the theory.)

Popper's proposal was that science was distinguished from non-science by two things:

1. The boldness of predicting as yet unobserved phenomena; especially phenomena which will pit the theory against its competitors and allow us to decide between them. Einstein was acutely aware of the need to compare his theory with its competitors.

2. The boldness of looking for tests and refuting instances. (I would also add: the boldness of accepting refuting instances, which is not implied by the boldness of looking for them.)

We may generalize the methodological conclusions of Popper's investigation as follows:

1. **Propound empirically testable theories;**
2. **Aim to refute them;**
3. **Given any theory T, aim to replace it by another theory T' which is more general and precise (has higher information content),[32]. one that explains the success of T, explains the refuting evidence of T and is moreover independently testable.**

In his early writings, Popper would have phrased 1. as 'Propound only empirically testable theories'. Popper later put much more emphasis on the importance of non-empirical theories, while retaining empirical content as the ultimate goal of theory development.

These are purely methodological rules. But there is also a historical thesis connected with them. It is Popper's conjecture that these ideals are responsible for some of the greatest leaps of man's scientific knowledge. Many commentators have confused Popper's methodological-normative analysis with his historical hypothesis. Kuhn is perhaps mostly responsible for this confusion, and others (for example, Boudon) have been led astray by relying on secondary sources. Chalmers also makes this mistake.[33]

There are two aspects to the demarcation criterion: one of attitude and one of pure logic. Firstly, the scientist must try to find falsifying instances to his theories. This is a matter of the correct attitude; the critical attitude. Secondly, the scientist must have at his disposal refutable theories. The possibility then arises of a scientist earnestly following the first injunction without realizing that the theory he is dealing with is empirically irrefutable. Equally, a body of theory may be logically capable of refutation, though its adherents have refused or neglected to look for refuting instances.

Since Popper is interested in the growth of knowledge he is most concerned to discourage the use of immunizing stratagems that flout the demarcation criterion, effectively reducing the information content of our theories. Kepler, for instance, could have described the planets that did not fit his master's model as not really planets. After all, he might have said, planets do not behave like that: a planet is essentially an object with a circular orbit. This would have been an example of what Popper calls an immunizing stratagem.[34]

Such a maneuver, Popper would say, saves the theory but at the price of a reduction in information content. As we have seen, Kepler's actual response greatly increased the informative content of astronomy, and is rightly admired for that.

Not all evasive moves are on the wrong side of the demarcation criterion. Some auxiliary hypotheses introduced to deflect a refutation from a valuable assumption have added greatly to our knowledge. One such auxiliary hypothesis was the prediction by Adams and Leverier of the existence of the planet Neptune. It had been observed that the orbit of the planet Uranus was not in accord with Newton's core theory (the laws of motion and the law of gravity) plus the then known initial conditions (assumptions about the gravitational influence of other planetary bodies). Newton's theory could have been regarded as falsified by this anomaly. However, Adams and Verrier proposed the existence of a previously unknown planet to account for the failure of the predictions, thus saving Newton's theory. But this particular evasion brought increased information content to the Newtonian system as was clear from the fact that the hypothesis was empirically testable by independent means (independent in the sense of doing more than simply checking whether the hypothesis agreed with the already observed perturbations of Uranus).

My view, contrary to Popper, is that immunizing stratagems are auxiliary hypotheses that are on the wrong side of the demarcation criterion and precisely those that while saving the original theory, as literally formulated, from refutation, effectively abandon it, replacing it with another theory. In our hypothetical example, Kepler's redefinition of planets as essentially circular in orbit would introduce a radically new theory and jettison the original claim. I will expand on this point later, after we have seen how Popper deals with the problem presented by metaphysical theories to his demarcation criterion.

METAPHYSICAL THEORIES CAN BE CRITICIZED

Popper was from the beginning aware of several problems with his demarcation proposal, whose solution is very pertinent to the idea that ideologies such as Marxism and Freudianism are safe, or can be made safe, from empirical refutation. I argue that Marxism and Freudianism do not save themselves from empirical criticism by assuming metaphysical form, and that even in the absence of empirical criticism there is potential criticism from other metaphysical theories.

Popper realized as early as 1934, the year of the first edition of the *Logic of Scientific Discovery*, that a metaphysical idea can inspire the creation of an empirically testable theory. In that book he gave a number of examples, such as atomism (which inspired John Dalton's atomic theory which explained the regular proportions in which elements combine); the corpuscular theory of light (which inspired Planck's photon theory); and the theory of terrestrial motion (Popper 1977, p. 278). However, Popper recalls that he had not been fully alive to the fact that metaphysical ideas are rationally arguable and in spite of being empirically irrefutable, are criticizable (p. 206, footnote 2). The boundary between science and nonscience is a vague one. More importantly for methodology, we may infer that a theory should not be discarded simply because it is metaphysical, for it may well inspire the formulation of a theory with more empirical content, one that can clash directly with experimental results. Many brilliant theories must begin their lives as half-baked, rough and ready formulations that flout the demarcation criterion. I infer from this that if the demarcation criterion were understood as a proscription on entertaining such ideas they would not have time to develop. I am unsure as to whether Popper would agree, but I suspect that the demarcation criterion is better understood as an ideal to strive for, simply because satisfying it brings more knowledge within our grasp.[35]

In 1957 Popper became very interested in the fact that metaphysical theories could be not only inspiring, but also arguable and open to criticism. He held that doctrines such as determinism that do not admit of empirical refutation are nevertheless open to criticism as to their effectiveness at solving the problem for which they were proposed (Popper 1958).

In the light of this discussion I would like to suggest that the three methodological rules discussed in the previous section may be simplified by eliminating Rule 1. Rule 3 takes into account the injunction to move from metaphysical speculations to empirically testable theories, as well as the injunction to move from less to more informative metaphysical theories.

If it is accepted that what is important is the move from less to more informative theories, then interesting conclusions follow. For example, even if Marxism has been made into untestable metaphysics, it could be made testable again. Equally, Freudianism could be made testable. A Marxist or Freudian could be shown how their theories could be interpreted empirically and promptly refuted. This need not be as arbitrary as it seems. Even lovers of metaphysics are constrained in their speculations by a whole network of what they regard as background knowledge (which may consist of both empirical and metaphysical theories) and by their problem situation.

Popper also realized that there is a rational function to resistance to criticism; one can be too sensitive to criticism. if refutation is avoided at all cost, then one gives up science. But on the other hand, if a theory is abandoned too easily in the face of apparent refutation, then the theory has no opportunity to show its strengths, which may only become apparent later in the course of debate. Popper concludes that there is room in science for dogmatism, by which he means sticking to a theory even against very strong arguments. Moreover, it may require considerable debate to discover that what at first seemed purely metaphysical is actually empirical. The actual information and logical content of a theory is not only a conjectural matter, but is mostly unfathomable, a point I touched on in Chapter 2 and will take up again later. The late physicist Richard Feynman made a similar point when he stressed how difficult it sometimes is to work out how a new physical theory might be tested in the laboratory because it is often not even clear what, if any, empirical implications it has. Another example is Planck's reinterpretation of Kaufmann's experiments of 1905, the result of which at the time was taken by everyone as bearing unfavorably on the Lorentz-Einstein theory and favorably on Abraham's classical theory of how an electron should behave in an electromagnetic field. Planck discovered that the failed Lorentz-Einstein prediction was no longer derivable from the theory if one were to reject an auxiliary assumption that both theories shared. We may draw the inference that the apparently 'irrational' stubbornness of some ideologues may in some cases be scientifically rational. The refutation of a complex theory is not an obvious and mechanical procedure. In itself, stubbornness in clinging to one's favored theories in the teeth of apparently contrary evidence, is not necessarily harmful and can be valuable.

Empirical versus Metaphysical Criticism

But more to the point, it does look as though the ideologies most infamous for their apparent obstinacy in the face of criticism, take on a metaphysical form. Marx held that for all economies based on wage labor and a market in factors of production (that is, capitalism) there is a tendency for industrial concentration to increase, limited only by the size of each industry, and ultimately by the size of all of industry. The tendency of capitalism, then, is for all production to become administered by a single gigantic organization. Administration of production tends to become more unified within capitalism, and this is one aspect of the process which leads to communism. In the communist revolution, the workers would be taking over an already 'socialized' and 'centralized' administration of production.

Apparently, Marx thought the revolution was not very far in the future. The Marxist, however, can always say that communism will arrive eventually: the tendencies to monopolization ('centralization of capital'), the Marxist might protest, have been temporarily countered by opposing tendencies, and will at any moment re-appear. Future-oriented systems can escape direct refutation by making their prophecies apply to some eventual future rather than by putting a definite date on the coming of the new era. Can they be criticized in that form without first interpreting them empirically?

To clarify the logic of the sorts of systems we're talking about and the possible empirical criticism to which they could be subjected, let's take an example from chemistry. A classic metaphysical sentence is: Gold has an acidic solvent. This is an irrefutable statement, for however far and wide one looks for such an acid without finding it, it is always possible to say that it exists at some other time or place. So is experience, our strongest critic, irrelevant to this type of statement? John Watkins has pointed out that experience can be brought in as a critic here indirectly via a well tested scientific theory which is directly testable (Watkins 1958). The metaphysical sentence in question is in fact incompatible with the well-tested theory that gold has no acidic solvent.

But is such an analysis relevant to the Marxist's attempt to evade criticism? Yes, for like the spatio-temporally unrestricted singular statement about gold, the Marxist's apology is also a spatio-temporally unrestricted singular statement. Both would require a systematic search of the whole of space and time for a direct empirical refutation (or confirmation), which is obviously impossible. (The Marxist's assertion covers only future time, though it might be made to cover the past if he were desperate enough.)

A Marxist is unlikely to adopt such an unrestricted prediction, at least not at the time of writing. Such a position might emerge after innumerable attempts to evade criticism, perhaps taking fifty to a hundred years to evolve. By that stage the morale of the Marxist apologist may well have sunk to an irrecoverable low. But even if a Marxist did resort to this desperate maneuver, he would still be open to an indirect empirical refutation. Ludwig von Mises argued that without a price system, which communism would eliminate, there could be no equally efficient way to allocate resources, so that capitalism's level of output could not be maintained (Mises 1935; see Steele 1992). Against the Marxist's hopeful belief in the possibility of communism, Mises pitted an argument drawing upon price theory, a theory which can be tested for its many detailed empirical predictions.

One might argue that economics does not make predictions of the same empirical precision as does chemistry. Some might even argue that economics is not empirical at all, but a very suggestive and true metaphysical theory. The analogy with chemistry would then be weakened. But we can certainly say that neoclassical price theory has greater informative content than the Marxist's unrestricted singular prediction, and may still help to undermine the Marxist's case.

It's easy to assume that empirical observation is the strongest critic. The implication would be that if a network of ideas succeeds in shielding itself from empirical counter-evidence, it will have evaded, if not all sorts of criticism, at least the most damaging both psychologically and logically. This may not be true. An interesting possibility is that opposing metaphysical theories may sometimes be of greater weight than empirical observations. Watkins has shown how metaphysical theories serve to filter out some possible theories before they even enter the body of science; these theories do not even get discussed because they conflict with the prevalent metaphysical background assumptions.

Watkins's discussion of the influential role of metaphysical doctrines ('haunted universe doctrines') is highly suggestive in this context:

> . . . what informs and integrates the heterogeneous ideas of Augustine, or Bossuet, or Condorcet, or Burke, or Comte, or Marx is in each case a distinctive view of history which both shapes each of their interpretations of historical facts and suggests a certain kind of moral and political outlook. . . . the moral-political suggestiveness of haunted universe doctrines indicates that large clashes of belief in the moral-political sphere need not have their origin in disagreement over moral principles or over observable facts. They may be generated, partly or wholly, by conflicting metaphysical interpretations of the world. (p. 360)

There are other methods of criticism that can be applied to metaphysical theories. Galileo suggests a charming way to criticize doctrines that fail to exclude rivals by empirical test. Galileo was able to report that his telescope showed that the Moon was not a perfectly smooth sphere as the Aristotelians expected, but was instead marked by craters and mountains. One of Galileo's adversaries tried to defend the Aristotelian doctrine by suggesting that an invisible substance filled up the craters and covered the mountains so that the Moon was actually perfectly spherical. When Galileo asked him how the substance was detectable, he said it was undetectable. Galileo responded by saying that he was quite prepared to accept the hypothesis of the invisible substance, but insisted that it was in fact piled up high on the mountains of the Moon in such a way that the Moon was even more uneven than the telescope could reveal. Galileo's rejoinder allows one to see the inadequacy of the immunizing move of making empirical testing irrelevant.

The same type of rebuttal can be applied to conspiratorial theories that have assumed an empirically untestable form. For example, suppose some cynical socialist asserts that all the setbacks in the socialist movement have been instigated by undetectable groups of capitalists operating behind the scenes. One could counter this by saying that the setbacks are real and there are conspiratorial capitalist groups working against the socialist movement; however, their efforts are always unsuccessful, because they are always thwarted by undetectable renegade socialist groups who are the actual cause of the setbacks in the socialist movement. If the conspiratorial theory is successful on account of its lack of empirical testability, then the propagandist is prompted by the logic of his situation to try to counter the rival conspiratorial theory. But he can do this only by augmenting his theory with testable content.

We may conclude that even if an ideology assumes the form of a metaphysical doctrine it may yet be criticized, not only by unproblematic empirical theories, but also by scientifically acceptable metaphysical assumptions. The Marxist's retreat to unrestricted prediction, does not save his position from criticism, but only creates other grounds for criticism.

Damaging versus Eliminating a System of Ideas

In correspondence, the late W.W. Bartley III, partly conceding my point, argued that:

> in a strict sense, the introduction of an immunizing stratagem may be tantamount to abandoning the position; but in practice it is more likely to be tantamount to damaging the position. (February 13th, 1988)

Jeremy Shearmur has made a similar criticism of my thesis. I think this contention is true, but misleading. Drastic revisions of a theory through the use of an immunizing stratagem are rare, for they are too obvious and unconvincing. The revisions are more often of a marginal nature.

Bartley's and Shearmur's disagreement with me rests on an unexamined assumption of theirs that there is a difference between modifying a network of ideas and making a new set of ideas, a form of essentialism that I view as mistaken. One might retort that a network of ideas may evolve yet survive, in the sense that the fundamentals are retained. My immediate response to this would be to ask how fundamentals of a network of ideas would be defined other than as: those elements of a modified network of ideas that are retained. Definitions are rarely important, but asking for a definition here could be revealing.

Even if we accept for the purposes of argument that to damage a position is not to eliminate it, the distinction breaks down when we look at the history of ideas. Metaphorically speaking, a sufficient number of injuries to a theory is always equivalent to its death. Each intentional or unintentional concession made by an ideologue may be individually insignificant; but a sufficient number of insignificant differences makes a significant difference. Successive, slight modifications may lead from orthodoxy to radically different interpretations—to what would earlier have been viewed as heresy. This is clear when we look at systems of ideas over many decades, periods of time in which the accumulation of injuries due to criticism has become conspicuously fatal. The Jehovah's Witnesses, for example, interpret each of the six biblical 'days' of creation as being seven thousand years long. Moreover, the Genesis creation account is interpreted as referring only to the creation of the Earth. The Witnesses have the reputation of being extreme Biblical literalists, and yet the original Genesis account of creation has been abandoned. I am not sure whether this current position was arrived at by a great number of marginal revisions, but one can easily imagine such a process.

This example prompted me to the thought that in analyzing the evolution of a network of ideas we ought to distinguish the following:

1. **The uninterpreted terminology of the doctrine as embodied in books and other sources;**

2. **The interpretation placed on the terminology;**

3. **The interpreter's theory about how his interpretation compares with previous interpretations (his own and others').**

If we wish to include ceremony and the like, we can substitute 'symbolism' for 'terminology'. The notion of an uninterpreted term is purely conceptual; in nature perhaps everything attended to gets some kind of interpretation.

It is important to recognize that #1 and #3 may remain constant while #2 changes quite dramatically. For example, in the simple case discussed, the words 'All swans are white' are retained, but the interpretation placed on them is altered considerably. We can also imagine that the person who proposed the claim about swans thinks that his later interpretation of his statement is exactly the same as his earlier interpretation—when challenged he might retort: I thought that all along.

The fact that old symbolism is often retained for new ideas is partly responsible for the overestimation of the stubbornness of ideologies. In European countries there are numerous 'socialist' parties, most of them formed over a century ago and some of them occasionally in power. In, say, 1930, 'socialism' was generally understood to entail something like this: abolition of private property in industrial means of production, conversion of all industry into public ownership, and abolition of all wide disparities in income among individuals. No one today understands the 'socialism' of the European 'socialist' parties in these terms. Distinctions between terminology and interpretation are particularly important in assessing the relevance of Lakatos's notion of a hard core versus protective belt in a theoretical system to ideological survival in the face of criticism.

Do All Immunizing Stratagems Abandon the Original Theory?

Many immunizing stratagems actually abandon the theory they were introduced to save, while many others lower the chances that the theory in question will be reproduced and successfully compete with other theories. But to take account of Bartley's and Shearmur's criticism I need to distinguish more precisely between a privileged subset T of a set of assumptions, and a useful but dispensable subset A. The more subtle claim then is that by tinkering with the subset of dispensable assumptions A, any T may be preserved in the face of any counter-evidence.

Suppose T & A yields as a consequence the implication e, but the accepted counter-argument implies $-e$. If the response of an ideology to criticism is to modify its assumptions then it may replace A by A' in one of three ways:

(1) T & A′ → − e, where A′ = − e. .

(2) T & A′ → − e, where − e is not derivable from either T or A′ alone.

(3) Such that neither T & A′ → − e, nor T & A′ → e.

If (1) then information content will be lowered and each successive theory will increasingly become a burdensome hotchpotch of unrelated hypotheses, sacrificing by incremental steps the preference for systematic organization. The system also becomes more difficult to learn and pass on. Moreover, there is no proof that a replacement A′ that is consistent with T can always be found (T and − e may be inconsistent).

If (2) then T is retained and also used systematically in the derivation of − e. There may even be an increase of information content. But this latter would make T & A′ even more open to criticism. Again, there is no general proof that for any counter-evidence - e against any theory T & A there is always a suitable A′ that in conjunction with T will yield − e.

If (3) then there is clearly a loss of information content. Weakening A so that T & A′ no longer implies e may also necessitate a loss of other implications that were important in solving problems for which T & A was initially adopted.

TYPES OF IMMUNIZING STRATAGEMS

Not all immunizing stratagems involve modification to the information content of a theory's assumptions. Some that at first do not seem to fall into this class can be interpreted this way, but not all. I have made a list of the types of immunizing stratagems, so that we can decide which ones involve the abandonment of the original theory and which impair the theory's chances of spreading:

1. **Denying the refuting evidence, *e*;**

2. **Reinterpreting the theory as a definition or the implication of a definition;**

3. **Adding other assumptions to T in the presence of which the resulting theory is consistent with or implies *e*;**

4. **Subtracting assumptions from T such that the remaining set of assumptions is consistent with or implies *e*;**

5. **Reinterpreting the theory as essentialistic;**

6. Introducing the idea that the theory is beyond the capacity of human reason to criticize or test (for example, 'God moves in mysterious ways');

7. Introducing ad hoc exclusion clauses to T for special cases;

8. Alternating between two or more versions of a theory.

1. *Denying the refuting evidence, e.* An example of the denial of evidence is Marx's attitude to the price of goods offered for sale that are not mass-produced commodities, such as valuable paintings, unworked mineral deposits, and so forth. In these cases, Marx asserts, the prices are "imaginary, like certain quantities in mathematics" (Volume I, p. 105). It may look as if Marx is saving the labor theory of value but he is substituting another theory instead, one that may well be implied by the original theory but certainly one of much lower information content.

Suppose the refuting evidence, *e*, is denied under all circumstances. For example, in the swan case, the person who advanced the theory that all swans are white may simply deny that any black swan presented to him is black.

At first glance this may not look like a case in which the original theory is abandoned. But let us look more closely. At least some of the information content of an empirical statement is logically equivalent to the class of basic statements with which (perhaps in the presence of other assumptions) it is inconsistent. In other words, the basic statement that constitutes *e* would be part of the meaning of T. Now if no basic statement is treated as inconsistent with a purported empirical statement, then we may infer that it is, after all, non-empirical. As a corollary, it follows that the original claim was either wrongly presented as empirical, or was empirical and was later abandoned for another theory with the same or a parallel terminology. In either case, the original claim has been abandoned.

2. *Reinterpreting the theory as a definition or the implication of a definition.* Reinterpreting a theory is in some cases abandoning the earlier theory; in some cases it is simply changing the conceptual structure without changing the theory. We will see in the case of Marx's Labor Theory of Value how the crucial term 'socially-necessary labor-time' is reinterpreted several times, the cumulative result amounting to an abandonment of both the original theory and the original problem (as these were announced by Marx at the beginning of *Capital*).

The assumption that one can modify a theory without abandoning it does have some truth to it. One can completely reorganize the conceptual structure of a theory without changing its empirical content. Popper himself was keen to make this distinction between a theory and the concepts in which it is expressed (Popper 1982, p. 42). The same theory may be formulated in many different ways and may use different conceptual schemes.

Changes in the conceptual system employed by a theory may function as protection against criticism, since they may disarm the critic—it may appear to the critic that the theory has been abandoned under the pressure of his criticism, whereas in fact the old theory is retained under the (intended or unintended) camouflage of the new concepts. However, such an effect has costs for the ideology's survival value that may be overlooked: the ideology has to be relearned—a transmission cost; and to the extent that the change of concepts is unintentional there is a loss of understanding of the theory. After all, if the ideologue believes that the conceptually transformed theory really is just the same theory, he cannot have a good grasp of the theory.

Can a propagandist guarantee that, by introducing ad hoc, purely abbreviative definitions to evade criticism, the system will not incur new unpredictable commitments that are themselves open to criticism? One might think that a purely abbreviative definition adopted as camouflage would be neutral, but as Popper argues, some abbreviative definitions are creative in the sense that they alter what can be derived from the theory (Popper 1982b, p. 170). A definition is creative if there are theorems not containing the defined term that cannot be derived without the help of the definition of the term. There is no routine way of telling whether a definition is creative or not, so even seemingly trivial evasive redefinitions may have unwanted but unforeseeable repercussions in the rest of the system, perhaps creating other more serious avenues for criticism. Moreover, even if an evasive definition is at first purely abbreviative, it may become creative by the removal or addition of an axiom to the system.

3. *Adding assumptions.* One might at first think that there are two main ways in which a theory T may be immunized through changes in the assumptions of the theory: 1. a move from T to T' (where T' is the conjunction of T and one or more auxiliary assumptions, denoted by B); 2. a move from T to X (where X is T minus some of its assumptions, perhaps with replacements). Only #2 represents the abandonment of assumptions of T, and its replacement by another theory. One might argue that #1 preserves the original theory within the substitute, and therefore immunization can preserve an ideology. Thus Lakatos says:

> For instance, we may have a conjecture, have it refuted and then rescued by an auxiliary hypothesis which is not ad hoc in the senses which we have earlier discussed. It may predict novel facts some of which may even be corroborated. (Lakatos 1970, p. 175)

But #1 is not a logically possible immunization. The modified theory cannot be consistent with the falsifying evidence if one simply adds extra assumptions that increase information content. For suppose theory T is false with respect to evidence e; then, since a conjunction is false if and only if one of its conjuncts is false, any conjunction consisting of T and an extra assumption B will also be false with respect to e.

This general point can be applied to Boudon's discussion of this issue. Boudon's failure to distinguish between different components of a theory allows him to infer that a refuted theory can be consistently retained by adding extra assumptions:

> Suppose that a physicist of Newton's time discovers that a planet is deviating from the orbit assigned to it by theory T. T could nevertheless be kept thanks to an adventitious hypothesis. (Boudon 1986, p. 161)

and because of exit costs of leaving T for T' (an alternative theory) and entry costs (such as learning a new terminology) of adopting T', people will try to keep T going by reducing the inconsistencies between T and the facts of the real world by means of adventitious hypotheses (Boudon 1986, p. 162).

This argument amounts to a simplification of Lakatos's argument, discussed below. As we will see, Lakatos makes a careful distinction between different components of the theory at issue.

To make this point clearer consider the case of Le Verrier and Adams. They did not reject Newton's laws of motion and gravity. Newton's theory, consisting of the laws of motion and of gravity conjoined with auxiliary assumptions regarding the number, mass, position, and acceleration of the planets and the Sun, was inconsistent with the observation reports of the motion of Uranus. Le Verrier and Adams introduced another assumption: the existence of the planet Neptune, with a certain mass, position and acceleration. Now if an ideology adopted this tactic it would be adding to knowledge and sustaining itself. But the augmented theory is now more open to criticism, so it is hardly being guaranteed against criticism.

But the above is not accurate enough. What Adams and Le Verrier did was to deny one of the auxiliary assumptions of Newton's theory:

that there were no other planets in the solar system but Mercury, Venus, Earth, Mars, Jupiter, Saturn, and Uranus. Therefore, the modified theory of Adams and Le Verrier actually contradicted Newton's full theory (though not Newton's laws of motion and gravity alone). If any ideologist did this he would be abandoning his ideology.

4. *Subtracting assumptions from T.* Subtracting assumptions that reduce the information content of an ideology effectively means that the original theory is abandoned. Though subtracting disjuncts may increase information content, for a statement p is logically stronger than 'p or q'. We will see below that Lakatos effectively replaces a conjunction of premises in Newton's theory by their disjunction and thereby empties the theory of much content.

5. *Reinterpreting the theory as essentialistic.* As we'll see in the case of Kepler, if he had tried to sustain his masters' position on the circularity of planetary orbits by asserting that the orbits of planets are essentially circular, he would have replaced a hypothesis with much content with one of possibly zero content. But not all essentialistic hypotheses are completely devoid of content. Hume says of the Peripatetics (the early followers of Aristotle) that when they were asked for the cause of a phenomenon, they would resort to faculties or occult qualities. They would say that bread nourishes by virtue of its nutritive faculty and senna (a laxative) purges by virtue of its purgative powers (Hume 1978, p. 73).

Hume took these hypotheses as devoid of content, but in fact they could be interpreted so that they ruled out some possibilities, such as the class of causes which lie outside the bread or senna. But as with the swan hypothesis, in making the interpretation, one would have to check it against the proposers' background knowledge and problem situation. However, if the theory is empirical in Popper's sense, then replacing it with an essentialistic theory will abandon much content. I argued in Chapter 1 that humans prefer to adopt ideas of higher information content. Essential explanations often imply an ultimate explanation. Essentialist immunizations run the risk of offending the desire for more information because they rule out further generalizations, explanations of greater depth. The idea may then lose in a competitive struggle with other ideas that address the same problems more fruitfully.

6. *Introducing the idea that the theory is beyond the capacity of human reason to criticize or test.* This sort of tactic is very interesting. Neither Marx nor Freud resorted to it as it would have been completely anathema to their Enlightenment inclinations, but it is a move that keeps cropping up in the history of the Abrahamic religions. It's an example of

what Bartley called a retreat to commitment. But its strength can easily be exaggerated. To function properly it must be kept under control, for it may backfire. For example, a skeptic may retort: If God moves in mysterious ways, how do you know that it is God and not Satan that speaks to you on any given occasion? God's command to Abraham that he sacrifice his son Isaac was, I suppose, a mysterious way of acting. But when Abraham obeyed God's command he did not first try to test the identity of the voice that spoke to him. But why not? It could have been Satan, as far as he knew—if, as you say, God moves in mysterious ways. So there is a counter-argument.

The original theory—that God exists—looks as though it has been retained. But has it? At first we had the confident assertion that a unique being answering to a definite description (all-powerful, all-knowing, completely benign) exists. This conception of God rests upon the tacit assumption that we can make sense of his actions. But since we can make no sense of such a being requiring us to kill our children, we may say that we can identify God regardless of our understanding of his actions, because God's motives are unfathomable. But now we have a different theory before us. The claim that God is unfathomable is at odds with the believer's wish to make definite statements about God and his actions. The doctrine that there is a completely unfathomable mysterious something seems to be almost no doctrine at all, and the closer we move to it, the less we can really claim about the something in question. How, for example, could we check that there is not more than one unfathomable God? And what is the difference between an unfathomable being who means us well and an unfathomable being who despises us or is indifferent to our welfare?

7. *Introducing ad hoc exclusion clauses for special cases.* The introduction of ad hoc exclusion clauses is also a mode of abandoning the original claim. For example, suppose someone advances the theory that bread nourishes, but then notices that a certain batch of bread kills some people. If he then says that bread nourishes, except that particular batch which killed those people, then he has reduced the content of his claim and therefore abandoned the original theory. As more counterinstances are dealt with in this way the theory becomes increasingly a hotch-potch of unrelated hypotheses, losing its systematic character. It not only becomes clumsy in application but more difficult to learn and pass on.

8. *Alternating between two or more versions of a theory.* The propagandist may alternate between what are really two or more theories. This is an interesting case in which the original theory is not completely

abandoned. It is quite possible that two interpretations of some canonical text are maintained, each being brought to the fore when powerful criticism makes it difficult to assert the other. Frank Cioffi has noted this phenomenon in connection with Freudianism:

> It is characteristic of a pseudo-science that the hypotheses which comprise it stand in an asymmetrical relation to the expectations they generate, being permitted to guide them and be vindicated by their fulfilment but not to be discredited by their disappointment. One way in which it achieves this is by contriving to have these hypotheses understood in a narrow and determinate sense before the event but a broader and hazier one after it on those occasions on which they are not borne out. Such hypotheses thus live a double life—a subdued and restrained one in the vicinity of counter-observations and another less inhibited and more exuberant one when remote from them. (Cioffi 1970, p. 474)

The bold version is still prized for its richness of information content and so is brought forward in certain circumstances. A classic example is Marx's historical materialism, which at first blush seems to make bold and surprising claims about human society. On being pressed, many Marxists quickly retreat to the assertion that economic factors are very important, an uninteresting proposition which no has ever disputed, while reverting to the original extravagant formulation at the next opportunity.

How does this phenomenon of switching back and forth between different versions of a theory fit into the evolution of an ideology? We may conjecture that this is a typical stage in the response of an ideology to powerful criticism. First we have the pristine doctrine promulgated faithfully with great confidence. Then, in response to criticism, we have the original doctrine supplemented by the immunized version, brought forward in appropriate circumstances. It's misleading to fasten on the 'success' this maneuver enjoys, while overlooking the increased burden of the excess theoretical baggage that this switching back and forth involves: new converts have to learn not only the original theory (usually quite cumbersome in itself) but also the adapted one. The likely consequences are increased errors of transmission and simple confusion, neither of which contribute to the morale of the movement and which may impair the propagation of the ideology.

It's my guess that this stage tends to be followed by one in which the original doctrine is completely supplanted by the adapted version. Thus we have, in chronological succession:

1. **Original doctrine;**
2. **Original doctrine plus adapted doctrine;**
3. **Adapted doctrine.**

In many cases the ideology may reach Stage 2 in the course of a single book. This seems to have happened with Freud's theory of dreams (*The Interpretation of Dreams*) and with Marx's Labor Theory of Value (*Capital*).

To further explore Bartley's suggestion that the use of immunizing stratagems may only amount to a modification and not an abandonment of the theory being 'protected', I must also consider Lakatos's distinction between a hard-core and protective belt and Duhem's Problem, since both of these seem at first sight to show that by tinkering with a system of hypotheses, refutation may be avoided and therefore a privileged sector of an ideology may be retained regardless of the facts. These ideas make more precise the suggestion that the 'essentials' of a system might be guaranteed from criticism and perpetuated even though the system evolves in response to criticism.

It turns out that all I need to sustain my claim that no system of ideas can be guaranteed against criticism is no more than Bartley and Shearmur concede: that the immunizing stratagem may simply 'damage the position'.

Hard Core versus Protective Belt

Imre Lakatos makes the distinction between the hard core of a theory, which is preserved in the face of unfavorable evidence, and a protective belt of hypotheses which may be changed to accommodate any unfavorable evidence. Lakatos argues therefore that no core scientific theory forbids any observable state of affairs. If this were true an ideology could in principle adopt this kind of stratagem to deflect criticism from a privileged portion of its structure. I argue that not only is this not always logically possible, but even if it were, it assumes superhuman powers of memory and reasoning.

First, most commentators have been too quick to assume that finding a suitable change in the protective belt is easy. But actually, creating such a protection may require more time, effort, and genius than creating an alternative core theory. Second, any attempt to guarantee that the changed protective belt will not adversely affect the hard core is doomed to failure: the line drawn between hard-core and protective belt is a conjecture, and one cannot always rule out the possibility that some remote logical consequence of the change to the protective belt will not be in conflict with the core theory. The same points apply also to Duhem's argument.

We can explain Lakatos's distinction between the hard core and the protective belt with the help of his story about an imaginary series of problems in Newton's research program (Lakatos 1979, pp. 100–01). A Newtonian using Newton's mechanics, law of gravitation plus generally accepted initial conditions, calculates the trajectory of a newly discovered planet, p. However, the planet deviates from the calculated trajectory. The question then is: Does our Newtonian place the blame on Newton's theory? No, he attributes the failure in prediction to his statement of the initial conditions: there is an as yet unobserved planet p' which perturbs the trajectory of p. The Newtonian calculates the mass and orbit of this planet p' and asks an astronomer to try and detect it. The astronomer fails to observe it, but undeterred the Newtonian sustains his allegiance to Newton's theory and conjectures that the planet p' is too small to be observed even with the most powerful of current telescopes, and applies for a research grant to build a more powerful telescope. In three years the new telescope is built and is trained upon the sky. The planet p' remains undiscovered. Yet, our Newtonian persists to deflect criticism from Newton's theory, suggesting that a cloud of dust hides the planet from us. He calculates the properties of the cloud and a satellite is sent up to detect it. By now the reader will be able to continue the story for himself for a while without much trouble. Lakatos's point is that with resolution and enough ingenuity, the Newtonian can select a part of his set of accepted statements as a privileged sector to be made safe from criticism by appropriate changes in other beliefs.

Lakatos supplies historical illustrations of research programs whose protective belts have gotten into trouble, but then saved not by revising the initial conditions, as in the above example, but by very fruitful advances in either fundamental theory (Soddy's contribution to Prout's program) or mathematical technique (Pauli's contribution to Bohr's old quantum theory). A modern version of Lakatos's story might focus on the hunt for the so-called dark matter, matter whose existence is postulated on the assumption that the universe is expanding despite gravitational attraction, but at a rate too slow given the relatively small amount of observable matter in the universe. This search has had a number of disappointments, but the researchers continued to search for a suitable particle, the most hopeful being the neutrino. However at first neutrinos could not even be detected, and when they were it was thought they were not heavy enough. But then several researchers were able to detect heavy neutrinos.

Lakatos drew the conclusion that in fact no scientific theory can be refuted because the theorist can always introduce auxiliary hypotheses to deflect criticism from the theory:

> exactly the most admired scientific theories simply fail to forbid any observable state of affairs. (p. 100.)

However, Popper has undermined this contention. Lakatos promises to back up his "characteristic story" with a general argument, but this general argument can only succeed if the most admired theories are denuded of part of their fundamental content. In assessing Lakatos's argument, Popper says, it is important to be clear that his thesis does not depend on arguing from defective observations:

> . . . even if there were a firmly established empirical basis to serve as a launching pad for the arrow of the modus tollens: the prime target remains hopelessly elusive. (p. 100)

Lakatos feels that he can generalize from the "characteristic story" to the most respected theories, such as Newton's. But, Popper argues, this would require the assumption that any deviations of a planetary orbit from its predicted path can be accounted for by Newton's theory by postulating the influence of some other planet (more generally, massive body). However, as Popper points out, there are an infinite number of planetary orbits which cannot be accounted for in this manner. For example, Newtonian gravitational theory cannot explain a square or a triangular orbit, no matter what is assumed about the mass or position of other planets. Lakatos's story, Popper concludes, cannot therefore be characteristic, but is in fact quite exceptional.

Lakatos asserts that

> some theories forbid an event occurring in some specified finite spatio-temporal region (or briefly, a "singular event") only on the condition that no other factor . . . has any influence on it. (p. 101)

Putnam argued the same point (in Popper 1974, p. 221). Lakatos draws from this the conclusion that such theories never alone contradict a basic statement, but at minimum (he says maximum, but the meaning is clear) the conjunction of a basic statement with a universal non-existence statement saying that no other factor is at work. What Lakatos overlooks is that his result is obtained at the price of emptying Newtonian theory of important content. Popper argues that Newton's theory of gravitation amounts to the thesis that all bodies in interplanetary space not only move according to Newtonian dynamics, but their movements can be explained by an appeal to *gravitational forces alone* (Popper 1974, p. 1008). If this is true, then Newton's theory does not allow the possibility that other factors may be at work, as Lakatos's ceteris paribus clause suggests, but actually denies their operation, making the theory much stronger logically. And this is why Newton's theory was refuted by the first rocket that traveled outside the Earth's atmosphere.

O'Hear makes the same mistake as Lakatos. O'Hear criticizes Popper's counterexamples to Lakatos's thesis, saying that the peculiar orbits of the planets could be produced by powerful rockets on the planets involved. We'll ignore for the moment that this state of affairs is ruled out by Newton's gravitational theory as interpreted by Popper, to see how strong O'Hear's argument is in other respects. It is not clear that such an arrangement could produce rectangular orbits, and O'Hear supplies no argument here. O'Hear finds it sufficient to say that Lakatos's general point is grasped: "that such explanations are always possible" (O'Hear 1980, p. 102). But O'Hear seems not to have taken heed of Popper's reply to Lakatos in the Schilpp volume, where he points out that Lakatos provides no general argument for such possibilities: it is far from obvious that such explanations are always possible.

Watkins agrees with and elaborates O'Hear's argument, making use of his notion of observational predicates. Watkins begins with a useful distinction between the "fundamental" assumptions of a scientific theory and "subsidiary" assumptions, which Popper calls the initial conditions. In Watkins's account the "fundamental" assumptions of a scientific theory are universal statements. In the case of Newton's theory the fundamental assumptions are the law of gravitation and the laws of motion. The subsidiary assumptions would be, for example, statements concerning the position, mass, number, and acceleration of the planets. Watkins calls the fundamental assumptions taken alone the "core theory," T, and the combination of this with subsidiary assumptions the "fleshed out theory", T & A. (Watkins 1980, p. 324). If we make this distinction, Watkins argues, then we may say, along with Lakatos, that all core theories fail "to forbid any observable state of affairs." This, Watkins says, is because the "core theory lacks the observational predicates needed for a possible conflict with observation reports" (p. 325). Only the subsidiary assumptions can supply these predicates. He infers from this that Popper's proposed examples of potential falsifiers of Newton's core theory do not count as such.

Paraphrasing O'Hear's conclusion Watkins writes:

> Newton's laws of motion plus his law of gravitation say nothing about the physical make-up of the planets; in particular they do not rule out the possibility that the planets are enormous rocket like devices that can accelerate themselves in all sorts of ways. (p. 326)

In a straightforward sense, it's true that Newton's core theory says nothing about the chemical constitution or size or mass or structure of the planets. However, the laws of motion rule out an infinite range of logically possible accelerated motions of objects with mass, and therefore motions of planets or rockets. According to Newton's core theory, therefore, rockets cannot 'accelerate in all sorts of ways'. Newton's core theory may not have the predicates 'rocket' or 'planet' but it certainly has the predicates 'acceleration' and 'mass', and all one needs to know about the planets is that they have mass for the core theory to rule out infinitely large classes of their possible motion. We could say, for example, that the second law of motion rules out the possibility of masses moving in accord with the law $F = ma^2$. This is a little unconvincing because in order for these laws to contradict one another one has to assume that bodies with mass exist.

But I have a more convincing argument. A rocket cannot accelerate from zero to any finite velocity instantaneously. To modify Popper's rectangular orbit example, we can imagine a rocket moving at constant velocity v along each of the borders of the rectangle, stopping instantaneously at each corner, remaining stationary for an hour, then moving off instantaneously with constant velocity v to the next corner. (v could be any one of an infinite number of finite velocities.) We can imagine this, but according to Newton's second law of motion alone it is impossible. Since force equals mass times acceleration, an instantaneous change in velocity would require an infinite force. Could an obstinate Newtonian just postulate the existence of infinite forces? No, for that would make the mass of the rocket indeterminate because arithmetic does not permit us to divide an infinity by an infinity. (For example, aleph zero divided by aleph zero can have any value from 1 to aleph zero.) But the meaning of Newton's law is that given any two of the values, F, m, a, the equation will yield a determinate answer for the third. Therefore, Newton's second law of motion taken alone rules out infinite accelerations.

In arguing against O'Hear and Watkins here I have allowed their argument considerable latitude and still found it wanting. I ignored the fact that the core of Newton's system contained the assumption that all the forces acting on the planets were gravitational. But this assumption is implicit in the way Newtonians solved their problems. It effectively rules out O'Hear's rocket-propelled planets; a report of such phenomena would constitute a falsification of Newton's core theory and so could hardly serve to protect it. Newton's core theory does not have to mention rocket propulsion for it to deny by implication rocket propulsion of the planets, since such propulsion implies that planetary motion is governed (at least partly) by non-gravitational forces.

A similar argument applies if instead of rocket propulsion the forces applied are gravitational. Taking the law of gravity: $F = Gmm'/r^2$. (Where F is gravitational attraction; G is a constant; m & m' are the masses of two objects; and r is the distance between these masses.) Substituting for F: $am = Gmm'/r^2$. Substituting * (infinity) for a, and cancelling m: $Gm'/r^2 = *$. Hence, either G or m' would have to be of infinite size, and we would again have the problem of indeterminacy for one of the variables.

In this counter-example I have excluded Newton's atomistic theory of matter, for when it is conjoined with the laws of motion instantaneous accelerations follow as a consequence, which in turn leads to an absurdity. If Newton's atoms or corpuscles are infinitely hard and incompressible, one may ask what happens when two of them collide? Since momentum is conserved they would have to rebound from one another with an instantaneous acceleration. Now, since Newton's second law of motion states that force equals mass times acceleration, such an instantaneous rebound would imply that repulsive forces of infinite magnitude were involved in all collisions, which is absurd.[36] But it again brings up the problem that the masses of the atoms become indeterminate.

Duhem's Problem

Pierre Duhem's problem is the problem of attributing the failure of a prediction. Suppose someone wants to test a theoretical statement B_1. If a set of assumptions $B_2, \ldots B_n$, are required in conjunction with B_1 to deduce a prediction g, and the result of the experiment, e, contradicts g, one cannot conclude that B_1 must be false. One can, however, deduce the falsity of the conjunction B_1 & $B_2 \ldots$ & B_n. Therefore, Duhem concluded:

> the physicist can never subject an isolated hypothesis to experimental test, but only a whole group of hypotheses. (Duhem 1991, p. 187)

Even if we know that exactly one hypothesis is false, no experimental outcome will enable us to decide which one.

To make this clearer let's examine one of the problems that confronted Mendeleev's theory of the periodic table of elements. Mendeleev's Periodic Law states that if the elements are arranged in order of their atomic weights, a periodic repetition of properties is observed. The table that Mendeleev constructed actually makes many very precise predictions about the specific heats, boiling points, densities, and reactivites of elements. However, early on Mendeleev noted that according to its valence and other chemical and physical properties iodine should be placed after tellurium and before xenon, but this would then put their atomic weights in the wrong order, contradicting the Periodic Law. These anomalies, of which there were several, were called reversed pairs.

Mendeleev could have rejected the Periodic Law but he realized that the predicted position of iodine was based not only on the periodic law but also on assumptions to do with the observations and measurements of some of the properties of iodine, tellurium, and xenon. He had a choice of where to direct the blame for the failed prediction. Mendeleev chose to deny that the gaseous iodine used to calculate the vapour density and hence the atomic weight of iodine was pure. Noting that the gas was dried over anhydrous calcium chloride, he guessed that some of the iodine had been replaced by lighter chlorine, bringing down the measured vapour density and hence the calculated atomic weight. The important point is that Mendeleev faced a number of options left open by the experiment.

The relevance of Duhem's argument to ideology is this. The ideologist may seek to protect a privileged part of his system of assumptions in response to empirical criticism by jettisoning those assumptions he regards as of little importance. This privileged part of the ideology would then be guaranteed against empirical criticism. Popper tries to show how in some circumstances such a defense would be ruled out because we could focus the criticism onto just one hypothesis by comparing two systems:

> Admittedly, Duhem is right when he says that we can test only huge and complex theoretical systems rather than isolated hypotheses; but if we test two such systems which differ in one hypothesis only, and if we can design experiments which refute the first system while leaving the second very well corroborated, then we may be on reasonably safe ground if we attribute the failure of the first system to that one hypothesis in which it differs from the other. (Popper 1957, p. 132n)

If this were valid it would also further undermine Lakatos's argument, for the crucial experiment may focus on what he calls the hard core. However, Watkins has shown Popper's argument to be invalid. Watkins begins by paraphrasing Popper's description of the two systems to be compared by a crucial experiment:

> denote that one hypothesis by B_1 and the large number of hypotheses common to both systems by B_2; and let B_1' be the hypothesis which replaces B_1. (Watkins 1984, p. 321)

Watkins compares theories to recipes. Suppose we have two recipes for a pudding, one uses cinnamon P and the other P' uses nutmeg instead of cinnamon. P' proves to be a better pudding. But this does not mean that nutmeg is gastronomically superior to cinnamon. Perhaps by keeping cinnamon and varying other ingredients in P the chef might produce a pudding even better than P'. Something analogous holds for theories:

> Perhaps B_1 is true and B_1' is false, but B_1' is the better partner for B_2 because there is an error in B_2 that is cancelled out by a compensating error in B_1'. (p. 322)

One may quibble with the assertion that the errors in the assumptions are "cancelled out," for the falsity content of B_2 & B_1' is no less than (and possibly greater) than the sum of the falsity contents of B_2, B_1' taken separately. Watkins's point may be stated more accurately: a conjunction of two or more false assumptions can yield true deductive consequences that none of the assumptions taken separately could yield.

An example in political theory would be the following:

B_2 = Communism will emerge in a society if and only if more than 70 percent of workers in that society are employed in industry and involved in unions.

B_1' = Russian society in 1987 had less than 20 percent of its workers employed in industry and involved in unions.

(Suppose B_1 = Russian society in 1987 had 71 percent of its workers employed in industry and involved in unions.)

Even though both B_2 and B_1' may be false, together they imply the true statement that communism did not emerge in Russian society in 1987. Whereas if the true statement B_1 is conjoined with B_2 we may deduce the false statement that communism emerged in Russian society in 1987.

In Watkins's interpretation of Popper's argument the two theories are treated as if they were telephone numbers of the same length, so that two theories differing in at most one hypothesis is analogous to two telephone numbers differing in at most one number position. But it seems not to take account of the situation in which the two theories that are put to the crucial test are exactly the same except that one has an extra hypothesis, symbolically T and T & A. But this is not a possible interpretation of Popper's suggested exception, for it is logically impossible to have both T → -e and T&A → e. The theories in Popper's proposal must be representable as T & A and T & -A.

I accept that it is sometimes possible for an ideologist to protect a particular sector of his assumptions from some counter-evidence that undermines his assumptions taken as a whole, by tinkering with what he regards as trivial auxiliary assumptions. But no one has yet proved that this can always be done for any particular system, for any counter-evidence. It has yet to be shown, therefore, that an ideology can always in principle be guaranteed from criticism on account of Duhem's thesis.

There is also a purely practical problem for the propagandist in protecting his privileged sector of assumptions. Propagandists have a limited reservoir of immunizing stratagems, especially in the short run, and persistent criticism will tax the most inventive apologist. Alan Musgrave makes a similar point in regard to theorists in science. Against Lakatos's idea that scientists can always defend the hard core of their research program, Musgrave points out that outstanding Newtonians tried for fifty years to explain Mercury's perihelion without having to abandon Newton's laws, but despite their undoubted ingenuity they failed (Musgrave 1978, p. 195). Moreover, each movement faces competition for adherents from many other movements; each has more critics than defenders. The 'protective belt' may then collapse.

Changing Demarcation between the Hard Core and the Protective Belt

Again, in assessing the relevance of Duhem's and Lakatos's idea to ideological survival, we must take a long-term view. Who is going to police the distinction between the hard core and the protective belt of an ideology down the centuries? The terminology of a system of ideas needs interpreting, so it's a conjectural matter as to whether the system of ideas is being reproduced or not. Thus error in a doctrine may be eliminated by error in transmission. Moreover, later adherents may well disagree, wittingly or unwittingly, with earlier adherents about what constitutes the privileged sector of beliefs, especially when the earlier adherents are no longer around to argue the point. These disagreements may be genuine mistakes in interpreting the work of their predecessors.

Marxism is a particularly good example here. Marx had a very definite idea of what communism was: an industrially advanced society immensely more productive and affluent than European capitalism in the late nineteenth century, without any buying and selling of factors of production. The absence of any market in factors of industrial production was regarded as one of the indispensable parts of Marxism. In the 1920s and 1930s a devastating attack on the possibility of communism (or socialism) in this sense was launched by Ludwig von Mises and then by his former pupil F.A. Hayek (Mises 1935, pp. 87–130).[37]

It took time for their arguments to sink in, but by the 1950s and 1960s so-called Marxists were returning to 'market socialism'. There had been no explicit acknowledgment of error (the errors were attributed to Mises and Hayek!) but the old message had been dropped by many. Today many self-styled Marxists are in fact but usually unwittingly espousing some form of pre-Marxist socialism; they are Owenites, Proudhonists, or Pecqueurians, not Marxian communists committed to the abolition of any market transactions in factors of production. Many new forms of 'Marxism' have also emerged, further threatening the original demarcation between the 'hard core' and the 'protective belt'.

I will now lay out a general argument to show that there are limits to the ability of a propagandist to defend that part of an ideology that Lakatos might call a 'hard core' and Watkins a 'core theory'. The logical ramifications (the information content and logical content) of a theory cannot be fully surveyed. Therefore, when modifications are made to the protective belt or subsidiary assumptions A, the theorist cannot always conduct a consistency proof to ensure that remoter consequences of the changes in A plus other assumptions remote from the core theory will be consistent with the core theory.

In the following argument I will adopt Watkins's terminology and distinctions, with additions, but the same argument would carry through using those of Lakatos.

T = The core theory of the ideology.

A = The subsidiary assumptions of the ideology.

A' = Modified A.

W = Total world view. The set of all assumptions, implied and asserted, that the individual maintains either in belief or in argument.

$b = A' \backslash A$ (that which is in A' but not in A).

Assume that T & A implies e, but a counterexample c, which implies not-e, is responded to by the replacement of A by A', which in conjunction with T implies not-e (or is at least consistent with c). Assume that the modification of the subsidiary assumptions A to make A' amounts to the assumption b. Now, it is quite possible for b to be consistent with $W \backslash T\&A'$ and consistent with T, but for W & b to be inconsistent with T. For the propagandist to guarantee, therefore, that the adoption of A' would save T, he would have to survey the whole of his world view, which is practically impossible (and I would argue, absolutely impossible in principle). I have assumed that the world view W of the ideologist includes and is larger than his ideology T & A. Both Gellner and Shils have pointed to the fact that the ideologist exists in a surrounding culture that they cannot fully divest themselves of (Shils 1968, p. 67). This seems to be an inescapable part of the logic of the propagandist's situation: even if we assumed quite unrealistically that the propagandist himself was but a cipher of his ideology, his audience and converts have a much broader and richer belief-system that may interact in unforeseeable ways with the ideology.

But the difficulty is even worse for the real-life propagandist. Ideologies are adopted by people partly because they provide explanations or interpretations of new and unforeseen events and developments. These may include particular events—*coups d'état*, wars, economic slumps—or theoretical developments. To do this an ideology has to adopt changes in the worldview of its adherents and new subsidiary assumptions A' to interpret or explain these. Even granting the propagandist superhuman powers that enable him to eventually perform a consistency proof for each modification, it may be some time before the contradiction comes to light. By that time the assumption b may have acquired great importance for explanatory or rhetorical reasons in maintaining adherence to the ideology. Costs in terms of learning alternative interpretations without b may also be considerable. Some of the content of T may then be sacrificed in order to retain b.

The history of the criticism of Marxism supplies an illustration. In 1908 Enrico Barone developed a system of simultaneous equations that described in general-equilibrium terms the structure of factor inputs and prices in an advanced industrial economy. Many Marxists who had been stung by Mises's 1920 argument later mistakenly turned to Barone's article as a vindication of their hope that an advanced industrial economy might be run according to a single plan. But Barone's work had actually been intended as a criticism of the Marxist idea of socialism, by way of arguing that any administration of an advanced industrial economy could not avoid sharing all the major features of capitalism. And acquaintance with Barone's argument helps one to understand how complex the problem of economic calculation is and to better understand Mises's argument. Having turned to Barone's argument with the intention of bolstering their position Marxists became, as an unintended consequence, more open to counter-argument.

My argument here takes Watkins's distinction between the core theory and the subsidiary assumptions for granted. It then shows that even with this clear distinction between the part of the theory to be preserved and the expendable part, there is no guarantee of maintaining doctrinal integrity and propagational success. But with ideologies such as Marxism and Freudianism, there is no clear or generally-accepted distinction between the core theory and the subsidiary assumptions. Thus these ideologies are even more open to such self-destructive developments than would appear at first sight in the light of a straightforward application of the analyses of Watkins, Duhem, and Lakatos (analyses applied primarily to scientific theories) to ideologies.

Ideological Movements Split

There's a tendency in ideological movements for different members of the original group of adherents to favor different ways of interpreting the ideology, leading to inter-factional disputes as ferocious as a family feud. The intensity with which separate organizations which began as factions squabble among themselves is usually greater than the intensity of their quarrel with incompatible groups completely outside the movement. Highly enthusiastic ideological groups display most hostility to those groups closest to them, a fact beautifully satirized in the segment in *The Life of Brian* dealing with the Judean People's Front and the People's Front of Judea. A Trotskyist has more venom for a Communist Party member than he has for a conservative, and most venom of all for a different brand of Trotskyist. A Randian Objectivist of the Peikoff denomination has more venom for a libertarian than for a socialist, and most venom of all for a Randian Objectivist of the Kelley persuasion.

The greater concern with close heretics than with distant opponents is a tacit recognition of the fact that marginal deviations, if not nipped in the bud, can eventually add up to great deviations and great schisms.

Throughout its history, the Catholic church has many times convened special councils to lay down explicitly what is to count as dogma, and Protestantism has also been marked by the periodic institution of various conferences which have issued 'confessions' or declarations of principle.

Since a choice of different immunizing stratagems is a choice of different interpretations of the ideology, it easily leads to factions and splits. This is a very definite cost to the employment of immunizing stratagems. With the formation of such factions the original demarcation between the hard core and the protective belt can easily become blurred and abandoned. In any living ideology there is a continual struggle between attempts to achieve conformity and deviations tending to the formation of factions and ultimately to schisms. It is a form of unstable equilibrium in two senses. Firstly, even in the most stable reproduction of the ideology, there is a continual oscillation between deviation and correction. Secondly, once distinct factions are formed, the forces leading to greater dissimilarity between the factions and to organizational separation increase dramatically.

Unfathomable Implications of an Ideology

The question naturally arises: could not some very determined propagandist settle the problem as to what stratagems will be needed and used in advance and so keep the faithful on the one true path? All new recruits could be specifically enjoined to keep to these and only these stratagems. This would be analogous to Lakatos's "positive heuristic."

However, this problem of propaganda is in principle unsolvable. This is because of certain logical properties of theories (including the doctrinal theories of all ideologies) which make it impossible for any individual or group to foresee what specific immunizing stratagems will be needed in response to awkward questions and criticism. The work of Alonzo Church and other logicians can be used to show that no ideologist could construct such a proven complete set of immunizing stratagems.

What our propagandist needs in order to guarantee his position in advance is an effective method of listing all and only the possible counter-examples to his ideology, so that he can check whether any proposed set of immunizing responses would meet all these possible difficulties. An effective method is one that can in principle be carried out by a machine: at any stage the method unequivocally determines how the computation shall proceed and terminate. According to Church's theorem of the undecidability of the predicate calculus this cannot be done.

Imagine an arbitrary set of sentences constructed according to the rules of the predicate calculus. Church's theorem amounts to saying that there is no mechanical way of sorting these sentences into two sets: the set consisting of those sentences that are tautologous consequences and the set of those sentences that are not tautologous consequences—because although any tautologous theorem will eventually be placed in the tautologous set, there is no way of telling of any sentence not so placed whether it is non-tautologous or whether the method has yet to class it as such. A consequence of Church's theorem is that any theory with universal and existential quantification ('all' and 'some' statements) plus unambiguous cross-referencing cannot be supplied with an effective negative proof of theoremhood.

In the propositional calculus the truth-table method can determine eventually whether any particular sentence is a logical truth or not. The truth-table method is an effective positive and negative test of logical truth for this system. However, only a positive test is available for the predicate calculus. But the predicate calculus describes the formal structure of the most interesting part of ideologies: the claims to universal significance.

Every non-tautologous theorem of a theory is false in some interpretation; that is: every non-tautologous consequence has a possible counter-example. It follows that there cannot be an effective method of constructing counter-examples, for if there were then there would be a effective method of determining of any sentence whether it is not a tautologous theorem, contrary to Church's theorem. Our propagandist cannot therefore determine in advance a set of immunizing stratagems that would deal with all and only the possible counter-examples to his ideology because he cannot even determine the set of possible counter-examples to check them against. Of course, the argument does not exclude the possibility of the propagandists' simply guessing correctly what the possible counter-examples to his ideology are. However, we will see below that even in principle such counter-examples cannot be listed: they are nondenumerably infinite.

The non-trivial implications of any theory are infinite. No individual or group could therefore survey all possible criticisms and prepare standard responses to deal with them. To develop this argument it is helpful to distinguish between two associated but different senses of the content of a statement or theory, which Popper has called 'logical content' and 'informative content'.

The logical content of a theory consists of the set of all (nontautological) consequences which can be derived from the statement of the theory. The informative content of a theory consists of the set of all those statements which are logically incompatible with the theory. The latter idea derives from the intuitive idea that a theory tells us more, the more it prohibits or rules out.

There is a one-to-one correspondence between the informative content and the logical content of a theory, for to every element of the one class there is an element in the other class that is its negation. Thus whenever logical content grows, informative content grows also and to the same degree.

Now the argument for the infinite size of the logical content of any theory can be presented as Popper presents it:

> Let there be an infinite list of statements a, b, c, ..., which are pair-wise contradictory, and which individually do not entail t. Then the statement "t or a or both" is deducible from t, and therefore belongs to the logical content of t. From our assumptions regarding a, b, c, ..., it can be shown that no pair of statements of the sequence "t or a or both", "t or b or both" ... entail one another. It then follows that the logical content of t must be infinite. (Popper 1976, pp. 26–27)

The following is a proof of the assumption that no pairs of the infinite sequence of statements entail one another.

> The statement "b or t or both" follows from "a or t or both" if and only if it follows from a; that is, if and only if it follows from "a and non-b". But this last statement says the same as a (because b contradicts a). Thus "b or t or both" follows from "a or t or both" if and only if t follows from a; and this, by assumption, it does not.

Popper argues that since the information content of any theory is infinite, we can never know all that we talk about. Thus since Einstein's theory is incompatible with Newton's theory it must be part of the information content of Newton's theory. Newton could hardly have been expected to know this. Indeed, there are an infinity of complex, non-trivial theories which are part of the information content of Newton's theory.

"t" could be: "Communism will be realized when market monopolization has increased to the point where there is only one capitalist agency. And under present trends p, this will occur in exactly n years". (Where p is a specification of the characteristics of the trend, and n is a finite number.) Then the infinite sequence of pair-wise contradictory statements can be constructed by substituting $n + 1$, $n + 2$, $n + 3$,.$n + y$, and so on for the rest of the natural numbers. Clearly, however large n is there remain an infinity of logically possible years in which communism could be established. The same can be done with the hypothesis about trends, p. But all these theories, even though they are but a variation on t, constitute an infinite set and every one of them contradicts t.

Each of the above arguments is sufficient to show that D.J. Manning made a serious error in saying that ideologists

> see all in the way of their belief and see all of what they believe. (Manning 1976, p. 141)

In putting his ideas into text the ideologist changes in a very special way the logic of his situation. He creates a set of ideas whose implications and ramifications go far beyond his comprehension and thus control. He cannot completely foresee how they will fare in argument or what sort of criticism they will provoke. In fact, this problem goes far beyond the capacity of any abstractly conceived predictor. In an important sense the ideologist becomes alienated from his own thought. Bartley was well aware of this implication, but in some respects did not apply it to the evolution of an ideology under criticism. (See especially Bartley's 'Alienation Alienated", Chapter 18 of Radnitzky and Bartley 1987.) More importantly for our problem, no leader of a movement can control how the various propagandists will deal with criticism, specifically which immunizing stratagem (in our example, which substitutes for n or p) will be created in response to each criticism.

As I argued in Chapter 1, the logic of the propagandist's situation is such that if an ideology is to survive and propagate, its chances of doing so are increased if its adherents actually propagandize. The various propagandists will then meet various counter-arguments. But some of these counter-arguments will be unpredictable. As Popper has argued, new ideas—which includes criticisms and defenses—cannot be predicted. If the number of propagandists is quite small, then they may continually consult with each other about the appropriate response to each criticism. On the other hand, if the number of propagandists is large, then their responses to counter-argument cannot be controlled by some kind of democratic decision or from a center. The responses must be improvized in the course of debate. The possibility is then open for different propagandists to improvize quite different 'immunizing stratagems'. This will facilitate the emergence of factions.

But the gulf between various factions runs deeper. In understanding a criticism one is understanding the theory being criticized, either because the criticism brings out a previously unnoticed implication or because one sees that it does not. If different propagandists improvise different immunizing stratagems, they are at the same time developing different (though perhaps overlapping) understandings of the original canonical theory. As is clear from the above example of a Marxist-style *t*, a propagandistic theory allows infinite room for divergence of opinion on what figure, $n + y$, to substitute for a falsified prediction n. (The substitution may occur not in response to a failed prediction but as a necessary consequence of other changes in the overall doctrine.)

In addition, each new immunizing stratagem brings its own problems. And since the argument is general, each problem may be solved in any of an infinite number of ways. So we have a rapid accumulation of possibilities for the emergence of factions, the various propagandists possibly holding increasingly divergent interpretations of the same symbolism.

The General Structure of Immunizing Responses to Criticism

I have maintained that the introduction of an immunizing stratagem will bring with it its own problems, which will need further immunizing moves. I have also maintained that this process gets us further and further away from the original theory. If I'm right and the succession of immunized theories are in fact different theories how do we account for the appearance of continuity, for the relatedness of the theories? Once we grasp the general structure of the process that spurs the ideologist on from one theory to the next, we will have the answer to this question.

The general pattern of ideological evolution under criticism conforms to a schema proposed by Popper for the development of science:

Problem 1 → Theory 1 → Error Elimination → Problem 2

The original theory is an attempt to solve a problem. But this solution often has unforeseen problems of its own, so we have Problem 2. This new problem then prompts the modification to the original theory to yield a different theory, Theory 2. The pattern is infinitely iterative. Popper argues that even the problems are theory-impregnated, and this is also true, though not at first sight, of practical problems. It might at first seem that some practical problems, such as pain or severe cold, are just felt. However, practical problems arise, Popper argues, because something has gone wrong because of an unexpected event. But this means that the organism has previously adjusted to its situation by some expectation, a pre-linguistic theory (Popper 1976, pp. 132–33).

To illustrate how this schema can be applied outside of what Popper would regard as science, we may point to the evolution of the idea of original sin. This example is taken from Wells 1988. The belief that God is just naturally leads to the expectation that the virtuous will be rewarded and the wicked punished (Theory 1). But the suffering of innocents makes it hard to believe that happiness and unhappiness are distributed according to this principle. Theists, therefore, had a problem in reconciling their belief with the world (Problem 1). Now the idea that God will compensate the innocent sufferer in heaven and punish the happy wicked in Hell was unavailable to the early Hebrews because they had no belief in personal immortality. So the Hebrews supposed that the innocent sufferer was paying for the sins of some wicked ancestor. After all, it's always easy to imagine some wicked ancestor; any possible refuting evidence is more difficult to collect since one can hardly survey the whole of anyone's ancestry. The Hebrews were then armed with a new and 'immunized' theory (Theory 2). But this in turn brought its own problem, since it implies that the good in every succeeding generation must be punished until the end of the world, and that there is nothing one can do about it (Problem 2). This then prompts the emergence of a revision in the earlier doctrine, an elimination of error. The Christian idea of Atonement is one such revision: we are cleansed of our inherited sins by the death of Jesus, providing we have faith in him (Theory 3).

The logic of the situation is often much more complex, as is hinted at in the above analysis of how immunizing stratagems may lead to the break-up of a movement. The situation is perhaps better rendered with a branching structure in which each node represents an emerging faction dealing with the same problem in a different way (or with different problems, since factions may even disagree on what are the problems).

The above schema will help us to understand how Marx and Freud were led from one position to another in response to criticism. The schema helps us to see how the successive theories are, though different, related to one another. The thread that seems to tie them together is a problem: specifically the sequence of unpredictable problems that the attempt to solve an original problem leads to. We also see that since the way criticism is dealt with cannot be predicted, any living doctrine must in one sense be a rambling structure. The rambling nature of the doctrine through time is no obstacle to our analysis, but its very object. (Over considerable time the importance of the various problems may shift considerably, either because later generations have forgotten the original primary problem or because they have different interests.)

The schema will also help us to identify immunizing stratagems. When identifying immunizing stratagems it's not sufficient to analyze individual statements. We have to relate the sequence of theories to the original problem that the first theory was meant to solve. (In some cases we're fortunate to be able to relate the alleged immunizing stratagem to the explicitly formulated objectives of the theorist and his intentions to solve it. We will see that we can do this quite clearly in the case of both Marx and Freud.) For example, in the case of the swan hypothesis talk of essence could be identified as an immunizing stratagem if the original problem was to give empirical information about all swans—which in the hypothetical example is taken for granted.

Case Study: Marxism

Now let's look at a less trivial example of Popper's. In *The Open Society* Popper argues that Marx's theory of social development was refuted by the Russian revolution of 1917:

> According to Marx the revolutionary changes start at the bottom, as it were: means of production changes first, then social conditions of production, then political power, and ultimately ideological beliefs, which change last. But in the Russian revolution the political power changed first, and then the ideology (Dictatorship plus Electrification) began to change the social conditions and the means of production from the top. The reinterpretation of Marx's theory of revolution to evade this falsification immunized it against further attacks, transforming it in to the vulgar Marxist theory that the "economic motive and the class struggle pervade social life." (Popper 1966, p. 43)

Popper's claim here is quite bold and interesting:

1. **The original theory is saved from falsification; and**
2. **Immunized against further attacks.**

The reinterpretation that Popper is speaking of here is no mere change of conceptual baggage; there is a change in informative content as one theory is replaced by another. The 'reinterpreted' Marxist theory is really a new theory which did not exist before the Russian revolution and in preference for which the original 'stages' theory of economic historicism was repudiated. In the competition of ideas, Marx's theory of revolution has lost, and this is true even if Marxists are unaware that they are no longer reproducing Marx's theory.

Is the theory immunized against further attacks? In a way it is, for it is no longer presented in debate for criticism (although the text is still accessible to criticism). 'Reinterpreted' Marxism clearly is subject to less criticism for it has less information content. Indeed, it may not be open to empirical refutation. This is the important truth in Popper's claim that the substitute theory (for that is what it is) is not open to further attack. But in so far as it makes any claim at all, it's still open to some possible criticism, and is therefore open to future attacks. Moreover, even if it's not open to criticism with respect to the truth, it is open to the methodological criticism that the substitution is unacknowledged and reduces information. We should not overlook the possibilities here for confusion, and the notion of the immunizing stratagem may do a lot to clarify to the Marxist what his theoretical maneuvers amount to.

Marx's Labor Theory of Value

Marx's Labor Theory of Value affords another example of a theory whose immunizing stratagems served to abandon the original theory. Early in Volume I of *Capital* Marx informs us that, in equilibrium, prices of commodities, including the price of labor-power, are proportional to the amounts of labor, measured in hours, currently required in the production of those commodities.

Marx intended to probe beyond the ceaseless fluctuations of supply and demand, which he considered superficial phenomena. Marx called those economists who accepted some form of the labor theory of value "classical economists" (Petty, Smith, Ricardo) while those economists who focused their attention on supply and demand (Nassau Senior, John Stuart Mill) he called "vulgar economists."

As Marx developed his theory in Volume I of *Capital*, he introduced a number of restrictions and qualifications which effectively repudiated his original statement of the labor theory of value, absorbing supply and demand into the very conceptual structure of his theory. The main immunizing stratagem is carried out through changes in the interpretation of the term 'socially-necessary labor-time'. These changes are not simply changes of conceptual structure, but changes in informative content.

In discussions about immunizing stratagems, it's normally taken for granted that the immunizing stratagem is introduced later than the original theory, only after the original has encountered embarrassing criticism from outside sources. Part of the charm of Marx's theory of value is that it was issued with its own immunizing stratagem. Despite his failure, one can see in this Marx's sincere attempt to come to terms with difficult facts and possible objections. It certainly cannot be said of Marx's theory that it disregards potential criticism.

THE PROBLEM MARX'S THEORY OF VALUE WAS MEANT TO SOLVE

As I pointed out earlier, to identify immunizing stratagems we must first understand clearly what the theorist's problem is and how he intends to solve it. Marx begins his exposition of the labor theory of value in Volume I of *Capital* with this rather interesting argument:

> Let us take two commodities, e.g., corn and iron. The proportions in which they are exchangeable, whatever those proportions may be, can always be represented by an equation in which a given quantity of corn is equated to some quantity of iron: e.g., 1 quarter corn = x cwt. iron. What does this equation tell us? It tells us that in two different things - in 1 quarter of corn and x cwt. of iron, there exists in equal quantities something common to both. The two things must therefore be equal to a third, which in itself is neither the one nor the other. Each of them, so far as it is an exchange value, must be reducible to this third. (Marx 1974, Volume I, p. 45)

Thus Marx's problem is to discover this third quantity which will explain the exchange-ratio of commodities, and hence their price. Marx conceived of his project as similar to John Dalton's work in explaining the ratios in which different chemical elements combine by postulating an underlying factor. However, Marx was also under the influence of Hegelian dialectic, which sometimes made him think that he could prove and derive scientific theories by mere argument. Yet Marx was not cocooned within this Hegelian approach and was not insensitive to empirical facts. David McDonagh has suggested to me that Marx's use of such aprioristic arguments has more to do with Marx's admiration for the work of Aristotle, especially, in this connection, his method of intuiting the essence of things.

At any rate, Marx proceeds with an argument by elimination to establish what this third quantity can be:

> This common "something" cannot be a geometrical, a chemical, or any other natural property of commodities. Such properties attract our attention only in so far as they affect the utility of those commodities, make them use-values. But the exchange of commodities is evidently an act characterised by a total abstraction from use-value. If we leave out of consideration the

use value of commodities, they have only one common property left, that of being products of labor. (p. 45)

It is less my concern here to point out the fallacy in this argument than to note that Marx begins by assuming that prices are equal to values, defined as quantities of labor-time. Defenders of this bold assumption from superficial criticisms have been keen to point out that Marx regarded this initial statement of the theory as a starting point for further development, a simple model which he is planning to complicate later. When he says it, he already knows he's going to take it back. (Recent examples are Roemer 1988, p. 47; Elster 1985, p. 121; Sowell 1985, p. 103.) What they have not noticed is that Marx not only qualifies this conclusion but completely contradicts it, finally producing a theory in which *actual, observable labor-hours play no independent explanatory role at all*. Marx begins by explaining prices in terms of labor-time, but through a number of redefinitions of the term 'socially necessary labor time' he produces a theory which explains quantities of labor-time in terms of prices. The final theory relies heavily on use-value (or utility), which Marx has here explicitly excluded.

Marx's theory of value was also intended to explain the following problem: how can a capitalist buy capital and labor at their equilibrium market value then sell the finished product at equilibrium market value and still make a profit, without the aid of theft or fraud? This problem had to be solved in tandem with showing that the profit thus made is made by exploiting workers. (Roemer 1988, p. 2, takes this to be the only point of the Labor Theory of Value.) This special part of Marx's project is effectively abandoned by Volume III, which presents something tantamount to a cost of production theory of price and profit, though ostensibly maintaining the ultimate determining influence of labor-time. Nevertheless, independently of this and prior to it, Marx has abandoned his stated original project in Volume I because of the way socially-necessary labor-time is eventually defined.

Inadvertently Self-Inflicted Injuries to Marx's Theory of Value

On the way to the final theory of Volume I, Marx can be seen struggling with counter-examples. And it is in trying to take account of these recalcitrant facts that Marx step by step abandons the original theory.

Marx begins by taking account of two obvious objections. If the laborer is lazy or inefficient, or uses inferior technology, then he would take longer producing his product. Would this make his product more valuable, would it fetch a higher price? Obviously not. Marx accommodates this by stipulating that it is not any labor that counts, but only *socially-necessary labor*.

> Some people might think that if the value of a commodity is determined by the quantity of labor spent on it, the more idle and unskilful the laborer, the more valuable would his commodity be, because more time would be required in its production. However, the total labor-power of society counts as one homogeneous mass of human labor-power, composed though it be of innumerable individual units. Each of these is the same as any other, so far as it has the character of the average labor power of society, and takes effect as such, so far as it requires for producing a commodity no more than is needed on average, no more than is socially necessary. The labor-time socially necessary is that required to produce an article under the normal conditions of production, with the average degree of skill and intensity prevalent at the time. The introduction of power looms into England probably reduced by one-half the labor required to weave a given quantity of yarn into cloth. The hand-loom weavers continued to require the same time as before, but for all that, the product of one hour of their labor represented after the change only half an hour's social labor, and consequently fell to one-half of its former value. What determines the value of any article is the amount of labor socially necessary. Each commodity is to be considered as an average sample of its class. (pp. 46–47)

Marx is saying that to calculate the value of each commodity we should take the total labor required to produce the whole supply of commodities of that particular kind, and divide by the number of commodities of that kind.[38]

But even if we only count socially necessary labor as here defined, some labor—we usually call it skilled labor—produces more value than other labor. Marx's response to this problem is to treat various types of skilled labor as multiples of unskilled labor—"simple, average labor" (Of course, if it is simple, that is, the labor yielding the lowest amount of value, it cannot be average.) But by what means do we reduce the one to the other?

Marx says that "Experience shows that this reduction is constantly being made" (p. 51). That is, the reduction is made by the processes of market exchange and competition. The ratio of skilled labor to unskilled labor is the ratio in which their products exchange. There is no independent (for instance, physiological) way to measure the relevant amount of 'skill'. Marx seems to have forgotten that the problem is to explain price in terms of labor-time, not labor-time in terms of price.

Eugen von Böhm-Bawerk seems to be the first to have noticed and criticized this aspect of Marx's argument (Böhm-Bawerk 1896). It's true that Marx also tries to deal with this in another way later by reducing skilled to simple labor via the labor expended by teachers in developing the skills. However, as Elster points out, this and subsequent attempts by defenders of the labor theory of value, have all failed.[39]

Suppose a great deal of socially-necessary labor-time has been spent on a thing which is useless. No one will buy it, so it will have no exchange-value at all. Marx sees this obvious objection, but his solution is far from happy. He simply stipulates that:

> nothing can have value, without being an object of utility. If a thing is useless, so is the labor contained in it; the labor does not count as labor, and therefore creates no value. (p. 48)

Here we have a contradiction of what Marx had said earlier:

> the exchange of commodities is evidently an act characterized by a total abstraction from use value. (p. 45)

If nothing can have value without being an object of utility (having use-value), then the exchange of commodities cannot be an act characterized by a total abstraction from use value. We no longer have the original theory as stated, but one in which socially-necessary labor-time depends upon use-value.

Is usefulness merely a necessary condition, given the satisfaction of which the exchange ratio is then determined by the number of socially necessary labor hours required, without further reference to use-value? That would still not be a total abstraction from use value, but the contradiction could then be viewed as no more than a matter of loose expression. But Marx says:

> Suppose that every piece of linen in the market contains no more labor than is socially necessary. In spite of this all the pieces taken as a whole may have had superfluous labor-time spent upon them. If the market cannot stomach the whole quantity at the normal price of 2 shillings a yard, this proves that too great a portion of the total labor of the community has been expended in the form of weaving. The effect is the same as if each weaver had expended more labor-time upon his particular product than is socially necessary.

So it is not merely that Marx stipulates that nothing can have value (meaning labor-value) unless it has use-value. He also says something additional to that, and going way beyond it. He maintains that the amount of socially-necessary labor-time allocated to production of some specific type of commodity will always be governed by the market demand for that type of commodity (and therefore by use-value, which he has informed us is entirely a matter of human wants expressed in market demand).

Thus we finally learn that how much labor-time counts as socially-necessary labor-time is itself defined in terms of the results of exchange, in terms of what it was supposed to explain, and furthermore is defined in terms of market demand! The semblance of a labor theory of value is maintained throughout by using the term 'socially-necessary labor-time', but in the development of this notion the original theory is jettisoned, and replaced by one that actually contradicts it. It is significant that ammunition for the criticism of Marx's doctrine can be found in the canonical text, and this fact has been very important in the evolution of Marxism—specifically, its lack of success in the British socialist movement.

In 1884, the economist, active socialist, and Unitarian Minister, the Reverend Philip Henry Wicksteed criticized Marx's economic theory in a socialist journal. George Bernard Shaw replied to this article, defending Marx's Labor Theory of Value. A debate ensued and Wicksteed, drawing on the material in *Capital*, convinced Shaw that the Labor Theory of Value was false and the new marginal theory true. (By marginal theory I mean the theory of marginal utility developed in the 1870s by Jevons, Menger, and Walras.) This debate played a part in ensuring that British socialism never became Marxist.

Wicksteed pointed out that Marx himself had said that, to produce value, labor must be *useful* labor. It followed that it is not true that the only thing in common between commodities is labor; they also have usefulness:

> If only useful labor counts, then when the wares are reduced to mere indifferent products of such labor in the abstract, they are still *useful* in the abstract, and therefore it is not true that "nothing remains to them but the attribute of being products of labor", for the attribute of being useful also remains to them.

Marx completed and published only Volume I of *Capital* during his lifetime. The next two volumes were composed by Engels from his notes and published after Marx's death. (The fourth volume, *Theories of Surplus Value*, a history of economic thought, was published even later than Volume III.) Even though Marx had explicitly worked out the analysis for Volume III of *Capital* several years before he published Volume I, it was sixteen years after the publication of volume I that Volume III was published.

Many have supposed that it was ill-health that delayed Marx. However, there is another possibility. It seems likely that Marx's slowness in getting *Capital* finished was due to his seeing the faults in the whole enterprise. The problems with the Labor Theory of Value became increasingly obstinate, leading Marx into contradictory positions which eventually (we may surmise) demoralized him. He couldn't complete it because he had come to realize that he couldn't see a way to complete it. It was only through Engels's pestering Marx continually that Volume I was completed, and Marx did virtually no work on the project for some years up to his death, despite the fact that Engels was supporting Marx financially, on the understanding that he was hard at work on it.

THE EVOLUTION OF THE LABOR THEORY OF VALUE IN VOLUME I OF *CAPITAL*

PROBLEM 1
What determines the equilibrium prices of commodities in capitalism?

THEORY 1
The relative amounts of labor-time required to produce each commodity.

PROBLEM 2
But any labor will not count: for example, lazy or inefficient or technically outmoded labor.

THEORY 2
It is the socially necessary labor-time that determines the price of a commodity (socially necessary labor-time defined at this stage only in terms of technical conditions of production).

PROBLEM 3
But skilled socially-necessary labor yields more value per hour than unskilled socially-necessary labor.

THEORY 3
Skilled labor is just a multiple of unskilled labor. We can calculate this multiple from observing the ratio in which products of skilled labor are exchanged for products of unskilled labor, that is, the ratio of their

prices. This violates the original intention of explaining product prices by something independent of prices and independent of 'vulgar' phenomena such as competition or supply and demand. We therefore have an immunizing stratagem, and moreover one that abandons the original theory.

PROBLEM 4

If a commodity has no use, it will not sell. But we have defined socially-necessary labor-time as being independent of use value.

THEORY 4

The labor that went into production of a non-useful product does not count as labor.

Socially necessary labor-time is now defined as necessarily useful.

Use value is introduced and therefore the original intention is violated.

We therefore have an immunizing stratagem. This also abandons the original theory.

PROBLEM 5

If a commodity is over-produced, not all units can be sold at prices corresponding with the labour-time (all the labor-time allocated to producing commodities of that type, divided by the total number of commodities of that type).

THEORY 5

In order for it to be 'socially-necessary' labor-time, the labor-time allocated to the production of all commodities of a particular type is determined by what the market will stomach. Thus, how much of the actual labor-time expended in any industry is 'socially-necessary' is determined by market demand. This gives up the original intention of explaining relative prices without bringing in market demand.

Abandonment of the Theory of Exploitation and Profit

My aim has been to show how Marx abandons his Labor Theory of Value in Volume I of *Capital*. I should, however, say something about how Marx abandons the theory of exploitation derived from his general theory of prices, and also how this collapse in Marx's project together with Böhm-Bawerk's classic refutation has affected contemporary 'Marxists'.

Recall that the purpose of the theory of surplus value (based on, or equivalent to, the Labor Theory of Value) is to explain how, without resort to fraud, theft, or violence, a capitalist, buying and selling goods at their value, can make a profit by exploiting workers. Some intellectuals before Marx, such as the English socialist John Bray and the notable contemporary of Marx, Pierre-Joseph Proudhon, had argued that interest and profit were made through swindling the workers. To prevent this occurring, Proudhon even proposed that interest be eliminated by making prices conform to labor values. Marx's method is to build a model of capitalism that ignores violence and fraud, in order to show that, even so, workers are exploited.

As Marx sees the problem of surplus-value, the capitalist pays for the various inputs into production and sells the product for a sum greater than what he has paid for all the inputs. But if value is governed by labor-time, then it would seem that the capitalist's profit, the excess of the selling price over the sum of the prices of all the inputs, cannot be accounted for.[40] Marx thinks he has found the solution to this puzzle in his distinction between labor and labor-power. In Marx's account, the capitalist does not buy the worker's labor, but his labor-power. The value of labor-power, like the value of everything else, is determined by the socially-necessary labor-time required to produce that labor-power, and that means: to produce the worker himself. In other words, wages are determined by the workers' subsistence. But the worker can produce more than his subsistence, and this 'surplus' becomes the capitalist's profit.

According to Marx's account, a capitalist hires a laborer to work for a period of time and can within this period legally command the laborer to produce more than his means of subsistence. If the laborer works for ten hours a day, and it takes five hours a day to produce the worker's subsistence, then the laborer is paid enough to cover the five hours corresponding to his subsistence. He actually works for five hours to replace his subsistence, and a further five hours to generate the capitalist's surplus or profit. The difference between the laborer's means of subsistence, counted in labor-time, and the extra labor-time the capitalist makes the worker perform is what Marx calls surplus-value. He takes this as a measure of exploitation.

If prices are proportional to labor-time, then it follows that profits will be proportional to surplus-value. Moreover, since Marx also maintains that labor-time is the sole determinant of value (or, as he sometimes says, is just the same thing as value) and therefore of equilibrium price, it follows also that machines, vehicles, raw materials, factory buildings, and other equipment, though made by labor, do not add any new value to the product, but simply pass on their labor-values to the product. Thus surplus-value is a necessary and sufficient condition of profits.

But this line of argument leads to an unacceptable conclusion. Marx's theory as laid out in Volume I logically entails that comparatively labor-intensive industries will have higher rates of return than comparatively capital-intensive industries, whereas (as Marx fully accepted) in real life, we never observe this: we always observe that rates of return are the same in all industries, except for brief periods of disequilibrium. And this must be so, because if there were a difference in rates of return, capital would swiftly be moved from the lower-return industries to the higher-return industries until the rates were equalized.

This meant that profits could not be proportional to surplus-value, except when the ratio between labor and capital (what Marx calls "variable capital" and "constant capital") is the same in all industries, which in fact it never is. Böhm-Bawerk showed in detail that Marx's attempt, in Volume III of *Capital*, to save the Labor Theory of Value from this hard fact is unsuccessful. Marx tacitly substitutes a cost of production theory for the labor theory of value, but tries to maintain the semblance of the original claim by various arguments intended to show that prices are in some sense still ultimately governed by what he calls "the law of value." This is the notorious 'transformation problem', in which Marx tries to mathematically 'transform' labor-values into what he calls 'prices of production', and to retain the idea that we cannot arrive at the 'prices of production' without starting from labor-values.[41]

Contemporary Marxists knowledgeable about the history of economic thought, such as Steedman and Morishima, have to a large extent absorbed the impact of Böhm-Bawerk's classic refutation of Marx's Labor Theory of Value. However, they try to retain some of the flavor of Marx's theory of profit by asserting that there still is some relationship between surplus labor and profit. Thus Morishima, for example, maintains, as the "fundamental theorem of Marxist economics," that a positive rate of surplus value is a necessary and sufficient condition of a positive rate of profit. But as Elster points out, a similar theorem can be demonstrated for any commodity employed in production (any factor input, such as paper, or iron, or electricity), and so does not show anything special about labor.

Obviously, profits are possible only if workers do not consume the whole net product. Similarly, profits are possible only if the electricity bill does not consume the whole net product. Moreover, such a theorem does not establish a causal connection (Elster 1985, p. 141). Thus, in order to retain some credible element of the Labor Theory of Value the proportionality between value and price is jettisoned. The result is a replacement theory of vastly lower information content than its predecessor—but one that is also open to obvious objections.

Many other so-called Marxists have trodden a similar path from the original theory propounded in *Capital*. For example, Clarke (1982, p. 99) reduces the Labor Theory of Value to the observation that within the labor contract characteristic of capitalism the capitalist can require the laborer to perform more work than necessary to furnish his subsistence. Clarke fails to notice that in emasculating the theory in this way he jettisons a determinate theory of price and profit. Furthermore, most workers receive wages or salaries many times what would suffice for their subsistence, so the claim that workers' level of pay is determined by their subsistence morphs into the claim that workers' level of pay may be any amount more than subsistence. All that's left is that we will not observe workers' pay rising to the point where there is no return on capital invested—where people put their savings into productive enterprises for zero return. This familiar fact is not in any way elucidated by Marx's theory.

Through many twists and turns and obscure incremental concessions to both internal and external criticism, the Labor Theory of Value has been substantially jettisoned either explicitly or by implication, at least by all Marxists who have a smattering of elementary economics and by all Marxists who have kept up with recent 'defenses' of Marxian economics.

Case Study: Freudianism

Here I mainly want to argue for the following points:

1. Some components of Freudianism are open to empirical falsification.

2. The basic theory, whatever that is, may not be falsifiable; it may be metaphysical in Popper's sense. But it is nevertheless open to sound arguments, and therefore its persistence is not guaranteed by its being closed to sound criticism in general.

3. These sound arguments can be psychologically and sociologically effective in undermining Freudianism. The perpetuation of Freudianism cannot be guaranteed, therefore, by immunizing stratagems or by adopting a metaphysical structure.

Popper's first argument against the scientific status of Freud's theory was propounded in 1919. This argument is intended to show that contrary to a good scientific theory, Freud's theory cannot clash with any particular observable behavior: whatever the conceivable behavior might happen to be, the theory can account for it. Popper argues that Freud's theory is different to Marx's theory, because whereas Marx's theory was empirical at first and only later became empirically irrefutable, Freud's basic theory was irrefutable from the beginning. Popper says that the theory does not need any immunizing stratagems to make it irrefutable. Thus in Popper's terminology it is a pseudo-scientific theory from the start.

Popper illustrates this with two radically opposite types of behavior. A man pushes a child into the water with the intention of drowning it; and another sacrifices his life in an attempt to save the child. According to Freud the first man suffered from repression (possibly of some element of his Oedipus complex) while the second man had achieved sublimation. The same fault characterises Adler's theory. According to Adler the first man suffered from feelings of inferiority (making him want to dare to commit a crime); and so did the second man (who wanted to prove to himself that he dared take a risk). Popper is saying that the basic theory of Psychoanalysis does not have any basic statements.

This argument only shows that Freudian theory does not predict specific behaviors. It does not show that Freudian theory is devoid of empirical implications which can clash with experiment. The theory may still be open to statistical tests. To illustrate what I mean, consider Eysenck's theory of personality. This theory predicts that most variation in personality between persons can be explained as occurring along two dimensions—extroversion-introversion and emotionality. This theory does not predict specific behaviors. Any particular behavior may be interpreted as either extroverted or introverted. Nevertheless, we do not reject this theory as being without empirical implications, since (for example) if a population of individuals is assessed by questionnaire for their specific position along these poles of variation we can then go on to make predictions about how the more extroverted will differ in their responses to various other tests from the more introverted. The predictions will concern 'more-or-less' response to the different tests, not precisely delineated behaviors; for example, that the more introverted will respond more to alcohol than the more extroverted.

Does Freud's or Adler's theory rule out any possibilities? Popper seems to accept S. Bernfeld's suggestion that Freud's theory predicts that the man will either repress or sublimate, but cannot tell which (Popper 1983, Volume I, p. 169). Is this verdict unfair? For example, it might be said Newtonian theory will not predict any particular event without the assistance of initial conditions: we do not thereby regard it as unscientific and closed to empirical refutation. Likewise, a Freudian interpretation must include details of the individuals whose behavior is being predicted or interpreted. Given such details we may then be able to decide in advance whether a sublimation or a repression is to be expected. But as we saw in our discussion of Lakatos's views, Newtonian theory does make some kinds of prediction without initial conditions; it does exclude some states of affairs within its domain. Indeed any empirical theory, Popper argues, allows the derivation of what we might call 'negative predictions'. From the theory 'All swans are white' we can derive the prediction 'You will not observe a black swan at 10:00 A.M. at place p on 14th February, 2024' (example adapted from Popper 1974, p. 998).

The important question for Popper is: Do Freudians supply such initial conditions in a way that is governed by the general theory? Newtonian theory will tell you what the variables are whose values must be specified; does Freudianism do this? It appears that for the basic theory no such initial conditions are specifiable. Moreover, there do not seem to be even observable negative predictions. One might say that one can derive the prediction 'Tomorrow at 10:00 A.M., if Jones is performing any psychologically important action, then he will not fail to be either sublimating or repressing'. But such a prediction is unobservable and therefore cannot be refuted.

So we cannot argue that Freudianism is on the same footing as Newtonian theory. Its predictions are more vague. Can it be argued that like the interpretations of everyday life, Freudian interpretations can be right or wrong and the subject of severe criticism, albeit criticism that is not as severe as that to which Newtonian theory is subject?

Jim Hopkins discusses this issue in his article 'Epistemology and Depth Psychology'. Arguing against Grünbaum's position that Freud's ascription of motives stands in need of inductive support, Hopkins says that psychoanalytic theory seems to be an extension of common-sense understanding, and therefore if common sense does not need inductive support—and Hopkins assumes it does not—then neither does psychoanalytic interpretation. In an extension of folk psychology, we try to apply motivational explanations to phenomena not covered by common sense. Hopkins illustrates his point in connection with Freud's theory of dreams:

In rational action motives produce willed intentions and real actions aimed at satisfaction. Here they produce wishes and mere representations of satisfaction, on the pattern of wishful imagining. (Hopkins 1988, p. 41)

Hopkins's argument is endorsed by Peter Binns (1990, pp. 531–552), but the argument seems to be invalid. A lot hinges on the extent to which psychoanalysis is an extension of common sense. Grünbaum might argue that if Hopkins's argument were allowed then one could argue by analogy that physics is in some sense an extension of common sense, and could therefore jettison its inductive procedures—clearly a non sequitur. Grünbaum might also retort that common sense employs induction, or even that Neo-Baconian rules of induction are an extension of common sense, so that Hopkins's recourse to common sense would not rule out Neo-Baconian rules of induction. Hopkins also fails to consider the possibility that common sense is at fault.

Popper's proposal is not that Freudianism be abandoned but that its advocates try to enhance its empirical content. Now while psychoanalysis may be an improvement on common sense in this respect (for it may at least be moving in the direction of increased content, if not empirical content), it's not sufficient to say that it has improved on common sense, if this is thought to exonerate it from any further demands. This last point is especially important if Hopkins thinks that the last word on psychoanalytic method is common sense.

Freud's Theory of Dreams Is Testable

Popper accepted Bartley's critical point that Freud's theory of paranoia is refutable. Freud's explanation of paranoia in term of repressed homosexuality seems to rule out active homosexual paranoids (Popper 1983, Volume I, p. 169). However, Popper says that this hypothesis is not part of the basic theory he was criticizing.

Nevertheless, whether Freudianism is refutable or not, my main contention holds: Freudianism, like Marxism, is criticizable and, moreover, has been abandoned by some former Freudians in response to criticism. But we can also say that at least some important components of Freud's theoretical edifice are empirically refutable. To illustrate this, I will focus on one of Popper's own examples: Freud's theory of dreams. We will then examine whether Freud's "basic theory" is refutable, and if not, the extent to which it is criticizable.

There is one theory of Freud's which is eminently refutable, since it is refuted every night: the theory of dreams. Popper argues that it is not refutable, or at least that it has been made irrefutable by the addition of a number of immunizing devices—specifically through the distinction between manifest and latent content, and finally by rejecting the original problem Freud set for his theory of dreams. Popper would accept that the theory is still open to criticism, for after all, that is the point of the term 'immunizing stratagem'. The adherent can still be taken to task for resorting to the immunizing stratagem. He may simply be unaware that the theory contains an immunizing stratagem; in which case, pointing it out may have a considerable impact on his belief. However, we may also argue that Popper's own analysis shows that interpreted properly, Freud's theory of dreams is empirically refutable too, and that Freud effectively gives up the theory, "without explicitly saying so" (Popper 1983, Volume I, p. 165).

In his *Interpretation of Dreams* Freud embarks on the project of "proving that, in their essential nature, dreams represent fulfilments of wishes" (Freud 1900, p. 286). These wishes arise from frustrated instinctual impulses which make use of residues of the day's experience to produce a symbolic visual representation of their satisfaction. The symbolic form of the satisfaction is a disguise to get past what Freud called the censor, another name for the super-ego or conscience, and to save the sleeper from waking. A dream, for Freud, then was a substitute gratification of impulses that are denied satisfaction in overt action because they contravene the dictates of conscience. More abstractly considered, Freud thought that a dream is a special way in which the psyche displays its general tendency to discharge tension.

As Popper points out, Freud was aware of one obvious objection to his theory: the existence of anxiety dreams and nightmares, dreams which represent the opposite of the fulfilment of a wish, the fulfilment of a fear.

Freud quotes several writers who are keen to point out that dreams are often of a distressing nature. He even makes reference to a study done by Florence Hallam and Sarah Weed on their own dreams which showed a preponderance of displeasure in dreaming. They found that 57.2 percent of dreams are disagreeable and only 28.6 percent positively pleasant. Freud writes:

> It does in fact look as though anxiety-dreams make it impossible to assert as a general proposition (based on the examples quoted in my last chapter) that dreams are wish fulfilments; indeed they seem to stamp any such proposition as an absurdity. (p. 215)

Here Freud looks like a model of the forthright scientist confronting and openly discussing the strong objections to his theory—rather like Kepler trying to fit the circular hypothesis to the facts. In this he conforms to

Popper's demand that a scientist look out for refutations. Popper would accept this, but, as is clear from our discussion of the demarcation problem, would also point out that it is the way the scientist deals with the apparent refutations that is just as important. Popper argues that this objection is dealt with by introducing a very powerful immunizing stratagem. The following is partly indebted to Popper's analysis of Freud's methodology, but my account differs to some extent in the hypothesized means whereby the shift from one theory to another is effected.

It is important to stress the meaning of Freud's earliest formulations of the theory. Careful reading of the text shows that as the problem of anxiety dreams looms larger in Freud's account, the formulation changes. The crucial word which is dropped from the later formulations is 'representation'. Originally, the theory is about what dreams represent; what dreams picture to us. In the end the theory is about what they are essentially, with little talk of what they represent.

Popper points out that in an analysis of one of his own dreams, Freud concludes that

> The dream represented a particular state of affairs as I should have wished it to be. Thus its content was the fulfilment of a wish and its motive was a wish. (p. 196)

Clearly the focus of Freud's discussion is what dreams depict, with their content. To reinforce Popper's point, this concern is reflected in further discussion:

> We have learnt that a dream can represent a wish as fulfilled. Our first concern must be to enquire whether this is a universal characteristic of dreams or whether it merely happened to be the content of the particular dream [the dream of Irma's injection]. (p. 201)

Careful reading of *The Interpretation of Dreams* shows that the last time we see the original formulation with Freud's original concern with what dreams represent is when he is discussing the dreams of young children:

> They [the dreams of young children] raise no problems for solution; but on the other hand they are of inestimable importance in proving that, in their essential nature, dreams represent fulfilments of wishes. (p. 286)

I also found this to be the first place at which the notion of essence comes into play and which is meant (in a Popperian kind of interpretation) to function as protection from criticism.

Popper argues that Freud proposed to overcome the objection posed by anxiety dreams by distinguishing between the latent and manifest content of a dream. Thus what appears to be an anxiety dream (manifest content) is in reality the representation of the fulfilment of a wish (latent content). But what we have here is not a protection, but an abandonment of the original theory.

> Almost straightaway Freud begins to modify (i.e. rejects) the original theory. We now have the theory that ". . . a dream is a (disguised) fulfilment of a wish." (p. 240)

The latent-manifest distinction marks the point at which Freud's concern has moved away from the problem of what dreams represent and on to what lies behind them, what motivates them:

> There is no question that there are dreams whose manifest content is of the most distressing kind. But has anyone tried to interpret such dreams? to reveal the latent thoughts behind them? (p. 215)

I conjecture that the transition from the early theory to the later one is assisted by the ambiguity of the word 'represent'. It can be synonymous with 'depict' or, more broadly, 'symbolize'; but it can also be synonymous with 'indicates', as a high body temperature may indicate illness. Freud uses it in the first sense in his original formulation but in the other sense in his later formulation in which the dream simply indicates the presence of a wish.

The latent-manifest distinction is supposed to be protection against criticism. Popper says that in Freud's mind this distinction solves the problem posed by anxiety dreams. Freud writes:

> The question raised was how dreams with a distressing content can be resolved into wish-fulfilments. We now see that this is possible if dream-distortion has occurred and if the distressing content serves only to disguise something that is wished for. (p. 227)

In Freud's theory the disguise is necessary to hide the wish from the superego, what we might call the conscience.

Clarifying Popper's point, we now see why the latent-manifest distinction is so powerful. Freud nowhere makes it plain how one would distinguish between a dream in which wish-fulfilment has been disguised and a dream which is not a wish-fulfilment. But this is necessary to make it an empirically testable theory. Any apparent counter-example can be dismissed as involving distortion and even counted as a verification. There are no limits set to the type and extent of distortion a latent dream content may be subject to. The illusion that limits are set is created, perhaps unwittingly, by the postulation of a certain number of processes of distortion: condensation, displacement, and secondary revision. But in reality the details of latent-content distortion are only constrained by the end product, the manifest dream. With sufficient intermediate steps one can condense, displace and secondarily revise any thought into any other thought. Freud's theory of dreams is rather like the theory that goblins and fairies exist, but with their magical powers they always manage to cover their tracks and always remain undetectable. Someone points out that no signs of goblins or fairies were observed despite extensive monitoring of their traditional haunts, to which the goblinologist retorts: 'See! I told you they always manage to cover their tracks; they are so clever. From what you have told me, they must have escaped your view in this way.'

In the light of Freud's attitude to experiment this should not surprise us. Freud was not interested in making his theories amenable to experimental testing. In a postcard to Rosenzweig in 1934, responding to Rosenzweig's attempts to study repression experimentally. Freud stated:

> I cannot put much value on these confirmations because the wealth of reliable observations on which these assertions rest make them independent of experimental verification. (As quoted by Eysenck 1986, p. 149)

Still, we must not lose sight of the fact that the original theory has been sacrificed in making room for an alternative theory that contradicts the original. This is an important point, not least because eminent interpreters of Freud's theory have taken the later causal theory to be the one and only basic theory of dreams propounded in *The Interpretation of Dreams*. There are in fact two theories:

a. All dreams represent wishes as fulfilled.
b. All dreams have wishes as their motives. These motives are the latent content of the dream.

The second of these actually replaces the first in the course of Freud's discussion. Adolf Grünbaum overlooks this transition when he asserts:

> Freud's wish-fulfilment theory of dream production is clearly a causal hypothesis. (Grünbaum 1989, p. 152)

The proposition 'All dreams have wishes as their motives' is a causal hypothesis, but the proposition 'All dreams represent wishes as fulfilled' is not. The latter is a universal interpretation of the content of dreams. In the case of the latent-manifest distinction we have an example of an immunizing stratagem that is tantamount to the rejection of the theory for which it was meant as protection (or that might be interpreted by Popper as protecting the theory). Moreover, it is a theory with less content, for the introduction of the latent-manifest distinction brings with it no independently testable consequences: the manner of distortion is inferred purely from the ways the dream deviates from the representation of a wish.

Popper's own account of Freud's attitude to apparent counterexamples shows that Freud effectively gives up the original theory. Popper quotes a passage from *The Interpretation of Dreams* which shows signs of Freud's demoralization over his theory:

> in order not to confirm the impression that I am trying to evade the evidence of this chief witness against the theory of wish-fulfilment whenever I am confronted by it, I will now give at least some hints towards an explanation of the anxiety dream. (p. 737)

This is in stark contrast to page 215, where Freud had confidently announced that

> there is no great difficulty in meeting these apparently conclusive objections.

Now Freud only promises "some hints" at a solution.

Popper points out that the hints are unsatisfactory even in Freud's eyes, and that Freud at last concludes that the whole topic of anxiety dreams falls outside the psychological framework of dream formation. Popper quotes a revealing sentence from the 1911 edition of *Interpretation of Dreams*:

> Anxiety in dreams, I should like to insist, is an anxiety problem and not a dream problem. (Popper 1982a, p. 167)

Thus Freud effectively abandons the theory, though Popper points out that it is not a conscious correction and admission of a mistake. But there are other comments by Freud which indicate this abandonment. In section ix of Freud's paper of 1923, Freud asserts unambiguously that some anxiety dreams are not wish fulfilments but "are the only genuine exceptions." However, this admission is not included in any edition of *The Interpretation of Dreams*.

I think we do have a genuine immunizing stratagem in Freud's attempt to develop his theory of dreams. Remember that we must identify an immunizing stratagem by noting first what the original problem was that the theorist intended to solve and then compare this with how difficult evidence is treated. We have seen that Freud actually abandons not only the original theory—all dreams represent the fulfilment of wishes—but also the original problem.

This digression into Freud's theory of dreams has revealed that at least some components of Freud's theoretical edifice are open to empirical refutation. We may also conclude that this openness to empirical refutation was effective in making Freud abandon the original theory, though without explicit acknowledgment. Freud abandoned the theory without perhaps realizing he had done so as an unintended consequence of trying to defend it.

We should now proceed to examine a further question. The original theory may have been empirically refutable, and Freud may have abandoned it. But is its replacement criticizable? Bear in mind Popper's position on the criticizability of metaphysical positions. My conjecture is that Freudians who embrace the replacement theory are confused and attribute more empirical content to the theory than it contains. But their confusion can be dispelled by comparing the theory with an equally weak theory that contradicts Freud's replacement. For example, one might as well hypothesize that all dreams represent not the fulfilment of a wish but the fulfilment of a fear, if not manifestly then latently. No matter what is represented manifestly in a dream one could always imagine some mechanism of distortion that would convert the latent fearful content of the dream into the manifest content. Such an argument might form part of a set of sound arguments that would prompt the Freudians to embellish their theory with greater testable content in order to escape from the uncomfortable situation of indecision. This would be predicted on the basis of Festinger's theory of cognitive dissonance.

One might at first think that a Freudian could defend Freud's theory of dreams from such a criticism by pointing out that the choice of a wishful, rather than a fearful, latent content and motive is not arbitrary but is constrained by the natural assumption that humans seek to achieve their ends and avoid pain and anxiety, specifically to live and reproduce happily. This is part of what Hopkins is suggesting when he refers to the relevance of common sense. This might be true for common sense, but there is no such recourse either in Freud's later developments of the theory of dreams in response to the problem of anxiety dreams or in the later developments of Freud's general theory. Fifteen years after the publication of *Interpretation of Dreams*, Freud was driven by the problem of anxiety dreams to say that anxiety and punishment in a dream may be exactly what is wished for, though perhaps not pleasant (Freud 1915–1916, p. 257). Freud maintained this position at least as late as 1932 (Freud 1932, p. 57), when he asserts that his division of dreams into wish-fulfilment, anxiety-fulfilment, and punishment-fulfilment keeps his theory intact. The anxiety and punishment are produced not by the instinctual wishes but wished by 'the other person', the censor. But this does not square with his intention quoted above of showing that the instinctual wish-fulfilling content of Irma's dream is not just an exception but "a universal characteristic of dreams." In the development of his general theory Freud postulated two fundamental drives: Eros and Thanatos. Eros is that instinct that strives to preserve and reproduce the organism; Thanatos is that instinct that strives to return the organism to the ultimate state of quiescence—death (Freud 1920). Thus the restraints on the attribution of different types of wishes are seemingly non-existent.

THE CRITICIZABILITY OF FREUD'S 'BASIC THEORY'

We have seen that at least some components of Freud's theory are empirically refutable, but we must return to the question that Popper's original criticism raised: is Freud's 'basic theory' open to empirical refutation? If it were not we would have to conclude that the only sound arguments that might undermine any movement based on the basics of Freudianism could not be empirical refutations. But would it then follow that Freudianism cannot be undermined by sound argument because it is uncriticizable in any way? What might be the structure of these non-empirical sound arguments?

Binns points out that "Freud's theory" really refers to a succession of theories, and so it is impossible to isolate the basic premises of the theory (Binns 1990, p. 533). Nevertheless, it is possible to analyze each conjectured basis of each theory. I will focus on Grünbaum's interpretation of the basis of Freud's theory, and argue that the theory thus interpreted is either open to empirical tests or must by implication be abandoned by attempts to save it by invoking the supposed special interpretive powers of psychoanalysts.

Grünbaum takes the centerpiece of Freud's theory to be the way that therapy is seen as confirming the truths of the theories that underlie it. This is expressed by Grünbaum in the following way:

(a) Only the psychoanalytic method of interpretation and treatment can yield or mediate for the patient correct insight into the unconscious causes of his neurosis.

(b) The patient's correct insight into the conflictual causes of his condition and into the unconscious dynamics of his character is in turn causally necessary for the durable cure of his neurosis. (Grünbaum, in Clarke and Wright 1988, p. 14)

Grünbaum calls this the "Necessary Condition Thesis" (NCT). Grünbaum argues that when this is conjoined with a clause to eliminate the effects of suggestion, we are left with a complete necessary and sufficient condition which is observable and thus open to refutation. Indeed, Freud accepted in 1926 that (a) was false because of the existence of spontaneous remission, and by 1937 Freud admitted that neuroses could recur even after therapy and so (b) was also false.

Since Freud made these admissions more experimental work has been done to test the NCT. There are many studies that show that control groups do as well or, in some cases better, than comparable groups treated by psychoanalysis (Farrell 1981; Eysenck 1985). In many cases the control group are given a placebo. Binns has questioned whether this would isolate the control group from unintentional psychotherapy, for the subjects may think they are receiving some cure and, more importantly, they are given an opportunity to talk about their problems to a supportive counselor. If it were impossible to separate psychoanalytic therapy from a control group, then the theory might not be open to empirical testing. However, Binns inaccurately describes the purpose of the placebo. A placebo is used in this context not to eliminate the influence of all beliefs, but rather certain ranges of belief that are thought to be collectively essential in psychoanalytic treatment. Presumably, thinking that one has been given a curative drug is not essential to psychotherapy, and believing that one is being helped in conversation is not sufficient. This avenue of criticism, therefore, is still open for empirical testing.

I suspect that psychoanalysts eager to maintain the integrity of their doctrine would be hesitant in adopting such a defense against the counter-evidence—because, if psychoanalysis may be given so frequently by accident, then another, seemingly more powerful defense would have to be sacrificed: what Gellner calls the monopoly of proper depth interpretation that the psychoanalytic guild claims for itself (Gellner 1985, p. 79). This power of decreeing what is and what is not a proper psychoanalysis and what is a cure is not constrained by publicly testable criteria and so it enables defenders to dismiss any allegedly failed psychotherapy as not really psychotherapy after all or alternative cures as not really deep cures. What Gellner overlooks is the great propagandistic cost of such a defense. If the identification of psychoanalysis becomes such an arbitrary matter, then what meaningful content exactly is being saved and perpetuated? In order to save face, it would seem, the psychoanalyst has to abandon the doctrine.

FURTHER EMPIRICAL REFUTATIONS

Eysenck has argued that Freudian theory is much more open to refutation than Popper would have us believe. In Eysenck's view, Freud's theory of repression, presumably a 'basic' part of Freud's theory, is quite amenable to experimental study. According to Freud, Eysenck says, "the essence of repression lies simply in the function of rejecting and keeping something out of consciousness." Repression is a kind of defense-mechanism to protect the individual from unpleasant emotional experiences. In one study two stories of a dream were used, one an Oedipal dream sequence and one a non-Oedipal dream sequence. Subjects were read either one or the other, and then had to recall the dream. Recall for the Oedipal sequence was significantly worse, as we would predict from Freud's theory (Eysenck 1985, p. 158). The actual result of the experiment is unimportant; what is important for my point is that Freud's theory can be interpreted in such a way as to make it falsifiable.

While one might see this experiment as predicated on a plausible interpretation of Freud's basic theory, can one be sure it is the correct interpretation? Perhaps it would be better to have psychoanalysts agreed on some criteria of falsifiability so that we can specify at least some potential falsifiers. We can always interpret any system of symbols as an empirical theory and impose on it our own class of potential falsifiers. But we want to know what the psychoanalysts are claiming, not what we might arbitrarily take them to be claiming. On the other hand, empirically testable interpretations of Freudianism need not be arbitrary: they can and must be constrained by our knowledge about the problems that psychoanalysis is trying to solve plus what it takes as background knowledge.

Refutation versus Elimination of Ideologies

The main conclusion to be drawn from the above examples of immunizing stratagems is the paradoxical one that an ideology may evolve by jettisoning its mistaken ideas in response to criticism without ever admitting a single mistake. An ideologist may abandon his ideology without explicitly recognizing that he has done so or that it was a refutation that led him to do so.

The importance of these immunizing stratagems is not that they guarantee the preservation of an ideology, but that they entail the repudiation of the ideology as the price of avoiding openly admitting a mistake in the light of refutation. We now see that the phenomenon of immunizing stratagems is not a rebuttal of the broad claim that ideologies cannot guarantee themselves against the impact of criticism, for in fact immunizing stratagems are a way of taking account of criticism.

Popper has often made the distinction between the refutation and the abandonment of theories. He has criticized Lakatos for ascribing to him a confusion of the two. Popper has this to say:

> while the former is, given the acceptance of a refuting state of affairs, a matter of logic, the latter is a question of methodology, and will depend among other things, on what alternative theories are available. (I have often stressed the need for working with more than one hypothesis in connection with both falsification ["falsifying hypotheses"] and the growth of science in general). (Popper 1974, p. 1009)

That Popper was aware of the distinction much earlier is clear from his remarks about Einstein in his discussion of the demarcation problem. Popper points to the fact that Einstein regarded his theory as false, as simply an approximation to the truth, but continued to work on it right to the end of his life.

To be more precise the distinction we are interested in is that between:

1. explicitly accepting a refutation

and

2. abandoning a refuted theory.

Thus it is quite possible for one Marxist or Freudian to explicitly accept that one of his theories has been refuted, but quite rationally to continue to work on the theory; while another Marxist refuses or simply fails to explicitly recognize a refutation, but nevertheless jettisons the theory. The consequence is that, if one could look behind the camouflage of face-saving devices and simple confusion, one might see the more scientific ideologist clinging more stubbornly to his theory (while recognizing its falsification) than the immunization-prone ideologist who simply jettisons parts or the whole of the ideology.

Part of the methodological import of Popper's discussion of the immunizing stratagem is that if we want to promote the growth of knowledge we must explicitly recognize error. Science has grown rapidly partly because of its adherence to this principle. But from our discussion we may conclude that while these rules expedite the evolution of theories in response to refutation, they are by no means necessary to such an evolution. Refutation can have a significant influence even in a non-scientific context: it may eliminate error surreptitiously, albeit with the risk of its surreptitious return.

To sum up my argument on the role of immunizing stratagems:

1. A network of ideas can evolve under the impact of refutation and criticism, with the elimination of error, without any explicit acknowledgement of error.

2. One of the ways this can happen is through the use of so-called immunizing stratagems. Immunizing stratagems which have this structure are better seen as face savers, not theory savers.

3. Immunizing stratagems do not prevent the critic from analyzing the ideologist's doctrine, pointing to the immunizing stratagem involved as a criticism in itself, and then providing an empirical refutation (or other criticism) of the reinterpreted doctrine.

4. Therefore, immunizing stratagems do not serve to preserve an ideology for which they have been instituted.

Conclusion

When an ideology looks to be threatened by criticism, its adherents will defend it by reinterpreting it so that the criticism can be fended off. At first blush, it seems that the ideology can be saved by reformulation. But this is not so, or rather, what is saved is not the same as what existed earlier: reformulation changes the ideology. Most often, it is the propagandist's face that is being saved, while the original doctrine is abandoned and replaced by a different one, though this may be concealed by retaining similar verbal formulas.

Many shifts and modifications of an ideology may not at first be recognized as such, even by those who originate them; they may be viewed as mere clarifications or routine applications of old principles to new circumstances. But over time the changes accumulate, so that the contrast between the old ideology and the new becomes more glaring. Long-lasting ideologies, even those that maintain a reputation for dogmatic inflexibility, can be observed to have revised their original beliefs, and critics (both inside and outside the ideological movement) can draw attention to the difference between the old and the new.

When we look closely at the various ways immunizing stratagems are carried out, we see that either they involve the abandonment of the original doctrine or they encumber the doctrine with new elaborations which may prove to be liabilities.

The theory that most people, or even all people, are irrational, in the sense that their minds are closed and it's a waste of time trying to reason with them, is tremendously popular, among both academics and the broader public. I have maintained the contrary: that humans just can't help being rational. I have tried to explain why I think this, and to expose the errors in the reasoning of those who believe that people are irrational.

The theory that people are irrational is not, of course, irrational: even those people who think that people are irrational are themselves entirely rational, though seriously mistaken. The theory that people are irrational is not irrational but *false*. As I have explained in some detail, its adoption involves various identifiable confusions, misinterpretations, and misconceptions. Widespread adherence to this false theory has ominous implications for social co-operation.

Naturally, some who claim that people are 'irrational' may mean merely that people are prone to error and sometimes stubborn in resisting the abandonment of their cherished beliefs. But, as we have seen, both of these qualities are elementary properties of the way human rationality works: evolved rational beings are bound to hold wrong opinions a lot of the time, and are bound to be reluctant to revise their key beliefs without a struggle. These phenomena corroborate—rather than refute—the theory that people are rational.

It won't do to say that when some writers say that people are irrational, they merely mean that people are often ignorant or unwise, or that they often resort to faulty algorithms, and that therefore these writers don't really disagree with me. I have quoted a number of authors (and could easily have quoted more) to show that they really do hold the theory of the closed mind: the theory that at least some proponents of some doctrines have found a way to insulate themselves from the force of reasoned argument, so that they can simply disregard criticism without paying any price for doing so. This is just not possible.

Although I do hold that all conscious humans are rational (though fallible), I have mostly defended a more modest claim: that those who set out to publicly propagandize for some doctrine are compelled by the logic of their situation to take criticism of that doctrine into account. They cannot shut themselves off from criticism without damaging their effectiveness as propagandists. Thus, even supposing there did exist an individual with a truly closed mind, that individual could have little success in persuading others of his opinions.

Our biological evolution has given us an innate preference for truth, logical consistency, and effective action. The result is that there is no way—logically, psychologically, or sociologically—to promote any doctrine while keeping that doctrine safe from criticism. Formidable and dangerous belief systems, such as Communism, Fascism, National Socialism, all kinds of cults or militant ideologies, even some of the major world religions, are always vulnerable to criticism, though they may be let off the hook for a while if their critics embrace the defeatist myth of the closed mind.

Notes

[1] Levine, in his 1984 study of over 800 members of religious movements, found that over 90 percent left within two years. Bird and Reimer, in their study of 1,607 adults in Montreal, found that 75.5 percent of participants in new religious movements were no longer involved five years later. The defection rate ranged from 55.2 percent for Transcendental Meditation to 100 percent for the Church of Scientology (Bird and Reimer 1983, pp. 221–22.)

[2] Karl Popper, 'The Beginnings of Rationalism', Chapter 5 of Popper 1963.

[3] For instance Marcuse 1972, p. 197.

[4] It's easy to conflate two quite different claims: 1. that by sound argument any person can be persuaded to give up any position violating the six rational filters listed above; and 2. that no person can guarantee that he will maintain such a position despite any sound argument to the contrary. I sympathize with the first theory, but I will be defending the second.

[5] It may also occur as a combination of the two processes. Hallpike (1988), arguing against a natural selectionist account of culture, makes much of the fact that for natural selection, variation has to be blind or random, whereas in human society variation can be the result of conscious action. However, Steele has pointed out that variation need not be entirely blind or random for natural selection theory to have some explanatory value. "When geneticists studying fruit flies deliberately stimulate certain kinds of mutations by, for example, radiation, this does not mean that the usual corpus of neo-Darwinian theory has to be abandoned" (Steele 1988, p. 126).

[6] In the light of these distinctions the statement that all erroneous positions are criticizable admits at least two interpretations: 1. Any person can be persuaded to give up any position failing the rational filters, using only true assumptions and valid inferences, where the arguments are persuasive qua their truth and validity; and 2. Any position failing the rational filters can be tested methodologically. We need to make this distinction because proof (or refutation) is not persuasion. Interpretation #1 presupposes Interpretation #2, but #2 doesn't presuppose #1. Given that my general argument implies #2 I need to examine this purely logical and methodological thesis. This enquiry will bring us into the debate over comprehensively critical rationalism, a doctrine developed by Bartley. We will see that #2 is easily satisfied since in fact all positions (true, false, or neither) can be criticized in a methodological sense.

[7] See for example Chapter 3 of Overy 2009.

[8] In the light of scientific theories certain descriptions in the Bible of particular events have become increasingly difficult to maintain in their literal interpretation. For

example, David Jenkins, now Bishop of Durham, wonders: "whether the actual discovery of the empty tomb was one of the preludes to discovering Jesus to be alive or whether the story came to be told as a symbol of the discovery that Jesus was alive" (Wells 1988, p. 70). This prompted the House of Bishops of the General Synod of the Church of England in 1986 to publish a statement and exposition of 'The Nature of Christian Belief'. The statement unequivocally affirms that the resurrection is "an objective reality, both historical and divine." But in partial concession to Jenkins, it allows that even though the canonical gospels assert that the tomb was found to be empty, this story may not be true. Jesus may have left his flesh and bones in the grave.

[9] Manning asserts that what makes an illegal seizure of power a revolution rather than a *coup d'état* or a counter-revolution for the Marxist is the fact that the former was committed by a Marxist and the latter by a Liberal or Nazi. This is a distinction supposedly made independently of the actions, which could be exactly the same. The argument here is invalid. From the fact that a distinction between two actions is not based on the intrinsic structure of the actions, it does not follow that the distinction carries no descriptive content about the world other than about who committed the actions. Manning has neglected to consider the philosophical argument that actions are individuated by their goals and the beliefs that the actor has about how they relate to the world, especially how they serve as means to the goals (Searle 1984). I may sign my name in the same way whether I'm filling out a cheque or concluding a letter, but these two actions are different. Both the Marxist and Nazi may take power by the same means, but their actions are distinguished by the differences in the theories they entertain regarding the place of the seizure of power within their scheme of means and ends. According to my thesis, therefore, the actions also differ with respect to the kinds of critical argument necessary to prevent them.

[10] Here I take for granted, in accord with an internal criticism, Popper's theory of propensities, as expounded in his *World of Propensities*.

[11] It is not formally inconsistent, but perhaps more accurately described as a case of Austin's infelicity.

[12] The main criticisms of C.C.R. are i. trivial synthetic truths and tautologies are uncriticizable; ii. C.C.R. is paradoxical; iii. C.C.R. is committed to logic, which is uncriticizable; iv. some doctrines are deliberately constructed so as to be uncriticizable (reinforced dogmatisms). i. Watkins contends that the statement "There exists at least one sentence written in English prior to the year two thousand that consists of precisely twenty two words." is uncriticizable because of its obvious truth. Another example is "I am more than two years old" said by a thirty year old man. Bartley's response to this is to claim that all he needs for his thesis is that it is logically possible to criticize any position. A clearer response is that of Miller, who argues that C.C.R. no more requires that any position be successfully criticizable than Popper's demarcation criterion demands that every scientific theory be successfully falsified. We have systematic methods of checking different sorts of claim; the fact that these methods apply to both difficult and absurdly easy cases is a consequence of the systematic nature of the methods and is no argument against their applicability. I would add that trying to exclude trivial cases in a systematic way may not even be possible; certainly, Watkins supplies no example of such methods. ii. Both Watkins and Post have produced arguments in an attempt to show that C.C.R. is paradoxical. Both Post and Watkins claim not that C.C.R. is not criticizable, but that the statement that C.C.R. is criticizable is not criticizable. Thus they show that a consequence of C.C.R. is uncriticizable. This latter statement is known as the C.C.R.

generalization. Watkins's argument proceeds as follows. (1) All propositions that are rationally acceptable are criticizable. (The C.C.R. generalization.) C.C.R. is meant to be acceptable, so we also have (2): (1) is rationally acceptable. Therefore (3): (1) is criticizable. Suppose we have shown that (3) is false; then, given (2), we would have shown that (1) is false. This would amount to a criticism of (1). But since this is what (3) asserts, (3) would be true. Thus our initial assumption that (3) is false leads to absurdity, and therefore there is no valid argument that (3) is false, and so it must be analytic (Watkins 1971). Bartley responded by contending that C.C.R., properly interpreted, applies to people not statements alone (Bartley 1983, p. 1158). Watkins then devised another version taking this into account, but he gave the argument a psychological twist: he took Bartley to be asserting that people are psychologically open to the criticism of any position (Watkins 1987, p. 273). Contrary to Watkins, it can be argued that Bartley's point is methodological. A sustainable interpretation of Bartley's position is that given any problem and the position that is meant to be a solution to that problem, one can always develop a method for checking whether it is in fact a solution, without falling into inconsistency, vicious circularity, infinite regress, or dogmatism. Post's argument is similar but uses only (1) and (3). The following is a compressed version of Post's argument, highlighting its general structure. Post argues that every criticism of (3) is a criticism of (1), because (1) implies (3). But no criticism of (1) is a criticism of (3) because a criticism of (1) would verify (3). Thus every criticism of (3) is a non-criticism of (1); there is no criticism of (3) (Post 1983). One response to both Post and Watkins, due to Miller, is to argue that a Comprehensively Critical Rationalist needs to assert that all positions are open to criticism, but he need not assert that they are open to criticism in every way. C.C.R. is not obliged to hold that every consequence of a criticizable position is itself criticizable. Miller draws an analogy with Popper's requirement that all scientific statements be potentially falsifiable. All empirically falsifiable statements are not made unfalsifiable by having unfalsifiable consequences. To expand on this, I would accept that a theory may contain metaphysical elements that reduce the theory's overall falsifiability, but our methodology can without difficulty require that such elements be removed. iii. It might be thought that in order for C.C.R. to be applied at all it presupposes logic, and so is committed to logic in the sense that it holds logic above criticism. Bartley himself accepts this. I would argue that even if one requires logic to carry through an argument, this does not mean that one presupposes it. One might be trying to show that logic is faulty by actually using it, as one might try to test a machine by using it. If logic were faulty (which it is not), one might obtain from such a test a good hint as to exactly what rules of logic are leading us into error. iv. The question of reinforced dogmatisms I leave for Chapter 4, in which I deal with so-called immunizing stratagems.

[13] Strangely, Gellner seems to repudiate this position in another essay: "Even in cases when they possess the political power to proscribe rivals, they do not really have the conceptual power to make rival positions unthinkable.... It is a most interesting and important trait of many, perhaps of all conceptual systems, that, unlike the artificial Newspeak of Orwell's 1984, they do not succeed in making dissent or heresy unsayable, unconceptualisable" (Gellner 1979, p. 124).

[14] The word 'blind' is used here instead of the word 'random', for a number of reasons. The variations may be far from random: equiprobability is absent in organic evolution and creative thought; statistical independence of variations is also unnecessary. On the latter point, certain systematic sweep scanning mechanisms are recognized as

blind in so far as variations are produced without any knowledge of which ones, if any, will produce a select-worthy discovery. There are three important connotations of the word 'blind': a. Variations are independent of the occasion of their occurrence; b. variations are uncorrelated with the solution, in that neither specific correct or incorrect trials are more likely to occur at any one point in a series of variations than at any other; c. variations do not make use of the direction of error of previous variations. (Such feedback processes are themselves regarded as higher-level blind variations.)

[15] An even broader characterization of the scope of economics is expounded by Kirzner in *The Economic Point of View*.

[16] Richard Gregory has given an explanation for our alternating perceptions of such ambiguous figures as the Necker cube and the girl/old hag: "We do not perceive the world merely from the sensory information available at any given time, but rather we use this information to test hypotheses of what lies before us. . . . We see this process of hypothesis testing most clearly in the ambiguous figures. . . . Here the sensory information is constant (the figure may even be stabilized on the retina) and yet the perception changes . . . as each possible hypothesis comes up for testing. Each is entertained in turn, but none is allowed to stay when no one is better than its rivals" (Gregory 1979, p. 221). Gregory does not generalize this insight to other types of belief: "Why should the perceptual system be so active in seeking alternative solutions, as we see it to be in ambiguous situations? Indeed it seems more active, and more intellectually honest in refusing to stick with one of many possible solutions, than is the cerebral cortex as a whole—if we may judge by the tenacity of irrational belief in politics or religion" (p. 222). His answer is that "The perceptual system has been of biological significance for far longer than the calculating intellect" (p. 222). Here Gregory comes close to seeing that evolution has a tendency to produce organisms that test all their beliefs, discarding false ones. But he assumes too quickly that political and religious beliefs escape the logic of evolution. He doesn't show why there has been too little time for evolution to produce flexibility in all our beliefs, and he fails to compass an alternative explanation. The explanation may lie in the fact that political and religious beliefs do not have as immediate a relationship to direct empirical testing as our perceptual beliefs. This may necessitate more protracted or indirect argument to change belief, but there is nothing irrational in a long or indirect argument.

[17] Research in psychology and physiology is consistent with this picture. All skills apparently involve scanning and correction of instantaneous belief by feedback mechanisms. It might be said (at least by someone from a geologically stable region) that it is hard to doubt the ground one walks on. But, even in walking, our brain continually tests its projections as to where the ground is.

[18] The Green Movement, for instance, may be based on fearful thinking, the fear being overpopulation, destruction of the tropical forests, and so forth. Where there is a fear there is a wish and *vice versa*, so we often find fearful and wishful thinking in the same movement. We may even conjecture that if a movement started by fearful thinking is unable to sustain wishful thinking (that the fearful possibility can be avoided or compensated for), then that movement would tend to collapse. Even movements like the Jehovah's Witnesses, who envision the destruction of the world, look forward to paradise. This would be an instance of instrumental rationality: if the Greens thought catastrophe were inevitable, they would see their propaganda as futile and cease to proselytize.

[19] The initial insight that wishful thinking might allow beliefs to be tested I owe to Jan Lester, who made this point in conversation with me on this issue in 1987. The rest of the argument presented here is my own fault.

20 What are the relationships between agreement, criticism, commitment, and understanding? It's often assumed that someone committed to a system (an ideology, lifestyle, or institution) will always have a greater understanding than a critic of the same system. But a critic may have a better understanding. Understanding a system consists in knowing at least some of its implications or aspects. If one makes a sound criticism of a system, this means that one has noticed an implication (or aspect) of the system that the committed have overlooked (assuming they are sincere). The general point is that a theory (including an ideology) has implications that are infinite. It follows that no psychological state, such as belief, commitment or understanding, can be correlated one-to-one with a theory's meaning or content. A theory or a contract has implications and ramifications that transcend anyone's understanding. In the case of patents this might be quite clear. It's always very difficult to describe an invention in such a way as to reap the maximum benefit from it. There always may be something that is overlooked. It therefore follows that the patentee can commit himself to something he does not fully understand.

21 This assumption is an elaboration of a much neglected discovery of John Locke's as expressed in his *Essay Concerning Human Understanding*. But there are major disagreements between my assumption and Locke's full position. I make the involuntariness of belief very general, whereas Locke puts many restrictions on it. In Locke's account a belief is involuntary if and only if an opinion is thought highly probable on the basis of the argument and evidence for it, and providing that there is no suspicion of any fallacy in the argument or the possibility of contrary and equally valid proofs yet undiscovered (Locke 1964, p. 425). Locke allows that in cases in which the evidence for and against a belief is not clear a person may indulge in wishful thinking or suspend his judgement. I maintain that, even if their explicit avowal may be voluntarily suspended, humans are continually making judgments that are involuntary. The process whereby a person acquires a belief never consists of a period of unbiased examination of evidence followed by a voluntary decision to accept or reject the belief. Rather, one approaches the problem guided by a prejudice. After thinking through the evidence one finds that one has come involuntarily to reject or maintain the prejudice, and that this cannot be revoked by an act of will but only by spontaneous variation in belief or by further argument. Locke's insight that even in the sphere of so-called divine revelation reason must judge whether a supposed revelation is in fact a revelation is correct but it has more importance for the history of religious thought (and other supposedly irrational systems of ideas) than he realized: "In propositions therefore contrary to the clear perception of the agreement or disagreement of any of our ideas it will be in vain to urge them as matters of faith. They cannot move our assent under that or any other title whatsoever" (p. 426). Locke seems close to giving argument a prominent role in the life of religious ideas, but then he avers that predominant passions may overrule beliefs thought to be highly probable (p. 439.); belief may be induced by force (p. 435.); by early education a belief can be made unresponsive to argument (p. 437); adherence to principles can render all argument vain against the adherent's beliefs (p. 438). If that is not a recipe for an absolutely closed system of ideas, it would be hard to think of one that was. Locke's idea that a belief may be induced by force seems to be inconsistent with his claim that belief is involuntary. It would be stretching the imagination to suppose Locke was thinking of forcibly operating by electrical or chemical means on people's brains to induce beliefs. Let us consider a plausible interpretation of Locke. Someone puts a gun to my head threatening to blow my brains away if I do not start believing that the moon is made of cheese. Can one choose to believe this proposition? Obviously not. Although force may

restrict enquiry, it cannot induce a specific belief. Other writers have rejected the idea that belief is voluntary: Quine 1987, p. 19; Williams, 'Deciding to Believe', in Williams 1973; Elster 1979, Chapter II; Winters 1979, pp. 243–256. None of these writers, however, takes an evolutionary perspective.

[22] The best analogy I have thought of is that of molecules moving completely randomly within the constraints of a bottle. We cannot predict the precise position of any molecule in the bottle, but we can predict that its position will lie within the precisely delineated shape of the bottle.

[23] Popper's idea is expounded in *Unended Quest* (1976), pp. 173–78). Popper there ponders the problem of orthogenic trends, that is: Why do so many evolutionary sequences appear to be in the same direction? This situation is contrasted with the concept of a 'random walk' (for example, the track made by a man who at every step consults a roulette wheel to determine the direction of his next step). Popper argues that changes in the organism's genetically permitted but not fixed preferences—because, say, some type of food has disappeared—may change genetically permitted but not fixed behavior which in turn puts a selection pressure on the organism's genetically determined range of preferences. This change then puts pressure on the organism's genetically determined range of skills, which in its turn puts a selection pressure on the organism's anatomy. The process can be represented by the following schema: P S A. The important point is that even though a classic change outside the organism may trigger an evolutionary change, the exact sequence may be significantly controlled by the internal relationships of selection and elimination between the internal structures of preference, skill, and anatomy. Popper presents a picture of organisms employing trial and error variation within the scope of their genetic make-up within their evolutionary niches. Their trials may lead them into a new niche. The organism is not a passive subject of evolutionary selection but partly the (unintentional) producer of it.

[24] On this, see Steele 2008, pp. 271–73.

[25] I owe this idea to David McDonagh.

[26] Walsby's book is a sustained attempt to argue that ideologies are irrational. His position rules out the rational selection of ideologies by the masses. The rational Darwinian filters I discuss have little room in Walsby's thesis.

[27] Popper had used the term 'conventionalist stratagem' in his *Logic of Scientific Discovery*. David Miller subsequently informed Popper of note 1 on p. 560 of Arthur Pap, 'Reduction Sentences and Dispositional Concepts', in Schilpp 1963, where Pap anticipates Popper's usage.

[28] Cohen points out that Copernicus placed the sun slightly away from the centre of the earth's orbit. It might be preferable to speak of a heliostatic rather than heliocentric system. But this does not affect the boldness of the conjecture. Cohen 1987, p. 44.

[29] Popper (1985) admits that this is an "oversimplification for Copernicus, but is almost certainly true of Aristarchus." Presumably, he is thinking of the bi-annual parallax of the stars that should be observable from the Earth if the Earth orbits the sun. This surely counted as the prediction of a new "appearance" and a crucial difference between Copernicus and Ptolemy's theory. It was only because of the great distance to the stars, and therefore a small parallax, that this effect was not observable until 150 years ago with the development of adequate telescopes. One could also add that with Copernicus it became possible to calculate the relative distances of the planets from the Sun, and Copernicus actually made these calculations. But though one could derive new observations from these calculations, Copernicus did not do so, presumably because the tech-

nology that would make those observations possible did not yet exist. Another crucial difference between the Copernican and Ptolemaic theories is that according to the Copernican theory the distances of the planets from the Earth vary and so the apparent size of at least a near planet, such as Venus, should also vary; but no such variation in apparent size was observed by astronomers.

[30] From Popper's work it may be inferred that he defines empirical refutation thus: the acknowledgment that an accepted basic statement, b, is inconsistent with either another basic statement, b', or a universal statement, U, and by inference classifying b' or U as false. A universal statement is a statement applying to every spatio-temporal region (for example, 'All swans are white', which is logically equivalent to 'There are no non-white swans'.) A basic statement is a singular existential statement describing an observable event at a particular spatio-temporal temporal region (for example, 'There is a white Swan at place-time k', or 'There is a black Swan at place-time k). There is also the proviso that the event is a reproducible effect, so that the basic statement can be inter-subjectively tested and the odd stray basic statement that contradicts the theory in question can be ignored. This kind of hypothesis is called a falsifying hypothesis (Popper 1934, pp. 86–87.) The term 'basic' does not imply that basic statements are untheoretical, or that they are a firm grounding for science. All basic statements are regarded as theory impregnated and tentative conjectures, which may in their turn be subjected to tests and rejected (p. 111). The term 'observable' does not imply a reference to immediate experience, as it might do in the works of other empiricist philosophers such as Carnap or Ayer. It can be defined in terms of the positions and movements of macroscopic objects (p. 103). Indeed, 'observation' can be defined quite harmlessly in terms of the positions and movements of macroscopic objects. This is clear when we say that a computer at Jodrell bank is making automatic observations of radio galaxies. It might even be programmed to perform refutations.

[31] The predictions concerned the bending of light rays by gravitational fields, elongation of the wavelength of radiation by gravitational fields, and the precession of the perihelion of the planet Mercury. From general relativity it can be predicted that the trajectory of light from a star passing near to the Sun will be bent towards the Sun at a certain angle. It is not strictly true that the bending of light was a radically new prediction, for Johann Georg von Soldner (1776–1833) showed that Newton's theory predicts bending by 0.875 seconds of arc for a ray grazing the Sun's edge. But Einstein's theory predicts a figure double this value: 1.75 arcseconds and Eddington's expedition obtained a figure of 1.60 + or − 0 .31 arcseconds, or 0.91 + or − 0.18 times the Einsteinian value (figures quoted from Will 1986, pp. 77–78). Einstein's prediction, therefore, was closer to the test results. The second prediction is that the frequency of electromagnetic radiation should be reduced by an increase in gravitational potential. Experiments carried out by R. Pound and G.A. Rebka showed that the frequency of gamma radiation on the roof of the physics building at the University of Harvard was higher than gamma radiation from the same source in the basement of the same building. This effect cannot be predicted from Newton's theory; Newton's theory is in fact silent on this question. The third prediction accounted for the anomaly in the precession of the perihelion of Mercury. Urbain Le Verrier discovered that Mercury's elliptical orbit rotates at 574 arcseconds a century. Le Verrier found that the Newtonian effects of the other planets were insufficient to account for all of this precession, leaving 38 arcseconds unaccounted for. (The modern figure is 43 arcseconds.) Einstein's theory gave a much closer prediction than Newton's theory; in fact, it coincides with the modern figure of 43 arcseconds.

[32] The concept of information content is derived from the intuitive notion that the more a statement prohibits, the more it tells us about the world. The methodological demand for greater generality and precision may be reduced to the demand for greater information content (cf. Popper 1934, p. 121). Popper defines the term 'information content' thus: "the set of statements which are incompatible with the theory" (Popper 1976, p. 26).

[33] This conjecture has often been confused with the purely methodological rule. For instance Thomas Kuhn asserts: "No process yet disclosed by the historical study of scientific development at all resembles the methodological stereotype of falsification by direct comparison with nature" (1970, p. 77). On the next page, Kuhn asserts that his alleged historical examples are "counterinstances to a prevalent epistemological theory." Although this is meant as an allusion to Popper's views, it is a gross misrepresentation. And if it is interpreted as suggesting that Popper's recommended methodology has had no role in the growth of scientific knowledge, then it is also mistaken. Popper may grant that knowledge has grown even when his rules have been neglected (he himself cites Copernicanism as a possible example; cf. Popper 1983, p. xxvi). A.F. Chalmers expresses a view similar to Kuhn's. Criticizing what he takes to be falsificationism, Chalmers says: "Given any example of a classic scientific theory, whether at the time of its first proposal or at a later date, it is possible to find observational claims that were generally accepted at the time and were considered to be inconsistent with the theory. Nevertheless, those theories were not rejected" (Chalmers 1988, p. 66). But there are hundreds of examples where knowledge has grown through the refutation of a theory. Rutherford's refutation of Thomson's theory of the atom is a particularly striking example. See the list on pp. xxvi–xxx of *Realism and the Aim of Science*. Popper does not claim that science has always proceeded in the correct methodological way; just that most of the major revolutions in science have been brought about by attempts to falsify theories. But the methodology itself is unaffected by what scientists happen to do. As Popper made clear (Popper 1934, Sections 10, 11) he does not regard methodology as an empirical pursuit, to be tested by the history of science. Popper's methodology is better characterised as based on metaphysical realism and a situational analysis of a scientist trying to discover a reality behind the appearances. Miller argues that even if the whole of science tomorrow rejected falsificationism, Popper's theory would remain untouched. After all, being fallible, every scientist could be wrong. So Kuhn is quite mistaken to suppose that his historical examples undermine Popper's methodological theory (Miller 1982). Popper's examples drawn from Newton, Einstein, Kepler, and Bohr were intended as suggestive case studies. They were arguably good examples of momentous advances in the approximation to truth, and so an analysis of them could be expected to suggest methodological rules. But once distilled, these rules would transcend what these particular scientists did or thought, and could even be used to correct their own faults.

[34] In discussions of Kepler's investigation of planetary motion it is generally assumed that Tycho's theory was explicitly applied to our Sun's planets identified independently of the law that planets move in circular orbits. The statement that all planets move in circular orbits, if construed as an essentialist definition, is empty of content; but if 'planet' is understood as equivalent to 'large, non-gaseous, Sun-orbiting body', then the circular hypothesis loses some of its information content but not all.

[35] Several writers have misunderstood the demarcation criterion in this way. For example it is often noticed that Freudianism does make some at least truth-like observations on human beings, and even that these observations and explanations are

akin to those we accept in everyday explanations of human action. It is then asked why Freudianism should be rejected; if it ought to be rejected so should all our daily explanations of people's actions—clearly an absurd position. Sebastion Gardiner (of Birkbeck College, London) suggested this at the Annual One-Day Conference on the Philosophy of Sir Karl Popper (26th May, 1990). The answer is that the demarcation criterion does not demand that Freudianism be rejected; only that its advocates try to increase its information content to the point at which it becomes empirically testable. Why settle for less knowledge? David Bohm (Bohm and Peat 2000) has misunderstood Popper's prescription that our theories be capable of and subject to severe criticism. Bohm points to the importance of encouraging the invention of new ideas and cultivating them in a noncritical environment. As an illustration of the benefits of this he points to the success of the method of brainstorming. In brainstorming, a number of people get together and for, say, half an hour will think of as many solutions as they can to a problem without subjecting them to any criticism. It it only after this open-door policy to ideas that possible solutions are whittled down through criticism. There is nothing in this method that is at odds with the method of bold conjecture and severe criticism or with the demarcation criterion. Brainstorming is simply a psychological tactic in the application of the strategy of bold conjecture and severe criticism.

[36] Kant seems to have been the first to notice this. See his *Metaphysical Foundations*, General Note to the Mechanic. This was the problem that led through the work of Leibniz, Kant, and Boscovic to field theory. Cf. section 20 of Popper 1982c and Popper and Eccles 1977, pp. 177–196.

[37] Also in Hayek 1935 are important essays by Hayek, Pierson, and Halm. Mises continued his argument in Mises 1951 and Mises 1949. With regard to 'market socialism', see F.A. Hayek's "Socialist Calculation III, The Competitive 'Solution'," in Hayek 1948.

[38] There are various muddles and mistakes in Marx's exposition which we will not pursue here, since we are merely noting Marx's concessions to reality. For example, in the passage just quoted, Marx doesn't seem to be sure whether the new price will be governed by the average amount of labor (the amount of labor required by both the new power-loom techniques and the still surviving hand-loom techniques) or whether it will be governed by the amount of labor required by power-loom production alone (and therefore not the average, as long as the hand-loom weavers are still selling some of their products). The statement that "each commodity is to be considered an average sample of its class" in this context tacitly assumes that the total amount of products of all the looms is somehow fixed independently of the price.

[39] Elster points out that the attempt to reduce skilled labor via the labor expended in education makes the value of all commodities sensitive to changes in the real wage, which, in a Marxist account, is in turn sensitive to the class struggle. Thus the value of commodities would be partly caused by the class struggle. But the purpose of the Labor Theory of Value is to explain not only the price of labor-power but also the nature of the class struggle, so this approach would put two carts before the horse. Even if this were allowed there seems to be an insuperable problem in the existence of non-producible skills, including natural aptitudes and skills whose acquisition becomes blocked after a certain time, such as language skills. Elster 1987, Roemer (a Marxist) 1988, and Blaug 1982 all agree on this point. Critics have also pointed to differences in equilibrium real wages caused, independently of differences of skill, by differences in the unpleasantness of the work required. As Elster points out, Steedman's attempt (1981, p. 88) to come to

terms with this fails to save Marx's theory because far from denying the near-obvious facts he tries to absorb them into the theory, making the value of commodities partly dependent on the subjective disutility of the labor process. My main point in mentioning these attempts to defend Marx is to illustrate how in attempting to defend Marx's system, it is being unwittingly replaced by modified versions much nearer to the marginalist (now standard) position from which most of the attacks have been mounted.

[40] This can easily be accounted for by accepting that capital equipment, corresponding to savings, makes a contribution to the value of products. But this is something Marx is determined to rule out; denying this possibility is the crucially distinctive point in his economic theory. If it is admitted that capital equipment makes a contribution to the value of output (rather than just passing on the labor embodied in it), there can be no 'exploitation' in Marx's specific sense.

[41] Marx's final defense is that without the use of values determined by labor-time, the amount of profit or surplus-value becomes indeterminate. To this there are two answers: 1. that in Marx's theory the return to capital is also indeterminate, since the level of wages cannot be explained by subsistence, and therefore has to be left unexplained; and 2. that the return to capital can be explained by theories encompassing the phenomenon of time preference. See Fisher 1930.

Bibliography

Alchian, A.A. 1968. Cost. *International Encyclopedia of the Social Sciences* 3, 404–415.
Argyle, Michael. 1957. Social Pressure upon the Modification and Distortion of Judgement. *Journal of Abnormal and Social Psychology* 54.
Ariely, Dan. 2009 [2008]. *Predictably Irrational: The Hidden Forces that Shape Our Decisions.* HarperCollins.
Allen, Joel. 1977. The Influence of Physical Conditions in the Genesis of Species. *Radical Review* 1.
Asch, S. 1951. Effects of Group Pressure upon the Modification and Distortion of Judgment. *Journal of Abnormal and Social Psychology* 54, 172–75.
Atran, S. 2002. *In Gods We Trust: The Evolutionary Landscape of Religion.* Oxford University Press.
Austin, John L. 1946. Other Minds. *Proceedings of the Aristotelian Society,* Supplementary Volume XX.
———. 1962 *How to Do Things With Words.* Clarendon.
Avron, A. 1990. Relevance and Paraconsistency. *Notre Dame Journal of Formal Logic.*
Axelrod, R. 1984. *The Evolution of Cooperation.* New York: Basic Books.
Barker, E. 1988. Defection from the Unification Church: Some Statistics and Distinctions. In Bromley 1988.
Barkow, J.H., L. Cosmides, and J. Tooby, eds. 1995. *The Adapted Mind: Evolutionary Psychology and the Generation of Culture.* Oxford University Press.
Barone, Enrico. 1935 [1908]. The Ministry of Production in the Collectivist State. In Hayek 1935.
Bartley, William Warren, III. 1971. *Morality and Religion.* St. Martin's.
———. 1983. The Alleged Refutation of Pancritical Rationalism. *Proceedings of the Eleventh International Conference on the Unity of the Sciences,* Volume II.
———. 1984 [1962]. *The Retreat to Commitment.* Open Court.
———. 1990. *Unfathomed Knowledge, Unmeasured Wealth: On Universities and the Wealth of Nations.* Open Court.
Battalio, R.C. 1973. A Test of Consumer Demand Theory Using Observations of Individual Consumer Purchases. *Western Economic Journal* 11 (December).
Beck, Aaron. T. 1976. *Cognitive Therapy and the Emotional Disorders.* International University Press.
Becker, Gary S. 1976. *The Economic Approach to Human Behavior.* University of Chicago Press.

Becker, Gary S., and George Stigler. 1977. De Gustibus Non Est Disputandum. *American Economic Review* 66.
Bergmann, Karl Georg Lucas Christian. 1847. Über die Verhältnisse der Wärmeökonomie der Thiere zu ihrer Grösse. *Göttinger Studien* 3:1.
Berman, David. 1988. *A History of Atheism in Britain: From Hobbes to Russell*. Croom Helm.
Binns, Peter. 1990. Experimental Evidence and Psychotherapy. *British Journal for the Philosophy of Science* 41.
Bird, F., and W. Reimer. 1983. *Of Gods and Men: New Religious Movements in the West*. Mercer University Press.
Black, M. 1964. *A Companion to Wittgenstein's Tractatus*. Cambridge University Press.
Blaug, Mark. 1982. Another Look at the Reduction Problem in Marx. In Bradley and Howard 1982.
Bohm, David, and F. David Peat. 2000 [1987]. *Science, Order, and Creativity*. Routledge.
Böhm-Bawerk, Eugen von. 1975 [1896]. *Karl Marx and the Close of His System*. Merlin.
Boole, G. 1952 [1854]. *An Investigation of the Laws of Thought*. Open Court.
Borger, Robert, and Frank Cioffi, eds. 1970. *Explanation in the Behavioral Sciences*. Cambridge University Press.
Boudon, Raymond. 1989 [1986]. *The Analysis of Ideology*. University of Chicago Press.
―――. 1989. *The Analysis of Ideology*. Chicago: University of Chicago Press.
Boyd, R., and P. Richerson, P. 1985. *Culture and the Evolutionary Process*. Chicago: University of Chicago Press.
Boyer, P. 2002. *Religion Explained*. Basic Books.
Bradley, Ian, and Michael Howard, eds. 1982. *Classical and Marxian Political Economy*. Palgrave-Macmillan.
Brafman, Ori, and Rom Brafman. 2008. *Sway: The Irresistible Pull of Irrational Behavior*. Random House.
Bromley, David, ed. 1988. *Falling from the Faith: Causes and Consequences of Religious Apostasy*. Sage.
Brown, J.A.C. 1972 [1963]. *Techniques of Persuasion*. Penguin.
Brown, Raymond E. 1993 [1977]. *The Birth of the Messiah: A Commentary on the Gospels of Matthew and Luke*. New York: Random House.
Brunvand, Jan Harold. 1989. *Curses—Broiled Again!* New York: Norton.
Burton, Robert. 2008. *On Being Certain: Believing You Are Right Even When You're Not*. St. Martin's.
Caldararo, Niccolo. 2006. Suicide Bombers: Terror, History, and Religion. *Anthropological Quarterly* 79:1.
Campbell, D.T. 1960. Blind Variation and Selective Retention in Creative Thought as in Other Knowledge Processes. *Psychological Review* 67.
―――. 1974. Evolutionary Epistemology. In Schilpp 1974.
―――. 1979. A Tribal Model of the Social System Vehicle Carrying Scientific Knowledge. *Knowledge: Creation, Diffusion, Utilization* 1:2.
―――. 1987. Neurological Embodiments of Belief and the Gaps in the Fit of Phenomena to Noumena. In Abner Shimony and Debra Nails, eds., *Naturalistic Epistemology* (Reidel).

———. 1993. Plausible Coselection of Belief by Referent: All the 'Objectivity' that Is Possible. *Perspectives on Science* 1:1.
Chakotin, Serge. 1940. *The Rape of the Masses: The Psychology of Totalitarian Political Propaganda*. Routledge.
Chagas, C., ed. *Recent Advances in the Evolution of Primates*. Vatican City: Pontificiae Academiae Scientiarum Scripta Varia.
Chalmers, A. F. 1988 [1978]. *What Is This Thing Called Science?* Open University Press.
Cioffi, Frank. 1970. Freud and the Idea of a Pseudoscience. In Borger and Cioffi 1970.
———. 1998. *Freud and the Question of Pseudoscience*. Open Court.
Clarke, S. 1982. *Marx, Marginalism, and Modern Sociology*. Macmillan.
Clarke, Peter, and Crispin Wright, eds. 1988. *Mind, Psychoanalysis, and Science*. Blackwell.
Cohen, Bernard. 1987. *The Birth of a New Physics*. Penguin.
D'Agostino, F., and Ian Jarvie. 1989. *Freedom and Rationality: Essays in Honor of John Watkins*. Springer.
Darwin, Charles. 2009 [1859]. *On the Origin of Species*. Penguin.
Dawkins, Richard. 1982. *The Extended Phenotype*. Oxford: Oxford University Press.
———. 1990 [1976]. *The Selfish Gene*. Oxford University Press.
———. 1993. Is God a Computer Virus? In B. Dahlbom, ed., *Dennett and His Critics: Demystifying the Mind* (Blackwell).
Deutsch, D. 1997. *The Fabric of Reality: Towards A Theory of Everything*. Allen Lane.
Deutsch, Morton, and Herald Gerard. 1955. A Study of Normative and Informational Social Influence Upon Individual Judgment. *Journal of Abnormal and Social Psychology* 51.
Duhem, Pierre. 1991 [1914]. *The Aim and Structure of Physical Theory*. Princeton University Press.
Durkheim, E. 1976 [1915]. *The Elementary Forms of Religious Life*. Allen and Unwin.
Edelman, G.M. 1987. *Neural Darwinism: The Theory of Neuronal Group Selection*. New York: Basic Books.
———. 1992. *Bright Air, Brilliant Fire*. New York: Basic Books.
Ellis, Ralph D. 1995. *Questioning Consciousness: The Interplay of Imagery, Cognition, and Emotion in the Human Brain*. Amsterdam: Benjamins.
Ellis, Ralph D., and Newton, Natika. 2010. *How the Mind Uses the Brain: To Move the Body and Image the Universe*. Chicago: Open Court.
Elster, Jon. 1979. *Ulysses and the Sirens: Studies in Rationality and Irrationality*. Cambridge: Cambridge University Press.
———. 1982. Belief, Bias and Ideology. In Hollis and Lukes 1982.
———. 1985. *Making Sense of Marx*. Cambridge: Cambridge University Press.
Eysenck, Hans J. 1986. *Decline and Fall of the Freudian Empire*. London: Penguin.
Farrell, B.A. 1981. The Standing of Psychoanalysis. Oxford University Press.
Festinger, Leon, H.W. Rieken, and S. Schachter. 1956. *When Prophecy Fails*. Minneapolis: University of Minnesota Press.
Fisher, E.B., Jr., Robin C. Winkler, Leonard Krasner, John Kagel, Raymond C. Battalio, and Robert L. Basmann. 1978. Economic Perspectives in Behavior Therapy: Complex Interdependencies in Token Economies. *Behavior Therapy* 9:3 (June).
Fisher, Irving. 1906. *The Nature of Capital and Income*. Macmillan.
———. 1974 [1930]. *The Theory of Interest: As Determined by Impatience to Spend Income and Opportunity to Invest It*. Kelley.

Flew, Antony. 1978 [1975]. *Thinking about Thinking*. Fontana.
Fodor, J. 1983. *The Modularity of Mind*. MIT Press.
———. 2001. *The Mind Doesn't Work That Way: The Scope and Limits of Computational Psychology*. MIT Press.
Frazer, J. 1922. *The Golden Bough: A Study in Magic and Religion*. Macmillan.
Freud, Sigmund. 1953–74 [1911]. Formulations on the Two Principles of Mental Functioning. In *Standard Edition of the Complete Works of Sigmund Freud*, Volume 12 (Hogarth).
———. 1976 [1900]. *The Interpretation of Dreams*. Penguin.
———. 1986 [1920]. *Beyond the Pleasure Principle*. Penguin.
———. 1988 [1932–33]. *New Introductory Lectures on Psychoanalysis*. Penguin.
———. 1989 [1915–17]. *Introductory Lectures on Psychoanalysis*. Liveright.
———. 1990 [1914]. *On the History of the Psychoanalytic Movement*. Norton.
———. 1991 [1913]. *Totem and Taboo*. Ark.
Fries, J. 1828–1831. *Neue oder anthropologische Kritik der Vernunft*. Heidelberg: Winter.
Galanter, Marc. 1989. *Cults: Faith, Healing, and Coercion*. Oxford University Press.
Garcia, J., and R.A. Koelling. 1966. Relation of Cue to Consequence in Avoidance Learning. *Psychonomic Science* 4.
Gardner, Dan. 2009. *Risk: The Science and Politics of Fear*. Virgin.
Gellner, Ernest. 1979. *Spectacles and Predicaments*. Cambridge University Press.
———. 1985. *The Psychoanalytic Movement: The Cunning of Unreason*. Paladin.
Gibbon, Edward. 1963 [1776]. *The History of the Decline and Fall of the Roman Empire*. Pelican.
Goertzel, B. 1993. Psychology and Logic. *Journal of Social and Evolutionary Systems* 16:4.
Graham, Angus C. 1989. *Disputers of the Tao: Philosophical Argument in Ancient China*. La Salle: Open Court.
Gregory, R.L., ed. 1979 [1966]. *Eye and Brain*. Third edition. Weidenfeld and Nicolson.
———. 1987. *The Oxford Companion to the Mind*. Oxford University Press.
Grünbaum, Adolf. 1976. Can a Theory Answer More Questions than One of Its Rivals? *British Journal for the Philosophy of Science* 27.
———. 1989. The Degeneration of Popper's Theory of Demarcation. In D'Agostino and Jarvie 1989.
Hallpike, C.R. 1986. *The Principles of Social Evolution*. Oxford University Press.
Hamilton, W.D., and R. Axelrod. 1981. The Evolution of Cooperation. *Science* 211.
Harris, Sam. 2006. *The End of Faith: Religion, Terror, and the Future of Reason*. The Free Press.
Hassan, S. 1988. *Combating Cult Mind Control*. Aquarian Press.
Hattiangadi, J.N. 1987. *How Is Language Possible?* Open Court.
Hayek, Friedrich A, ed. 1935. *Collectivist Economic Planning*. Routledge.
———. 1944. *The Road to Serfdom*. Routledge.
———. 1948. *Individualism and Economic Order*. University of Chicago Press.
———. 1960. *The Constitution of Liberty*. University of Chicago Press.
Hitler, Adolf. 1939 [1925–26]. *My Struggle*. Hurst and Blackett.
Hoffer, Eric. 2002 [1951]. *The True Believer: Thoughts on the Nature of Mass Movements*. Harper.

Hofstadter, D.R. 1983. On Viral Sentences and Self-Replicating Structures. *Scientific American* (January).
Hollis, Martin, and Steven Lukes, eds. 1982. *Rationality and Relativism*. Blackwell.
Holloway, R.L. 1974. The Casts of Fossil Hominid Brains. *Scientific American* 231:1.
———. 1983. Human Paleontological Evidence Relevant to Language Behavior. *Human Neurobiology* 2.
Honey, Charles. 2008. Belief in Hell Dips, but Some Say They've Already Been There. *The Pew Forum on Religion and Public Life* (August 14th).
Hopkins, Jim. 1988. Epistemology and Depth Psychology. In Clarke and Wright 1988.
Hume, David. 1904. Of the First Principles of Government. In Grant Richards, ed., *The Essays of David Hume* (World Classics).
———. 1977 [1748]. *An Enquiry Concerning Human Understanding*. Indianapolis: Bobbs-Merrill.
———. 1978 [1739]. *A Treatise of Human Nature*. Fontana.
———. 1990 [1779]. *Dialogues Concerning Natural Religion*. Penguin.
Jarvie, Ian. 1972. *Concepts and Society*. Routledge.
Jarvie, Ian, and J. Agassi. 1967. The Problem of the Rationality of Magic. *British Journal of Sociology* 8:2.
Kant, Immanuel. 2004. *Metaphysical Foundations of Natural Science*. Cambridge University Press.
Karmiloff-Smith, A. 1996. *Beyond Modularity: A Developmental Perspective on Cognitive Science*. MIT Press.
Katz, D. 1937. *Animals and Men*. Longmans.
Kahnemann, Daniel, P. Slovic, and A. Tversky, eds. 1982. *Judgment Under Uncertainty: Heuristics and Biases*. Cambridge University Press.
Kaufman, F. 1933. On the Subject Matter of Economic Science. *Economica* 13, 390.
Keynes, John Maynard. 1936. *The General Theory of Employment, Interest, and Money*. Macmillan.
Kirzner, Israel. 1960. *The Economic Point of View*. Sheed and Ward.
Kolakowski, Leszek, and P.S. Falla. 1978. *Main Currents of Marxism*. Three volumes. Clarendon.
Kramer, Samuel N. 1963. *The Sumerians: Their History, Culture, and Character*. University of Chicago Press.
Kuhn, T.S. 1970. *The Structure of Scientific Revolutions*. University of Chicago Press.
Lakatos, Imre. 1970. Falsification and the Methodology of Scientific Research Programmes. In Lakatos and Musgrave 1970.
Lakatos, Imre, and A. Musgrave, eds. 1970. *Criticism and the Growth of Knowledge*. Cambridge: Cambridge University Press.
Laqueur, Walter. 1977. *The Age of Terrorism*. London: Weidenfeld and Nicolson.
Le Bon, Gustave. 1979 [1895]. *The Crowd*. Liberty Press.
Levine, S. 1984. *Radical Departures: Desperate Detours to Growing Up*. San Diego: Harcourt Brace.
Levinson, P., ed. 1982. *In Pursuit of Truth: Essays on the Philosophy of Karl Popper*. Atlantic Highlands: Humanities.
Locke, John. 1964 [1689]. *An Essay Concerning Human Understanding*. Collins Fontana.
Loparic, A., and N.C. Da Costa. 1984. Paraconsistency, Paracompleteness, and Valuation. *Logique et Analyse* 27.
Lorenz, Konrad. 1977 [1973]. *Behind the Mirror*. Methuen.

Malinowski, B.K. 1926. Anthropology. In *Encyclopedia Britannica*. Thirteenth edition, Supplementary Volume I.
Manning, D.J., ed. 1980. *The Form of Ideology*. Allen and Unwin.
———. 1976. *Liberalism*. Dent.
Maranon, G. 1924. Contribution à l'étude de l'action émotive de l'adrénaline. *Revue Française d'Endocrinologie* 21.
Marcus, Gary F. 2008. *Kluge: The Haphazard Construction of the Human Mind*. Houghton Mifflin.
Marshack, A. 1985. *Hierarchical Evolution of the Human Capacity*. American Museum of Natural History.
Marx, Karl H. 1974 [1867, 1885, 1894]. *Capital: A Critique of Political Economy*. Three Volumes. Lawrence and Wishart.
McKenzie, R.B., and Gordon Tullock. 1981 [1975]. *The New World of Economics*. Third edition. Irwin.
Meyerson, Denise. 1991. *False Consciousness*. Clarendon.
Meyerson, E. 1908. *Identité et Realité*. Vrin.
Mill, John Stuart. 1836. On the Definition of Political Economy; and on the Method of Investigation Proper to It. *London and Westminster Review* (October).
———. 1874. *Essays on Some Unsettled Questions of Political Economy*. Second edition. Longmans, Green, Reader, and Dyer.
Miller, David. 1975. The Accuracy of Predictions. *Synthese* 30.
———. 1977. The Uniqueness of Atomic Facts in Wittgenstein's Tractatus. *Theoria* 53.
———. 1982. Conjectural Knowledge: Popper's Solution of the Problem of Induction. In Levinson 1982.
———. 1994. *Critical Rationalism: A Restatement and Defence*. Open Court.
———. 1960 [1933]. *Epistemological Problems of Economics*. Van Nostrand.
Mithen, S. 1999. *The Prehistory of the Mind: The Cognitive Origins of Art, Religion, and Science*. Thames and Hudson.
Minogue, Kenneth. 1984. *Alien Powers*. Blackwell.
Mises, Ludwig von. 1935 [1920]. *Economic Calculation in the Socialist Commonwealth*. In Hayek 1935.
———. 1949. *Human Action*. Hodge.
———. 1951 [1922]. *Socialism*. Yale University Press.
Mithen, S. 1999. The Prehistory of the Mind: The Cognitive Origins of Art, Religion and Science. Thames and Hudson.
Monod, Jacques. 1970. *Chance and Necessity*. Fontana.
Moore, G.E. 1903. *Principia Ethica*. Cambridge University Press.
Mouton, Jane, Robert Blake, and Joseph Olmstead. 1956. The Relationship Between the Frequency of Yielding and the Disclosure of Personal Identity. *Journal of Personality* 24.
Munz, P. 1985. *Our Knowledge of the Growth of Knowledge: Popper or Wittgenstein?* Routledge.
Musgrave, Alan. 1978. Falsification, Heuristics, and Anarchism. In Radnitzky and Anderson 1978.
Nozick, Robert. 1974. *Anarchy, State, and Utopia*. Blackwell.
———. 1993. *The Nature of Rationality*. Princeton University Press.
O'Hear, A. 1982. *Karl Popper*. Routledge.
———. 1988. The Evolution of Knowledge. *Critical Review* 2:1.

Ollman, Bertell. 1979. *Social and Sexual Revolution: Essays on Marx and Reich*. South End.
Orwell, George. 1977 [1949]. *Nineteen Eighty-Four*. Penguin.
Overy, Richard. 2009. *The Twilight Years: The Paradox of Britain between the Wars*. Viking.
Pagels, Elaine. 1990 [1979]. *The Gnostic Gospels*. Random House.
Pap, Arthur. Reduction Sentences and Dispositional Concepts. In Schilpp 1963.
Pape, Robert A. 2005. *Dying to Win: The Strategic Logic of Suicide Terrorism*. Random House.
Pears, D. 1984. *Motivated Irrationality*. Oxford University Press.
Penton, M.J. 1988 [1985]. *Apocalypse Delayed*. University of Toronto Press.
Pinker, S. 1998. *How the Mind Works*. Allen Lane.
———. 2003. *The Blank Slate: The Modern Denial of Human Nature*. Penguin.
Plamenatz, John. 1988 [1971]. *Ideology*. Macmillan.
Plato. 1988. *Phaedrus and Letters VII and VIII*. Penguin.
Plotkin, H. 1995. *Darwin Machines and the Nature of Knowledge*. Penguin.
Polanyi, Michael. 1958. *Personal Knowledge: Towards a Post-Critical Philosophy*. Routledge.
Popper, Karl R. 1957. *The Poverty of Historicism*. Routledge.
———. 1958. On the Status of Science and Metaphysics. *Ratio* 1. Reprinted in Popper 1969.
———. 1966 [1963]. *The Open Society and Its Enemies*. Two volumes. Routledge.
———. 1969 [1963]. *Conjectures and Refutations*. Routledge.
———. 1974. Replies to My Critics. In Schilpp 1974.
———. 1976. *Unended Quest*. Fontana.
———. 1977 [1934]. *The Logic of Scientific Discovery*. Hutchinson.
———. 1979 [1972]. *Objective Knowledge*. Oxford University Press.
———. 1982a. *Realism and the Aim of Science*. Volume I of *Postscript to The Logic of Scientific Discovery*. Rowman and Littlefield.
———. 1982b. *The Open Universe*. Volume II of *Postscript to The Logic of Scientific Discovery*. Rowman and Littlefield.
———. 1982c. *Quantum Theory and the Schism in Physics*. Volume III of *Postscript to The Logic of Scientific Discovery*. Rowman and Littlefield.
———. 1987. Natural Selection and the Emergence of Mind. In Radnitzky and Bartley 1987.
———. 1990. *A World of Propensities*. Thoemmes.
———. 1994. *The Myth of the Framework*. Routledge.
———. 2001 [1998]. *The World of Parmenides: Essays on the Pre-Socratic Enlightenment*. Routledge.
Popper, Karl R., and John C. Eccles. 1983 [1977]. *The Self and Its Brain: An Argument for Interactionism*. Routledge.
Quine, W.V. 1953. *From a Logical Point of View: Nine Logico-philosophical Essays*. Harvard University Press.
———. 1977 [1966]. *The Ways of Paradox*. Harvard University Press.
———. 1987. *Quiddities: A Philosophical Dictionary*. Harvard University Press.
Radnitzky, G. 1986. Towards an 'Economic' Theory of Methodology. *Methodology and Science* 19.

Radnitzky, Gerard, and William Warren Bartley III, eds. 1987. *Evolutionary Epistemology, Rationality, and the Sociology of Knowledge*. Open Court.
Radnitzky, Gerard, and G. Andersson, eds. 1978. *Progress and Rationality in Science*. Reidel.
Rapport, D. 1971. Optimization Models of Food Selection. *American Naturalist* 105.
Rawls, John. 1980 [1972]. *A Theory of Justice*. Oxford University Press.
Robbins, Lionel. 1945 [1932]. *An Essay on the Nature and Significance of Economic Science*. Macmillan.
Robinson, T.J. 1980. Ideology and Theoretical Inquiry. In Manning 1980.
Roemer, J. 1988. *Free to Lose*. Radius.
Ruse, M. 1986. *Taking Darwin Seriously*. Blackwell.
Russell, Bertrand. 1938. *Power: A New Social Analysis*. Allen and Unwin.
Rycroft, Charles. 1968 [1966]. *Psychoanalysis Observed*. Pelican.
Sargent, W. 1963 [1957]. *Battle for the Mind*. Pan.
Schilpp, Paul A., ed. 1963. *The Philosophy of Rudolf Carnap*. Open Court.
———, ed. 1974. *The Philosophy of Karl Popper*. Open Court.
Schachter, S., and J.E. Singer. 1962. Cognitive, Social, and Physiological Determinants of Emotional State. *Psychological Review* 69.
Schilcher, Florian von, and Neil Tennant. 1984. *Philosophy, Evolution, and Human Nature*. Routledge.
Schweitzer, Albert. 1914. *The Mystery of the Kingdom of God*. Dodd, Mead.
———. 1954 [1906]. *The Quest of the Historical Jesus*. Black.
Searle, John R. 1984. *Minds, Brains, and Science*. Penguin.
Seligman, M., and J. Hager, eds. 1972. *Biological Boundaries of Learning*. Appleton-Century-Crofts.
Shils, Edward. 1968. The Concept and Function of Ideology. *International Encyclopedia of Social Science*, Volume VII.
Simon, Julian. 1993. *Good Mood: The New Psychology of Overcoming Depression*. Open Court.
Smith, H.P. 1921. *Essays in Biblical Interpretation*. Allen and Unwin.
Sowell, Thomas. 1985. Marxism: Philosophy and Economics. ???
Sperber, D. 1996. *Explaining Culture: A Naturalistic Approach*. Blackwell.
Spiro, M.E. 1979. *Gender and Culture: Kibbutz Women Revisited*. Duke University Press.
Staal, F. 1967. Indian Logic. In Paul Edwards, ed., *The Encyclopedia of Philosophy*, Volume 4 (Collier Macmillan).
Stark, Rodney. 1997. *The Rise of Christianity: How the Obscure, Marginal Jesus Movement Became Dominant in the Western World in a Few Centuries*. Harper Collins.
Steedman, Ian. 1977. *Marx After Sraffa*. Verso.
Steele, David Ramsay. 1988. How We Got Here. *Critical Review* 2:1.
———. 1992. *From Marx to Mises: Post-Capitalist Society and the Challenge of Economic Calculation*. Open Court.
———. 2008. *Atheism Explained: From Folly to Philosophy*. Chicago: Open Court.
———. 2010. Is God Coming or Going? *Philosophy Now* 78 (April–May).
Stigler, George J. 1961. The Economics of Information. *Journal of Political Economy* 69:3 (June).
Tarski, A. 1943–44. The Semantic Conception of Truth. *Philosophy and Phenomenological Research* 4.

Tichy, P. 1974. On Popper's Definitions of Verisimilitude. *British Journal for the Philosophy of Science* 25.
Tillich, Paul. 1949. *The Shaking of the Foundations*. SCM.
Tobias, P.V. 1983. Recent Advances in the Evolution of the Hominids with Special Reference to Brain and Speech. In Chagas 1983.
Tooby, John, and Leda Cosmides. 1992. The Psychological Foundations of Culture. In Barkow, Cosmides, and Tooby 1992.
Trigg, R. 1977 [1973]. *Reason and Commitment*. Cambridge University Press.
———. 1985. *Understanding Social Science*. Blackwell.
Vedantam, Shankar. 2010. *The Hidden Brain: How Our Unconscious Minds Elect Presidents, Control Markets, Wage Wars, and Save Our Lives*. Random House.
Voltaire. 1971 [1764]. *Philosophical Dictionary*. Penguin.
Wächtershäuser, G. 1984. Light and Life: On the Nutritional Origins of Sensory Perception. Paper presented at a Symposium at the 150th National Meeting of the American Association for the Advancement of Science. Reprinted in Radnitzky and Bartley 1987.
Walsby, Harold. 1947. *The Domain of Ideologies*. McLellan.
Ware, Timothy. 1963. The Orthodox Church. Penguin.
Wartofsky, Marx. 1977. *Feuerbach*. Cambridge University Press.
Watkins, John W.N. 1958. Confirmable and Influential Metaphysics. *Mind* LXVII, NS #267 (July).
———. 1971. C.C.R.: A Refutation. *Philosophy* 46 (January).
———. 1984. *Science and Scepticism*. Hutchinson.
———. 1987. Comprehensively Critical Rationalism: A Retrospect. In Bartley 1987.
Weber, Max. 1968. *Economy and Society: An Outline of Interpretive Sociology*. Bedminster.
———. 1968. *Max Weber on Charisma and Institution Building: Selected Papers*. University of Chicago Press.
Wells, G.A. 1988. *Religious Postures: Essays on Modern Christian Apologists and Religious Problems*. Open Court.
———. 2009. *Cutting Jesus Down to Size: What Higher Criticism Has Achieved and Where It Leaves Christianity*. Open Court.
Will, C.M. 1986. *Was Einstein Right?* Basic Books.
Williams, Bernard A. 1973. Deciding to Believe. In Williams, *Problems of the Self* (Cambridge University Press).
Wilson, E. 1967 [1940]. *To the Finland Station*. Fontana.
Winkler, Robin C. 1973. An Experimental Analysis of Economic Balance: Savings and Wages in a Token Economy. *Behavior Therapy* 4 (January).
Winters, Barbara. 1979. Willing to Believe. *Journal of Philosophy* 76.
Wolpert, L. 2006. *Six Impossible Things Before Breakfast: The Evolutionary Origins of Belief*. Faber and Faber.
Zahar, Elie. 1989. *Einstein's Revolution: A Study in Heuristic*. Open Court.
———. 2007. *Why Science Needs Metaphysics: A Plea for Structural Realism*. Open Court.

Index

Abraham (Biblical), 46, 228
Adams, Gerry, 21
Adams, John Couch, 215, 226–27
Adler, Alfred, 37, 260–61
advertising: rationality of, 162; emotion and, 202–03
affectual action (Weber), 103–04
Agassi, Joseph, 35
Al Kindi, 44
Al Farabi, 44
Al Ghazali, 44
Al-Qaeda, 111
Albigensians, 70
American Psychoanalytic Association, 166
anarchists, 196
Anaximander, 21
Anderson, Benedict, 113
Anselm: *Proslogion*, 49, 50
apartheid, 175
Aquinas: *Summa Theologica*, 49
Aristarchus, 212, 280n29
Aristotle, 44–45, 227, 250
Asch, Solomon, 167–68
astrology, 34
atheism, 167
atheists, 33, 95, 112
Austin, J.L., 118–19, 143
Averroes, 44
Avicenna, 44

Bacon, Francis, 91
Barth, Karl, 51, 71, 72, 73
Barker, Eileen, 16

Barone, Enrico, 240–41
Bartley, William Warren, III, 22, 117, 150, 162, 184, 196–97, 220–21, 230, 245; attribution of closedness to argument to some belief systems, 57, 60–62, 90, 139; comprehensively critical rationalism, 26, 58, 275n6, 275n6, 276–77n12; evolution of ideas, 150; on liberal Protestantism, 69–75, 159; *The Retreat to Commitment*, 70, 159; and situational analysis, 62
Begin, Menachem, 21
belief: and determinism, 134; contrasted with faith, 8; involuntary, 8, 133–36, 159, 279–260n21; like a searchlight, 123; stubbornness of, 136–37, 156, 163
Bergmann, Carl, 35
Bergson, Henri, 133
Berman, David, 167
Bernfeld, S., 260
Bernstein, Eduard, 165
biases, 3, 9, 12–13, 29,36, 148; to believe agency is at work, 14; to confirm what you already believe, 8; and brain modules, 85–87, 96; to believe what you want to believe, 4–5; of visual system, 136; *see also* fearful thinking; wishful thinking
Bible, 48, 62, 66, 73–75, 275n8
Binns, Peter, 262, 269, 270
blank slate view of human nature, 28, 82
Böhm-Bawerk, Eugen von, 253, 256, 257–59
Bohr, Niels, 211, 231

Book of Mormon, 5
Boudon, Raymond, 56, 170–71, 185, 214
Boyer, Pascal, 42–43, 44
Brahe, Tycho, 212
brain: modules, 3, 9, 13, 29, 42, 83–87, 94, 96
Braithwaite, R.B., 71
Bray, John, 257
Brown, J.A.C., 183
Brown, Father Raymond E., 76
Burmese Days (Orwell), 199

Caldararo, Niccolo, 113
Campbell, Donald T.: evolutionary epistemology, xvi, 87, 90
Cannan, Edwin, 101
Carnot, Nicolas, 55
Castro, Fidel, 181
Chakotin, Serge, 202; *The Rape of the Masses*, 175–77, 180–82, 184, 188, 189, 190
Chalmers, Alan F., 214
charismatic leaders, 39
children: curiosity about the world, 41, 86; ability to form hypotheses, 81; understanding of persons' motivations, 81; understanding of logic, 11, 81, 95
Chomsky, Noam, 28
Christian Science, 49
Christianity, 32, 52, 163, 166, 167
Christians, 123
Church, Alonzo, 242–43
Cioffi, Frank, 229
Clark, John Bates, 101
Clarke, S., 259
closed mind: emotion and, 4; false theory of, 1, 4–13; indirect refutation of existence of, 97–98; trade-off of closedness for spreadability, 40, 65
Cohen, Jack, 3, 84
communism (hypothetical social system), 6–7, 129, 131, 175, 193–94, 218, 237–38; impossibility of, 131, 195–96, 219, 239, 244–45
Communism (political movement), 1, 15, 16, 23, 67, 136–38, 241

Comprehensively Critical Rationalism (C.C.R.), 26, 58, 275n6. 276–77n12
conjecture and refutation, method of, 91, 197, 281n30
Copernicus, Nicolaus, 212, 280n29
Cosmides, Leda, 9, 84, 95–96, 148
creationism, biblical, 1
critical rationalism, 57–59, 60, 95; comprehensively critical rationalism, 26, 58, 275n6, 276–77n12
cults, 9, 24, 29, 39
curiosity, 2, 3, 122–23; *see also* children, curiosity about the world

Dalton, John, 216, 250
Darwin, Charles, 2, 68; *Essay* of 1844, 89; *Natural Selection*, 89; *Origin of Species*, 89;
Darwin Machines, 87
Dawkins, Richard, 10, 15, 16, 18, 22; on memes, 31, 150; on religion, 95
Deutsch, David, xvi
Dick, Philip K., 117
Duhem, Pierre, 92, 230, 235–38, 241
Dubois, Paul, 173
Durkheim, Émile, 200; *Elementary Forms of Religious Life*, 171, 175–180, 185–86, 190,

Eastern Orthodox Church, 76
economic rationality, 3, 9, 19, 21, 29, 56, 81–87, 90, 96–99, 103–09, 146–47, 156, 189
economics: 18–19; innate human compliance with, 2; marginal revolution, 159; explains martyrdom, 78–79; Robbinsian conception, 101–02
Edison, Thomas Alva, 88, 95
Einstein, Albert, 47, 91, 211, 212, 244, 281n31
Elster, Jon, 127–130, 159, 258–59, 283–84n39; *Making Sense of Marx*, 128
emotion: and absolute values, 113–14; and advertising, 202–03; arousal, effect on transmission of ideas,

181–82; as barrier to reason, 20–21, 29, 169–173; controlled by beliefs, 4, 30, 156, 169–170, 194–95, 199; cognitive, 156, 171, 176, 180, 194–95; impervious to argument, 4; and the masses, 176–77; strategically serving the intellect, 4; and terrorism, 20–21, 171; *see also* fearful thinking; wishful thinking
Engels, Friedrich, 194, 254–55
Epictetus, 172, 177
epistemology, evolutionary, 87–95
eucharist, 75–76
Euclid: *Elements*, 100
evolution: of humans, 2, 3, 140–41, 199; origin of human characteristics, 2, 3, 28, 146–47, 199; gives humans rationality, 28, 81–83, 140–41, 147
evolutionary epistemology; *see* epistemology, evolutionary
exploitation of workers by capitalists, 192–93, 195, 256–59, 284n40
Eysenck, Hans, 271

Facebook, 201
faith, 7, 15, 18,
fanaticism, 106–114
Faraday, Michael, 47
fanatics, 20–21; *see* terrorism
Fascism, 198
Fascists, 196
fearful thinking, 4–5, 125, 132–33, 137; *see also* wishful thinking
The Federalist Papers, 202
Festinger, Leon: *When Prophecy Fails*, 159; cognitive dissonance, 268
Feuerbach, Ludwig, 124
Feynman, Richard, 217
Fisher, Irving, 102
Fodor, Jerry, 42, 85, 135
Freud, Sigmund, 29, 36–37, 166, 211, 227, 247; *Interpretation of Dreams*, 230, 263, 264, 267; mendacity of, 167
Freudianism, 22, 118, 163, 166, 282–83n35; empirical tests of, 259–271; as impervious to argument, 22, 36–38, 43, 63, 206, 216

Freudians, 118, 163, 213, 268
Fries, Jakob Friedrich: trilemma, 59–60
Frink, Horace, 37

Galanter, Marc, 24
Galileo Galilei, 21, 43, 211, 219–220
Gellner, Ernest, 37, 47–48, 51, 68, 122, 166, 240, 270–71, 277n13
guesses: irrefutability of some, 13–14; need for under uncertainty, 14
Gibbon, Edward: *Decline and Fall of the Roman Empire*, 46, 64
Gladstone, William Ewart, 175
Gnostics, 165
God, 11; Design Argument for the existence of, 49, 81; definitions of, 74
Gödel, Kurt, 55, 141
Goldwater, Barry, 189
Gregory, Richard, 134, 278n16
Grünbaum, Adolf, 262, 266–67, 269–270

Hallam, Florence, 263
Hallpike, C.R., 30, 150, 275n5
Hamas, 111
Harris, Sam, 7; on permissibility of killing those who think incorrectly, 15; on religion being responsible for terrorism, 112
Hassan, Steven Alan: *Combating Cult Mind Control*, 167
Hattiangadi, Jagdish, 68
Hayek, Friedrich August, 76, 239; *Collectivist Economic Planning*, 283n37; *The Road to Serfdom*, 188
Heath, Edward, 189
Heraclitus, 55
Hezbollah, 111
Hicks, John, 51
Higher Criticism, 76
Hitler, Adolf, 39–40, 81, 107, 155, 201; theory of propaganda, 174–75, 175–76, 180, 188–190, 200
Hoffer, Eric, 22–23, 133, 136–137; *The True Believer*, 201
Holocaust revisionism, 1

Holy Thorn, miracle of the, 69
Homo economicus, 101
Homo habilis, 141
Homo sapiens, 3; *Homo sapiens sapiens*, 147, 199; pre-*Homo sapiens*, 140–43
Homo sociologicus, 101
Hopkins, Jim, 261–62, 268
Hume, David, 2, 23, 49, 92, 195, 196, 202, 227; *Dialogues Concerning Natural Religion*, 49; *An Enquiry Concerning Human Understanding*, 49; *An Enquiry Concerning the Principles of Morals*, 49; government based on opinion, 137; on induction, 95
ideological movements: evolution of doctrines of, 18, 31, 67–69; splits in, 18, 66; turnover of adherents, 16–17, 30, 160–61, 275n1
ideologies (belief systems): emergence, maintenance, abandonment of, 171; apparent imperviousness to argument of, 163–68; memetic evolution of, 157–163; as rationalizations of irrational emotions, 170–73; unfathomable implications of, 242–46
immunization of a belief system against possible refutation, 22–23; *see* immunizing stratagems
immunizing stratagems, 6–7, 32, 37–38, 71, 205–273; involve abandonment of original theory, 206, 209, 215, 220–23, 224, 228, 268, 272; origin of the term, 206, 280n27; types of, 208–210, 223–230
instrumentally rational action (Weber), 103–04
intellectuals and masses, 175–77, 181
International Psychoanalytic Association, 37
involuntariness: of belief, 2, 133–36, 138–39, 159, 279n21; of sense perception, 2, 134
Irenaeus, 165
The Iron Heel (London), 199
irrationality, 17, 183; in cults, 9; emotions and, 4; distinguished from proneness to error, 18; what it would look like, 19–20; and Wason's experiment, 148–49; *see* closed mind, false theory of; rationality
Islam: fundamentalism, 1; response to Aristotle, 44–45

Jehovah's Witnesses, 1, 48, 50, 160–61, 221
Jesus, 68, 72, 73
Jevons, William Stanley, 254
Johnson, Lyndon B., 189
Jones, Reverend Jim, 24, 187
Jonestown, 24, 187
Jung, Carl Gustav, 37
justificationism, xvi, 60, 124–28, 130, 183–84

Kahnemann, Daniel, 36
Kant, Immanuel, 50, 283n36; *Critique of Pure Reason*, 49
Kaufmann, Walter, 217
Kautsky, Karl, 181
Kelley, David, 241
Kepler, Johannes, 211–13, 215, 263
Keynes, John Maynard, 188
Khomeini, Ruholla, 187
Knox, Ronald, 22
Kolakowski, Leszek, 15, 22–23, 99, 137
Kuhn, Thomas S., 6, 214, 282n33

Labor Theory of Value (Marx), 190–94, 224, 230, 231–35, 249–259, 283–84n39, 284n41
Laden, Osama bin, 98
Lakatos, Imre, 226, 230, 231, 239, 242
Lamarck, Jean-Baptiste, 83
Lamarckism, 146, 150
Laqueur, Walter: *The Age of Terrorism*, 21, 107–09; *Weimar*, 188
Le Bon, Gustave, 22, 107–08, 162, 167
Le Verrier, Urbain, 215, 226–27, 281n31
Lenin, Vladimir Ilyich, 181
Lester, Jan C., xvi, 278n19
Levinson, Paul, xvi
Liberal Party (UK), 164

Life of Brian, 241
List, Friedrich, 189
Locke, John, 202; *Essay Concerning Human Understanding*, 279–280n21
logic: favored by evolution, 140–41; ghostly, 13; innate human respect for, 2; people's ability for, 8–10, 148; applicability to reality, 140; similar in all cultures, 143; of the situation, *see* situational logic
logical consistency, 25
Lukács, Georg, 33, 129–131; special epistemological position of the proletariat, 129–130
Lysenko, Trofim Denisovich, 128, 156–57

Makarios, Archbishop Michail, 21
Mannheim, Karl, 129, 130
Manning, D.J., 16, 22, 56, 117–18, 245, 276n9
Mao Zedong, 68, 82, 181
marginal revolution, 159
Marshall, Alfred, 101
martyrdom, as a rational technique, 78–79
Marx, Karl H., 24, 159, 166, 211, 227, 147; *Capital*, 174–75, 181, 193, 224, 230, 249–259; assumption that communism is possible, 194–95, 219, 239; prediction of increasing industrial concentration, 218; socially necessary labor-time, 249–259; transformation problem, 257–59
Marxism, 6–7, 31, 87, 115, 118, 124, 152, 163, 166, 239; draws on earlier theories, 157; as impervious to argument, 22, 36–38, 43, 63, 206, 216; privileged character of, 129
Marxists, 7, 69, 123, 188, 213
Maxwell, James Clerk, 47
McDonagh, David, xvi, 250
McGovern, George, 189
memeplex, 31–32
memes, 10–11, 31; evolution of, 152–57; Hellfire, 151–56; logical content of, 10–11, 32

Mendeleev, Dmitri: Periodic Law, 236
Menger, Carl, 254
Mew, Melita, xvi
Meyerson, Denise, 137–39
Meyerson, Émile, 53–55, 152
Microtus epiroticus (sibling vole), 36
Mill, John Stuart, 100
Miller, David W., xvi, 57, 276–77n12, 282n33
Millerites, 160
mind viruses. *See* memes
Minogue, Kenneth, 55, 118, 190–94
Les Misérables, 113
Mises, Ludwig von, 20, 104–06, 198–99, 200, 239, 241
modularity of mind; *see* brain modules
Moeller van den Bruck, Arthur, 189
Monod, Jacques, 45–47, 51, 53, 100
Moonies. See Unification Church
Moore, G.E., 196
Morishima, Michio, 193, 258
Mormons (Latter-Day Saints), 5
movements, religious and political. *See* ideological movements
Munz, Peter, 147
Musgrave, Alan, 238

National Socialism, 1, 87, 115, 174–75, 189, 198
Newspeak, 6, 68
Newton, Isaac, 2, 43, 47, 49, 211–13, 226, 231, 232–35, 238, 244
Nicea, council of, 165
Niebuhr, Reinhold, 71
9/11 atrocity, 20
Nineteen Eighty-Four (Orwell), 6, 8
Nixon, Richard, 189
Notturno, Mark Amadeus, xvi
Nozick, Robert: experience machine, 116–17

Objectivism (Rand), 200
Objectivists, 241
O'Connell, Daniel, 201
Ollman, Bertell, 191–92, 195
Orwell, George, 6

O'Hear, A., 147, 233, 235
Owenites, 239

Packard, Vance, 162
Paley, William: *Natural Theology*, 50, 81
papal infallibility, 75
Pape, Robert: *Dying to Win*, 110–13
paradigm, 6
Pareto, Vilfredo, 101, 179–180, 183, 190
Parmenides: theory of block universe, 55
A Passage to India (Forster), 199
Pauli, Wolfgang, 231
Pavlov, Ivan, 175, 176, 178
Pears, David: *Motivated Irrationality*, 125–26
Pecqueurians, 239
Peikoff, Leonard, 200, 241
Penton, M. James: *Apocalypse Delayed*, 48
People's Temple, 24, 187
Percival, Frank, xvi
Percival, Paul, xvi
Peripatetics, 227
PKK (Kurdish political group), 113
Planck, Max, 216, 217
Plato, 3; *Meno*, 93; *Phaedrus*, 120
Plotkin, Henry, 87
Popper, Karl R., 6, 22, 94, 148, 172, 184, 225, 233, 244, 247, 272; attribution of closedness to argument to some ideologies, 36–37, 57–60, 90, 133, 139; on Darwinism, 89, 146; demarcation problem, 206, 211–15, 282–83n35; arguments against determinism, 134, 158; merit in dogmatic defense of a theory, 164, 217; evolutionary epistemology, 87; on the exploratory drive, 123; falsifiability, 52, 206, 216; on immunizing stratagems, 206–211; *Logic of Scientific Discovery*, 216; metaphysical concepts, 34–35, 216, 217–220; *The Open Society and Its Enemies*, 248; *The Open Universe*, 134; impossibility of predicting new ideas, 158; propensities, 134–36, 276n10; and situational analysis, 62; *Unended Quest*, 280n23
Post, F.J., 61, 276–77n12
Powell, Enoch, 189
probability, propensity account of, 134–35
propaganda: long-term, 188; spoken and written word, 201–02
the propagandist, 22, 26–27; logic of the situation of, 25–26, 121–22, 185, 210
propensity theory of probability, 134–36, 276n10
Proudhon, Pierre-Joseph, 257
Proudhonists, 239
Prout, William, 231
psychoanalysis: as effective treatment, 270; *see also* Freudianism
Putnam, Hilary, 232

Quine, Willard Van Orman, 92, 184

racists, 175, 182, 198
The Ragged Trousered Philanthropists (Tressell), 199
Rand, Ayn, 24, 200
Rapport, David, 98–99
rationality: of humans, 1, 103–04; given by evolution, 25, 28; exploratory, 122–23; of insane persons, 63, 100; instrumental, 115–16; of microscopic animals, 98–99; of wishful and fearful thinking, 4–5, 124–25, 132–33, 137; of zombies, 19
Rawls, John, 114
Reagan, Ronald, 111
religion, 7, 152; Abrahamic, role of logic in, 44–45; defection rate from religious affiliations, 275n1; not immune to criticism, 43; as offering a true account of the world, 43
Revisionism, 165
Ricardo, David, 157; labor theory of value, 56
Robbins, Lionel: *Essay on the Nature and Significance of Economic Science*, 101–02

Roemer, John, 192, 197–98
Roman Catholic Church, 62, 66, 67, 75–76, 165, 198, 242
Rosenzweig, Saul, 266
Russell, Bertrand, 45, 124, 162, 183
Russell, Charles Taze, 160
Russia, Soviet, 136–37, 157, 237–38, 248
Rutherford, Joseph Franklin, 160

Sabbataians, 160
Saint-Simonians, 157
Santayana, George, 52
Sapir-Whorf hypothesis, 6
Sargent, William, 202
Saudi Arabia, 20,
schism, 69; *see also* ideological movements, splits in
Schopenhauer, Arthur, 88
Schilcher, Florian von, 150, 156–57
Schweitzer, Albert, 71
Scientology, 1, 17, 49
Shakers, 70
Shakespeare, William: *Othello*, 16, 169
shame at having been wrong, 165
Shaw, George Bernard, 192, 254
Shearmur, Jeremy, xvi, 221, 230
Shils, Edward, 56, 240
situational logic, 26–27, 30, 62–69
Skinner, B.F., 28
Smith, Adam, 114, 201; *Wealth of Nations*, 201
Smith, H.P., 52
Smith, Winston, 6, 8
Social Democrats (Germany), 165, 188
Socialist Party of Great Britain, 33
Socrates, 120–21
Soddy, Frederick, 231
Soviet Union; *see* Russia, Soviet
Sombart, Werner, 189
Spengler, Oswald, 189
Spencer, Herbert, 200
Sraffa, Piero, 193
Staal, F., 143
Stalin, Joseph, 67, 68, 157, 181
Star Trek, 3, 84
Stark, Rodney, 78

Steedman, Ian, 192–93, 258
Steele, David Ramsay, xvi, 194, 219, 275n5
Stentor coerulus, 98–100
Stoics, 4, 172
Storr, Anthony, 166
strategic analysis; *see* situational logic
stubbornness in sticking to beliefs, 5
Sugar, Alan, 98
suggestion: as simple assertion, 182–84; as implicit argument, 184–85
Svalbard, 36

tarot, 34
Tennant, Neil, 150, 156–57
terrorism, 20–21; effectiveness of, 108–09, 108–113; suicide, 20–21, 109–11
Tertullian, 165
Thales, 21
Tillich, Paul, 51, 71, 72, 74–75
Total Recall, 117
totemic symbols, 177–78
traditional action (Weber), 103–04
Trigg, Roger, 71, 72
Trotsky, Leon, 181
Trotskyists, 241
truth: as an advantage for the spread of ideas, 25, 41, 43, 46–48, 55–56
truth-likeness; *see* verisimilitude
Tschachotin, Sergei; *see* Chakotin, Serge
Tullock, Gordon, 189
Twitter, 201

UFOs, 41
Uncle Tom's Cabin (Stowe), 199
Unification Church (Moonies), 1, 16,

value-rational action (Weber), 103–04
values: absolute, 113–14; conflict over fundamental, 198
verisimilitude (truth-likeness), 25, 47, 55, 56, 93, 147, 156–57, 282n35
Veyne, Paul, 128, 159
Viet Minh, 113

Virgin Birth, 76
Voltaire (François-Marie Arouet), 49

Walras, Léon, 254
Walsby, Harold, 280n26
Ware, Timothy, 76
Wason, Peter, 8, 10, 148–49
Watkins, John W.N., 35, 61, 158, 218, 233, 237, 239, 241, 276–77n12
Weber, Max, 177; charismatic leadership, 171, 185–87; classification of human action, 103–06
Weed, Sarah, 263
Wells, G.A., 69, 142–43, 161
Whewell, William, 92
Whorf, Benjamin Lee, 6

Wicksteed, Philip Henry, 254
Wilson, Edmund, 174–75, 188, 189, 202
wishful thinking, 4–5, 124–139; conducive to exploration, 132–33; and fearful thinking, 4–5, 124–25, 132–33, 278n18; rationality of, 125
Wolpert, Lewis, 144

Xenophanes, 21, 184

Yerkes-Dobson Law, 181

Zahar, Elie: *Einstein's Revolution*, 53–54

www.ingramcontent.com/pod-product-compliance
Lightning Source LLC
Chambersburg PA
CBHW030107010526
44116CB00005B/134